SEPHARDI, JEWISH, ARGENTINE

INDIANA SERIES IN SEPHARDI AND MIZRAHI STUDIES

Harvey E. Goldberg and Matthias Lehmann, editors

SEPHARDI, JEWISH, ARGENTINE

Creating Community and National Identity, 1880–1960

ADRIANA M. BRODSKY

INDIANA UNIVERSITY PRESS
Bloomington & Indianapolis

This book is a publication of

INDIANA UNIVERSITY PRESS
Office of Scholarly Publishing
Herman B Wells Library 350
1320 East 10th Street
Bloomington, Indiana 47405 USA

iupress.indiana.edu

© 2016 by Adriana M. Brodsky

All rights reserved

No part of this book may be reproduced or utilized in any form or by any means, electronic or mechanical, including photocopying and recording, or by any information storage and retrieval system, without permission in writing from the publisher. The Association of American University Presses' Resolution on Permissions constitutes the only exception to this prohibition.

The paper used in this publication meets the minimum requirements of the American National Standard for Information Sciences—Permanence of Paper for Printed Library Materials, ANSI Z39.48-1992.

Manufactured in the
United States of America

Library of Congress Cataloging-in-Publication Data
Names: Brodsky, Adriana Mariel, 1967– author.
Title: Sephardi, Jewish, Argentine : creating community and national identity, 1880–1960 / Adriana M. Brodsky.
Description: Bloomington and Indianapolis : Indiana University Press, [2016] | Series: Indiana series in Sephardi and Mizrahi Studies | Includes bibliographical references and index.
Identifiers: LCCN 2016019128 (print) | LCCN 2016019819 (ebook) | ISBN 9780253022714 (cloth : alk. paper) | ISBN 9780253023032 (pbk. : alk. paper) | ISBN 9780253023193 (ebook)
Subjects: LCSH: Jews—Argentina—History—19th century. | Jews—Argentina—History—20th century. | Jews, Oriental—Argentina—History—19th century. | Jews, Oriental—Argentina—History—20th century. | Jews, Oriental—Argentina—Social life and customs. | Jews, Oriental—Cultural assimilation—Argentina. | Sephardim—Argentina—History. | Argentina—Ethnic relations.
Classification: LCC F3021.J5 B76 2016 (print) | LCC F3021.J5 (ebook) | DDC 305.800982—dc23
LC record available at https://lccn.loc.gov/2016019128

1 2 3 4 5   21 20 19 18 17 16

Contents

- *Note about Translation and Transliteration* vii
- *Note on Previously Published Material* ix
- *Acknowledgments* xi

Introduction 1

1. Burying the Dead: Cemeteries, Walls, and Jewish Identity in Early Twentieth-Century Argentina 25

2. Helping the Living: Philanthropy and the Boundaries of Sephardi Communities in Argentina 53

3. The Limits of Community: Unsuccessful Attempts at Creating Single Sephardi Organizations 90

4. Working for the Homeland: Zionism and the Creation of an "Argentine" Sephardi Community after 1920 113

5. Becoming Argentine, Becoming Jewish, Becoming and Remaining Sephardi: Jewish Women and Identity in Twentieth-Century Argentina 140

6 Marriages and Schools: Living within Multiple Borders *173*

- *Postscript* *205*
- *Notes* *213*
- *Bibliography* *249*
- *Index* *265*

Note on Translation and Transliteration

ALL TRANSLATIONS FROM SPANISH ARE MINE, UNLESS OTHERwise noted. I did not translate into English the Hebrew names of the organizations I discuss in the book, unless it was necessary to convey to the reader the type of work the organization engaged in. In most cases, the names chosen by the societies—most taken from biblical phrases—did not indicate the nature of the work carried out. I believe this approach preserves the language choices these Jewish Argentines made for the names of their societies. When transliterating Hebrew terms, I have generally followed the Library of Congress system, unless a different spelling was used as the legal name of an organization. In such cases, I retained the original spelling because in the early twentieth century there were no standard transliteration systems; rather, ad hoc solutions were employed, using Latin letters to attempt Hebrew pronunciation for Spanish speakers. Thus using a modern transliteration system would have meant that, in most cases, the names in this book would look very different from the ones these Argentine Jews used. Finally, I have chosen *Sephardi* over *Sephardic*, which sounded closer to the Hebrew and Spanish oral rendition of the same word.

Note on Previously Published Material

PARTS OF CHAPTER 2 PREVIOUSLY APPEARED IN SPANISH IN "Re-configurando Comunidades: Judíos Sefaradíes/Árabes in Argentina, 1900–1950," in *Arabes y judíos en Iberoamérica: similitudes, diferencias y tensiones* (Madrid: Dykinson, 2008). Sections of chapter 4 and chapter 5 appeared previously in "Electing 'Miss Sefaradí', and 'Queen Esther': Sephardim, Zionism, and Ethnic and National Identities in Argentina, 1933–1971," in *The New Jewish Argentina: Facets of Jewish Experiences in the Southern Cone*, edited by Adriana Brodsky and Raanan Rein (Leiden: Brill, 2012). Sections of chapter 6 appeared previously in "Educating Argentine Jews: Sephardim and Their Schools, 1920s–1960s," in *Returning to Babel: Jewish Latin American Experiences and Representations*, edited by Amalia Ran and Jean Cahan (Leiden: Brill, 2011).

Acknowledgments

IT DEFINITELY DOES TAKE A VILLAGE TO PRODUCE A BOOK; IN fact, we may even say that it takes several villages. Throughout this project, I have traveled across countries and oceans, meeting friends who discussed this project with me, invited me into their homes, and continued to help me in countless ways even from afar. I am indebted to them all; any of the book's shortcomings, however, are mine alone.

Crossing oceans and borders, and finding time to write, was achieved by financial support from several institutions. A Kluge Fellowship at the Library of Congress was instrumental in providing the best writing and research atmosphere any scholar could wish for. Sharing my research with Oana Godeanu-Kenworthy, Thierry Rigogne, and Peter Wien while there was a wonderful treat that helped bring several chapters into sharper focus. The Maurice Amado Foundation also provided financial support early on. Faculty development grants from St. Mary's College of Maryland allowed me to visit archives and conduct interviews. Being able to revisit some of the archives I had spent time in while writing my doctoral dissertation proved to be invaluable in defining the book project.

The ideas in this book were shaped, in part, through conversations with colleagues in a variety of professional settings. The research conferences of the Association of Jewish Studies, the Conference on Latin American History, and the Latin American Jewish Studies Association were wonderfully fertile (and friendly) ground in which to present and discuss the ideas I offer here. In particular, the following workshops allowed me to test ideas and further develop many of the issues I explore in these chapters: Tel Aviv University in 2007 ("Arabes y Judíos en América Latina: Simposio Internacional"); the Maurice Amado Program in Sephardic Studies at UCLA, and the 2011 program of their Center for Jewish Studies ("Crossing Borders: New Approaches to Modern Judeo-Spanish [Sephardic] Cultures"); the Center for Advanced Holocaust Studies at the United States Holocaust Memorial Museum; the Department of History at the University of Washington (Seattle); the Samuel and Althea Stroum Jewish Studies Program at the University of Washington, Seattle, in 2013 ("Sephardic Jewry and the Holocaust: The Future of the Field"); and the Center for European Studies, the Duke Center for Jewish Studies, the Center for Latin American and Caribbean Studies at Duke University, and the Duke Islamic Studies Center in 2013 ("The Jewish and Muslim Diasporas in Latin America: New Comparative Perspectives").

So many colleagues have contributed with their knowledge, their professional example, and their support. Argentineanists Daniel James, Mark Healey, Pablo Palomino, Sandra McGee Deutsch, Donna Guy, David Sheinin, José Moya, Ben Bryce, and Kristen McClearly helped me along the way with questions big and small, and just by being there. Colleagues I have known since my days at the Consortium in Latin American and Caribbean Studies at the University of North Carolina at Chapel Hill and Duke University, Jody Pavilack, Bianca Premo, Jon Beasley-Murray, John French, Ivonne Wallace-Fuentes, Jane Mangan, and David Sartorius, among others, continue to inspire me with their work and encourage my own intellectual pursuits. Sephardi and Jewish Studies scholars Sarah Abrevaya Stein, Devi Mays, Devin Naar, Ethan Katz, Julia Phillips Cohen, Paula Dacarrett, Judah Cohen, Barbara Mann, and Yaron Ayalon provided invaluable help in reading sections of the manuscript and answering questions at all hours of the night (and from all parts of the globe!). Malena Chinski and Ariel Noijovich searched archives for me, and helped me figure out the answer to important questions. Adriana X. Jacobs, David Brodsky, and Ronnie Perelis helped me with key Hebrew translations. Jeffrey Lesser, Bea Gurwitz, Alejandro Meter, Evelyn Dean-Olmstead, Ariana Huberman, Margalit Bejarano, Edna Aizenberg, Efraim Zadoff, Santiago Slabodsky, Natasha Zaretsky, Mollie Lewis, and many other Latin American Jewish Studies Association members and colleagues have followed and contributed to this project for a long time. A special thanks goes to my dear friend Raanan Rein for his intellectual guidance and mentorship and to Esti Rein for opening up her house and making me feel at home on my many visits to Givatayim.

In Argentina, Marcelo and Liliana Benveniste and Mario Cohen, loyal supporters of Sephardi culture, helped me in myriad ways. I cannot thank them enough for their work and help. Ricardo Djaen was always eager to answer my questions about his grandfather Rabbi Djaen, and provided me access to his personal archive. My wonderful and longtime friends Rosana Avelino, Gustavo Aznarez, Alberto Bononi, Gabriela Scalone, Nora Rabadan, Roberto Barreira, Graciela Colombo, and Alfredo Bernal opened their homes during my many visits and let me talk (ad nauseam) about the ideas I present here. Martin Lyon (without whom I could not have created the databases I used), Marcela Harris, Kevin and Sandra O'Reilly, Victor Wolansky, and Cristina Meier have become my local *comunidad Argentina* in northern Virginia. Over *asados* and *mate* afternoons, they help me feel at home in this hemisphere.

St. Mary's College of Maryland has been another wonderful home away from my many homes. The Media Services Department, and in particular Justin Foreman, was instrumental in fixing all things technical. History Department colleagues Gail Savage, Tom Barrett, Christine Adams, Chuck Holden, Linda Hall, Garrey Dennie, Charles Musgrove, and Kenneth Cohen provide a wonderful intellectual community with which to share my work. My thanks to all of them. Former students Monica Louzon, Gabriel Young, and Alison Curry helped me in more ways than they probably know.

This book is better because of the hard work of wonderful editors Katharine French-Fuller, Ruth Anne Phillips, and Karen Adams. They helped me figure out what I was saying and then improved on how I had said it. The editors of the Indiana Series in Sephardi and Mizrahi Studies, in particular Matthias Lehmann, encouraged me to publish this work as part of the series. I believe the book has found a good home.

My family is owed the greatest thanks. I know my mother, Luna, would have been very proud of this book; I only wish I had been able to share it with her. My father, Sergio, his wife, María del Carmen, my brother, Ariel, and my nephew, Iván, believed in this project and never doubted that I would finally finish it. My partner, Greg, has done more than his fair share at home so that I had time to work on this seemingly never-ending project. His love and unwavering support made it all possible. David and Leah, my children, have lived with the book since they came into this world. For their patience, love, and blind faith, I dedicate it to them.

SEPHARDI, JEWISH, ARGENTINE

INTRODUCTION

ISTANBUL NATIVE ESTELA LEVY RECALLED IN HER AUTO-biography:

> On the night of January 12, 1919, violent riots marked the beginning of a working-class outburst that later came to be called "The Tragic Week." We lived far from Once, the [Buenos Aires] neighborhood [in] which congregated a great number of Ashkenazi Jews and where these virulent acts were taking place.[1] Those Jews suffered serious damage to their lives and possessions. We, the Sephardim, were still protected by [people's] ignorance of our origins. We were thought to be turcos.[2]

The riots, which began early in January as the police and the army attempted to disperse striking steelworkers in outlying working-class neighborhoods, drew in upper-middle-class nationalist young men who, fearing the influx of foreign ideologies, attacked areas in the center of Buenos Aires where "Russians [rusos] and Catalans" lived.[3] The Hipólito Yrigoyen government, elected in 1916, read this working-class activism as a threat to the social order. In its view, this activity was carried out by "foreign antisocial groups," and thus brought the issue of immigration—its dangers and benefits—to the fore. In this context of impending revolution and the need to defend the nation, the term *rusos*, in particular, came to be synonymous with "maximalists" (those who took up the extreme socialist position advocated by Russian Bolsheviks), "stateless-ness," and "Jews."[4] The events of the night of January 12, then, targeted *some* but not *all* Jews. Levy and her family were saved from these nationalist attacks, she claimed, not because of the geographic distance between the events and the neighborhood where she resided, but because of the *imagined* distance between Sephardim and Ashkenazim,

1

a distance so ample that Sephardim were not considered Jews in Argentine society.

This short passage from Estela's memoirs suggests at first glance that Argentines held one image of what a Jewish immigrant looked like, and Sephardim, to their advantage in this instance, did not fit that model. Sephardim were *invisible* as Jews to Argentines as they were linguistically different from Ashkenazim, lived in different Buenos Aires neighborhoods, wore different styles of clothing, and had cultural and political practices learned and acquired in the lands they had migrated from that were not associated with Jewishness in Argentina. The publication of Levy's memoir hints at more significant issues. The subject that concerned her when the memoir was published in 1983 was that Sephardim—precisely because they had been invisible as Jews—were also written out of narratives that stressed the contributions of these immigrants in the making of modern Argentina. "We should tell the story of Sephardim," she pleaded, "those [of us] who did not come to these lands in the painful and precarious conditions [as] our brothers from faraway Russia did, escaping the horrors of persecution, misery and intolerance. Our arrival," she added, "was unaided by organizations like Baron Hirsh's [sic]; it was individual, each of us providing our own means, each of us managing our own destinies."[5] Thus Levy at once affirmed the role of these "different Jews" in the making of Argentina as well as stressed the more independent nature of Sephardi immigration. This independence, she subtly asserted, constituted a stronger loyalty to Argentina on the part of Sephardim, because of their individual investment in the migration experience.[6] While Ashkenazim became "Jewish gauchos" in agricultural colonies with the help of the philanthropic Jewish organization of Baron Maurice de Hirsch, Sephardim labored on their own, risked their savings in their own ventures, and succeeded. To Levy, Sephardim were not only less disruptive politically but had also contributed to the growth of Argentina without external aid.

Levy's memoirs constitute a telling example of how Sephardim, in the last decades of the twentieth century, engaged in the not-so-subtle project of claiming visibility, asserting both their difference from Ashkenazim as well as their belonging to Argentina and to its organized Jewish community.[7] Levy, a visible figure among Sephardim as a contributor to Sephardi magazines, the author of two books on Sephardi topics,[8] and member of the Sephardi branch of the Women's International Zionist Organization (WIZO), framed her efforts at visibility in the context of what she thought was the slow disappearance of Sephardi culture: "Those of us who are still alive at the end of this turbulent century," she wrote in 1983, "are blending with Ashkenazim and even gentiles. This is not a reproach, but an irrevocable reality," she claimed.[9] Her family tree, included in her memoir, also made this assertion visible: her children, and nieces and nephews, married mostly Ashkenazim and, to a lesser degree, Argentines of Italian and Spanish descent. To this image of slow disappearance that she so vividly expressed, we should juxtapose the reality of Sephardi *visibility*. For example, in 1998, almost eighty years after the Semana Trágica (Tragic Week) massacre, Rubén Beraja, an Argentine Sephardi who maintained close contacts with local and international Sephardi organizations, headed the Delegation of Argentine-Jewish Organizations (DAIA) that linked the organized Jewish community to the Argentine state. Three other Sephardim had previously led the DAIA: Moisés Cadoche, in the 1940s; Enrique Ventura, in the 1950s; and Sión Cohen Imach, in the 1980s.[10]

This book presents answers to the questions raised by Levy: How did Sephardim—Jews who were not Jews in the eyes of Argentines—come to represent all Jews in Argentina by leading their main community organization at the close of the century? How did Ashkenazim and Sephardim negotiate and contest their cultural differences? How did Sephardi Jews construct their public "Jewishness" without turning into Ashkenazim, the Jewish majority? How did Sephardim become Argentines in these processes, as well?

Levy's astute observations throughout her book also uncover other, not-so-openly stated issues that relate to the construction of ethnic and diasporic identities, including the unstable meaning and use of the very term *Sephardim*. In the first pages of her book, she defined *Sephardim* as all those Jews who were *not* Ashkenazim [rusos]. They arrived not from Russia and Poland, she noted, but "from Istanbul, Izmir, Rhodes, Salonika, Tétouan and the Middle East, Aleppo, Beirut and Damascus." Yet, as if immediately aware of the weakness inherent in defining a group by stating that it is *not* something, Levy added a few sentences later that these Jews more importantly shared a common past and history: "the people I talk about in this book are linked by a fine thread to the Sephardim, the once glorious people of Spain." Sephardim were connected, Levy proudly continued, "to those who excelled in the worlds of science, poetry, and the arts, [to those who] opened the doors of knowledge during truly dark times, [to the likes of] Maimonides, Yehuda Halevy and Spinoza."[11] *Not* being Ashkenazi connotes absence, an identity based on *not* being part of an experience presumed to represent all Jews; a shared historical land and culture suggests a presence, a *being* something.[12] Levy's claim to group identity based on these premises—even if not completely accurate, as a significant number of Syrian Jews were autochthonous and had never lived in medieval Spain—made Sephardim their own diasporic group *and* worthy of the visibility she believed was denied them.[13]

Levy's effort in the early pages of her memoir to define Sephardim as a group that shared commonalities is central to her project of attesting to Sephardi visibility. Yet throughout the book she appears acutely aware that the shared diasporic past she identifies as the basis for that group identity is an illusion, at best, and an insurmountable obstacle often. As her narrative progresses, the Sephardim that appeared as a cohesive unit in her first pages vis-à-vis the Ashkenazim become a complex mixture of peoples from different areas that are defined by their different experiences, and not by shared ones. Levy's family, Ladino-speakers from Istanbul, settled in the neighborhood of La Boca where a large community of Jews from Damascus lived. It is among these Arabic-speaking Jews that Levy's father's business grew, and from whom Levy and her sister chose husbands. The differences between the Arab Jews and her family, as well as the relationships between the different organizations these groups founded, are central in the memoir. But while her father "learned [that] strange language" and even joined the "synagogue of the Arabic-speaking Jews" as a member of its steering committee,[14] Levy recalled "barely understanding the words [uttered by her sisters-in-law]."[15] She found "Oriental Jews"[16] to be "bound by strict laws of an underdeveloped environment,"[17] following rites "that they had inherited from the Arabs, with whom they had lived for centuries," and with rules of etiquette that were "fixed and primitive."[18] And if Levy, in the end, "learned how to comprehend their ways," she noted how "Sephardi Jews" in Córdoba, the city where she lived after her marriage, could not overcome these different "origins, customs, ways of thinking and feeling, inherited from the climate and the land" in which they had lived for centuries.[19] Until she left Córdoba in the 1950s, Jews from Syria and those from Izmir lived in different neighborhoods and worshiped in different synagogues.[20] Levy discovered that while her definition of *Sephardim* seemed to stress similarities among the groups, there were differences. "I was with them, but never *of* them," she noted.[21]

Levy, like other Sephardim I introduce in this book, encountered these contradictions of group belonging and multiple identities. In Argentina, they constructed a single Sephardi identity when it served their purposes even as they struggled with invisibility against an Ashkenazi majority and an Argentine society that did not quite even see them as Jews, but equally important, they chose to maintain the differences that existed among them, based on their origin, when deciding where to pray, where to dance and socialize, and where to bury their dead. Sephardim, I argue, crafted their diasporic identities, writ large (Sephardim) and small (Moroccan, Ottoman, Aleppine, and so on), as they simultaneously became Argentines. This study, then, can help us understand both the construction and use of diasporic identities, always in the plural, and how these dovetailed with national identities.

MODERN JEWISH IDENTITIES, SEPHARDIM, AND MULTIPLE DIASPORAS

Scholars have stressed that Sephardim indeed constituted their own diasporic group, one that arose from experiences of expulsion from the Iberian Peninsula, and the resulting consequences of their forced move. Sephardim, explained Jonathan Ray, are not simply part of the broader historical and cultural phenomenon of Jewish exile, but rather a subethnic group that came to be, in part, defined by their own diaspora.[22] He rightfully bemoaned the failure of diaspora scholars to view Sephardim as their own group, as well as Jewish scholars' reticence to use the tools developed by diaspora studies in the analysis of its history. In this light, Sephardim are not Jewish exceptions to the Ashkenazi narrative and culture, but a group with their own constitutive trajectories. Levy, and the Jews I present in this book, strongly believed in the centrality of this Sephardi diasporic identity.

In addition, Jewish scholars have pointed out that Jews have built strong connections to different and multiple homelands. In the past scholars have described the Jewish diaspora as an exilic condition resulting from Jews' expulsion from the biblical Holy Land; new studies, however, have begun to question that proposition by noting that desire for the *prohibited homeland* did not exclusively define Jewish identity.[23] Rebecca Kobrin, in her study of Jews from the city of Bialystok (located in present-day Poland), has masterfully demonstrated "the ways in which immigrant Jews harbored different, at times competing, longings and loyalties," and how these loyalties were manifested and maintained during periods of mass emigration from Eastern Europe.[24] Although scholars had previously noted the organizational structure of immigrant groups around their cities or region of origin (*landsmanshaftn*), Kobrin's approach is novel in that it demonstrates the weight of these ties *across* national borders. The immigrants Kobrin studied were bound by their "undying loyalty" to Bialystok, and they maintained their connection to the city even as they settled in the United States, Argentina, Australia, and Palestine.[25] What united them in these different destinations was not only their Jewishness but their being *from* Bialystok. Levy and the Sephardim presented in this study also found themselves willingly bound to others who remained in, or originated from, the same specific cities and regions in faraway lands.

This book is situated within these academic crossroads: the realization that Jewish diasporic identity is not only related to the biblical "promised land" but to other "realized lands," where Jews in fact lived and to which they developed strong connections, and that Sephardim, partly because of that fact, should be understood as a specific subgroup within the larger Jewish ethnic category. This study, which focuses on the experiences of the numerically small Sephardi communities in modern Argentina, highlights the existence of multiple and equally important diasporas. These diasporas are linked to a variety of real and imagined centers that uncover the constructed nature of the very term *Sephardim*.

Introduction

In particular, this study uncovers several interrelated (and concurrent) processes that shaped Sephardi experiences in Argentina. First, Sephardim constructed their Sephardi identity not only by stressing connections to a Spanish past but also through shared experiences with other Argentines: what united them was a memory of a distant shared history and the concrete realities of living together in Argentina. Previous scholars who focused on Sephardim defined their object of study as either "all the non-Ashkenazi communities... whose religious rituals, liturgy and Hebrew pronunciation bear the imprint of a common non-Ashkenazi tradition," or, more narrowly, as those who were "expelled from Spain and Portugal and maintained the Hispanic tradition."[26] Yet it will be clear in the chapters that follow that *being* Sephardim and *acting* as a single group was a *choice*. Even when these communities shared "non-Ashkenazi traditions," in many cases they saw themselves as separated by the many differences resulting from their various origins (Moroccans, Syrians, Ottomans, and so on), while in many other cases they chose to act as one.[27] While Ashkenazim encompassed many Jews who were also bound together by their loyalty to specific cities, regions, and nations, they did not find the need to construct their group identity vis-à-vis Sephardim. This book argues then that Sephardi identity was never a given, an essence that was brought along from the Old World, but the product of the realities lived in new diasporic destinations, among other Jews, other immigrants, and Argentines, which bound them to others outside Argentina, as well.

This book also argues that diasporic identities are reinforced by, and not erased by, the process of creating new ones. Sephardim living in Argentina became *both* Jewish and Argentines (in their eyes and in the eyes of Argentines and Ashkenazim). Not imagined as Jews by Argentines, and not fully accepted by the Ashkenazim, Sephardim claimed their belonging in the organized Jewish community through their actions: they participated in the construction of the Jewish hospital in Buenos Aires, and represented the organized Jewish community at public events in provincial towns, alongside Ashkenazim. But this process always involved presenting themselves *as* Argentines. Successfully joining other Jews and Argentines did not mean that Sephardim were shedding any group identity based on strong identification with place of origin: they donated money for the building of the Jewish Orphanage (in Buenos Aires) so it could be used for "Sephardi" foundlings; in 1945, they sent money to the Jewish World Congress so it could purchase food and clothing to be sent to the (Sephardi) communities of Greece; they created a religious court (Bet Din) for Sephardim, and its leader met important Argentine government officials; they sent money to the World Zionist Organization (WZO) requesting to specifically help the Sephardi community in Palestine. Sephardim lived in multiple real and imagined diasporas, with real attachments and loyalties to their old and newfound homes.

Because of the focus on how diasporic/regional identities dovetailed with ethno-national ones, the book also contributes to a lively ongoing debate within the field of Latin American Jewish Studies regarding the theoretical frameworks used to study Latin American Jews/Jewish Latin Americans.[28] While the field was initially focused on understanding the experiences of Jews in the Americas, with the tacit objective of comparing their experiences with those of Jews elsewhere, current scholarship is shifting, focusing on the need to understand Jews as an ethnic group in the nations in which they settled. Raanan Rein and Jeffrey Lesser call for a "shift ... [in] the paradigm about ethnicity in Latin America by returning the 'nation' to a prominent position just at a moment when the 'trans-nation,' or perhaps no nation at all, is often an unquestioned assumption."[29] The focus, then, turned away from attention to migratory experience and diasporic identity to the ethno-national context and the fluid boundaries that demarcated ethnic groups and the nation. Yet another group of scholars has suggested that such focus on ethno-national communities prevents us from being able to analyze and understand the processes of "diasporization, de-diasporization and re-diasporization" of these communities (that today have restrengthened their links to the nations their parents or grandparents left from); in short, they alert us to the limitations of the "ethnic" approach in understanding new realities in an era of globalization.[30]

While the book does not focus on the re-diasporization of Jewish Latin Americans, its findings strongly suggest that diasporic identities and ethno-national loyalties and identifications reinforced each other, came into conflict with each other, and coexisted with each other at different points in time and over various issues.³¹ By offering a detailed description of the *historical* processes of the construction of multiple diasporic and national-ethno identities in the first half of the twentieth century—processes that tend to be associated mostly with the realities of the late twentieth century—the study can provide a model of how to be attentive to these interrelated processes. Moreover, paying attention to the contested nature of ethnic identities, and rejecting the tendency to essentialize ethnic groups, this book also contributes to the literature of the "new" ethnic studies in Latin America.³²

The centrality of the local context in the reconfiguration of identity should not hide the participation of other transnational actors, both individual and group, who insisted on maintaining these varied diasporic belongings at the forefront. Sephardim, for example, were visited by Sephardi leaders from the Old World as well as from Palestine and later Israel in the hopes that they continued imagining themselves and acting as members of the Sephardi (or Moroccan, Ottoman, or Arab-Jewish) diaspora. Moroccan Jews living in the province of Mendoza, for example, were asked to contribute to the building of the Moroccan synagogue in Buenos Aires, to raise funds to build a cemetery wall in the city of Tétouan, Morocco, to finance the creation of a Zionist Sephardi World Union, and aid other Sephardim living in Jerusalem. They were imagined as members of different but overlapping diasporas.

SEPHARDIM, DIASPORAS, AND SEPHARDI HISTORY

The different groups of Sephardim who arrived in Argentina as part of its large immigrant population had been living in their countries of origin for many centuries. Many had lived as part of the Sephardi diaspora; expelled from Spain in 1492, and from Portugal in 1497, they had settled in the Ottoman Empire, North Africa, the Italian Peninsula, and even as far as in Britain, the Netherlands, and towns in Palestine. Sephardim generally enjoyed good relationships with the rulers of their new homelands, thanks to the creation of semi-independent administrative units, and lived relatively unbothered for centuries. But in the late nineteenth-century and early twentieth-century, these Jews initiated other new diasporas as they left the towns, cities, and regions their ancestors had settled and moved to Argentina (as well as to other parts of the Americas, Palestine, and later Israel). Some newcomers had, in fact, never lived in Spain before leaving the Middle East for their new homes in Argentina.[33]

The reasons for the emigration of Sephardi Jews were primarily economic. Although Sephardim had become quite prominent in trade, banking, and science after their expulsion from Spain, with the passing of centuries their influence was lost to other groups. As historian Aron Rodrigue aptly put it, in the Ottoman Empire "from the end of the sixteenth century onwards . . . the community as a whole began a slow but steady process of decline in most areas, a decline that was to last until the nineteenth [century]."[34] In her memoir, Levy recalled that her father left Istanbul because of "economic hardship," as did her future brother-in-law, who was "born in Damascus."[35]

International political events also contributed to the emigration of Sephardim to Argentina. After the 1908 revolution of the "Young Turks," many Jewish males left the Ottoman Empire for fear of conscription. The two Balkan Wars of 1912–1913 and World War I increased the poverty of many Jewish communities, starting the movement of some families to safer areas.[36] The postwar breakup of the Ottoman Empire also affected its Jewish communities. As Rodrigue points out, "These communities were correctly seen by the new rulers as having strongly supported the old Ottoman regime, and anti-Semitic acts and incidents marred relations between Jews and non-Jews."[37] Jews in Syria also suffered with the rise of Arab nationalism, and Jews in Izmir were persecuted when the city fell into the hands of the Greeks (1919–1922). Also, as late as 1967, after the Six-Day War, many Jews still living in Morocco and Syria made the voyage to Argentina.[38]

By focusing on the emigration of Sephardim out of the Old World, this study allows us to avoid a teleological narrative of Sephardi culture that peaks with the Golden Age in Spain, begins its demise with the expulsion of Sephardim from Spain, and ends with the disappearance of Sephardi communities in Europe (during the Holocaust), and in northern Africa and other Arab countries of the Middle East (after the creation of the state of Israel). By focusing on the Americas (and Israel), we clearly see that most of Sephardi life did *not* tragically end in the mid-twentieth century. Other historians have offered descriptions of Sephardi life in these areas. Aviva Ben-Ur, for example, has focused on Sephardim who settled in New York City, and charted the ways in which they fought, whenever possible, against the invisibility they were subjected to as a group by Ashkenazim living in the area.[39] Susan Miller, in a study of Moroccan Jews in the Amazon in the nineteenth century, also presents a picture of Jews who found in the Americas a place to re-create their communities.[40] Edna Aizenberg and Margalit Bejarano recently edited a collection of essays on Sephardim in the Americas that reminds us of the rich and vibrant life created by these Jews on the continent.[41] My study contributes to this literature by focusing on the ways in which Sephardi identity (assumed in many of these works as a fait accompli) was always in the process of being contested and created.

Literature on Sephardim in the Americas has also focused on their experience during the Spanish and Portuguese colonial period, even though most Sephardi immigration into the Americas dates from the late nineteenth to the twentieth century. Prone to inquisitorial persecution, Crypto-Jews figure prominently in studies that describe the ways in which they (unsuccessfully) fought—most often losing their lives—to maintain their traditions.[42] This desire, perhaps not scholarly, to highlight the presence of Sephardim in the Americas dating from its colonial past constitutes an attempt to legitimize Sephardi presence on the continent "right from the start," creating "a myth of belonging not available elsewhere."[43] "[This] Iberian link," explains critic Edna Aizenberg, "gave Sephardim the right to be part of Latin America, of its Luso-Hispanic cultures and languages."[44] Levy clearly made use of this strategy in her memoir. But this study focuses on the concrete actions that these Jews took in modern Argentina as they helped shape its multicultural present.

IMMIGRANT ARGENTINA AND ASHKENAZI AND SEPHARDI JEWS

The choice made by Sephardim to come to Argentina was similar to those made by many other immigrants. Argentina is one of the six countries that received the greatest numbers of overseas immigrants at the turn of the century.⁴⁵ Although the country was a distant second in number of arrivals, it experienced the most dramatic increase in population: the country had only 1.7 million inhabitants in 1869, which increased to more than 20 million by 1959 (a more than tenfold increase in a period of ninety years). Argentina's experience was also unique in that immigrants came to account for a huge percentage of the population as a whole. In 1914, for example, a third of the inhabitants were foreign-born, while in Buenos Aires this figure was close to 60 percent.⁴⁶

Large numbers of immigrants chose Argentina in part because of immigration policies adopted by liberal ruling governments starting in the second half of the nineteenth century. Imbued with the positivist ideas of the era, Argentine authorities sought to attract European immigrants in order to regenerate ("whiten") the local population, which was imagined to be backward and not prone to improvement, and to exploit the rich lands recently made available by the forceful elimination of indigenous peoples.⁴⁷ This desire to bring in primarily northern European men and women, however, was not fulfilled; most of the immigrants came from South and Eastern Europe, as well as from regions in the Mediterranean and the Balkans. And although most of the newcomers were Catholic, Argentina also became home for non-Christian minorities, including Jews and Muslims.

The number of Jewish immigrants who settled in Argentina was indeed lower than the number of Italian and Spanish immigrants, but the Jewish community they built became, with time, the largest in Latin America. A combination of poor record keeping, the loss of important census returns, and the fact that authorities were interested in recording national origin as opposed to religious affiliation all make it hard to calculate this migration with any certainty.⁴⁸ In 1914, Jews accounted for 1.49 percent of foreign-born inhabitants of the city of Buenos Aires compared with 20 percent for Italians and 19.5 percent for Spaniards. By 1930, the Jewish population, including Argentine-born Jews, was around two hundred thousand, and by 1960, close to three hundred thousand of the nation's twenty million inhabitants were Jews.⁴⁹

Argentine immigration policies—usually characterized by scholars as haphazard—oscillated between a desire to foster agricultural production specifically (by facilitating a move to the interior provinces, and by making land accessible to newcomers) and a more general need to address a shortage of labor in urban areas.[50] In the countryside, the native worker (usually referred to as *gaucho*) then had to compete with immigrants who had (slightly) more support from national and provincial government agencies. Liberals' belief in the improvement of Argentina through a regeneration of its Spanish/indigenous/black population made it hard for gauchos (mestizos with indigenous and black ancestors) to survive the new reality brought about by the presence of such immigrants in large numbers.

But as gauchos were struggling against immigrants, the compulsory military draft, railroads, and large landowners who curtailed the freedoms they had enjoyed for many years, their symbolic weight grew. Especially in the last decades of the nineteenth century, and in the first few of the twentieth century, urban writers and intellectuals contributed to turning the gaucho into an icon of Argentine national identity.[51] The gaucho characters in iconic literary works such as José Hernández's epic poem "Martín Fierro," and the 1926 novel *Don Segundo Sombra,* by rancher Ricardo Güiraldes, among others, highlighted the qualities this icon was to have: loyalty, bravery, intelligence, strong work ethic, and self-reliance. Within this discursive imaginary, immigrants found in the gaucho an ideal to emulate in order to facilitate their inclusion into the nation.

As Levy noted in her memoir, the history of Jews in Argentina almost exclusively focused on the experiences of the Ashkenazi majority, and, in particular, as the Jewish gauchos of the colonies. Life in the agricultural colonies founded by the Jewish Colonization Association (JCA) played a central role in the construction of Jewish (Ashkenazi) identity in Argentina precisely because of the ways in which it matched the ideology espoused by the liberal governments. While the Argentine government wished to regenerate the population and encourage its agro-export economic model, Baron Maurice de Hirsch founded the JCA in order to fund agricultural colonies that could provide persecuted and destitute Eastern European Jews with a livelihood. As Louis Horowitz points out, the program of rural colonies in Argentina was part of larger efforts made to "reconstitute the myth of the Jew as a man of the land in response to the anti-Semitic charges associated with the commercial

Jew."⁵² In Argentina, JCA colonies were located mostly in the northeastern and central provinces of Entre Ríos and Santa Fé (see figure I.1).

Later generations of Jewish and non-Jewish intellectuals promoted the image of the "Jewish gaucho," working the land next to the Argentine campesino, to claim that Argentina had indeed been built with the help of Jewish hands, making Jews an inextricable part of the new nation. In 1910, Alberto Gerchunoff, an Argentine writer and journalist whose family had lived in a JCA colony, wrote *Los Gauchos Judíos*, a now famous collection of stories.⁵³ Written in commemoration of the first centennial of Argentina's independence, the book would come to symbolize (Ashkenazi) Jewish commitment to Argentina and suggest the path to becoming an Argentine.⁵⁴ In fact, the JCA had clearly stated that their objectives were "to make good Argentine farmers" out of the Eastern European Jews who settled in their colonies.⁵⁵ The project was imagined as assimilationist: Jews would be able to erase their distinctiveness and become part of the nation in which they settled.

However central this experience to the construction of a Jewish (Ashkenazi) identity linked to Argentine land, the numbers show that agricultural production was not an activity that *most* Jews engaged in. In fact, few did. Sources estimate that in 1896 there were slightly less than seven thousand colonists. That number grew as JCA purchased more land, and in 1925 the size of the population in the colonies reached its peak, with close to twenty-one thousand farmers. Yet that merely amounted to 12.9 percent of the total Jewish population living in the country.⁵⁶ By 1960, only around 9,573 farmers still remained in these agricultural centers, representing 3.19 percent of the estimated total Jewish population.⁵⁷

The majority of Jewish Argentines, including Sephardim, lived in urban centers. Most Sephardi immigrants arrived in Argentina after 1890 but before 1930.⁵⁸ Table I.1, derived from the Argentine census of 1960, shows from where and when the immigrants who were still alive in 1960 had arrived. This data confirmed what had been gleaned through other sources: most of the Arabic-speaking Jews arrived before 1930, as did those from Turkey; the late arrival of many from the Balkans, Italy, and France responded to problems faced by Jews during the rise of fascism and World War II; the early Moroccan Jewish population

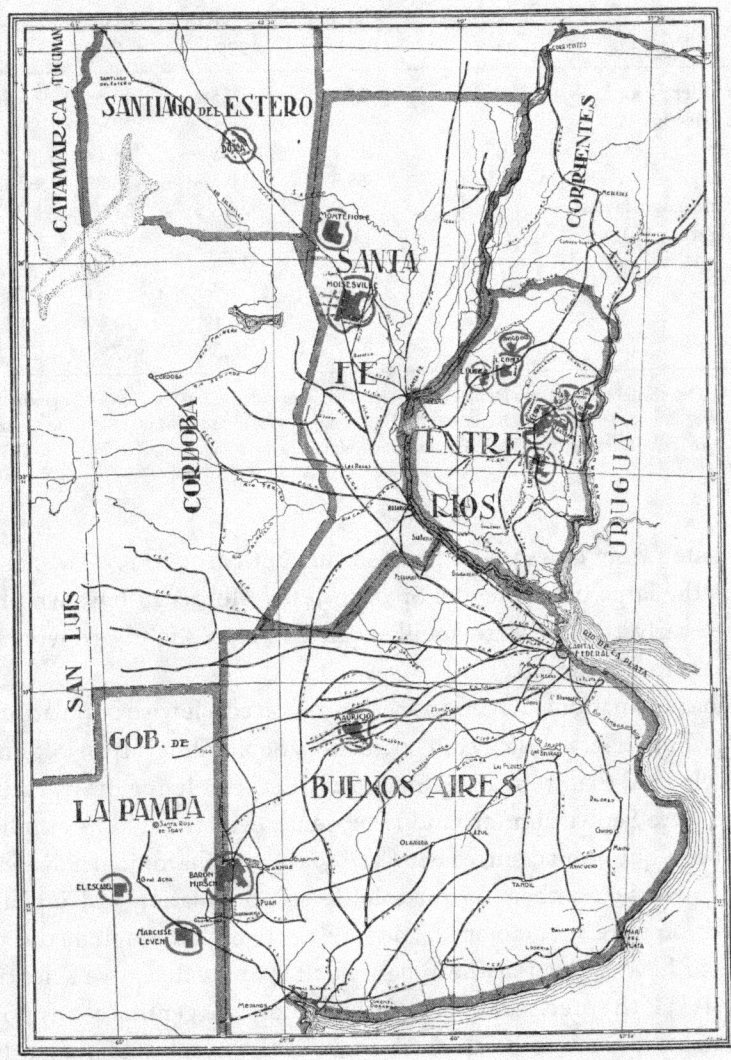

Figure I.1. Jewish Colonization Association Colonies. From the Jewish Colonization Association, *Su Obra en la República Argentina, 1891–1941* (Buenos Aires: n.p., 1942), 14–15.

Table I.1. Sephardim in Argentina: Dates of Arrival

Place of Origin	Absolute Number of Foreign-Born Jews Alive in 1960	Arrived up to 1919 (%)	Arrived from 1920 to 1929 (%)	Arrived from 1930 to 1939	Arrived from 1940 to 1960
Syria (Aleppo and Damascus)	3,569	36.%	47.5%	11.5%	5.%
Turkey	3,534	35.1%	45.5%	13.1%	6.3%
Palestine	1,016	25.3%	30.7%	13.9%	30.1%
Balkans (Yugoslavia, Bulgaria, etc.)	949	11.9%	26.5%	21.9%	39.7%
Africa (Morocco)	833	34.4%	24.2%	6.%	35.4%
Italy	1,079	12.8%	28.7%	35.4%	23.1%
Spain	706	50.2%	26.1%	10.4%	13.3%
France	585	24.7%	16.3%	17.%	42.%

From U. O. Schmelz and Sergio Della Pergola, *Ha-Demografyah shel ha-Yehudim be-Argentinah uve-aratsot aḥerot shel Amerikah ha-latinit* (Tel Aviv: n.p., 1974), cited in Mario Eduardo Cohen, "Aspéctos Socio-Demográficos de la Comunidad Sefaradita de la Argentina," *Sefárdica* 3 (1985): 57–78, 63.

originated from cities under Spanish rule until around 1956, which explains the large percentage of Spanish Jews. Moroccan Jews who had arrived early, though, were not likely alive in 1960, slightly skewing the numbers for this group.

The 1960 national Argentine census reported a Jewish population of 291,877, but understandably did not identify Sephardim.[59] In 1936, Simon Weill claimed that from an estimated 253,242 Jews living in Argentina, 43,228 were Sephardim (around 17 percent), even though his numbers have been questioned since then.[60] In 1940, a Sephardi journalist suggested that the numbers for the total Jewish population and Sephardi population were 300,000 and 35,000, respectively, although he did not claim to have arrived at these figures after any exhaustive scientific analysis.[61] If the precise number of Jews living in Argentina at any point in time has proven to be an elusive figure, the number of Sephardim within the Jewish community has been even harder to ascertain; however, given the figures provided by scholars, it would seem safe to argue that Sephardim never accounted for much more than 10 percent of the total Argentine-Jewish population.[62]

Introduction

The first Sephardim who arrived and settled in Argentina were Moroccan Jews. They arrived from the Moroccan cities of Tétouan, Tangier, and Larache, as early as 1859 to 1860, as a result of the Spanish-Moroccan War and the subsequent Spanish occupation of Tétouan.[63] Latin America, though, in particular Brazil and Venezuela, had attracted many Moroccan Jews as early as the 1810s. In Brazil, a decree passed on May 12, 1838, in Pará, required that certain foreign merchants buy a license to operate their businesses, and within two months, several Moroccan Jews, acting in their own names or on behalf of various companies, paid the authorities to continue operating in the region. Río de Janeiro, the Amazon, and later the Brazilian northeast (especially during the rubber boom) provided excellent opportunities for young Moroccans to make modest fortunes peddling goods, and eventually to own their own wholesale stores.[64] In some cases, these Jews would return to Morocco, where newly acquired Brazilian passports and a better economic situation would make them attractive as potential spouses and provide them with a sense of political protection in such uncertain times. Argentina was sometimes the last country these Jews chose to settle in, after having tried their luck in other South American regions.[65]

In Buenos Aires, Moroccan Jews settled in the Sud (later called Constitución) neighborhood (see figure I.2). Strategically placed close to the city port and the commercial downtown area, the neighborhood housed all their institutions until the late twentieth century. In the rest of the country, these Jews chose the northeastern provinces, with high concentrations of Moroccan Jews settling in the northern cities of Santa Fé, Chaco, and Corrientes. Most of them spoke Spanish, and some Haketía (Jewish-Moroccan Romance language spoken mostly in northern Morocco), but had also learned French at the schools founded by the Alliance Israélite Universelle (created in 1860 and focused on educating Jews particularly in the Middle East and the Ottoman Empire).[66]

Arabic-speaking Jews in Argentina organized burial, religious, social, sport, and philanthropic institutions around their city of origin. Most of the Jews from Damascus (*ashwams*) arrived between 1910 and 1925, and those from Aleppo (*ḥalabim*) traveled between 1914 and 1924.[67] Regardless of origin, Syrian Jews became involved in commerce. They marketed and sold merchandise, usually using family and

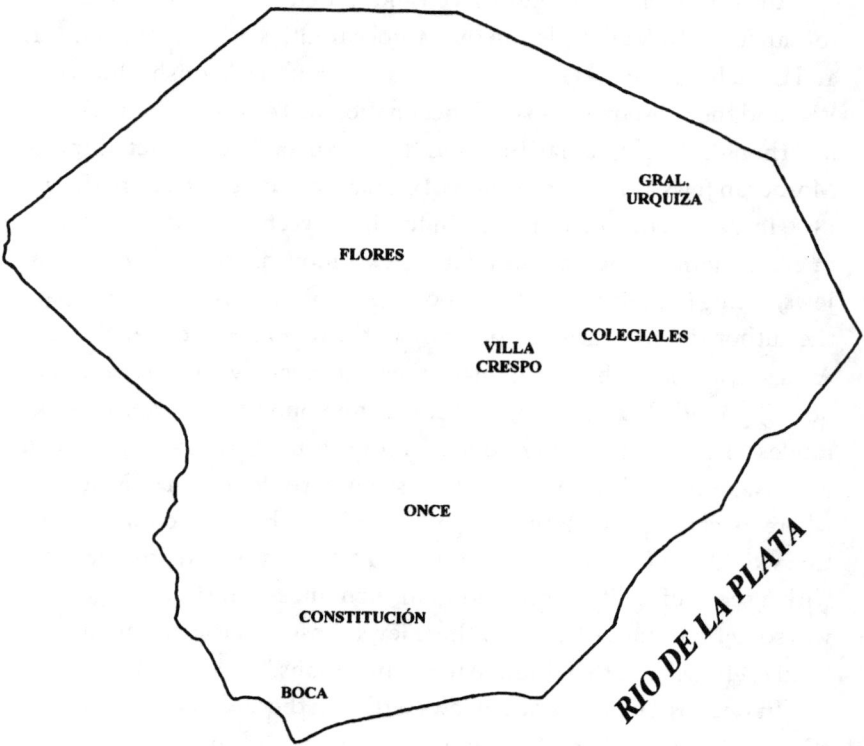

Figure I.2. Buenos Aires neighborhoods where Sephardim settled and founded their organizations.

social connections to establish wider trade networks. Some Syrian Jews, following a pattern also shared with non-Jewish Syrians, became prominent in the silk and textile trade, and established close contact with the existing Syrian community in Manchester, England.[68] In Buenos Aires, those from the city of Damascus settled in the neighborhoods of La Boca/Barracas, and Flores, and those from the city of Aleppo set up their organizations in Once, Flores, and Ciudadela (a suburb outside Buenos Aires city limits; see figure I.2). In the provinces of Córdoba, La Rioja, Salta, Rosario, Corrientes, and Entre Ríos, Syrian Jews founded their own institutions and also maintained close ties with the non-Jewish Syrian population.[69]

Introduction

Ladino-speaking Jews came mostly from former Ottoman lands: the city of Salonika, the island of Rhodes, Balkan countries, and many cities now in present-day Turkey. In Buenos Aires, these Jews founded organizations in Villa Crespo, Once, Colegiales, Flores, and Villa General Urquiza, sometimes gathering those from similar cities/regions (see figure I.2). In the interior of the country, Ottoman Jews settled in the cities of Tucumán, Rosario, Santa Fé, Posadas, and Córdoba, where they also founded religious and social institutions. Speaking Ladino (*djudeo-espanyol*) proved to be an asset, aiding an easier transition to the new land, as the language was based on sixteenth-century Spanish. Other (smaller) groups arrived from Palestine, Italy, Bulgaria, and Samarkand.

For many, Jewish life in Argentina started *not* in Buenos Aires, the port city that became the most active center of Jewish life, yet there is no history of the Sephardim in Argentina that shows the strong links that developed between Jews living in Buenos Aires and those settled in the rest of the country. Instead, like much of Jewish-Argentine history in general, the history of Sephardi life has almost exclusively focused on their various organizations in Buenos Aires.[70] If these texts make reference to Sephardi presence in the provinces, descriptions are focused primarily on a few of the most important provincial capitals, like Santa Fé, Córdoba, and Posadas. Sephardi life in the interior provinces, I argue, cannot be understood apart from the religious, social, and cultural centers of communal life in Buenos Aires. These acted as an anchor to the many Sephardi Jews who settled in the interior cities of the country, as they looked toward organizations and networks in Buenos Aires for unity, support, and continuity of their traditions. Various organizations in Buenos Aires also depended on those living in the rest of the country for the maintenance of their organizations, however, even when those same people were struggling to create institutions in their own towns. It was there, in these small urban contexts, that we can see clearly the interactions among Sephardim, Ashkenazim, and Argentines.

Negotiations among Jews belonging to different diasporas took place in particular Argentine realities that defined how these immigrants integrated themselves into the nation.[71] Policies that encouraged the arrival of immigrants, unlike those instituted by the United States after

World War I, continued to welcome new arrivals until 1930, when economic depression and the first military coup of the same year ended these open-door policies. While the Semana Trágica of 1919 disproportionally affected Jews (15.6 percent of all arrested by the police during these events were Jews, at a time when the Jewish population would not have been more than 2 percent), anti-Semitism, prevalent within the Catholic Church, the military, and many on the right, was never hegemonic and was, in fact, fiercely fought by liberals and the Left.[72] Immigration policies were further tightened during the rise of fascism and World War II, although many Jews still found their way to Argentina. Juan Domingo Perón, president from 1946 to 1955, returned to more favorable policies for immigrants, even granting amnesties to those who had entered illegally during the previous decades.[73]

None of the neighborhoods in Buenos Aires were exclusively Jewish. Once on Argentine soil, Jewish immigrants, like others, chose to settle close to those who had preceded them.[74] Whether in certain neighborhoods in Buenos Aires or in certain provincial cities, immigrants tended to settle where coreligionists had settled before. But it is important to stress that while some areas may have received larger numbers of Jewish immigrants, such as the neighborhood of Once in Buenos Aires, for example, they were never exclusively Jewish. Buenos Aires neighborhoods, as well as provincial towns and cities, facilitated interaction among immigrants and Argentines. Levy recalled her surprise that the La Boca neighborhood, where her family had settled and where many Arabic-speaking Jews lived, as well, "was not an Arab republic, but a conglomerate of Italians and Spaniards who had also come to Argentina." She added, "One could hear Spanish melodies and Italian *canzonette* [songs] emanating from their homes."[75] Interactions among immigrants and Argentines were more the norm than an exception.

Integration into Argentine society was also mediated by participation in the political system. The Radical Party in particular developed strategies to attract new citizens or their children after the passage of the 1912 Sáenz Peña Law, which made male voting mandatory. Participation of Jews in the Socialist and Communist Parties was also not only possible but noticeable, as Jewish candidates began competing for office and supporters were active in electoral campaigns.[76] A significant number of women activists also participated in the political process.[77] This participation became prominent during the presidency of Juan Domingo Perón, when some Jewish Argentines occupied prominent positions in government institutions and even founded the Organización Israelita Argentina (OIA) (Argentine Jewish Organization), which openly supported Perón.[78]

This book is attentive to some of the mechanisms that allowed Jews to become part of the nation, but it does not center on state policy per se. Rather, it untangles the ways in which Jews constructed their ethnic and subethnic identities in conversation with their sense of being Argentines, a process that in fact solidified those identities, as well. The book also illustrates that these processes were concurrent with the reconstruction of their diasporic identities. Such a focus meant reading institutional documents and community publications with an eye to these interactions, paying attention to social events, celebrations, and arguments and conversations among and between groups. The objective was not to write institutional or community histories, but to use institutional and community records to uncover how people constructed their belonging to a variety of collectives, and how they navigated these overlapping loyalties, too.

The organization of the book is not chronological, but thematic. This topical approach allows, I believe, for a better understanding of Sephardi life in Argentina, as the chapters show how identities, and their boundaries, were built not out of some essence but as a result of conflict, consultation, and agreements over specific issues.

In chapter 1, I argue that cemeteries provide invaluable information on how Argentine, Jewish, and Sephardi identities were negotiated. The processes by which communities decided when, where, and how to organize cemeteries varied. In some interior towns, Sephardi groups (of various origins) decided to pool their resources in order to have their own cemeteries and not have to bury their dead with the Ashkenazim. In other towns, the Jewish community acted as one group, and no distinctions were made between Ashkenazim and Sephardim. In still other parts of the country, each Sephardi group founded its own cemetery, so that each group (Moroccans, Ottomans, Syrians from Aleppo and those from Damascus) kept its dead within community grounds. I argue, then, that the choices made about where to build the walls separating cemeteries suggest that group boundaries were purposefully constructed based on local circumstances.

Chapter 2 focuses on the role of philanthropy in creating and recreating identities among Sephardim. The chapter explores the settlement pattern of each Sephardi group in Buenos Aires and the creation of the different religious and communal organizations. This geographic cohesion among different groups did not exist in the provinces, where Sephardi communities were more inclusive and less geographically oriented. Yet this did not mean that in the provincial settings these Sephardim would forgo their identification with their individual communities of origin. It was not uncommon for Sephardim in small towns to support both the local Sephardi organizations (which usually gathered Sephardim from various origins) and also organizations in Buenos Aires that had been founded by individual Sephardi groups. And Sephardim in both Buenos Aires and the provinces continued to contribute to important causes in their birthplaces across the Atlantic. While the study of cemeteries helps us understand the connections made *to* the land, given the economic realities in which Sephardim lived in Argentina, the flexibility of contributing financially across geographies reminds us that they also constructed new ties *while* keeping old ones alive.

Chapter 3 analyzes several failed attempts by Sephardim to create and sustain institutions that invoked an all-encompassing "Sephardi" identity. The failure of the Consistorio Rabínico Sefaradí (Sephardic Rabbinical Consistory) in the early 1930s to become *the* Sephardi religious authority in Argentina highlights the tenuous weight of the category "Sephardim." Communities (and their leaders) were unwilling to compromise what they perceived to be their "independence" for a centralized organization that sought to help them with religious, cultural, and educational concerns. While Sephardim wanted to ensure proper religious observance, the need to standardize religious practice was not an imperative for them. The unsuccessful consistory and other institutional attempts of later decades remind us of the Sephardim's desire to build strong *lay* communities, not religious ones.

Sephardi communities sought to preserve their own distinctive cultural and religious practices vis-à-vis one another and the Yiddish Ashkenazi majority. This picture of internal fragmentation among different Sephardi groups changed, however, during the interwar years and especially after World War II and the creation of the state of Israel. At that point, Sephardim were able to forge a new identity partly because Zionist ideology opened up social, political, and cultural spaces that did not conflict with distinctive Sephardi and Ashkenazi identities or with their national identity as Argentine Jews. Chapter 4, then, discusses Zionism and the role it played in helping Sephardim to defend their identity as a single group vis-à-vis the Ashkenazi majority. Sephardi participation in the Zionist movement was the result of both local and outside organizing. The local Ashkenazi Zionist centers and the WZO attempted to bring Sephardim into organized Zionism by sending delegates to Argentina to recruit Sephardi support. But from the start it was difficult for Sephardim to participate as a group that was clearly in the minority. Sephardim, then, succeeded in creating two Zionist groups that refused to participate with the Federación Sionista Argentina (FSA) (Argentine Zionist Federation), the umbrella organization led by Ashkenazim. The defense of their own subethnic identity in the face of the Ashkenazi majority was accomplished not only by appealing to a long-gone past, when all Sephardim had actually lived together in Spain and Portugal, but also by emphasizing their identity as Argentines. In the end, it was by acting as Argentine Sephardim that they were able to defend their individuality vis-à-vis the Ashkenazim. Sephardi participation in the movement allowed for the emergence, by the 1960s, of a more inclusive identity that, although premised on becoming Jewish Argentines, did not erase the particularities of each Sephardi group; they had become Jewish *Argentines* who were also *Sephardi*.

Chapter 5 moves beyond institutional history to explore the roles played by Sephardi women in articulating identity and belonging. Sephardi women, I argue, transformed the Sephardi and broader Jewish community, both in the public and private sphere. This was accomplished in the public sphere through philanthropic social events such as *té danzantes* (dancing soirees) that were prominent in the Sephardi/Jewish social world, or through the diaspora dynamics that they cultivated in Zionist philanthropy, while in the private sphere, it was accomplished primarily through the transmission of food traditions, or lack thereof, to later generations. The chapter demonstrates that although Jewish men may have been in positions of communal power and leadership, Jewish/Sephardi women were at the forefront in articulating precisely what it meant to be Jewish, Sephardi, and/or Argentine—notions always modeled after upwardly mobile, elite Argentines—and how these layers of affiliation overlapped, sometimes conflicted, and changed over time.

Chapter 6 closes the book with a discussion of education and marriage patterns. Although Sephardi Jewish educational institutions were almost always defined as *only* religious in purpose, Sephardi communities actively participated in discussions about what it was to be Argentine, Jewish, and Sephardi. Attention to Sephardi educational institutions also allows us to see the ways in which all Jews (Sephardim and Ashkenazim alike) participated in the process of becoming Argentine *while* safeguarding their Jewish identity. A focus on marriage helps delineate the process of the construction of a *Jewish-Argentine* identity; one that ultimately, and by the 1960s, did not pay so much attention to the geographical origin of earlier generations. Jewish-Argentine and Sephardi identities had by then entered a new era, and they were predicated on a different relationship to the state of Israel, to Argentina, and to the many diasporas to which the people belonged.

ONE

BURYING THE DEAD

Cemeteries, Walls, and Jewish Identity in Early Twentieth-Century Argentina

> Jews bury themselves the way they live.
> Nathan Englander, *The Ministry of Special Cases*

> Only death requires that we be precise.
> Yehuda Amichai, "The Clouds Are the First Fatalities"[1]

THERE LIES AN OLD WALLED-IN JEWISH CEMETERY IN AVELlaneda, a suburb to the south of Buenos Aires. The tombs, still bearing sepia pictures of the deceased and blurred Yiddish inscriptions, were once adorned with expensive marble monuments; now they are almost all destroyed by the passage of time, occasional vandalism, and a wish to forget. The cemetery abuts that of the Moroccan Jewish congregation, and the differences between the two graveyards could not be starker. In contrast to the unkempt grass and damaged tombs of the walled cemetery, that of the Moroccan Jews displays carefully maintained and finely decorated monuments.

The identity of those buried in the walled cemetery holds the key to understanding this vivid contrast. They were members of the Zwi Migdal, an infamous mutual aid association of Jewish pimps and madams involved in the international traffic of Jewish women known as "white slavery."[2] The embarrassing presence of large numbers of organized Jewish pimps and prostitutes threatened the broader Jewish community's standing within Argentine society—precisely because these outlaws insisted on identifying themselves as Jews—in early twentieth-century Buenos Aires, which already had a reputation as "the capital of vice." Shunned by the broader community, the traffickers nevertheless worked to create and sustain their own Jewish institutions, such as the cemetery, and a synagogue. The Zwi Migdal had originally requested burial space from the majority Ashkenazi community but was "informed that the separation between purity and impurity was extended even to the dead."[3] Its members were thus forced to establish their own cemetery, outside communal boundaries. Although the small Sephardi Moroccan community eventually shared a common wall with the Zwi Migdal, even *they* carefully walled the cemetery off, and left to neglect the burial ground of the "impure" when the organization was dismantled by the Argentine police in 1930.

Walls went up among "pure" Jews, as well. The four main Sephardi immigrant groups, as soon as they arrived in Buenos Aires, organized burial societies, raised money, and negotiated with Argentine authorities, among themselves, and with Ashkenazim to purchase lots to bury *their* dead. By 1957, Sephardi societies had founded six separate cemeteries close to the city of Buenos Aires, and had opened up five burial grounds (see figure 1.1 and table 1.1). Some of these groups shared land, but their dead lay separated by walls.

Outside Buenos Aires, however, Sephardim tended to be less divided by origin when founding their cemeteries. In towns across Argentina, Sephardim usually came together to bury their dead, even sharing these cemeteries with Ashkenazim, at first. Ashkenazim would eventually open up their own burial grounds, sometimes a single wall away from Sephardim. Yet in even smaller provincial towns the Jewish community, represented by a handful of members from differing origins, Ashkenazim and Sephardim, managed to achieve unity inside one cemetery wall.

The walls that Jews built around their dead are the focus of this chapter. Anthropologist Fredrik Barth argued that ethnic groups are defined by the boundaries that enclose them rather than by the "cultural stuff" encircled within. These social boundaries are, of course, not static; they are modified and validated through interaction with others, an ongoing process that makes it necessary to continually redefine the line that divides those inside from those outside. This theory places "differ-

Burying the Dead

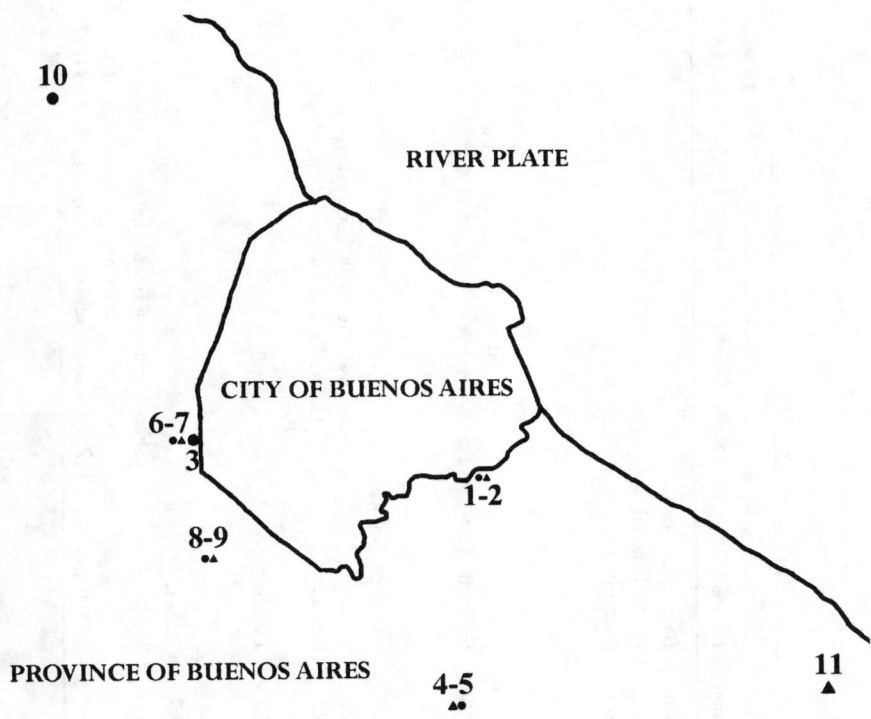

Figure 1.1. Jewish cemeteries close to Buenos Aires. For key, see Table 1.1, p. 28.

ence" at the center, as ethnic boundaries delineate just that. In Barth's words, the boundary "implies a recognition of limitations on shared understandings, differences in criteria for judgment of value and performance, and a restriction of interaction to sectors of assumed common understanding and mutual interest."[4] Such difference is not likely to disappear even though ethnic groups live in constant interaction with others. "The persistence of ethnic groups in contact," contends Barth, "implies not only criteria and signals for identification, but also a structuring of interaction which allows the persistence of cultural difference."[5] Stuart Hall likewise favors a definition of cultural identity which incorporates "difference" as constitutive of that identity.[6] In a discussion of diasporic communities, he claims that they do share a common element, yet that essential element is also necessarily modified by what the community becomes in each diasporic context. The idea of

Table 1.1. Jewish Cemeteries Close to Buenos Aires

Number on Figure 1.1	Organization	Origin	Year of Opening	Location	Notes
1	Guemilut Hasadim	Morocco	1900	Barracas al Sud (Avellaneda)	
2	Sociedad Israelita de Socorros Mutuos Varsovia (Zwi Migdal)	Ashkenazi	1909	Barracas al Sud	Share a wall.
3	Ḥevra Kedusha Ashkenazi	Ashkenazi	1910	Liniers	Sephardim (except Moroccans) buried their dead here until their own cemeteries opened.
4	Sociedad Israelita de Socorros Mutuos Dr. Theodor Hertzl	Ashkenazi	1913	Lomas de Zamora	
5	Bene Emet	Damascus	1915	Lomas de Zamora	
6	Ḥesed Shel Emet Sefaradit	Aleppo	1929	Ciudadela	Share a wall. Ḥesed Shel Emet also purchased a piece of the land and buried their dead until 1951.
7	Ḥevra Kedusha Ashkenazi	Ashkenazi	1929	Ciudadela	
8	Asociación Hebrea Argentina de Socorros Mutuos	Ottoman	1930	Tablada	Share a wall.
9	Ḥevra Kedusha Ashkenazi	Ashkenazi	1935	Tablada	
10	Ḥesed Shel Emet	Ottoman	1951	Bancalari	Shared land with Ḥesed Shel Emet Sefaradit (Ciudadela) until they purchased Bancalari. Purchased by Ḥevra Kedusha Ashkenazi in 1957.
11	Ḥevra Kedusha Ashkenazi	Ashkenazi	1957	Berazategui	

"difference" is stressed brilliantly by Daniel Boyarin and Jonathan Boyarin: "diasporic cultural identity teaches us that cultures are not preserved by being protected from 'mixing' but probably can only continue to exist as a product of such mixing."[7]

Using Barth's and Hall's focus on difference as central to ethnic identity, I argue that the walls around the dead built by Sephardim and Ashkenazim in Argentina show how ethnic, subethnic, and diasporic identities were understood and experienced, and how these separations were informed by local realities. In this chapter, we see that what so outraged Ashkenazi Rabbi Joseph regarding Moroccan Jews in Buenos Aires "and their ridiculous [burial] practices," which signaled to him the need for Ashkenazim to found a separate burial ground, did not bother Ashkenazim in Vera, in the Santa Fé province, when they came to be buried among Moroccan Jews. The issues that prompted the creation of six different Sephardi cemeteries close to the city of Buenos Aires were not apt in provincial settings, in which the Jewish population overall (and Sephardim in particular) was small. Cemetery walls underscored differences between many groups: Jews (Ashkenazim and Sephardim) from non-Jews in towns with a small Jewish population; Sephardim (regardless of origin) from Ashkenazim in larger provincial cities; and Sephardim from other Sephardim around Buenos Aires. But this chapter also shows that those differences could be overcome, even if for short periods, so that Jews in Argentina, Sephardim and Ashkenazim, Moroccan, Arabic, and Ladino speakers could negotiate common walls or shared burial grounds. The boundaries around these groups were thus not marking *essential* differences, but delineating *strategic* ones; they were malleable indeed.

Scholars have studied cemeteries for a variety of reasons. Latin American historians in particular have focused on cemeteries in order to understand the contested process of secularization that wrought control of cemeteries from the church to the state after the Wars of Independence.[8] These studies have drawn connections between new cemeteries and modern discourses on medicine and health, as secularization was embedded in the larger project of Latin American modernization. Ethnic cemeteries and ethnic societies that provided burial in city cemeteries have also been the focus of several studies.[9] These have stressed the persistence of ethnic identity in the new lands, and the role played by death in accentuating ethnic loyalties. Jewish cemeteries in particular have received much scholarly attention. In many cases, the focus of these works has been the historical recovery of Jewish presence in areas where Jews no longer live.[10] My reading of Jewish/Sephardi cemeteries aims to uncover the contested nature of the walls that encircled and divided the dead, as well as the dialogues that death spurred and made possible among the living.

THE FIRST JEWISH ARGENTINE CEMETERIES IN SANTA FÉ

Jewish cemeteries were founded in JCA colonies as they were created. The first dates from 1891, founded in the colony of Moisesville in the province of Santa Fé.[11] Like the schools, synagogues, and libraries built in the colonies, cemeteries belonged to the JCA, and it was not until later that they were sold to each colony's Hevra Kedusha (Burial Society).[12] In any Jewish community, this organization's main role is the preparation and care of the body for ritual interment, but besides its burial function, the Hevra Kedusha purchases a plot for the construction of the cemetery and then oversees its maintenance. This role usually involves dealing with secular authorities in obtaining licenses and passing inspections.

What would become the first Sephardi cemetery was founded in the city of Santa Fé in 1895. Unlike the many ethnic groups who came to the province to work the land, the Sephardim in the capital city were not colonists themselves, but rather lived off the increasing activity brought about *by* colonization. The population of the province exploded, as evidenced by the number of towns, which went from four in 1869 to sixty-two in 1895.[13] It was in these small villages that Sephardim settled. In the city of Santa Fé, for example, in 1886 and 1887, a few Moroccan Jews bought permits (*patentes*) to sell goods out of humble "stores," which were no more than movable trays on wheels. By 1895, several Jews had managed to buy their own, more permanent shops in key locations such as the city's commercial area and around the train station, and had founded their first institutions.[14]

The cemetery was a Jewish, not exclusively Sephardi, burial ground when it opened. In fact, the first interment was the reburial of an Ashkenazi child who had died in 1892, and was probably originally buried in the municipal cemetery.[15] The first burial was an Ashkenazi boy, as well. The only Jewish organization in town, the Ḥevra Kedusha that bought the cemetery, was founded by forty members, of whom seven were Ashkenazim.[16] The cemetery became Sephardi in 1915, with the founding of an Ashkenazi Ḥevra Kedusha and the subsequent purchase of a plot in 1916 for their own dead.

It is unclear what prompted the Ashkenazim to invest in their own plot in this case. But Santa Fé's Jewish cemeteries, the first in Argentina, confirm important contentions. First, that the history of Ashkenazi Jews in Argentina requires a careful look at Santa Fé, along with Entre Ríos, Buenos Aires, La Pampa, and Santiago del Estero, as these were the areas where the JCA founded their agricultural colonies. Yet the location of the first Sephardi cemetery reminds us that we should also look to the interior of the country to find the first vestiges of Sephardi life. The opening of the Sephardi cemetery on June 5, 1895, also shows that the provincial government had by then clearly recognized that religious minorities had the right to bury their dead in their own space and following their own traditions. In 1867, the province of Santa Fé had taken cemeteries away from the control of the church, and placed them under the jurisdiction of municipal governments. The city of Santa Fé, following this decree, reserved a part of the local cemetery for "Arabs, Jews, and Protestants."[17] But in 1871, the provincial government, through another decree, made it possible for the various religious communities to have their own cemeteries rather than share space in the municipal burial grounds. Taking advantage of this provision, the small Jewish community raised the money to buy a lot adjacent to the city cemetery. These acts—the creation of a Ḥevra Kedusha, the raising of funds, the purchase of the property—are also evidence of a commitment to maintain the cemetery rather than use the existing section in the municipal cemetery. The fact that there were no recorded burials in June 1895 indicates the purchase and creation of the cemetery had not been prompted by an individual's death or an epidemic. Jews were in Santa Fé to stay. This story further suggests that (only) from 1895 to 1916, Ashkenazim and Sephardim had found ways to negotiate their differences in order to embark on a common project.

BUENOS AIRES: FROM NO JEWISH CEMETERY TO TWO JEWISH CEMETERIES

Before the two Jewish cemeteries opened in the first years of the twentieth century, Jews in Buenos Aires had solved their burial needs by using the (second) Dissidents' Cemetery,[18] a term given to burial grounds not consecrated by the Catholic Church, so both Jews and Protestants were allowed to follow their own burial traditions there. This cemetery, on the outskirts of Buenos Aires at its founding, was closed in 1892, as the expanding city encroached on its borders; the remains were disinterred and relocated to burial grounds farther outside city limits. The British and German communities obtained from the city government a parcel (Disidente Section) in the recently opened Cementerio del Oeste (Western Cemetery), later to be named Cementerio de la Chacarita (Chacarita Cemetery), and Jews continued to bury their coreligionists alongside the dead of these communities until 1900 (see table 1.2).[19] But by 1898, it was clear that the British and German community section could not accommodate the growing Jewish community's burial needs. In fact, in 1897, the German and British communities informed the Jews that no more burials could take place in the section they managed.[20] It had become clear that Jews required a society that would ultimately secure a parcel for their own community, even while the Dissidents' Section in the Cementerio del Oeste provided temporary respite.

Two Hevrei Kedusha were created as answers to this need: one Ashkenazi, the other Sephardi. In order to found the Ashkenazi Hevra Kedusha in 1894, differences between Western and Eastern European Jews, as well as different political ideologies, were successfully set aside.[21] The Congregación Israelita de la República Argentina (CIRA) (Jewish Congregation of the Republic of Argentina) had, from early on, lobbied the city government for a solution to the Jewish burial question.[22] This congregation was made up mainly of Western European Jews (from Germany, France, and Britain), although there were a few Moroccan

Table 1.2. Jewish Burial Spaces in Buenos Aires

Name	Dates of Jewish Burials	Notes
Second Dissidents' Cemetery	1833 to 1892	Dates cemetery was in operation.
Western Cemetery (Chacarita): Dissidents' Section	1892 to 1900	Jews were assigned to their own section: 6.
Flores	1900 to 1935 (with very few burials after 1910, when Liniers Cemetery opened)	About 887 Jews were buried here; some were transferred to Liniers Cemetery when it opened.
Jewish Cemetery in Punta Alta	None	Approved by the city in 1925, but permits were revoked in 1926, before the cemetery opened.

members.[23] The other group interested in participating in the purchase of a cemetery parcel was the Poale Zedek (Sociedad Obrera Israelita), whose members were Russian (mostly working-class, leftist) Jews.[24] But the Ḥevra Kedusha (formed by the coming together of members from these two groups) intended to act as an independent body, and therefore, it was agreed that the burial society should not be linked to any particular organization or congregation.

The decision to form alliances in order to build a cemetery was fundamentally a financial one. The construction of synagogues (and sometimes even the rental of a room to hold services for the High Holidays) was made difficult by the shortage of cash, so finding the necessary resources to buy and upkeep cemeteries was extremely challenging. Small congregations or societies would find it very difficult to finance this project on their own. Religious, secular, Zionist, Bundist, Communist, and even Jews who married out of the faith, all came together around Jewish burial and a Jewish cemetery.[25]

Guemilut Ḥasadim, the Moroccan community Ḥevra Kedusha, was founded in 1897. The few Moroccan Jews who were part of the mostly Ashkenazi burial society became members, as did Moroccan Jews living elsewhere in the country, some from as far as Tucumán province in northwest of Argentina.[26] Like the Ashkenazi society, Guemilut Ḥasadim provided their membership with the right to rituals associated with death (such as watching over the dead body, washing and preparing the body for interment) and to financial assistance for burial.

Although the Ashkenazi Ḥevra Kedusha managed to obtain from the German and British an extension that allowed them to continue using the Dissidents' Section until 1900, the need for a Jewish cemetery became more pressing as time went by. In 1898, the now all-Ashkenazi Ḥevra Kedusha invited the recently formed Moroccan Guemilut Ḥasadim to their meetings to discuss a future collaboration. Guemilut Ḥasadim insisted on contributing only a quarter of the needed capital, as the Moroccan community was not as numerous as the Ashkenazi one. In addition, they demanded the freedom to charge their own members independently of the prices fixed by the Ashkenazi society.[27] The Ḥevra Kedusha seemed ready to receive less capital from the Moroccans than they wished, but it was unwilling to let the Moroccans have control over their own members. Although conversations between the two groups continued for the rest of the year, it soon became clear that no agreement could be reached. By June 1898, the Ḥevra Kedusha suggested that individual members of the Guemilut Ḥasadim donate money toward the cemetery fund rather than the burial society. The joint venture ultimately failed, as a result of financial considerations and power struggles.

The Ashkenazi burial society was also approached by the *t'meym* (impure) while the Ḥevra Kedusha and the Moroccan burial society were still negotiating. The t'meym was a group of Jewish men and women involved in the white slave trade who had brought this activity from Eastern Europe and was taking advantage of the gender imbalance created by the migratory patterns.[28] Although Jewish prostitutes were a minority within this activity (between 29.9 percent and 33.3 percent of the total number of registered prostitutes from 1899 to 1924 were Jewish), their presence, as well as the existence of Jewish pimps, embarrassed the nascent Jewish community.[29] As much as possible, the "pure" Jewish community tried to avoid the infiltration of "impure" elements into their organizations; they implemented strict controls for membership, sometimes even rejecting donations if it was not clear who had contributed the monies.[30] Such restrictions "forced" these Jews to set up their own societies, which included, among others, a temple, a burial society, and a self-help organization. The Sociedad Israelita de Socorros Mutuos

Varsovia (Jewish Mutual Aid Society Warsaw), founded by the t'meym in 1906—likely linked to a previous organization in existence since the 1880s—helped support the widows and orphans of members, paid for some form of health insurance, owned a mansion on Córdoba Street, and provided burial services.³¹ According to the Ashkenazi Ḥevra Kedusha, the t'meym offered an "important sum of money" to participate in purchasing land to be used as a Jewish cemetery, stressing that they did not wish to be accepted as members. The story, according to the Ḥevra Kedusha, is that the money was rejected and these two groups went their own separate ways—a telling that is borne out in that there is no joint cemetery in existence.

While the Ashkenazi Ḥevra Kedusha continued searching alone for land on which to build their cemetery, the Guemilut Ḥasadim managed to purchase a plot in Barracas del Sud (present-day Avellaneda). At that time, Barracas al Sud was a small town in the province of Buenos Aires, just across the river from the city. The cemetery, located next to the municipal burial ground, opened in 1900.³² Today, this cemetery shares a wall that once also belonged to the "impure" Zwi Migdal.³³ Although contemporaries claimed that the Moroccan and the "impure" pooled their resources in order to buy the land from the municipal authorities,³⁴ the Moroccans insist even today that they had nothing to do with the "unwanted" community.³⁵ Evidence strongly supports this contention: the two cemeteries were purchased by two different associations, years apart: Guemilut Ḥasadim (1900) and Sociedad Israelita de Socorros Mutuos Ashquenasi de Barracas al Sud y Buenos Aires (1909).³⁶ Because these parcels were located across from Barracas al Sud's municipal cemetery, it is likely they were chosen because of their location in a cemetery-approved zone. No permissions to open burial grounds could have been granted otherwise.

At the opening of the new century, then, Moroccan and "impure" Jews had their own cemeteries, and Ashkenazim continued their search for their own land. In 1930, the Zwi Migdal was declared illegal, its properties were confiscated, and its members prosecuted and sentenced to prison. The fate of the cemetery remained in a legal limbo until the late 1980s, when the municipal government made the Moroccan community responsible for its upkeep. Behind the high wall, the abandoned tombs and monuments, so close to the "pure" Jews, continue to be a reminder that divisions among living Jews were also reflected in and enacted among the dead.

THE ASHKENAZI ḤEVRA KEDUSHA: FROM BURIAL SOCIETY TO SINGLE ASHKENAZI ORGANIZATION (KEHILA)

In 1910, the Ashkenazi Ḥevra Kedusha was finally able to purchase its own cemetery in Liniers, just outside the Buenos Aires city limits. Until then, it had obtained permission from Argentine authorities to bury its members in the Flores Cemetery, another cemetery on unconsecrated land (see table 1.2).[37] But it soon became clear that even the newly purchased cemetery in Liniers would not be able to accommodate the growing number of Jewish people living (and dying) in Buenos Aires. The burial society then negotiated with the municipal authorities to acquire a new plot of land in Punta Alta close to the Cementerio del Oeste, within city limits. The request was rejected at first, yet after an appeal to the municipal council, Buenos Aires city authorities granted the permit.[38] The Ḥevra Kedusha bought the property and began construction of a fence and an administrative building. When the buildings were finished,[39] in December 1925, the Ḥevra Kedusha requested final permission to open the cemetery, which was granted by the council.[40]

In 1926, however, the municipal council withdrew its permission. On April 23 and May 11, the council signed resolutions retroactively applying a law passed in December 1925—as the Ḥevra Kedusha were finishing construction—stating that "no private cemeteries and burial grounds can be built within city limits."[41] The Ḥevra Kedusha was forced to temporarily address the problem by purchasing more land to enlarge the Liniers cemetery, in 1928, and again in 1929, it bought a section in the cemetery owned by the Aleppo Jewish community in Ciudadela, in the province of Buenos Aires. Thus the cemetery had become a key pawn in a political struggle on which the future role of the Ḥevra Kedusha rested.

By 1930 there was a growing concern about the need to centralize Jewish (Ashkenazi) communal life. "Let me tell you," the secretary of the organization informed a journalist from *Mundo Israelita*, "that if the

Ḥevra Kedusha is left without a cemetery, or if we have to move it outside of the city, this powerful institution will suffer."[42] At stake was whether the Ashkenazi Ḥevra Kedusha could become the principal Jewish (Ashkenazi) organization if a full-size cemetery (ideally within city limits) was not secured for the community. A single and strong organization was necessary to, first, accomplish many of the tasks that were fulfilled by myriad small societies and, second, represent the (Ashkenazi) community to the Argentine government and to the rest of the world.[43] Several attempts had been made in the past—the Federación Israelita Argentina (Argentine Jewish Federation), formed around the need to control ritual butchering (1908–1909); the Federación Israelita (Jewish Federation) (1913–1914); and the Alianza (1920s)[44]—all of which had failed. A central organization was not viable precisely because of the internal ideological, religious, and ethnic fractures that existed among Jews. Some argued it would be easier and less problematic to change an existing organization into the Jewish Kehila of Argentina, and the Ḥevra Kedusha appeared ideal. Not only did this organization have a long history of activity but it had demonstrated that it could neutralize internal divisions around ritual and burial. Further, the supporters of this measure insisted, the Ḥevra Kedusha was already in charge of two of the most important activities of a Kehila: charity and education.[45] In 1931, some of the burial society's board members presented a revised constitution to the governing body suggesting that the organization "formalize the activities that the Ḥevra Kedusha in fact already performs, and that are not included in its present constitution, that is to say, to represent legally all the Jews, thus preventing that anyone speak in their name, and to intensify and practice systematically social welfare and Jewish instruction."[46] The burial society seemed poised to become the first (Ashkenazi) institution able to recruit most, if not all (Ashkenazi) Jews living there.

But in order to succeed, the Ḥevra Kedusha of Buenos Aires needed to be the only such society among Ashkenazim. Thus the cemetery was important symbolically; it carried the potential to secure the preeminence of Ḥevra Kedusha, to make it the central institution within the community. As Leon Horischink, its secretary, aptly put it:

> I cannot emphasize enough the importance it [the cemetery] has for the very existence of the Ḥevra Kedusha: most of its members only belong to this organization because of the cemetery.... All those who belong to the Ḥevra Kedusha envision a future that includes many other responsibilities within the community... yet this will only be achieved if the Ḥevra Kedusha continues to administer the cemetery.[47]

The insistence on Buenos Aires as the location for the future cemetery was deliberate. As the society's secretary pointed out when the city refused permission to open the Jewish cemetery in Punta Alta, "this [the rejection] was not only unjust, but we are also being humiliated as a *colectividad* [community] because others who belong to [other] religions or dissident sects, already have their own [cemeteries within city limits]."[48] The Jewish community wanted to be treated the same as other religious communities, and if indeed the Ḥevra Kedusha wanted to act as spokesperson for the whole (Ashkenazi) Jewish community, it had to be able to provide the cemetery and defend the community's position vis-à-vis the other immigrant groups.

The cemetery within city limits, as explained, never materialized, but the monopoly over Ashkenazi death and burial remained in the hands of the Ḥevra Kedusha, which later changed its name to Asociación Mutual Israelita Argentina (AMIA) (Argentine Jewish Mutual Aid Association) to better reflect its objectives. In 1935, it finally bought a significant parcel of land from a Sephardi organization in La Tablada, a town in the province of Buenos Aires, and in 1957 it purchased its last parcel, in the town of Berazategui in the same province.[49] By 1960, then, fifty years after the purchase of the first cemetery in Liniers, the Ashkenazi community could bury their members in Liniers, Ciudadela (in the section bought from the Aleppine Jews), La Tablada (which was later enlarged to meet the growing need for space), and Berazategui. These cemeteries assured the association the ability to provide burial plots for all its members.

Thus the Ashkenazi Ḥevra Kedusha traveled a long way: from a handful of men belonging mainly to the CIRA, whose main responsibility was to assure Jewish ritual burial in Protestant and municipal cemeteries, to an organized body in charge of the purchase of a parcel to be used exclusively by Jews; from managing a section of Dissidents' Cemeteries to owning four; from Ashkenazi and Sephardi to only Ashkenazi; from an Ashkenazi burial society to an (Ashkenazi) Kehila. Other Jewish Ashkenazi organizations gathered around class, ideological, religious, and political lines, but the importance of Jewish burial meant that the Ḥevra Kedusha could blur those divisions and represent the interests of all.[50]

OTHER SEPHARDI CEMETERIES IN BUENOS AIRES: BUILDING WALLS

Like the Ashkenazi Ḥevra Kedusha, Sephardi burial societies and the cemeteries they purchased and managed became centralizing institutions within their communities. Although each Sephardi group established various philanthropic, educational, and religious societies, there tended to be only one Ḥevra Kedusha and only one cemetery. Here, I briefly outline the histories of the creation of these organizations as well as their cemeteries, which bear many similarities. In most cases, burial societies became priorities very early on in the institutional history of different migratory groups; the purchase of cemeteries tended to centralize institutional life, as all societies (social, religious, educational) contributed financially, and (most) Jews belonged to them; in many cases, the power of burial societies was challenged by other groups precisely because of the power they held.

Challenges to power of burial societies were common. The Moroccan Guemilut Ḥasadim's position within the community, for example, was tested in 1905, with the creation of a new *hermandad* (brotherhood): Ḥesed VeEmet. In return for the payment of a monthly fee, members were eligible for, among other things, burial services.[51] Then from 1905 to 1920, the societies worked alongside each other, burying their own members in the Moroccan cemetery. But in 1920, the leadership of these organizations decided that Guemilut Ḥasadim would be the sole organization in charge of burials (ritual and costs) and Ḥesed VeEmet would focus on philanthropy among the Moroccan community.[52]

In 1913, Damascene Jews founded the burial society Bene Emet in Lanús, in the province of Buenos Aires. Members announced the purchase of a parcel of land in Lomas de Zamora (in the same province) to be used for their cemetery, for which they paid cash, suggesting that they may have been actively raising money for some time. The cemetery opened in 1915 after meeting municipal requirements and receiving official permission. Although primarily a burial society, Bene Emet also aided members of the community. In turn, money to support the work of the organization (mainly the purchase and upkeep of the cemetery) was provided not only by the fees paid by members of the society but by collections carried out in other Arab-Jewish organizations founded by Jews from Damascus. For cemetery construction, for example, Bene Emet received donations from various Damascene congregations in La Boca and Lanús.[53]

The other Arab-Jewish community from the city of Aleppo founded their own Ḥevra Kedusha in 1923, which they named Ḥesed Shel Emet Sefaradit.[54] Until then, the organization buried its members in the Liniers cemetery, through agreement with the Ashkenazi Ḥevra Kedusha. The arrangement worked well for some time; however, as they announced in 1927, "[our own] cemetery would fill a major need in our community." The parcel they managed to procure was indeed large, and they were able to sell parts of it to the Ashkenazi Ḥevra Kedusha,[55] and to the Ladino-speaking community, whose burial needs had not yet been resolved.[56] These sections were walled off and independent from each other.

In 1916, the Ladino-speaking community founded their Ḥevra Kedusha (Ḥesed Shel Emet). In 1919, however, this organization joined the efforts of Kahal Kadosh (later Asociación Comunidad Israelita Sefaradí de Buenos Aires; ACISBA) to raise money to buy their own synagogue, which opened in 1919. Until 1951, when they finally purchased their own cemetery (in Bancalari, province of Buenos Aires), the community met their burial needs by joining the Ashkenazim in Liniers and by purchasing a small parcel together with the Aleppine community in their Ciudadela cemetery.

There was another group of Ladino-speaking Jews, those who had originally settled in the downtown area of Buenos Aires, who placed the purchase of a cemetery plot at the top of their communal objectives. In 1929, the Jews who belonged to congregation Etz HaḤaim and the El Socorro philanthropic group joined the Ladino speakers who had settled in Villa Urquiza (a northern neighborhood in the city) to form the Asociación Hebrea Argentina de Socorros Mutuos (AHASM) (Argentine Jewish Mutual Aid Association). It was this new society that, in 1930, managed to purchase a parcel of land in La Tablada to create the first Ladino-speaking community cemetery, although only those belonging to the AHASM could be buried there. The purchase of the land has become a central part of this community's institutional memory: It is seen as, first, a victory over the "shortsightedness" of the other Ladino-speaking group, which had purchased a parcel that was not big enough to meet its burial needs, and, second, as a source of pride because of the large size of the parcel purchased. Part of the land was sold to the Ashkenazi Ḥevra Kedusha, solving that organization's needs.

As recounted by a former president and secretary of AHASM, the story of the purchase of the La Tablada land is simple: the friendship between Alejandro Arruguete, the son of one of the past presidents of the association, and Manuel Fresco, the son of the governor of the province of Buenos Aires, resulted in the largest concession of land given to any Jewish institution. The narrative stresses that Arruguete placed the objectives of the community above all else by suggesting that his friend's father solve the issue of Jewish burial. Fresco, according to the narrative, responded to the request by having President Uriburu (who had just come to power after the military coup) sign a degree granting a vast parcel of land in Tablada, province of Buenos Aires.[57] The parcel was so large (and expensive) that AHASM approached the other Ladino-speaking community, asking them to share the cost of the purchase, but the invitation was rejected. Then, as the story goes, they approached the Ashkenazi Ḥevra Kedusha, who gave AHASM the money needed to seal the deal. The story for AHASM, in the end, highlighted the fact that it was thanks to the *criterio buenísimo de muchacho judío* (wonderful common sense of a Jewish boy) that the burial needs not only of their society, but also of the larger (Ashkenazi) Jewish community, were finally met and solved.[58] Ownership of a large parcel that solved burial needs for many years to come became evidence of financial solvency and independence.

Other Sephardi groups, much smaller in size, decided from early on not to invest in their own cemeteries and joined other Sephardi groups for their burial needs. Italian and Yugoslav Sephardim, alongside Jews from Rhodes and Salonika, worked with the Ladino-speaking community that purchased the Bancalari cemetery in the early 1950s. The Jews originally from Jerusalem joined in the Aleppo community for their burial needs.

BRIDGING WALLS

The recounting of the cemeteries and burial societies obscures the many conversations that took place between and among these groups in their search for a solution to burial needs. Some of these attempts at working together ended up in agreement, if only temporarily, while others failed almost immediately. In some cases, initial refusal turned into later acceptance; in others, agreement meant only that difference and distance was legitimized. Ultimately, paying attention to these conversations, to the bridges and walls built by Jews among and around cemeteries, highlights the contingent nature of the boundaries that defined and constituted the identity of these subethnic groups in the new land.

The Ashkenazi Hevra Kedusha agreed to bury Sephardim in the lots they had secured, but not without conflict. Rodolfo Ornstein, past vice president of the Congregación Israelita de la República Argentina and the president of the Hevra Kedusha in 1895, protested that members of the Congregación Israelita Latina de Buenos Aires (Spanish Jewish Congregation of Buenos Aires), (Moroccan Jews) "demand that the ... [burial society] pay for nurses for their sick, something which is against our constitution ... and likewise demand that the *shomrim* [the attendant of the burial society] be obligated in some cases to watch the dead for two nights for the same price [as one]."[59] Ashkenazi leaders also complained that Sephardi traditions were too "different" and othered all Jews in the eyes of the broader Buenos Aires community, thus bringing unwanted attention from the city's non-Jewish majority. For example, Rabbi Joseph, the head of the Ashkenazi burial society and rabbi of the Congregación Israelita de Buenos Aires, complained that when they bury a coreligionist, "the members of the Congregación Israelita Latina ... hold ridiculous ceremonies in public that attract the attention of the populace, and could provoke a conflict with the [general] population and authorities."⁶⁰ Although there is no clear explanation of what constituted a "ridiculous ceremony" for the Ashkenazim, Moroccan Jews (as well as other Sephardi groups) practiced some unmistakably non-European rituals, including the famous loud ululations made by mourners at the grave and the practice of burial without coffins (which were burned at the cemetery).⁶¹ The Ashkenazi community and their "modern" Jewish leaders, in their wish to foster a "modern" Jewish identity in Buenos Aires, might have viewed these burial rites as "intolerably other."⁶² This attitude helps us understand why they declined to work with the Moroccan Guemilut Hasadim to purchase a shared lot.

Yet this initial objection to Sephardi practices and rituals did not prevent the Ashkenazi Hevra Kedusha from striking agreements with other Sephardi communities, probably as a result of its realization of the power (and income) such a position would generate. Until the opening of their own cemeteries, all Sephardim (with the exception of the Moroccans, who already had purchased theirs) were buried in the Ashkenazi plots of Liniers, and the section managed in the Flores municipal cemetery. Bene Emet, for example, paid the Ashkenazi Hevra Kedusha for the burial of several members who were laid to rest in Liniers.⁶³ But the relationship between these various institutions and the Ashkenazim was not devoid of conflict, nor was it always over the ritual itself. The problem was financial; it was over what prices to charge for burial, and whether favorable payment terms for those with little or no means could be obtained. The Aleppine community leaders knew that the rich had no problem negotiating with Ashkenazim. "But the poor," they noted, "in their painful moments, always have to depend on the charity of other members; sometimes waiting until the money [to pay for expenses] is raised prevents a quick burial, and two or three days would pass before it is possible."⁶⁴ The implication was that the Ashkenazi Hevra Kedusha did not make distinctions between poor and rich, therefore leaving the impoverished members of the Aleppine community even more vulnerable. Complaints leveled by the Ladino-speaking Hesed Shel Emet also ran along the same lines: "the Ashkenazi burial society, when dealing with poor Sephardim, did not treat them right."⁶⁵ Burying their own members was a highly regarded mitzvah, but burying those who belonged to other communities seems to have been a mere financial transaction.⁶⁶

Although these Sephardi groups used the Ashkenazi cemetery even while privately voicing their concerns, that tenuous association with the Ashkenazim made it more pressing for them to find an alternative. At the same meeting in which members of the Ḥesed Shel Emet (Ladino-speaking community) cited the difficulties of the needy, they launched a discussion of the cemetery options available to them. One group wished to continue their relationship with the Ashkenazi society, in the hope that the new proposed cemetery in Punta Alta (a much bigger parcel than Liniers) would ease tensions between the two associations; another group found a parcel in the town of Vicente Lopez, in the province of Buenos Aires, which would be completely theirs; and yet a third group wished to join the Aleppine Jews in their search for a parcel.[67] Eventually, the joint venture with the Jews from Aleppo was deemed the most financially advantageous. It solved the community's burial problems until 1951, when they finally purchased their own separate land in the town of Bancalari.

The burial society of the Aleppine community purchased a cemetery in 1927 that opened in 1929 and was divided into three sections. One was sold to the Ladino-speaking community for their burials; another area was managed by the Ashkenazi Ḥevra Kedusha (which had by then lost the bid for the cemetery in Punta Alta); and the third area was administered by the Aleppine community's Ḥevra Kedusha. So while these organizations were able to cooperate in the purchase of the cemetery and successfully negotiated a sharing agreement, in practice three separate cemeteries with three different burial societies only catered to their specific communities; they used the rituals they wished and provided financial support to whomever they deemed needed it. Aleppine community leaders also offered Moroccan Jews a section of the newly purchased land. The Moroccan cemetery was quickly filling up, and they had been discussing ways to obtain more space. Yet after several meetings and conversations, an agreement was not reached, so there would not be a fourth section managed by yet another Ḥevra Kedusha.[68]

In 1909, the Damascene Ḥevra Kedusha (Bene Emet) approached Moroccan Sephardim about burial space in the Moroccan cemetery in Barracas al Sud, which was used by both Guemilut Ḥasadim and Ḥesed

VeEmet. But rather than approach the Guemilut Ḥasadim (the Moroccan Ḥevra Kedusha and the owner of the cemetery), members from the Bene Emet initiated discussions with Ḥesed VeEmet, which provided an array of philanthropic services, including burial assistance. Although Ḥesed VeEmet did not completely reject the possibility of a joint venture, the response to Bene Emet's request was negative. Ḥesed VeEmet claimed that they wanted to accept these Syrian Jews as members, but said that the Guemilut Ḥasadim would not accept non-Moroccan dead in the cemetery they owned. The Guemilut Ḥasadim, they explained, had bought the cemetery, and decisions as to who could be buried there remained under their control. Torn between the possibility of enlarging their membership, but aware that Bene Emet's reason for joining their mutual aid society was mainly to secure access to the cemetery for *their* members, Ḥesed VeEmet insisted that they would do everything in their power to obtain space for the "international" Sephardim, but guaranteed no success.[69] This joint project never materialized. The Damascene Ḥevra Kedusha thus set up a relationship with the Ashkenazim for burial spaces in Liniers and eventually opened their own cemetery in 1915.

The reasons provided by the Moroccan Sephardim to justify the rejection of the shared burial ground illustrate the ways in which the living—their conflicts and jealousies—defined the walls built (or not) around the dead. Ḥesed VeEmet claimed that if Syrian Jews were granted rights for burial, they would end up occupying their already "reduced space," as the number of Moroccan Jews was significantly smaller than those of the Syrian community from Damascus. But, more important, Moroccan leaders stressed that only "those international Sephardim with irreproachable behavior" could be allowed to be buried in the cemetery.[70] Ḥesed VeEmet declared that it was not able to ascertain whether these individuals were of "irreproachable behavior," since they did not know them while they were alive.

Such worries about behavior were not just a convenient excuse for rejecting Syrian Jews. Respectability was an important concern that Jews discussed in a variety of settings, but it is a topic that has, among scholars of Jewish Argentina, unfortunately only been framed within discussions of "prostitutes and pimps."[71] Honor and good reputation were qualities that mattered greatly for membership in communal organizations, and an attack on one's reputation was considered an inexcusable affront to one's good standing in the community.[72] These affronts were always challenged by the "victim," who requested that there be a public recanting of the accusation. These events were mediated by the ethnic societies to which both "victim" and "victimizer" belonged.[73]

Proving "good behavior" was done through community contacts, people who vouched for one's moral standing.[74] Families and commercial networks usually acted in the name of individuals to provide the support required. In Argentina, such considerations continued to be important and decisive, but it became a contentious issue, especially when people of different communities of origin requested acceptance. Family and commercial ties were not common among those from different lands, so it was hard to prove "irreproachable behavior" when applicants and organizations were of different origins. Ḥesed VeEmet eventually understood that it was impossible for the Guemilut Ḥasadim to accept the request of the Syrian Jews. To be buried in their cemetery, it was required that knowledge of the dead and of the living be available, something that could not be guaranteed if the living had not shared common grounds.

SEPHARDIM AND THEIR DEAD IN THE REST OF ARGENTINA

The story of Jewish cemeteries in the rest of Argentina shows that the borders and walls that Jews of different origins built around their dead in and around the city of Buenos Aires were not demarcating essential differences. Rather, this story stresses how identity boundaries obeyed local realities, specific to where the walls were built. This section briefly recounts the founding of the cemeteries in cities of the interior, paying specific attention to how all Sephardim, regardless of origin, found common ground to build shared institutions, and how Ashkenazim participated alongside or not in these projects. While Sephardim in these towns did not highlight the distinctions around origin they maintained in Buenos Aires, the Sephardim-Ashkenazim divide was indeed kept.

Initially, capital cities in the interior of the country had only one Jewish cemetery, and, as such, it accepted all Jews living in those towns

Burying the Dead

and those around it. As previously noted, the first Sephardi cemetery opened in Argentina was located in the city of Santa Fé. The next Sephardi cemetery was inaugurated in 1912, by the Ḥesed VeEmet of Resistencia, Chaco.[75] In 1917, the first burial in the Sephardi cemetery in the city of Corrientes took place.[76] The location and dates of these cemeteries also show how much earlier Sephardim had been able to organize, petition, and purchase burial grounds compared with the Sephardi organizations in Buenos Aires.

As Sephardi immigration to interior towns took place before the settlement of significant numbers of Ashkenazim, the Sephardi societies organized in those towns also congregated those Jews who arrived later.[77] This was particularly true not so much for purposes of prayer but specifically for purposes of burial.[78] For example, in Santa Fé, seven of the members of the burial society that bought the cemetery were Ashkenazim, and five of the first six dead buried in the newly acquired plots were also Ashkenazim.[79] In Resistencia, until the creation of the Ashkenazi cemetery, there were twelve burials of members from that community in the Sephardi plot.[80] In Corrientes, there are also around thirteen Ashkenazi members buried in the Sephardi cemetery.[81] The cemetery (founded by mostly Sephardi members) acted, at first, as the only collective "Jewish" institution, while the other social and philanthropic organizations remained subethnically divided.

As the Ashkenazi communities grew in these cities, they eventually established their own cemeteries, but in many cases, not immediately. In Santa Fé, the Ashkenazi cemetery opened on October 1, 1916, fifteen years after the inauguration of the first cemetery.[82] In Resistencia, the Ashkenazi community purchased their cemetery in 1938, almost twenty-six years after the Sephardim had opened theirs; in Corrientes, the Ashkenazi cemetery dates from the late 1930s, more than ten years after the opening of the first one. Because it was already possible to ensure Jewish burial in a Jewish cemetery, it seems that Ashkenazi communities opted to create other institutions before spending money on a parcel of land for their own cemeteries.

In the few cases in which it has been possible to document the relationship between Sephardim and Ashkenazim in the interior of the country regarding burial, it can be argued that friction, although it existed, never provoked the later founding of an Ashkenazi cemetery. In 1933 in Resistencia, for example, an Ashkenazi commission requested from the Sephardi Ḥesed VeEmet the burial of one of their members. There are no records of negotiations, and the Ashkenazim paid m$n 400[83] (then about US$125) that was charged for the plot and service.[84] Even in the case of subsidizing the burial, which was a point of contention in Buenos Aires between the Sephardi organizations and the Ashkenazi Ḥevra Kedusha, there seems to have been a working understanding between the two groups. In January 1933, an Ashkenazi father was charged only "the minimum sum stipulated in our bylaws" (m$n 200; then about US$63) to bury his baby girl, as he was not a member of the community but "his economic situation was dire."[85] In October of the same year, another Ashkenazi Jew requested permission to bury his stillborn baby. The father was charged only m$n 10 (then about US$3.13) as "he does not have much money."[86] Unless the situation between Ashkenazim and Sephardim soured in the following five years (which is the date for the founding of the Ashkenazi cemetery), these exchanges between the two societies suggest that the groups had developed an amicable relationship; they agreed on prices and changed the costs of services depending on family need.

But while Sephardim expressed no problems with accepting Ashkenazi burials, and they even lent them other property, it was clear that matters of ownership of the cemetery would not be even discussed. In 1935, Ḥesed VeEmet in Resistencia received a letter from the president, secretary, and treasurer of the Ashkenazi community, who were asking to buy part of the cemetery for their organization's use.[87] This transaction did not take place, although a few years later, Ḥesed VeEmet allowed the same organization to use their upstairs room for their religious school.[88]

Other incidents recorded in the surviving minute books of the Sephardi society of Resistencia suggest that issues of ritual were also under the supervision and control of the Ḥesed VeEmet. In 1928, the executive committee of Ḥesed VeEmet decided not to accept the burial of Alfredo Shomke "as no documents or existing family can prove the dead man was indeed Jewish."[89] On January 1, 1930, the minutes book refers to an article in *La Opinión*, a local newspaper, which "censured the way in which Ḥesed VeEmet handled the death of a boy belonging to the Ashkenazi community."[90] Although the minutes are not explicit about the issue in question—and the original article has yet to be located—it is possible to infer that it had to do with either the "Jewishness" of the boy or the manner of death.

Disagreements existed not only between Sephardim and Ashkenazim but between the Ḥesed VeEmet and Sephardi families whose members had died. In February 1933, a Sephardi Jew accused the community of not allowing the burial of his daughter. Ḥesed VeEmet requested that it be established whether the baby was stillborn, or if she had indeed been born alive, as the distinction would determine the type of burial—whether in the general section or not—required.[91] The argument over this issue produced a rift that ended with all the executive committee resigning.[92] The degree of ritual observance required by the burial society is quite surprising, and the negative response to the forcing of religious orthodoxy was quite clear, as well.

In Santa Fé, the Ashkenazim decided to form their own Ḥevra Kedusha and raise money for their own parcel "because there is no more space in the section of the municipal cemetery reserved for dissidents."[93] This reason suggests that the Ashkenazi community was using the municipal cemetery for their burials, and not the already open Sephardi cemetery. Yet the number of Ashkenazim buried in this cemetery before the opening of their own contradicts the impression that tension existed between the two communities: eighty-two members, including some relatives of the founders of the Ashkenazi Ḥevra Kedusha, were laid to rest in the Sephardi cemetery. Again, this example suggests that financial and practical decisions played an important role in deciding where to be buried, not ritual or cultural matters.

In other big provincial towns, the division between Ashkenazim and Sephardim was not made evident by the founding of two separate pieces of land but by a wall that divided a cemetery into two sections. This was the case in Córdoba, Salta, San Juan, and La Rioja, in which the two communities, Sephardi and Ashkenazi, pooled their resources to buy a big parcel, and then divided it according to their membership and financial capabilities. In Salta, for example, the Sephardi community bought, as early as December 1917, a plot for a cemetery.[94] Soon after the purchase, the Sociedad Israelita Salteña "La Union" de Socorros Mutuos (Jewish Mutual Aid Society "Union" of Salta) sold part of the land to the Ashkenazi community.[95] In Córdoba, the Sephardim bought a plot in 1923 and gave part to the Ashkenazi community in exchange for construction of the surrounding wall.[96]

In other (usually smaller) towns, Jews were buried together, regardless of their origin, and divided by no walls. In Catamarca, Tucumán, Formosa, San Luis, Villa Mercedes, Vera, Rosario, Posadas, and Presidencia Roque Sáenz Peña (cities with a significant number of both Sephardim and Ashkenazim), the purchase of the cemetery lot was either done by the majority Jewish organization (and the smaller group was accepted without any problems) or the cemetery was bought by an organization that was of mixed origins. In Rosario, for example, burial was always in the hands of the Ashkenazi organization even when Sephardim were indeed numerous. No evidence exists that they wanted to buy their own land.[97] In Roque Sáenz Peña, on the other hand, the association that bought the cemetery (and has administered it since) was made up of both Ashkenazim and Sephardim.[98] In Tucumán, although the cemetery belongs to the Ashkenazi community, there were two Ḥevrei Kedusha, and families chose which rabbi performed the burial.[99] In Paraná, however, the provincial government had to intervene and create a "mixed" Ḥevra Kedusha to resolve internal issues between Sephardim and Ashkenazim (though the sources do not say exactly what the issues were).[100]

Jewish cemeteries in provincial towns were also used by the smaller Jewish communities living close by who had not yet founded (and probably never would) their own cemeteries. The cemetery in Vera, province of Santa Fé, for example, was bought thanks to donations made by Jews living in various small nearby towns: Colonia Romang, Reconquista, Calchaquí, and Margarita.[101] The cemetery in Resistencia, Chaco, for example, buried people from the city of Corrientes, La Sabana, and Villa Angela.[102] In Chaco, those Jews who belonged to the Ḥesed VeEmet of Resistencia (which owned the cemetery) but lived in Presidencia Roque Sáenz Peña, rescinded their membership when the Jewish community of the small town founded their own cemetery.[103] Catamarca and Salta sent their Jewish dead to Tucumán (to the Dissidents' Section of the municipal cemetery) until the local Jewish cemeteries opened.[104]

CONCLUSION

These stories of conversations, agreements, and disagreements bring us to an important realization. Sephardi/Jewish identity, as reflected in the number of cemeteries and burial societies, was constructed as the result of particular events related to establishing new lives and how the living interacted among themselves. It has been assumed that the various Sephardi groups that arrived and settled in Argentina had an essential commonality derived from their expulsion from Spain, the maintenance of religious traditions born from their experience in Spain, and from their attachment to Spanish culture and Sephardi ritual.[105] All these elements are understood to have constituted, throughout time, an "essential" Sephardi identity. Yet scholars, even as they describe how *different* these groups had become as a result of their wanderings in the various diasporic contexts after the expulsion from the Iberian Peninsula, still seem surprised when confronted with difference.[106] The few studies of the Sephardim in Argentina, for example, stress the lack of unity that characterized these groups.[107] Why, it is asked, did the various groups of Sephardim not become *one*? Why, in the case of Buenos Aires, did they create five cemeteries? Why did they insist on stressing their differences rather than focus on their similarities?

The only "constant" difference marked by all these cemetery walls was that of "Jewishness."[108] Whether by religious conviction or cultural identification, (most) Jews requested to be buried in "Jewish" cemeteries, and Jewish communities responded to this wish by purchasing a space in which Jewish practices could be observed. The Jews who are buried inside the Jewish cemetery walls (no matter which Jewish organization owns it) mark, above all, this *chosen* difference with the rest of society. In Buenos Aires, for example, the need to maintain this difference moved Jews to acquire land rather than use the space provided by the city in the Dissidents' Cemetery, and later in a section of the Chacarita plot. The same reason motivated the purchase of the Jewish cemeteries in the interior towns, like Santa Fé, Resistencia, and Vera.

The walls in Jewish cemeteries—and the existence of various Jewish cemeteries in one city or town—did not (and still do not) mark only "Jewishness" but also a desire to highlight origin. Although it is true that for Argentine society that distinction may have been (and still may be) lost (Argentines probably read any Jewish cemetery's wall as a basic differentiation between Jews and Catholics), it was a distinction that some Jewish communities wanted to maintain. In Buenos Aires, the different Sephardi groups each founded and fought for their own burial grounds; in some interior cities, the Ashkenazim preferred to have their own community cemetery; in other towns, internal walls divided Sephardi and Ashkenazi graves.

Difference did not override commonality. The (Ashkenazi) cemetery in Liniers, for example, was used by almost all Sephardi communities until they were able to buy their own grounds; Ashkenazim initially used the Sephardi cemeteries in Resistencia, Santa Fé, and Corrientes. Rather, the wish to preserve difference, or the lack of need to do so, speaks to boundaries that are constructed, arranged, and rearranged, and do not follow some "essential" characteristic of Jewishness or even "Sephardiness." Each Jewish community in Argentine cities and towns decided on and constructed boundaries that differentiated and therefore constituted its own "Jewish" identity.

The cemetery walls were not built to divide only the dead. The boundaries constructed around the graves signified a much larger set of differences and commonalities. Because burial societies were part of a net of community "services," which included medical, religious, and philanthropic activities, these walls also clearly marked difference among the living. In a sense, difference in origin translated (or not) into a set of groups, societies, and social organizations of which the cemetery was one. If Jews of different origins together founded social clubs, they also buried their dead together. If they socialized depending on origin, walls around cemeteries also were put up. It is to the boundaries around the living that we now turn our attention.

TWO

HELPING THE LIVING

Philanthropy and the Boundaries of Sephardi Communities in Argentina

> Our society should be like a family.
>
> Legion de Voluntarios Kanfe Yona (1927)[1]

IN 1927, SEVERAL DOZEN MOROCCAN JEWS FOUNDED THE LEgion de Voluntarios Kanfe Yona (Volunteer Legion, Kanfe Yona) in Buenos Aires. The objectives of this philanthropic society were varied: to facilitate medical attention and provide access to medicine; to create hospitals; found retirement homes, orphanages, and clinics; to visit the sick and provide comfort to those suffering; and to provide charity.[2] Its reach was inclusive: any Sephardi man, woman, or child over the age of thirteen—member or not, resident of Buenos Aires or settled in another part of the country—was eligible to receive its help. Especially during its early years, the community responded enthusiastically to the organization. The society boasted four hundred members in the first few months after its creation,[3] and it was still active until at least the early 1950s.[4] Membership fees were a symbolic one peso (m$n) but by 1932 Kanfe Yona had raised enough money to open its own *tefilá* (temple). It reported that, by that date, Kanfe Yona:

> has distributed the respectable sum of m$n11,200 (around US$400); we have alleviated much suffering, helped many helpless and forgotten women; we have visited hospitals, assisted patients with tuberculosis, provided a fixed income to heads of families unable to work. We have secured jobs for many people who had lost hope; we have paid for numerous travel tickets; and have contributed to charity in Morocco.[5]

Kanfe Yona was not alone in providing help to the Sephardim who settled in Argentina. In fact, it was only one of a myriad of organizations (even within the small Moroccan community) created to assist coreligionists when they faced difficult periods in their lives. The Sephardim brought the concept of these organizations from their countries of origin; although similar to those in the Old World, these new philanthropic societies supported the birth of new identities. While delimited by the geographical proximity of their members and by the gaze of the state in the Old World, the organizations Sephardim founded in Argentina acted as the foundations on which these communities reimagined their identity boundaries in the new land. Kanfe Yona, for example, attempted to include, even if only discursively, all Sephardim both as members and as potential recipients;[6] members of the association could be found many miles away;[7] and Kanfe Yona used some of the money it raised in Argentina to aid Jews living in Morocco. In short, Kanfe Yona encouraged, through the dispensation of aid, the idea of an all-encompassing Sephardi community whose members were not necessarily always Moroccan, not necessarily always living in the same city, and not even always on the same side of the Atlantic.

This chapter uses the various institutions created by Sephardim in Argentina, and the ties the leaders of these organizations created with individuals and other organizations, as a window into the construction of ethnic boundaries. I briefly describe Sephardic philanthropic organizations in the Old World, and move on to those created by Sephardim in Buenos Aires and the rest of the country to address financial or medical need. Burial organizations, such as the Ḥevrei Kedusha, were more fully examined in chapter 1 but are a part of this discussion, as some dispensed aid beyond that required for burial. Schools, social or sporting societies, and women's auxiliaries—even when dedicated to philanthropy—are not included here, as they are the focus of chapters 5 and 6. This chapter concludes by focusing on the ways in which these exchanges of aid and communication created spaces for the birth of new identity ties, no longer based exclusively on geographical origin but on shared experiences as Argentines.

PHILANTHROPY, JEWS, AND DIASPORA

Prior to the arrival of modernity, 613 commandments, or mitzvot, governed traditional Jewish life, and observing these ethical, legal, work, and ritual rules defined a Jew's place in these communities. Several of these mitzvot refer to *tzedakah*, a term that has been translated as "charity" or "philanthropy," but these English terms lose the element of obligation embedded in the meaning of the Hebrew. These acts of kindness included, among others, visiting the sick, providing a dowry for poor young brides, providing for the needs of the elderly and orphans, attending to the needs of the deceased and mourners, and even ransoming captives in times of war.

Even as the processes of secularization and modernization unfurled in Europe and in the Ottoman Empire, and (modern) states took responsibility for education and welfare from the church, Jewish communities continued to take care of their own. Historians of Jews in Western Europe argue that this was because of existing perceptions of the "semiautonomous nature" of Jewish communities, with some historians contending that Jewish elites saw in philanthropy a tool with which to reduce anti-Semitism.[8] Meanwhile, historians of Jews in the East, with a very different modernization process under way, have emphasized the role played by the Ottoman state, and by the active philanthropic institutions from the West that had settled there.[9] This historiographical divide is thus based on geography, and perhaps also the fact that, with the advent of modernity, the meaning of philanthropy changed. This modernization period, scholars stress, witnessed the shift from the notion of "charity" to that of "welfare," which had important implications for both modernization and nationalist projects.[10] In addition, new studies of Jewish diasporic groups have highlighted the ways in which mass immigration into the New World reconfigured the very borders of these communities, and the central role philanthropic organizations played in recrafting these identities.[11]

Just as scholars understand the importance of tzedakah in Jewish life, even at a time of profound changes, Sephardi immigrants to Argentina also emphasized the centrality it played in their lives prior to migration.[12]

In fact, tzedakah constitutes one of the most frequently used images of life prior to immigration; one that confirms, in immigrants' minds, the traditional character of that experience. One such immigrant, Mesody (last name not given), remembered that her mother-in-law, a haute couture seamstress in Tangier, during the summer months would "go to the *Alliance Israelite Universelle* school with other women and sew clothes for poor girls' *ajuares* [trousseaus]. The clothes [they made] would be distributed before Rosh Hashanah. I can still see her, bent over her needlework with the *mejerma* [headpiece] covering her hair."[13] Mesody continued:

> No meal would be eaten before something was prepared for those who had nothing to eat. Tzedakah bread was a spiritual obligation, a sacred ritual. In all Jewish homes, every Thursday, bread for Shabbat would be baked.... Among all the loaves my mother made, there was always a special one, round and very big, "the Tzedakah bread" that three men would come to get, house by house, and would later distribute among the most indigent.[14]

Because of the central role of tzedakah in everyday Jewish life, informants would also recall the pervasive presence of the societies created in order to fulfill these commandments. Jaime Angel remembered, for example, how the Bikur Ḥolim (organization to help the sick) helped poor people in Kavala (city in Northern Greece) obtain medical attention, medications, and even milk for their children.[15] In Salonika, the Matanot Laevionim (organization to help the poor) was in charge of providing daily lunches to students of the community schools, who were usually orphans.[16] In Rhodes, Rosa explained, the poor were asked to perform some activity in return for the help they received, such as accompanying mourners and praying for the dead.[17] In Tétouan, Morocco, these communal organizations helped as many as 160 families in 1889.[18]

In these recollections, tzedakah is remembered as part of the *community's* Jewish identity. It was the community's duty to ensure a decent livelihood for their own, and they did so by raising communal taxes (a fiscal right obtained from the state) to fund their activities and by donating willingly (money and/or time) to the organizations of their choice. The responsibility of helping their own rested entirely on themselves, and helping those in need (not only in their own communities but also in the Jewish world in general) united them, as a community, in action. Tzedakah, as well, involved personal interactions. Those living in the *dzhudería* (Jewish quarter) knew one another, and although most of the work was done through the actions of societies, acts that brought together those who helped and those who were helped were common.[19] As noted, the poor would be invited to eat either before or after a wedding or circumcision banquet in Salonika and Tétouan;[20] they would eat in the garden of those who could feed them on Friday night in Çeşme (seaside town close to Izmir),[21] or get free coal from those who could afford it.[22] For every Jewish festivity, women in wealthier families would send their daughters or granddaughters with plates full of the delicacies baked for the occasion to distribute among the less fortunate.[23] Poor people in Rhodes would go from door to door, collecting what people could give them so they could eat during the Sabbath.[24] In these recollections, tzedakah is seen to reinforce communal ties and identity.

CROSSING THE ATLANTIC WITH THESE SOCIETIES: SEPHARDI (AND IMMIGRANT) ARGENTINA

Sephardi organizational life in Argentina cannot be understood outside the context of this previous experience. Jews adjusted their practices as they arrived in Argentina, at the same time that the country was establishing itself as a liberal, modern state. First, Jews were never imagined as semiautonomous communities by the Argentine state. They were not "required" to organize themselves, for example, to levy taxes on members as a means to obtain communal income, nor were they required to provide their own firemen or legal courts to settle matters among Jews. In fact, Argentina, echoing the ideals of the French Revolution, had started dismantling special legal privileges during the Wars of Independence (1810–1816), and would continue to do so throughout the nineteenth century. In that same vein, Argentina had come to define itself as a liberal country that stressed separation of church and state and whose process of secularization was under way, especially in education and other civil matters.[25]

Still, Argentina's welfare state was far from being established. Although local governments would indeed develop social policies to address problems brought about by massive immigration, it would be up to the immigrant communities themselves to create institutions that could provide those services, or they would need to rely on existing philanthropic groups.[26] In 1914, the national census listed 1,202 mutual aid societies (not all ethnic in character) providing a variety of services such as health, education, and other forms of subsidies. By 1926, the number had slightly declined to 1,141.[27] These associations supported about half a million immigrants in times of need and raised money to support these activities through events that provided opportunities to socialize in an environment that was familiar and safe. Historians of ethnic communities, gender, and labor have all noted the central role these societies played in the formation of the working class and the welfare state, and in aiding both assimilation to the new country and retaining connections with the country of origin.[28]

The Argentine government, however, was baffled by how to define Jewish philanthropy. In the 1926 national census on mutual aid organizations produced by the Congress, Jewish philanthropic organizations were not included among the basic three groups identified by the study: (1) "mutual aid organizations per se" (those that help members); (2) "individual companies' benefit packages" (*Cajas Patronales*); and (3) "pseudo mutual aid organizations," which were divided into "for profit," usually institutions providing medical care, and "religious and political" organizations, mostly Catholic Workers' Circles.[29] Jewish (*israelitas*) organizations were placed in a category all on their own, as they:

> cannot be defined as "mutual aid organizations," even though they clearly are; they regard ritual burial as central to their activities; medical services—including medication dispensaries—are not well developed; and they resemble charitable organizations: there seems to be no distinction made between members and non-members when it comes to receiving aid, and steering committees have large discretionary power regarding the amount of the sums distributed.[30]

Only eleven organizations were listed in the "Israelita" section of the national census, a very small figure even for this early period.[31] This may suggest that Jews themselves viewed their organizations as different from "mutual aid" societies and did not respond to the Congress's call for information. The Argentine government's confusion about Jewish societies stemmed from the fact that each organization, in many cases, provided a variety of services that not only benefited paying members but Jewish men and women in the community at large.

During Juan Domingo Perón's first and second presidencies (1946–1955), the welfare state was massively expanded. Partly, this was achieved thanks to Perón's strategy of "co-opting key issues that had been supported by others and adopt[ing] them as his own."[32] Philanthropic and mutual aid organizations were brought under closer state scrutiny even before his election. In 1943, control over state subsidies granted to these organizations migrated from the Ministry of Foreign Relations and Religion to the Ministry of the Interior, a move that also signaled an intent to take away the right of immigrant and religious organizations to dispense aid. In this way, the expansion of the welfare state would, in the words of historian Donna Guy, "become intimately identified with the Perón regime."[33]

Regardless of the legal status of these philanthropic/mutual aid institutions, Sephardim (as well as Ashkenazim) understood the ways in which their societies were situated at the intersection of the two realities they recognized and belonged to: the traditional organization based on concepts of tzedakah and Jewish philanthropy—not mutual aid—and the universe of institutions all immigrant groups had created in Argentina. In 1929, Kanfe Yona members stressed in a manifesto that their objective was "to create a ḥebra [society] similar to the ones in our country of origin called 'Ḥebra Rebbi Schimhon' [sic]." But they quickly added that they desired to "found a hospital and orphanage, *since all* [immigrant] *communities have theirs except for us* [emphasis mine]."[34] Sephardim understood not only that it would be difficult to provide coreligionists with medical treatment unless they created philanthropic organizations but that by founding such institutions they would make their community comparable to the Spanish, French, Italian, British, German, Irish, and other communities that had already organized theirs. Sephardim would, through such institutions, claim their own space in Argentina among the other immigrant groups.[35]

SEPHARDI BUENOS AIRES

In Buenos Aires, each Sephardi migratory group settled in a different part of the city and created organizations and societies in close proximity to one another (see table 2.1). Throughout this process, they constructed distinct pockets of Sephardi life much like in the old country. Although the physical barriers that had sometimes divided Jews and non-Jews in the Old World no longer existed (many Jewish quarters were walled off), the proximity in which they now chose to live in the new land resembled, in many ways, the quarters from which they had emigrated.[36] "Community" in the city was a very tangible notion: it was the people who lived nearby and could be identified as belonging; it was also the network of help set up around its members.

Starting in the 1940s, Sephardi institutions in the city of Buenos Aires experienced a process of consolidation as a consequence of both shifting identity parameters (moving away from "Jewish" neighborhoods in the second half of the twentieth century, for example) and financial and organizational considerations. Each immigrant group created a kehila of sorts, a single organization that even today continues to be in charge of most of the religious, burial, educational, social, and philanthropic needs of its members. Descendants of Moroccan Jews congregated around Asociación Comunidad Israelita Latina de Buenos Aires (ACILBA) (Spanish Jewish Community Association of Buenos Aires), while Ottoman Jews belonged to the ACISBA but attended various synagogues, depending on place of residence. Damascene Jews belonged to the Asociación Israelita Sefaradí Hijos de la Verdad (Bene Emet) (Sephardi Jewish Association Sons of Truth—Bene Emet) and Aleppine Jews belonged to the Asociación Israelita Sefaradí Argentina (AISA) (Sephardi Jewish Association of Argentina), although they also attended various synagogues depending on their residence. Sephardi life in the first half of the twentieth century was characterized by the large number of organizations created to fulfill social, religious, and philanthropic needs among their own.

Table 2.1. Buenos Aires: Sephardi Philanthropic and Religious Organizations

City	Community Origin	Organizations	Active Years
Buenos Aires	Moroccan	Asociación Comunidad Israelita Latina de Buenos Aires (ACILBA)	1976–present
		Congregación Israelita Latina	1891–1976 (joined ACILBA)
		Guemilut Ḥasadim	1897–1976 (joined ACILBA)
		Hes Hayim	1905–?
		(Temple) Aleluya	late 1920s–1976
		(Temple) Bet Rachel (or Etz HaḤaim)	1931–1976
		(Temple) Ḥaverim	1970s–?
		Kanfe Yona	1927–1950s?
		Ḥesed VeEmet	1905–today
		Ozer Dalim	1916–1934 (joined Ḥesed VeEmet)
	Ladino-speaking Jews	Asociación Comunidad Israelita Sefaradí de Buenos Aires (ACISBA) (V. Crespo)	Until today
		Bene Sion (Once)	1917–?
		Sociedad Israelita para Culto y Beneficencia Bene Mizraḥ (Once)	1931–present
		Sociedad Kahal Kadosh y Talmud Torah "La Hermandad Sefaradí" (V. Crespo)	1914–present
		Asociación Israelita Sefaradí Pro-Medicamentos (V. Crespo)	
		Chalom	1926–present
		Etz HaḤaim (Downtown)	1910–?
		El Socorro (Downtown)	
		Asociación Hebrea Argentina de Socorros Mutuos (AHASM) (Once)	1929–present
	Damascene Jews	Asociación Israelita Sefaradi Hijos de la Verdad (Bene Emet)	1913–present
		Or Torah (La Boca)	1920–present
		Agudat Dodim (Flores)	1913–present
		Ahavat Aḥim (Lanús)	1921–present
		Shaare Tefila	1952–present
		Guemilut Ḥasadim	1920s
		Bikur Ḥolim	1930s
		Asociación Argentina Sefaradí de Cultura y Beneficencia	1940–present

(continued)

Table 2.1. (continued). Buenos Aires: Sephardi Philanthropic and Religious Organizations

City	Community Origin	Organizations	Active Years
	Aleppine Jews	Asociación Israelita Sefaradí Argentina (AISA)	1923–present
		Yesot Hadat	1920–present
		Habad Tsedek	1920s?
		Shaarei Sion	1920s
		Asociación Israelita Sefaradí de Ciudadela	1930s
		Shuba Israel	1940s
		Yeshurun	1950s
	Yugoslavia	Asociación de Israelitas oriundos de Yugoslavia en la Argentina	

Moroccan Jews

Moroccan Jews settled in the Sud neighborhood, and in 1891 they organized the Congregación Israelita Latina de Buenos Aires (also known as Congregación), the second Jewish organization in the city.[37] Its bylaws indicate the variety of objectives members wished to fulfill with such an institution (philanthropic, educational, religious ritual, medical, burial) and most other Sephardi groups followed this model.[38] With time, Moroccan Jews created other organizations, in many cases to fulfill one or just a few of these objectives.

The Congregación built its temple in 1919 (the first Sephardi temple in the city of Buenos Aires), but it was not the only prayer house for Moroccan Jews (see figure 2.1). In 1905, there is evidence a temple called Hes Hayim existed,[39] and by 1930, there were at least two other temples within a radius of ten blocks, and each with a significant number of members: Aleluya and Etz HaḤaim-Bet Raquel (Raquel). These two would combine memberships for a few years in the 1970s (creating the collective Templo Raquel-Aleluya), and would all later join the Congregación in 1976. For a few years in the 1970s, too, there was a third praying house called Ḥaverim.

The existence of several houses of prayer served many purposes. On the one hand, they anchored the community to the neighborhood. As new immigrants arrived, they sought to live close to those from their home country who had previously settled. The Sud neighborhood was conveniently close to the port and therefore to newly arrived Moroccan Jews, but the neighborhood also attracted "internal migrants," Moroccan Jews who had been living in the interior provinces. For example, Marcos Botbol, the founder of Temple Aleluya, in late 1920 came to Buenos Aires from Vera, in Santa Fé province, where he had lived for at least twelve years. Aleluya, also known as Jolita after a woman who lived there, provided housing for new arrivals, whether from the provinces or abroad, until they found permanent housing in the big city.[40] "Newcomers," recalls a Moroccan Jew, "would go to Jolita and gather there because there was always food [available to those who stopped by], olives, and those sweet cakes known as *'pasta real.'* "[41] Whether looking for a place to worship or a familiar space in which to spend time until moving on, these religious institutions brought Moroccan Jews together in this neighborhood and supported them in times of change.

Scholars of Argentine Sephardim have read the existence of multiple synagogues in close proximity to each other as evidence of disunity.[42] They claim that it was only around the burial society that the community came together. While this may be true, to equate one "single organization" with "unity" obscures the vibrancy that the existence of many organizations suggests. One synagogue per community had never defined Sephardi life in the Old World. In 1866, Tétouan had seventeen prayer houses, all of which were inside the Jewish quarter. A hundred years later, in 1967, after years of massive emigration overseas and even to other parts of the city outside the Jewish *mellah* (Jewish quarter), the number of prayer houses was still high, with twelve functioning synagogues inside the walled quarter.[43] By 1880, Aleppo had two *public* synagogues and Damascus had seven, while the rich had their own in their homes.[44]

The existence of multiple organizations all vying for membership among a limited (and small) community exposed intracommunity class conflict. David Mehaudy was a wealthy individual whose powerful position among all Moroccan Jews derived, in part, from his role as president of Temple Raquel in its later years. After the Congregación absorbed both Aleluya and Rachel, Mehaudy became a central figure in the administration of the now centralized Moroccan community.[45] Likewise,

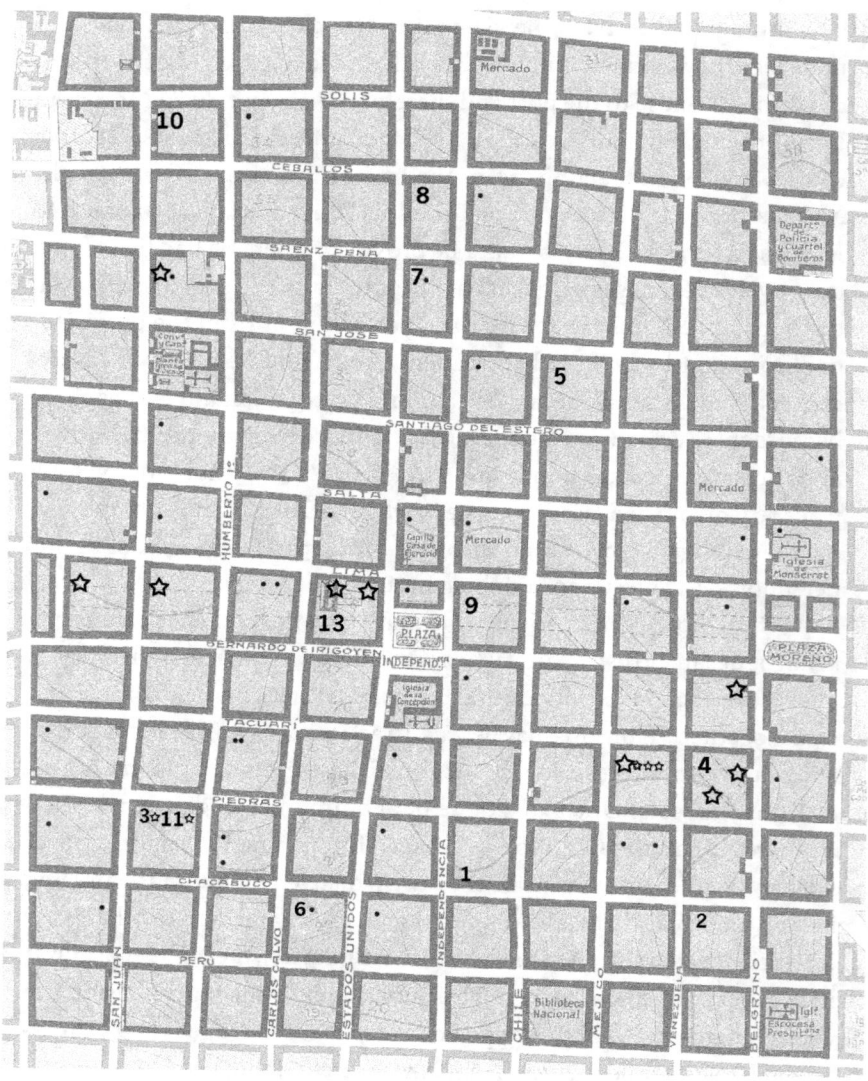

Figure 2.1. Buenos Aires: Sud neighborhood. Locations of major Moroccan Jewish institutions and homes of members. Created by author.
Key:
• Homes of members of Ozer Dalim (1917), and addresses culled from marriage licenses (1919).
☆ or ✮ Stores owned by Moroccan Jews (taken from *Israel* advertisements).
1 Congregación Israelita Latina de Buenos Aires (1903–1905). Independencia 664.

a short-lived congregation called Haverim challenged the hegemony of the more affluent Congregación. This congregation was formed in the early 1970s when a group of members left the newly merged Templo Raquel-Aleluya. As hinted at in the name (*haverim* means "comrade"), congregants left looking for a more egalitarian organization. In the words of one of its founders, Haverim was specifically conceived as a reaction to the Congregación and Raquel-Aleluya practices that stressed class distinctions. "Haverim was more democratic," explained José Roffé. "In the other temples, it was money that allowed you to participate in religious rituals." He continued, "If you wanted to carry the Torah around the temple—during the High Holidays, for example—you had to 'buy' that distinction."[46] Haverim prided itself for not allowing money to dictate privileges.

Evidence also suggests that the relationships among the different prayer houses (and other societies these organizations supported) and their leaders were not divisive but cordial. The Congregación sent a representative from the steering committee to the opening of the Raquel temple in 1930, and the president and teacher of the Talmud Torah were both present when Raquel opened its permanent synagogue in 1933.[47] The leader of Raquel, as noted above, became one of the heads of the Congregación, and Roffé, a Haverim founder, was named later general manager of ACILBA. In September 1950, the Congregación organized a celebration in honor of General Don José de San Martín, an Argentine military leader who was instrumental in liberating South America from

---

2 Congregación Israelita Latina de Buenos Aires (1905–1919). Venezuela 594.
3 Congregación Israelita Latina de Buenos Aires from 1919. Piedras 1164.
4 Hes Hayim temple (1905). Venezuela 783.
5 Aleluya temple (1920s and 1930s). Kanfe Yona used this address on their stationery. Chile 1380.
6 Aleluya temple (late 1930s). Chacabuco 980.
7 Aleluya temple (from 1940s until 1976). Estados Unidos 1461.
8 Club Alianza (from 1919 to 1940s). Estados Unidos 1532.
9 Club Alianza (from 1940s until 1962). Lima 734.
10 Club Alianza (from 1962). Solís 1056.
11 Talmud Torah (until 1925). After 1925, it moved to Piedras 1164. Piedras 1100.
12 Raquel temple (1931–?). Perú 808.
13 Raquel temple. Carlos Calvo 1060.

Spain and whose centennial was commemorated then—and "invited all members of Moroccan organizations and *sister congregations* [emphasis added]."⁴⁸ The event, they claimed, turned out to be "magnificent."

In order to specifically fulfill the objectives of philanthropy, Moroccan Jews founded other organizations, as well. In many cases, organizations had similar objectives and were undoubtedly created in order to challenge the power of leaders. For example, Guemilut Hasadim (the Hevra Kedusha) had been founded in 1897, but in 1905, a new organization called Hesed VeEmet challenged its standing.⁴⁹ The latter's founding responded, in its words, to the needs of "the proletariat class of Buenos Aires," who now found itself without a friendly organization since previous ones had disappeared.⁵⁰ The aims of the association were to help members with the burial costs and support them in sickness (visiting them regularly and providing deathbed care).⁵¹ Later, conflict between these two societies was resolved when Guemilut Hasadim became the organization mostly in charge of burials, and Hesed VeEmet continued only with "beneficence, in its broader sense."⁵² In 1943, the latter spent most of their money on helping poor families, purchasing medicine, and contributing to the Hospital Israelita Ezrah (Jewish Hospital Ezrah) to subsidize the treatment of Moroccan Jewish patients. By 1934, when Ozer Dalim, a new philanthropic group, joined Hesed VeEmet, it became the most important Moroccan beneficence organization, and it is still in existence today.⁵³

Ozer Dalim was founded on September 1, 1916, to "bring help to all the homes desolated by misery and to all people [illegible] who are not able to provide the most basic means for life and the curing of diseases which might affect them."⁵⁴ The activities supported by this organization were diverse, ranging from paying the rent for those who could not afford to do so to providing a father with the funds to pay for the circumcision of his son and for a party to celebrate it.⁵⁵ In 1917, however, the members of this organization limited their range of support, stressing that they would focus on the sick and on parturient women.⁵⁶ In 1934, they joined Hesed VeEmet.

Kanfe Yona, as noted previously, was created in 1927 by a group of men belonging to both Aleluya and the Comunidad. The arrival of Kanfe Yona on a philanthropic scene that included two other organizations prompted animosity, especially among the members of these other institutions. Both in 1929 and in 1935 (after the merge of Ḥesed VeEmet and Ozer Dalim), members of Kanfe Yona insisted in letters sent to the magazine *Israel* that their organization wished "to unite, not to dissolve."[57] They added, "We do not want a society in conflict with those that already exist but to collaborate in objectives they have already set."[58] Although no minute books belonging to Kanfe Yona have survived, conflict seems to have quieted down as the society continued its work. It was still functioning in the early 1950s alongside Ḥesed VeEmet.

Arabic-Speaking Jews

Arabic-speaking Jews settled according to their city of origin. In Buenos Aires, the ḥalabim (Jews from Aleppo) moved to the neighborhoods of Once, Flores, and Ciudadela (Buenos Aires province), and the ashwam (Jews from Damascus) set up their communities in La Boca, Barracas, and Flores. Jews from Damascus settled in various neighborhoods joined forces in 1913 to create Bene Emet, their burial society, which also dispensed aid. The Damascene founded two main congregations in Buenos Aires: in 1913, Agudat Dodim, in the neighborhood of Flores, and in 1920, Or Torah, in the La Boca-Barracas area. They also created Ahavat Aḥim, a congregation in Lanús in Buenos Aires province, and much later, in 1952, Shaare Tefilá in the neighborhood of Once.[59] At the beginning, however, and in a pattern that resembled the Moroccans, there were at least seven other *minyanim* (prayer groups for men) in the areas in which they settled.[60]

With its founding, Or Torah's main objective was to buy a property large enough to house a synagogue and a Talmud Torah. Members of smaller houses of prayer soon joined the effort.[61] They managed to build their temple in 1929, on Brandsen Street, and until then carried out their activities (religious, educational, and welfare) in various houses they rented and/or owned (see figure 2.2). While the main objective remained the construction of the temple, Or Torah also participated actively in charity by helping other Damascene philanthropic societies. In 1920, a six-member subcommittee was created to help Guemilut Ḥasadim raise funds for poor families.[62] The fundraising activities of Bikur Ḥolim were

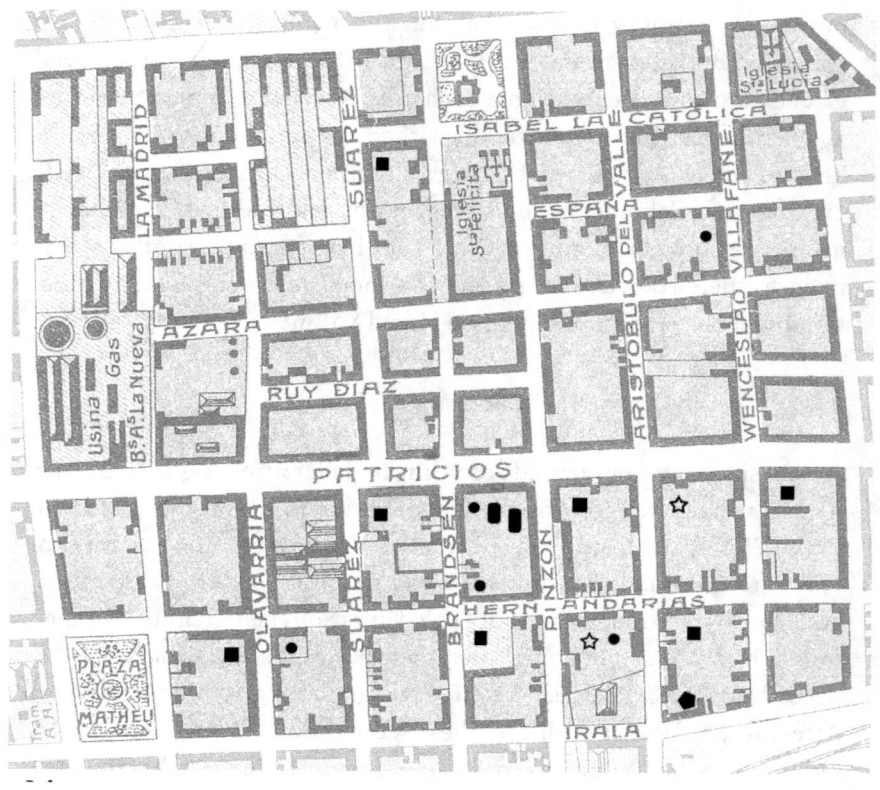

Figure 2.2. Buenos Aires, La Boca neighborhood. Locations of Damascene Jewish institutions and homes of members. Created by author.
Key:
- Temples
- Private homes
- Ritual baths/Mikvaot
- Butchers
- Stores

supported by letting three of its members speak to congregants during Saturday morning services.[63] Finally, the Asociación Argentina Sefaradí de Cultura y Beneficencia (Sephardi Argentine Association of Culture and Beneficence), an organization exclusively devoted to philanthropy, was created in 1940, and it would eventually run the first Sephardi senior citizens' home.[64]

Agudat Dodim was founded in the neighborhood of Flores in 1913 by members of the Damascene community who settled in the area. Several smaller prayer houses existed, as well, and donations from these congregations were sent to Agudat Dodim to support a school, kosher butcher, and for philanthropy.[65] In 1944, the community boasted 573 members, placing the number of Jews living in the area at, at least, 1,700.[66] Agudat Dodim also kept strong ties with other Damascene and Sephardi organizations. In 1937, for example, it contributed money to Bene Emet, Guemilut Ḥasadim, and Bikur Ḥolim.[67]

The Jews from Aleppo founded their main organizations in the neighborhood of Once, under the leadership of Rabbi Saúl Sutton Dabbah, who led the community from 1912 to 1930.[68] Besides the Ḥevra Kedusha (Ḥesed Shel Emet),[69] founded in 1923, they created the Congregación Sefaradí de Enseñanza, Culto y Beneficencia Yesod Hadat (Sephardi Congregation for Education, Worship, and Charity, Yesod Hadat), which was in charge of their Talmud Torah, Beit Din (Rabbinical Tribunal), and kosher butcher shop.[70] This organization spent 2 percent of its income on philanthropy in 1933, and 31 percent in 1943. Education was another significant expenditure: support for its Talmud Torah went from 31 percent in 1933 to 40 percent in 1943.[71] Under the leadership of Nissim Teubal (a wealthy textile businessman), on Lavalle Street they built a synagogue that also housed medical offices and Habad Tsedek, a society to dispense aid.[72] Other congregations formed include, in the 1920s, Shaarei Sion in Flores; in the 1930s, Asociación Israelita Sefaradí de Ciudadela (Sephardi Jewish Association of Ciudadela), province of Buenos Aires; in the 1940s, Shuba Israel in Once, and in the late 1950s, Yeshurun in Palermo.[73]

Ladino-Speaking Jews

The Ladino-speaking Jews came mostly from various cities in present-day Turkey and Asia Minor (Izmir, Istanbul, Aydın, Urla, Edirne, Çeşme, Milas, and Bodrum) but also from Rhodes, Salonika, and Balkan countries. At first, they tended to congregate according to city of origin, establishing their communities in different parts of Buenos Aires. The Jews from Turkey lived near the port (on 25 de Mayo and Reconquista Streets),[74] and later moved to Villa Crespo. They founded Etz HaḤaim, their synagogue, in 1910, and Ḥesed Shel Emet, their Ḥevra Kedusha, in 1916. In the same area close to the port, Jews from Rhodes created, in 1917, their first organization, Bene Sion, whose aim was to organize a Talmud Torah.[75]

In 1931, having moved away from the downtown neighborhood, the Jews from Istanbul formed the Sociedad Israelita Para Culto y Beneficencia Bene Mizraḥ (Jewish Society for Worship and Charity, Bene Mizraḥ), and they later built a synagogue in Once. The Jews from Izmir who settled in Villa Crespo (see figure 2.3) founded in 1914 the Sociedad Kahal Kadosh y Talmud Tora "La Hermandad Sefaradí" (Kahal Kadosh Society and Talmud Torah-Sephardi Brotherhood), as "a cultural and mutual aid institution." Their aims, as stated in their bylaws, were to "[provide] instruction to the children of its members, and dispense charity." They had initially met for prayers in a small room, and later bought the land on which they built their synagogue on Camargo Street. In 1946, this society spent more than half its income (collected from dues and donations) on "social welfare."[76] This included monthly support for the needy and widows, onetime sums dispensed to alleviate specific problems, food, High Holiday supplies, student loans, and medical assistance. This last service was provided by the Asociación Israelita Sefaradí Pro-Medicamentos (Sephardi Jewish Association for Medical Aid), which had its own property and medical offices by the 1930s, and was later incorporated into ACISBA.[77]

Other groups of Ladino-speakers settled in Colegiales, where many immigrants from Rhodes had settled, and founded Chalom[78] congregation on September 11, 1926.[79] A collection of membership requests dating from the late 1940s to mid-1950s reveals that, although mostly men from Rhodes, Salonika, and several "Turkish" towns were applying for admission, men from Damascus, Egypt, and even Warsaw who had moved into the neighborhood did so, as well.[80] Chalom continued to be an "Ottoman" institution, but it also became the Colegiales Jewish option for many new to the area.

In the neighborhood of Flores, there was yet another group of immigrants from Izmir and Aydın who, after settling there in the early 1920s, founded a temple and a social center. Their centers were religious

Figure 2.3. Buenos Aires, Villa Crespo neighborhood. Locations of Ottoman Jewish institutions and homes of members. Created by author.

Key:
- Members' homes.
1 Asociación Israelita Sefaradí Pro-Medicamentos (1930s). Acevedo 589.
2 Sociedad Kahal Kadosh synagogue (1918). Acevedo 218.
3 Sociedad Kahal Kadosh synagogue and Talmud Torah (1914). Gurruchaga 421.
4 Synagogue built in 1919, still standing today. Camargo 870.

(synagogues) and social in nature, and the sources suggest that they relied on the larger organizations in the neighborhoods of Villa Crespo and Villa Urquiza for philanthropy.

In 1929 the Ladino-speaking Jews of Etz HaḤaim and the society El Socorro, from the downtown area, formed the AHASM in conjunction with Sephardi Jews living in Villa Urquiza. By 1932, the society had formed two committees in charge of providing charity and medical assistance, and moved to Once, where they opened a temple and a social hall.[81] The committee in charge of dispensing aid in the form of cash employed an inspector to visit and vet those who requested help if they were not known personally by members of the organization.[82]

There were also Jews from Jerusalem and other cities in Palestine.[83] This group, as explained in chapter 1, joined the Aleppine Jews for their burial needs but founded their own synagogue in the 1920s, their Talmud Torah "Hatikva," and a kosher butcher. Other groups of Sephardim, much smaller in number, came from Italy, Yugoslavia, and central Asia. Italian Sephardim never organized on their own and joined the Ladino-speaking Jews from Camargo Street for religious activities, and burial and philanthropic purposes. The few Jews from Yugoslavia (Sarajevo, Travnik, Debernka, Monastir, and Belgrade) created in the 1940s the Asociación de Israelitas oriundos de Yugoslavia en la Argentina (Association of Jews from Yugoslavia in Argentina), which had social and charitable objectives. As the Italians did, these Jews joined ACISBA for religious services and burial.[84]

In Buenos Aires, Sephardi communities stressed geographical proximity by choosing to settle in areas where the first institutions had been created. If Jews moved out of the area (a trend that was more noticeable in the larger communities), their philanthropic institutions unsurprisingly followed them. These institutions created a closely knit web around them, supporting one another, either financially—by donating or loaning money—or by facilitating the use of the buildings for meetings or fundraising events.[85] The support dispensed to people in the community also helped strengthen already existing ties: those Jews coming from the same towns and cities across the Atlantic felt themselves *again* members of a whole that lived close by and helped its members.

SEPHARDIM IN THE PROVINCES

Sephardi settlement in the provinces, regardless of origin, followed similar patterns. It was mostly urban, as these Jews usually engaged in commercial activities. They peddled goods, sold lottery tickets, and owned stores—usually clothing or general stores, but they engaged in many other ventures, from furniture factories to owning bars—or other activities that benefited from an urban setting. These urban centers were found along railroad lines (or close to navigable rivers) and new settlements would often spring up as the train extended its rail lines. Although the following section might read as a mere list of where Sephardim settled and what societies they founded, I believe it presents evidence of the extent of Sephardi presence in the interior (see table 2.2). It will also help better understand the connections set up by Jews in these areas and those of Buenos Aires and across the Atlantic.

The organizations set up by the Sephardim in provincial capitals or important cities acted as anchors not only to those living in those cities but also to the settlers in other parts of these provinces. As Sephardim tried their commercial ventures away from these organizational centers, they maintained close ties with those societies. They paid dues and helped in fundraising activities. With the passing of time, if the number of Jewish settlers in the peripheral areas became significant, new local organizations were created and ties with the provincial centers were weakened. In other cases, the provincial capitals exercised a strong pull, and the central organizations would regain those members (or their children) who had left to try their luck elsewhere. Sephardim created numerous organizations aimed at providing social, cultural, religious, and burial services. As the century went on, many organizations merged, consolidating their work under one main society, or two, as in Buenos Aires.

Many Moroccan Jews settled in Santa Fé early on, in particular along the railroad line in the west of that province (see figure 2.4). In the city of Santa Fé, evidence of Moroccan Jews dates from as early as 1886. This small community opened their cemetery on June 5, 1895.[86] In the same year, a few months later, they formed the Congregación Israelita Latina Sefaradím de Santa Fé, which requested to be accepted as a legal

Table 2.2. Provinces of Argentina: Sephardi Philanthropic and Religious Organizations

Province	Community Origin	Organization and City	Date Created
Santa Fé	Moroccan	Congregación Israelita Latina Sefaradím de Santa Fé (Santa Fé)	1927
		Asociación Israelita Aḥinu Atah (Rosario)	
		Débora (Vera)	
	Ottoman	Sociedad Israelita Shalom VeReut (Santa Fé)	1931
		Sociedad Israelita Sefaradí Etz HaḤaim (Rosario)	1909
	Moroccan and Ottoman	Sociedad Hebrea Sefaradí (Santa Fé)	1949
	Arabic-speaking (from Aleppo and Damascus)	Asociación Israelita Sefaradí Shevet Aḥim (Rosario)	1930s
Misiones	Ottoman	Asociación Israelita de Beneficencia Hijos de Sión (Posadas)	1924
Corrientes	Moroccan	Sociedad Jóvenes Israelitas Sefaradím (Latinos) de Corrientes (Corrientes)	1914
Entre Ríos		Sociedad Israelita Sefaradí Shevet Aḥim (Paraná)	1925
		Asociación Agudat Israelita Sefaradí de Concordia (Concordia)	
Chaco	Moroccan	Sociedad Israelita Latina Ḥesed VeEmet (Resistencia)	1910
Córdoba	Ottoman	Sociedad Israelita de Beneficencia Sefaradí (Córdoba)	1914–1943*
		Sociedad de Beneficencia Rofe Ḥolim (Córdoba)	1929–1943* (joined CISC)
	Arabic-speaking Aleppo	Shevet Aḥim (Córdoba)	1914
	Damascus and Aleppo	Sociedad Israelita Sefaradí Talmud Torah (Córdoba) (later, Sociedad Israelita Siria)	1921
Tucumán	Izmir, Beirut, and Jerusalem	Asociación Israelita de Beneficencia (Tucumán)	1921
Salta	Syria, Izmir, Beirut, and Jerusalem	Sociedad Israelita Salteña La Unión (Salta)	1917

Province	Community Origin	Organization and City	Date Created
		Centro Argentino de Socorros Mutos (Salta)	
Catamarca	Ottoman	Asociación Israelita Sefaradim de Socorros Mutuos (Catamarca)	1929
Mendoza		Sociedad Israelita de Socorros Mutuos Rofe Ḥolim (Mendoza)	1920s
San Juan		Sociedad Israelita Latina de Socorros Mutuos de San Juan (San Juan)	1923

*When they joined the Comunidad Israelita Sefaradí de Córdoba.

society (*Personería Jurídica*), but the request was not granted by the provincial government.[87] The main objective of the organization was to facilitate the practice of "Sephardi rites," but the bylaws listed a procedure for requesting aid, stressing their philanthropic orientation, too. The Moroccan organization was finally recognized by the province in 1927 after two societies joined forces: the original Congregación and the Ḥevra Kedusha Ḥesed VeEmet de Socorros Mutuos (Mutual Aid Organization for Burial and Beneficence), which gave the new society its name. In the same city, in 1931, the Sociedad Israelita Shalom VeReut (Jewish Society Shalom VeReut) was founded by Sephardim from Turkey.[88] Finally, in 1949, Moroccan and Turkish Jews joined together and formed the Sociedad Hebrea Sefaradí (Sephardi Jewish Society).

In Rosario, the first Sephardi organization was founded in 1909 by Jews from Turkey: Sociedad Israelita Sefaradí Etz HaḤaim (Sephardi Jewish Society, Etz HaḤaim).[89] By 1930, they had created two social and cultural societies, the Círculo Cultural Israelita Sefaradí (Sephardi Jewish Cultural Circle) and the Círculo Juvenil Israelita (Jewish Youth Circle).[90] The Moroccans gathered around their own Asociación Israelita Aḥinu Atah (Jewish Association Aḥinu Atah), and in 1933 founded the Centro Israelita Argentino (Jewish Center of Argentina).[91] Syrian Jews also created their organizations, at first keeping different synagogues depending on city of origin (Aleppo and Damascus) but later joining efforts to create the Asociación Israelita Sefaradi Shevet Aḥim (Association of Sephardi Jews Shevet Aḥim).[92] By 1928, the Arabic-speaking

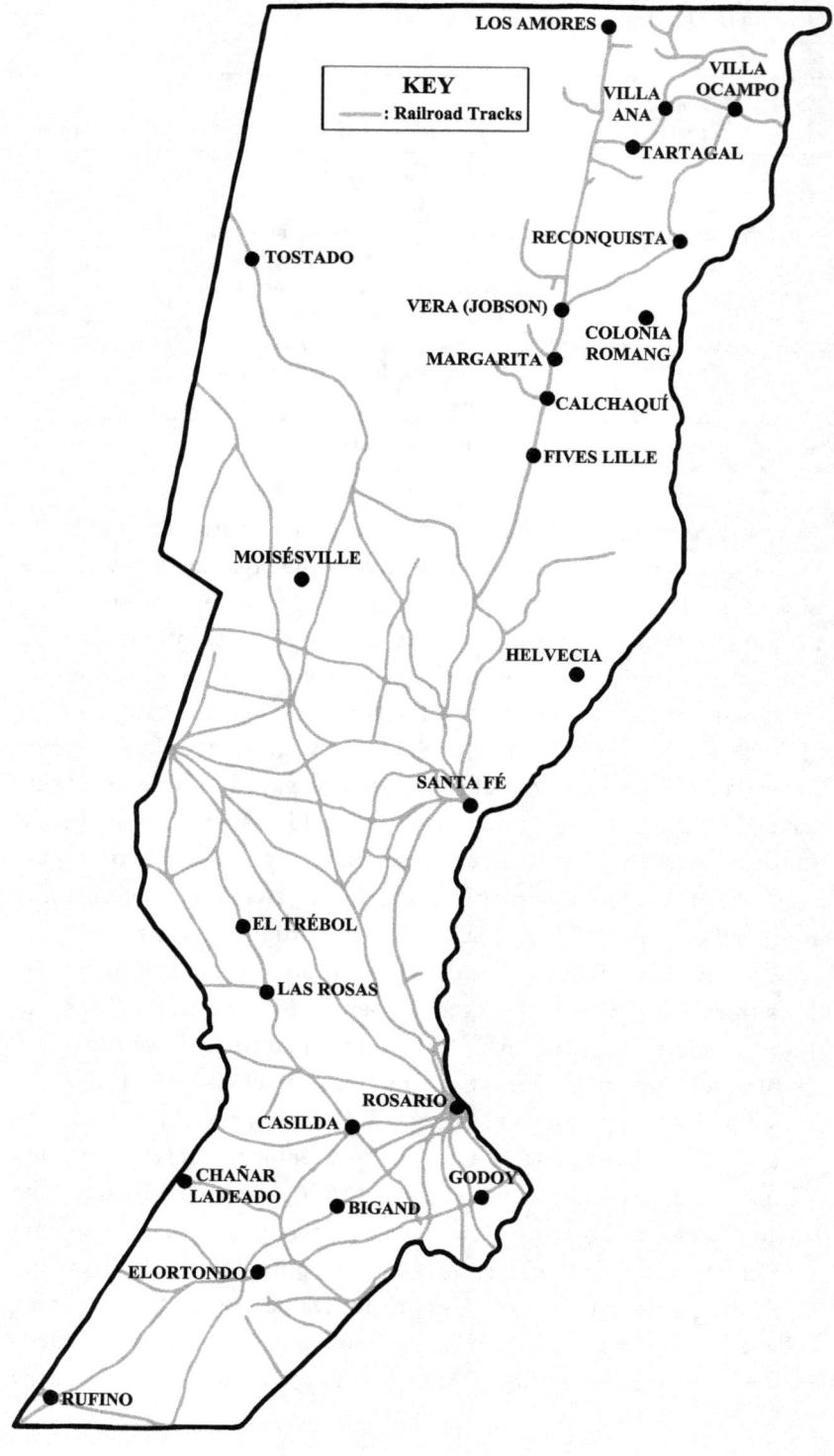

Figure 2.4. Province of Santa Fé: Towns where Sephardim settled.

Jewish community had built a mikvah and supported a Talmud Torah. There was also an association of Sephardi women who did charity work.[93] In 1920, there was an attempt at unification led by Etz HaḤaim. They issued a call for joining efforts as "we profess the same ideals," with the intention of building a synagogue and organizing a school.[94] Etz HaḤaim and members of the smaller "Palestinian" community joined forces, but the Arabic-speaking Sephardim and the Moroccan group continued their independent activities.[95]

Sephardim, mostly Moroccan Jews at first, also settled in many small towns along the railroad line or close to the Paraná River (see figure 2.4). The magazine *Israel* appointed local "representatives" in these towns and would regularly publish their reports in the section entitled "Jewish events." One of the largest communities was in Vera, where Jews had a mutual aid organization, called Débora, which raised money for philanthropy and for a cemetery that opened in 1918.[96]

In Misiones, Sephardim, mostly from the city of Izmir, founded the Asociación Israelita de Beneficencia, "Hijos de Sión" (Jewish Benevolent Society, Sons of Zion) on October 5, 1924.[97] The organization stated in its bylaws that "the objectives of the society are mutual aid among its members, to encourage culture and the spirit of solidarity and unity, and to care for the cemetery of this association."[98] By the 1930s the society had built a social center and opened a cemetery.[99]

In Corrientes, the first Sephardim arrived as early as 1894 from Tétouan, Aleppo, and Izmir.[100] They founded the Sociedad Jóvenes Israelitas Sefaradím (Latinos) de Corrientes (Sephardi [Spanish] Jewish Youth Society of Corrientes) in 1914, built their synagogue in 1928, and bought their own cemetery.[101] Smaller groups of Jews lived in other towns in Corrientes, like Sauce, Curuzú Cuatiá, Paso de los Libres, Esquina, Goya, Mercedes, and Alvear.[102]

In Entre Ríos, the Sephardim founded congregations in Paraná and in Concordia. In Paraná, the Sociedad Israelita Sefaradí Shevet Aḥim (Sephardi Jewish Society, Shevet Aḥim) was created in 1925, and they built their first social center in 1931. Originally, they had their own cemetery, but in 1947 they merged with the Ashkenazim of the city in order to share philanthropic, social, educational, and funeral services.[103] In Concordia, there were two Sephardi organizations, Centro Cultural y

Recreativo Sefaradim (Sephardi Cultural and Recreational Center) and the Asociación Agudat Israelita Sefaradí de Concordia (Sephardi Jewish Union of Concordia), although only the latter was devoted to religious services and philanthropy.[104]

Moroccans were the first to arrive to Chaco (it was a national territory until 1943), following the railroad tracks (see figure 2.5). They opened up small stores to supply the (mostly railroad) workers in these areas. In La Sábana, there was a significant Moroccan settlement attracted, undoubtedly, by the presence of La Forestal, a company that extracted tannin from trees.[105] Meri Benasayag, a small girl in La Sábana at the beginning of the twentieth century recalls, "I still see the stores [in my mind].... they sold fine cloth, Japanese cloth.... I say [the town] was a *judería* [Jewish quarter], because there were Jews in all the homes. All were Jews."[106] Salomón Bentolila recalls working for La Forestal in a "huge tent, alongside Indians [sic]."[107]

In Resistencia, the provincial capital, the Moroccan Jews founded the Sociedad Israelita Latina Hesed VeEmet (Spanish Jewish Society, Hesed VeEmet) in December 1910. The society helped members by providing money when needed, by helping defray medical costs, by providing medical assistance to those in need, or by visiting sick members of the community.[108] In 1912, they bought and opened a Jewish cemetery, and in 1932, they built their own social center. The community in Resistencia grew in the 1920s, attracting Jews who had originally settled in smaller towns around it, and as new Sephardim arrived from Izmir and Istanbul. Although Moroccan in origin, the Sociedad Latina Israelita ended up attracting all arriving Sephardim.[109]

In Córdoba the community was bigger and could afford to be divided into three groups at first (as had happened in Rosario): Syrians, who gathered in two groups, depending on city of origin, and Jews from Turkey. By 1910, the Jews from Izmir had already formed a group around León Rubin, who had arrived in 1904, and founded the Sociedad Israelita de Beneficencia Sefaradí (Sephardi Jewish Society of Beneficence) in 1914.[110] In 1929, a new Sociedad de Beneficencia Rofe Holim (Beneficence Society Rofe Holim) opened a medical office and formed a women's auxiliary to distribute food and clothes to those in need. These two charity organizations joined forces in 1943 and the new group was

Helping the Living

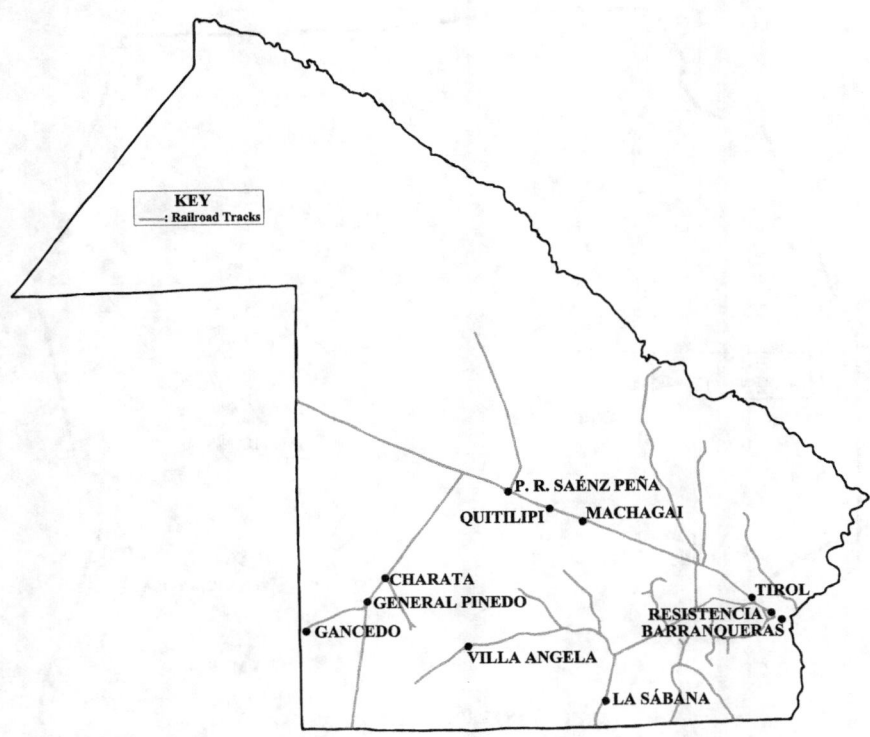

Figure 2.5. Province of Chaco: Towns where Sephardim settled.

called Comunidad Israelita Sefaradí de Córdoba (Sephardi Jewish Community of Córdoba).[111] Arabic-speaking Jews also organized as soon as they arrived. In 1914, the Jews from Aleppo formed the society Shevet Aḥim. In 1921, they joined the Jews from Damascus and founded the Sociedad Israelita Sefaradí Talmud Torah (Sephardi Jewish Society Talmud Torah), which later changed its name to Sociedad Israelita Siria (Syrian Jewish Society).[112] This society also bought land and founded the Jewish cemetery, which they shared with the Sephardim from Turkey.

Again, the list of contributors to the magazine *Israel* gives us hints as to where else Sephardim in the province of Córdoba settled (see figure 2.6). But as was the case with the Sephardim living in small towns in Santa Fé, the number of Jews in each town was not that large. Esther

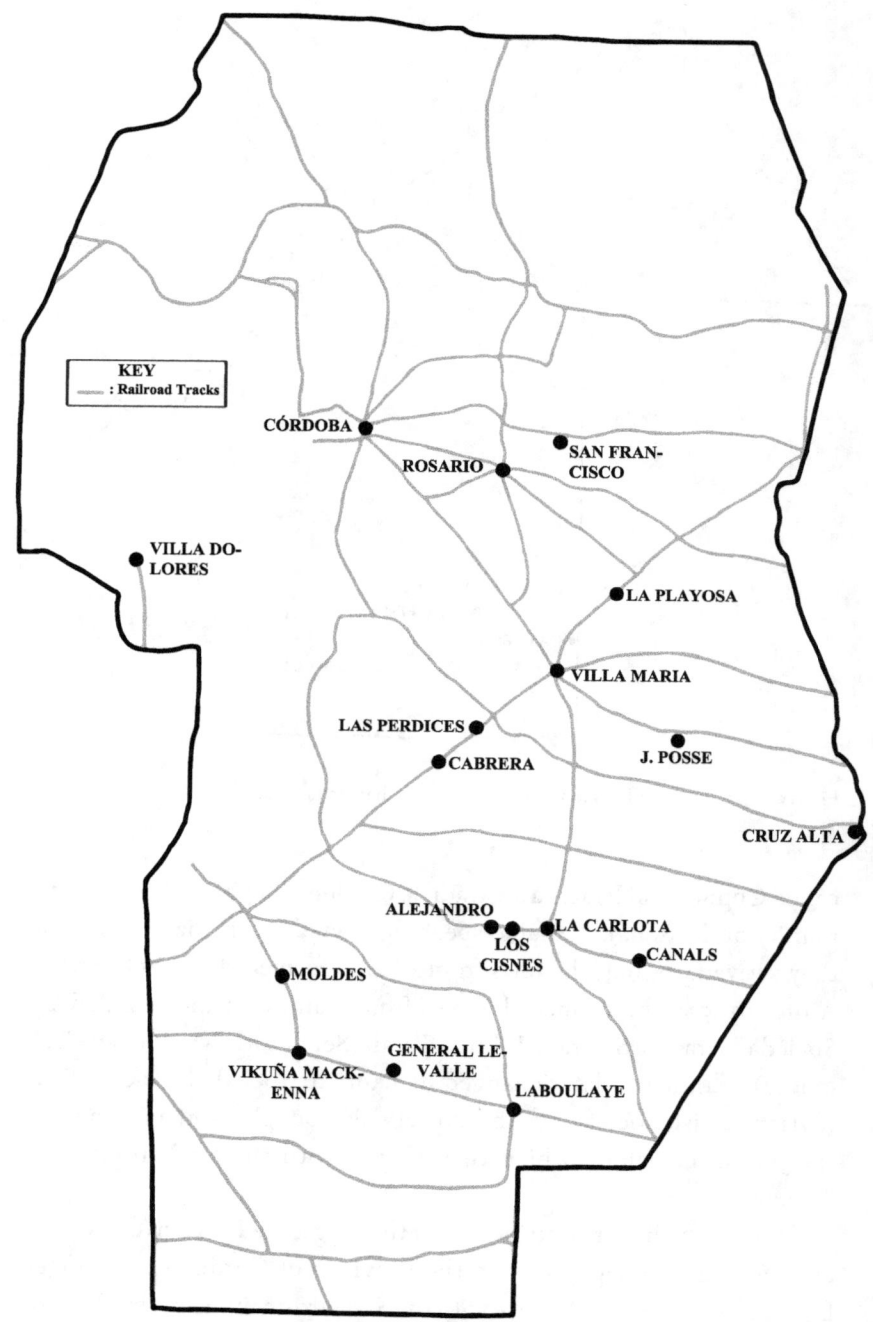

Figure 2.6. Province of Córdoba: Towns where Sephardim settled.

Acrich, an informant, described how her father, who lived in General Levalle, would travel with the other Sephardic men to Laboulaye for the High Holidays, as the bigger town had a *myniam* (required number of men for a religious service).[113]

In the city of Tucumán, the story is similar. Although there was an unsuccessful attempt in 1917, it was not until 1921 that the Jews from Izmir, Beirut, and Jerusalem founded their first society: Asociación Israelita de Beneficencia (Jewish Association of Beneficence). Their aim was "to aid those members in need and carry out all matters related to beneficence" and "build the social center."[114]

In the northwestern province of Salta in 1917, Sephardim, mostly from Syria, Izmir, Beirut, and Jerusalem, founded the Sociedad Israelita Salteña La Unión (Jewish Society of Salta, The Union). Made up of never more than eighty families, they still managed to own a cemetery (bought in 1917), opened a Jewish school, and built an important social center.[115] For a short time, there was another Sephardi organization named Centro Argentino de Socorros Mutuos (Argentine Center of Mutual Aid).[116] They also founded a Zionist organization, which joined its Ashkenazi counterpart in 1932.[117] In another northwestern province, Catamarca, there was a small Sephardi community, mostly Ladino speakers, who in 1929 established the Asociación Israelita Sefaradim de Socorros Mutuos (Sephardi Jewish Association of Mutual Aid), to "gather for beneficence purposes.... encourage mutual aid.... and to found our own cemetery, which would follow our rites."[118]

In the province of Mendoza, Sephardim had created their own institutions of mutual aid, along with their religious congregation: Sociedad Israelita de Socorros Mutuos Rofe Ḥolim (Jewish Society of Mutual Aid, Rofe Ḥolim), and Sociedad Israelita Sefaradi de Mendoza (Sephardi Jewish Society of Mendoza), respectively.[119] Although there is some indication that Moroccan Jews traveled there first,[120] by 1931 the community was made up of Sephardim from Turkey, Morocco, and some Arabic speakers.[121] In the province of San Juan, the Sociedad Israelita Latina de Socorros Mutuos de San Juan (Spanish Jewish Mutual Aid Society of San Juan) was founded in 1923, and it sent a member to Buenos Aires so he could train as a mohel and shoḥet.[122]

HELPING SEPHARDIM

The flow of aid between Sephardim in Buenos Aires and those in the interior provinces was indeed significant and placed philanthropy at the center of the reconfiguration of communal identity. The story of charitable societies in the rest of the country and their relationship with the organizations of the big city also helps us rethink the description of "separateness" that emerges from the study of Buenos Aires and focus much more on the diverse and contiguous boundaries created by the Jewish communities in the places in which they settled. The communities in the interior kept strong ties with the centers in Buenos Aires, and with other Sephardic groups close by, especially during the first years of migration. Connections with Buenos Aires worked both ways, as the interior communities needed those in Buenos Aires as much as the ones in Buenos Aires needed the support of those in the rest of the country.

In their calls for help, communities in the interior sought aid in matters of ritual and economic support. One item that was requested very often was a Torah scroll. Aḥinu Atah in Rosario, for example, from 1926 to 1932, used Torah scrolls lent by the Moroccan Congregación of Buenos Aires.[123] Or Torah also lent several scrolls to Sephardim in Chivilcoy and Ciudadela, small towns in the province of Buenos Aires. Payment for the use of the scrolls ranged from a onetime donation to a monthly fee.[124] The Syrian congregation in Lanús also borrowed a Torah from Or Torah, the Damascene community in La Boca. A small community in Villa María, province of Córdoba, requested a scroll from the Ottoman community in Buenos Aires.[125]

The smaller communities in the interior also sought economic help from their coreligionists in Buenos Aires. Usually, when raising money to buy land for a cemetery or to build a social center, the congregations organized raffles and sent tickets to the Buenos Aires societies. Or Torah, for example, received several tickets from the Talmud Torah in Rosario (a Syrian association) in 1923.[126] The Asociación Israelita de Beneficencia Hijos de Sión in Posadas sent raffle tickets to the Moroccan Congregación in 1929.[127] Ḥesed Shel Emet, organized a collection for a temple in San Luis.[128] To help the Sephardim in San Juan purchase their cemetery, three commissions were created in Buenos Aires among the Moroccan, Aleppine, and Turco communities.[129]

In other cases, communities in the interior requested help to pay for medical services or costs associated with hospitalization. The Syrian association in Córdoba once asked Or Torah to help them with a man who was sick with tuberculosis, and Or Torah agreed to be billed for the cost of transportation to Buenos Aires.[130] The funeral expenses of another tuberculosis casualty, who died in a hospital in Córdoba, were paid by Bene Emet.[131] Ḥesed VeEmet in Buenos Aires received a letter from the Sephardi society in Resistencia soliciting support to send a member's child to the Hospital Israelita Ezrah in Buenos Aires.[132]

Small communities or individuals in the provinces likewise sought the help of other communities in the interior. The community in Corrientes, for example, sent several tickets for a raffle to the community in Resistencia.[133] In Quitilipi, province of Chaco, the birth of a girl prompted a donation to the society Ḥesed VeEmet in Resistencia.[134] For the purchase of the Sephardi cemetery in San Juan, mentioned above, collections were carried out in the provinces of Chaco, Corrientes, and Mendoza.[135]

The surviving documents of Ḥesed VeEmet in Resistencia allow for a more detailed picture of the exchanges of help between smaller societies and the larger parent organization. Three books containing the names and places of residence of members from 1922 to 1929 and 1934 to 1936 show that many members of the organization did not, in fact, live in Resistencia.[136] Between 1922 and 1929, the society had one hundred constant members, of which twenty-seven lived in other smaller Chaco towns.[137] There were seven other members who listed one place of residence in the first book and a different location in the other. This might mean that they initially lived in Resistencia and moved to another location later or that they lived in those towns from the very beginning (1922) but that fact was only recorded later. (The extant documents are sometimes illegible, or notations were written in pencil and are no longer visible.) I identified fifty-eight names who were only members for a short time. Of those, sixteen lived in other towns in Chaco, but this figure may be higher, as I have assumed that if no indication was made in the book to suggest otherwise, the member lived in Resistencia. The second cluster of data (books from 1934 to 1936) shows that the number of people living in other towns is smaller, but the records are incomplete.[138] This may suggest that Sephardim may have chosen, after a few years living in small towns, to move to larger urban centers.

Although Ḥesed VeEmet in Resistencia was founded in 1910, it was only in 1932 that they had enough money to build their own social center and synagogue. The years of growth for the association, then, are those during which a considerable number of its members lived far away from Resistencia, in smaller towns. Those members helped in the construction of the social hall, in the upkeep of the cemetery, and in collections for the charity fund. They might have thought that they would return to Resistencia at some future time, that they could use the organization's benefits even while living elsewhere, or that it was just what one did because they (and their families) were part of that community, even if they lived elsewhere in the province.

The availability of the minute books of this society also hints at how the flow of aid between Resistencia and Jews living in other towns worked. On May 31, 1931, the steering committee read a letter sent to them by "several members living in Tirol" (a town) who requested help for one person. The association ended up rejecting the appeal, but not because "the person [was] not a member," or was not living in Resistencia, but because "we had already offered him a job and [he] did not want to accept."[139] Ḥesed VeEmet made the decision to move away from simply handing out money in favor of providing a means for self-subsistence. On November 30, 1930, another member of the association sought a loan "because [he] has no job. . . . and would give some jewelry as collateral for the money received." This request was granted.[140]

Requests for help between congregations in interior towns and those in the city of Buenos Aires went both ways. When Ozer Dalim, a Moroccan mutual aid organization in the city, was formed, they appointed representatives in the interior provinces to collect money.[141] Close to half the members of this association lived in the interior of the country.[142] Also, when the Congregación Israelita Latina de Buenos Aires was raising money to build the temple on Piedras Street, they chose "agents in the interior to sell commemorative medals of the opening of the temple."[143] The Ottoman Jewish community also sent donation calls to those living in interior towns to raise money to buy the land for their synagogue on Camargo Street.[144] When building its temple on Brandsen Street in La Boca, Or Torah appointed local agents to raise money in five provincial towns: Chivilcoy and Bahia Blanca (province of Buenos Aires), Rosario and Santa Fé (province of Santa Fé), and Córdoba City (province of Córdoba).[145] A Damascene Jewish organization in the city of Rosario sent money to Bene Emet in Buenos Aires to support the purchase of land for a cemetery.

Sometimes the congregations in Buenos Aires would receive donations from coreligionists in the provinces. The Sociedad Israelita Sefaradí Etz HaḤaim in Rosario, for example, sent an artistic menorah, hand-painted by one of its members, to the Congregación in Buenos Aires.[146] Moisés Levy, living in Resistencia, "donated a ritual glass.... and $50 in memory of a deceased friend" to the Congregación in Buenos Aires.[147] Samuel Mehaudi, from Calchaquí, province of Santa Fé, also donated to the charity fund of the Congregación.[148]

Communities in Buenos Aires also kept connections with communities in the old countries and with Palestine. Or Torah received a telegram from Ḥesed Shel Emet, the Syrian women's association, soliciting funds to help build the walls of the cemetery in Syria. Or Torah, answering the call, sent letters to the various Damascene organizations in order to raise even more money.[149] They also helped support an old people's home in Jerusalem and wired money to a number of rabbis who were living in poverty.[150] In 1910, the Moroccan community raised money for the victims of political unrest in Casablanca.[151] In 1926, Moroccan brothers living in the province of Córdoba campaigned to raise money to build the walls of the Jewish Cemetery in Alcázarquivir (Morocco), having already raised significant amounts to help the poor in Tétouan and the Benchimol Hospital in Tangier.[152] In 1931, the Jewish community of Tétouan requested that money be raised to build the walls of the Jewish cemetery in that city. To that effect, commissions were formed in the interior provinces and in Buenos Aires.[153]

Supporting "Jewish" Institutions

Although Sephardi societies listed the creation of hospitals among their many objectives, pooling resources and raising significant sums to support such an entity was hard to do.[154] Nonetheless, Sephardim were able to provide access to doctors and funds to defray the cost of medical treatment and medicines.[155] For example, the AHASM had a commission that paid for medicines;[156] two doctors provided free services in the name of Bene Emet; there were medical offices in the synagogue of Yesod Hadat; and the Asociación Israelita Sefaradí Pro-Medicamentos in Villa Crespo even opened up its own building in 1947.[157] In 1946, this last organization assisted 3,761 patients for clinical and pediatric issues, gynecological problems, "nervous" conditions, and ear, nose, and throat ailments.[158] Hesed VeEmet and Ozer Dalim helped members purchase medicine,[159] and the Damascene community in Flores founded the Liga Antituberculosa Israelita Sefaradí (Sephardi Anti-Tuberculosis League).[160] This league was a "Sephardi" branch of the Liga Israelita Argentina contra la Tuberculosis (Argentine Jewish League against Tuberculosis), founded in 1916 by Ashkenazim. According to Jaime Favelukes, the director of the Liga Israelita, 11.6 percent of Jews had died from tuberculosis from 1917 to 1928. With offices in the Jewish neighborhood of Once in Buenos Aires, and a special arrangement with the National Hospital Santa María in the province of Córdoba, the organization helped 11,342 patients in 1930.[161] The Sephardi branch, founded in 1933, sent two young men to the province of Córdoba to be treated for tuberculosis, for example.[162] The organization received support from Bene Emet and Agudat Dodim, and periodically held fundraisers on their behalf at their synagogue as well.

Each community did not build their own hospital nor did Sephardim get together in order to build one. Instead, Sephardim (although by no means all) decided to support and utilize the Hospital Israelita "Ezrah," which opened its building in 1921 with the help of the main Ashkenazi institutions of the early twentieth century (CIRA, the Hevra Kedusha, Bikur Holim, Talmud Torah, and the philanthropic organization Ezrah). The hospital was sustained thanks to fundraising efforts carried out in Buenos Aires (with commissions in many neighborhoods) and interior cities.¹⁶³ Although Ashkenazim complained that Sephardim refused to contribute to the institution—even going as far as labeling them separatists—Sephardim made yearly contributions to the hospital's maintenance and periodically sent "their own sick" to be treated there (as opposed to, say, another ethnic community's medical institution).¹⁶⁴ There was talk that they should build a "Sephardi wing" of the hospital, but this never materialized.¹⁶⁵

Jewish orphanages (for girls and for boys and old men) were other Ashkenazi institutions that Sephardim decided to support, rather than fund their own. The Sociedad de Damas Israelitas (Jewish Women's Society) was founded in 1919, and in 1927 built the Asilo Argentino de Huérfanas Israelitas (Argentine Jewish Girls' Orphanage), an impressive three-floor building with the capacity to board three hundred orphans.¹⁶⁶ Although the institution would receive a small state subsidy beginning in 1943, the cost of upkeep was the Jewish community's responsibility. Sephardim sent not only monthly or yearly contributions but carried out collections in synagogues and supported events like "Semana de la Huérfana" (Orphan Girls' Week).¹⁶⁷

An old men's home was founded in 1916 and opened a wing for orphaned boys in 1921. In 1943, thanks to the donation of an Argentine philanthropist (who was not Jewish), both institutions were moved to Burzaco (province of Buenos Aires) where they functioned jointly until recently.¹⁶⁸ Although there were talks between the institution and Sephardim to build a "Sephardi ward" that would house orphans "on the same conditions as Ashkenazim," this proposal did not pan out.¹⁶⁹ Sephardi societies made monthly payments and organized fundraising events to support the orphanage,¹⁷⁰ and the Sephardi press listed the Sephardi boys who were housed in the institution in order to obtain donations.¹⁷¹ Much later, in the 1980s, Sephardim in Flores founded the first Sephardi senior citizens home.¹⁷²

Supporting Non-Jews

There is evidence of Sephardim and their philanthropic institutions supporting non-Jewish organizations, as well. In 1936, Bene Emet purchased fifty raffle tickets sent by the Sociedad de Beneficencia Pro-Hospital

Sirio-Libanés (Philanthropic Society for a Syrio-Lebanese Hospital).[173] Sephardim participated in fundraising for victims of natural disasters in Argentina. In 1929, Guemilut Ḥasadim sent money to alleviate the problems caused by the earthquake of Villa Atuel (province of Mendoza), and in 1939 Bene Emet called Damascene organizations to request help for the survivors of an earthquake in Chile. They purchased one thousand each of blankets, shoes, and shirts.[174] Finally, Sephardi institutions supported, through donations from their philanthropic funds, neighborhood associations. Ḥesed Shel Emet, for example, distributed food, clothes, and money to poor families in Once during Argentine national holidays (*fiestas patrias*) and gave money to the local public school, to the first aid society in Ciudadela, and to the police station.[175]

CONCLUSION

As any immigrant community in Argentina did, Jews created their own philanthropic institutions, in conversation with the practices of their countries/cities of origin. Victor Mirelman distinguished three levels at which these organizations were active. First, they maintained a connection between the Old and New World. Jews in Argentina raised money to aid coreligionists who faced poverty, religious persecution, and even natural disasters in their old countries across the Atlantic.[176] Second, Jewish organizations were important in solving problems immigrants faced on a daily basis. Hospitals, medical assistance, schooling, and work were some of the areas in which these organizations were active, and the reasons for their success were, according to Mirelman, the lack of state services and poor attention given to specific cultural concerns of immigrants, such as ritual and language needs. The third area in which these societies participated was combating white slavery. Worried that the existence of such criminals would endanger the Jewish community's standing within Argentine society, and to participate in a worldwide Jewish effort to end white slavery, several organizations were created to solve some of the problems that had made it all too easy for Jewish pimps to obtain young women and girls.

I suggest that the study of these societies, and the decisions their members made in terms of how and whom to aid, tells us significantly more than merely what Jews decided to organize about; it speaks about the ways in which Sephardim (re)constructed the boundaries of their communities after they settled in a new land. They imagined themselves part of a diasporic community, still connected to their communities of origin and to Palestine through concrete acts of philanthropy. Yet being in Argentina created *new* ties and forms of identification. Sephardim settled in specific neighborhoods in Buenos Aires and grounded their presence in the buildings they constructed and the organizations they created. In the provinces, Sephardim founded institutions that incorporated Sephardim from many different origins and that provided aid to those who left to try their luck in other nearby areas, and to Sephardi institutions in Buenos Aires. They also began to consider themselves part of a larger-than-Sephardim group and supported institutions founded by Ashkenazim. They also contributed to Argentine causes, and aided non-Jewish groups with whom they shared significant connections. The boundaries of the community of origin had extended; in fact, they had been "translated" and become more flexible.

It was stressing the diasporic boundaries that helped these Jews see themselves as Argentines. Being Sephardim in a new land brought them together, and by deciding to help fellow Sephardim in Argentina, they cemented their identity as Argentines. Argentina was "realized" through acts of philanthropy. Building a social center and synagogue in Resistencia, sending donations for the construction of the synagogue on Piedras Street in Buenos Aires, raising money to help rebuild the walls of cemeteries back in Tétouan, and donating to earthquake victims in Villa Atuel were all acts that created and recreated Sephardi and Argentine identities.

THREE

THE LIMITS OF COMMUNITY
Unsuccessful Attempts at Creating Single Sephardi Organizations

> It was imperative to create a sovereign organization that could, when necessary, speak on behalf of all, and take a position.
>
> *Israel*, July 1931

IN 1933, THE SOCIEDAD ḤESED VEEMET OF RESISTENCIA, CHACO, requested help in dealing with two issues: Could Jewish men married to non-Jewish women be buried in the Jewish cemetery? And could the non-Jewish women married to Jewish men be buried there?[1] Most likely the result of a real situation they faced, and given a clear lack of knowledge about ritual matters, the Ḥesed VeEmet deferred the decision and consulted those they considered capable of providing advice. They wrote four letters: one to the Moroccan congregation in Buenos Aires;[2] another to Saúl Sedero, a Moroccan Jew also living in that city;[3] a third letter went to Samuel de A. Levy, director of the magazine *Israel*; and the last missive went to David Elnecavé, editor of the magazine *La Luz*. Ḥesed VeEmet received replies from the three individuals (although Elnecavé requested more time to respond in full), and they decided that society members should vote on which suggestions to follow.[4]

Ḥesed VeEmet was not the only organization to request help in deciding ritual matters. Sheila Saidman, a historian who studied the Jewish community of Posadas, Misiones, noted that the Sephardi community there sent similar questions to the Comunidad Israelita Sefaradí in Buenos Aires. The questions concerned reburial in the Jewish cemetery (after interment in the municipal cemetery), which documents legitimately proved conversion for the purpose of marriage, and whether children of non-Jewish mothers could attend religious school.[5] The Ḥevra Kedusha in Mendoza, as well, sent a letter to the Guemilut Ḥasadim (the Ḥevra Kedusha of the Moroccan community in Buenos Aires) including five questions in matters of "religion."[6]

These were precisely the types of questions the Consistorio Rabínico Sefaradí, founded at the end of 1928, wished to provide answers to. In the program it sent to Sephardi communities in Argentina, the consistory stated a need to create "a single religious institution, a rabbinate, so that a man, able to lead the people, be heard ... and guide the religious, spiritual and cultural destinies of our communities, currently dispersed and somewhat incoherent."[7] With the existence of such an institution, the Sephardim in Resistencia would have had only to consult the consistory-appointed grand rabbi to find answers to their questions. But by 1933, when the letter was sent from Chaco, the Consistorio Rabínico no longer existed. Grand Rabbi Sabetay Djaen was back in Europe, in Romania. If in 1933 there was still the need for religious/ritual leadership, why had the consistory not been successful a few years before? Why did this organization fail?

This chapter explores unsuccessful attempts to construct Sephardi collectives.[8] While the previous chapters focused on the elasticity of community boundaries with regard to burial and philanthropy, moments when origin did not matter, moments when it was clear that it was "practical" to act together, the histories of the Consistorio Rabínico Sefaradí, the Confederación Israelita Sefaradí (Serphardi Jewish Confederation), and the Unión de Asociaciones Israelitas Sefaradíes de la República Argentina (Union of Sephardi Jewish Associations in the Argentine Republic) show that Sephardi identity was not necessarily a given easily invoked and applied. In the case of the consistory, I argue that although there were personality clashes, the reasons for its failure relate to changes brought about by immigration and the impossibility of re-creating communities as they had existed in the Old World. The stories of these failed organizations show the difficulty in deciding *who* would speak on behalf of all Sephardim, and even whether it was important or necessary to speak in one voice. Ultimately, these failed organizations allow us a glimpse into the contexts that created commonality and difference: Sephardim attempted cultural and religious unity through the Consistorio; in response to an attack by the Ashkenazi community they created their Confederación; and as a result of international events they attempted the creation of the Union of Associations. The fluid nature of identity boundaries is highlighted by the fact that the idea of unity was abandoned in the wake of these events.

CONSISTORIO RABÍNICO SEFARADÍ

Religious life in Argentina during the initial years of migration to the country was likely very trying. Most Sephardi immigrants created institutions and settled in new lands without religious authorities in their midst. Ceremonies were usually performed by "learned" men who were trained as shoḥets and mohels but lacked the standing and education of rabbis. (The Spanish word used in documents was *oficiante*.) It was even more difficult for communities founded in the country's interior, far away from the opportunities provided by the large Jewish population in Buenos Aires. Mohels traveled around the country—if families could afford to bring them—and they also advertised their wedding services in Jewish magazines.[9] For Passover, matzo could be purchased in Buenos Aires and mailed to the provinces, but access to kosher meat was more problematic. Unless kosher butchers existed—and they likely did in larger provincial cities—it was hard to transport meat from Buenos Aires.[10]

The communities from Damascus and Aleppo were exceptions, however, since the main institutions they created had the support and presence of learned men from the start. Ḥakham ("wise," a term used by Sephardim to mean rabbi) Shaul Setton Dabbah, who was born in Aleppo in 1851 and arrived in Argentina in 1912, was instrumental in the creation of Yesod Hadat one of the main Aleppine organizations in Buenos Aires. He closely regulated ritual slaughter and kashrut (which provided the institution with a significant source of revenue) and established a Beit Din (rabbinical court).[11] Shortly after settling in Buenos Aires in 1928, and in conjunction with Aharon Goldman [*sic*], the Ashkenazi rabbi of the JCA colony of Moisesville—and with the approval of Yosef Yedid, the rabbi of the Aleppo community in Jerusalem—Ḥakham

Dabbah (as he was known) passed a now-famous ban on conversions in Argentina. Claiming that:

> life in this city is exceedingly wanton, and everybody does as he pleases.... [and that] there is no rabbi serving the Jewish community, whose authority is respected by the government or by any other party ... anyone who wishes takes an unconverted gentile woman for his wife or chooses lay persons at random (to serve as witnesses) and "converts" her in their presence.... Therefore I dispersed [sic] announcements that it is forbidden to accept converts in Argentina until the end of time, for several reasons which we three rabbis endorse.[12]

Although it has been claimed that Dabbah was in fact originally more lenient when it came to interpretations regarding conversions than Rabbi Goldman was (Dabbah, for instance, was much readier to accept conversions done by others), he was instrumental in obtaining approval of the prohibition from the chief rabbis of Palestine and in publishing it.[13] The ban came to be accepted in Aleppine and Damascene communities in New York and Brazil, and by Aleppines in the rest of the diaspora.

Although living in Argentina, Ḥakham Dabbah maintained contact with his peers back in Aleppo and Palestine. Even before the ban, in 1926, Dabbah contacted religious authorities in Palestine, seeking support for his decision to use Arabic or Spanish rather than Hebrew as the language of instruction in Yesod Hadat's Talmud Torah. They concurred with his interpretation, which had been challenged by Jacobo Setton, president of Yesod Hadat, who wished to introduce the teaching of Hebrew as a colloquial language.[14] Ḥakham Dabbah also maintained correspondence with rabbis in both Aleppo and Palestine, and hosted Hizkiya Shabtai, chief rabbi of Aleppo, when he visited Buenos Aires in 1927 and 1929.[15]

Dabbah's death in 1930 did not leave the community without religious leadership, although the ḥakham who succeeded him found it harder to keep the community close to tradition.[16] This transitional period within the Aleppo community—until 1953—would also be marked by the presence of non-Aleppine rabbis as religious leaders of the community: Rabbi Dr. Panigel (former rabbi of Jerusalem and Baghdad) and Rabbi Dr. Abraham (Amram) Blum (Ashkenazi).[17] The period came to an end with the 1953 arrival of Itzjak Chehebar, another rabbi from Aleppo.[18] Ḥakham Chehebar would bring this community back to Orthodoxy, the path that characterizes this community still.

The Damascene Sephardim of Buenos Aires were able to initiate their religious communities with the aid and presence of "learned" men (although not necessarily rabbis), as well. Ḥakhamim Iaacov Mizrahi (who had been trained in Damascus), Iaacov and Elias Suli, Isaac Levy Hara, and Nissim Freue were connected with Or Torah in La Boca from early on. Ḥakham Iaacov Cohen Salama and his son Isaac were the religious leaders of Agudat Dodim in Flores and were instrumental in the creation, in the 1920s, of that congregation and the Talmud Torah. Interviews with elder members of these two Damascene congregations showed the central role these learned men played in both keeping religious traditions alive and aiding assimilation into the new society.[19]

In the early years of settlement, however, the rest of the Sephardim in Argentina did not have trained religious leaders among them, so a Sephardi rabbinate would come to fill an important need. In May 1927, the Congregación Israelita Latina de Buenos Aires, whose members were originally from Morocco, received a letter from Isaac García, president of Club Alianza, stating the "desire [existing] within the community to form a rabbinate in Argentina." García was requesting CILBA's support and he noted too that the rabbinate would be supported by "Oriental" Jews (a reference to the Ottoman community of Villa Crespo). The Congregación wrote back and agreed to pay m$n 500 (100 of which would come from the Ḥevra Kedusha, and another 100 from Club Alianza), but requested that the Ottomans pay m$n 800, given their numerical majority. They also requested "the rabbinate be located at our congregation and that the mission [of the rabbi] be purely religious, forbidding [him] to express his opinions about the community. . . . or to hurt it in any way."[20]

Although it would take more than a year for this proposal to become a reality, and some alterations would be made to the original proposal made by García, the rabbinical institution was linked to Rabbi Sabetay Djaen (see figure 3.1) from the beginning.[21] The initial conversations began in 1927, during his visit to Argentina on behalf of the World

Figure 3.1. Rabbi Djaen in Monastir, 1924.

Confederation of Sephardi Jews. Djaen was received by most Sephardi communities in Buenos Aires and by those in the larger provincial cities. During a visit to Club Alianza, Djaen and representatives of the "various institutions specifically invited" to the meeting discussed the creation of such an organization.[22] "Your presence here," declared the president of the Congregación Israelita Latina, "becomes even more necessary after noting that our activities push us apart and prevent us from contributing to a common objective."[23] A few days after this meeting, Djaen mentioned in an interview to a non-Jewish newspaper in Córdoba that the "proposal to name him Gran Rabino Sefaradí in Argentina [was] almost official."[24]

Born in Belgrade in 1883 into a family of rabbis and Zionists, Djaen studied in the Rabbinical Seminary of Istanbul before accepting positions as a Hebrew teacher in many cities of Bulgaria, Bosnia, and Serbia. Clashing with conservative religious men owing to his unorthodox activities, Djaen was eventually named rabbi of the city of Bitola in 1924, when the city belonged to Serbia. There he continued his Zionist work, bringing in, for example, a Hebrew teacher from Palestine to prepare children to make aliyah, as well as campaigning on behalf of the Jewish National Fund (JNF), founded in 1901 to buy and develop land in Ottoman Palestine for Jewish settlement. He founded many philanthropic organizations, soliciting donations from Bitola émigrés in North America. During his travel to South and North America in 1927, he initiated negotiations to found the Consistorio, and he finally migrated to Argentina in 1928. In Argentina, he became rabbi of the Ottoman community on Camargo Street, the Grand Rabbi of Argentina, Uruguay, and of the Consistorio; positions he held until 1931, when he returned to Europe and was named Rabbi of Bucharest and Grand Rabbi of the Association of Sephardi communities of Romania. During World War II, Djaen was repeatedly imprisoned while attempting to help the Jews living there, but he managed to survive thanks to the Turkish ambassador to Romania, who granted him a diplomatic passport.[25] Djaen escaped to Argentina, where he died in 1947 after giving a Zionist speech in the city of Tucumán.[26]

The Sephardim in Argentina particularly liked Djaen during his visit in 1927 because he was "modern," a Jew who "without leaving behind his traditions, marches alongside [modern] times."[27] While visiting their synagogues, their Talmud Torahs, and even their Zionist organization (which will be discussed fully in chapter 4) Centro Sionista Sefaradí (CSS) (Sephardi Zionist Center), Djaen captivated all with his famed oratory. It was perhaps his ability to move comfortably among religious leaders (he met with Ashkenazi Grand Rabbi Samuel Halphon and Aleppine Rabbi Dabbah, for example), government officials (he was visited by the Yugoslav representative in Argentina and met with the president of Argentina), community leaders (he was offered a lunch by the Teubal brothers and visited the homes of community leaders), Argentine Zionist leaders (he visited the Federación Sionista Argentina and met the Sephardi Zionist authorities), and regular people that convinced Sephardim that Djaen was indeed a man who earned the respect of all.

The many talents that endeared Djaen to Sephardim were put to use in the Consistorio. Although its name suggests a religious focus, and the figure of the rabbi was central, its work was not simply religious, and it was not created only to decide matters of ritual and law, as was Dabbah's Bet Din. In fact, newspapers and magazines highlighted the Consistorio's active involvement in cultural and educational matters. The rabbi planned to give Hebrew courses,[28] presented "Esther," a play he had written,[29] suggested the creation of a Sephardi youth center,[30] and gave presentations to many different audiences on different topics.[31] He traveled to the interior of the country and contacted many of the Sephardi communities settled there, and in an effort to involve them in the work of the Consistorio, he sent them a questionnaire. His educational objectives were clear, as he visited Talmud Torahs and handed out prizes to the best students to encourage Jewish education.[32] He was "the principal of all existing schools; control[led] the curricula; [taught] all unlicensed teachers; organize[d] visits to the schools and [oversaw] the activities of the students."[33] This commitment to education was evident even prior to his return to Argentina in 1928, as he had, while traveling on behalf of the World Union of Sephardi Jews to Palestine, "recruited Hebrew teachers [from Jerusalem] for nine schools in Latin America."[34]

From the program that was sent to institutions in the provinces, we learn that the rabbi also had specific ritual and religious obligations: he would keep a register for births, marriages, and deaths, perform wedding ceremonies, and would help those with "religious" queries.[35] He was in charge of regulating the "prayers" in the different synagogues, as well as scheduling services and festivities. He "controlled *shohatim* [sic] [ritual butchers] so that meat would be ritually compliant, following the regulations of our religion,"[36] and there is evidence that he granted a license for the sale of kosher cheese under his supervision.[37] In short, he was "the mainstay of Jewish Religion [sic] and [did] whatever was needed in order to comply with Jewish law."[38]

In the participating congregations' minute books, we find evidence that Rabbi Djaen attempted to enforce the "ritual" work of the Consistorio and contribute to the centralization of Sephardi ritual life. For example, in the Ottoman community, there is reference to a letter he sent to the steering committee that was setting rules regarding circumcisions and other life events, "so that people would register, as soon as it was convenient."[39] But it is clear too that he met some resistance. Djaen had to request that Moroccan community leaders post a sign in the synagogue reminding the members that "the grand rabbi was cloaked in religious authority."[40]

Although Sephardim thought very highly of Djaen, it is evident that there was some apprehension before the Consistorio was created. The 1927 proposal requested that the "rabbinical council be formed by six members plus a president; [the six members] would be made up of three members from our community [Moroccan Congregation] and three from the [Ottoman] community."[41] The final makeup of the rabbinical council, and the powers vested in it and in the rabbi, suggest that negotiations took place to address concerns of the lay leadership. First, representatives of the Jerusalemite community joined (there were three members from each of the three participating groups). The council thus ended up being larger (eleven members, including a president and the rabbi, among others), not simply because of the addition of the Jerusalemite group but because of the addition of more members at large (secretary, treasurer, pro-treasurer, and so on). It was also the president (a Moroccan Jew was elected to this position) who named the rabbi, reserving a more visible role for the lay leadership. In the pamphlets printed by the organization it was made clear that "any educational, cultural or religious issues of interests to the communities that the grand rabbi wishes to sponsor, should be presented to the council and only then, if approved, could they be implemented by the grand rabbi."[42] In addition to this clause limiting the power of the rabbi, the language of the program is replete with expressions that reveal the lay leadership's fear that the organization could become, if not checked, too independent from the communities themselves: "with the approval of the participating congregations," and "with the support and collaboration of the communities."[43] There may have existed a need for a religious leader and institution but not at the expense of the lay leadership.

Coupled with the language that gave communities clear visibility within the Consistorio, there was from the beginning a discourse, evident both in Sephardi publications as well as in Ashkenazi and Argentine ones, that placed Rabbi Djaen in the role of "savior" and "sage." For example, in *El Semanario Hebreo,* published by José Lutzky, Djaen is described as "the guide and adviser of this numerous Sephardi-Jewish colony, which lacked, until now, energetic leaders." Lutzky encouraged "Sephardim to appreciate the presence of such celebrity,"[44] which they do; Sephardim described him as "kissed by God on his forehead at birth," as "the shining light of world Sephardim," and as having come "to organize [them] and energize their spent souls."[45] This language, although certainly earned by Djaen for his many accomplishments, perhaps echoed prevalent ideas about the "cultured" European, even when, in this case, Djaen himself was from the Ottoman Empire, located at best on the margins of Europe. He came to represent what the European Jewish elite had been fighting for: an Ottoman Jew "renewed" by education. This discourse placed Djaen above the rest of Sephardim, who were imagined to be inferior and in need of guidance. This idea would eventually contribute to the demise of the organization.

However striking the journalistic coverage the Consistorio generated during its first months, the speed with which it disappeared is notable, as well: within a year, it fell from view. On November 17, 1929, the Moroccan community voted on "whether we should continue our link to the rabbinate, since given the original commitment of a year, we should resolve the matter in a general assembly."[46] Although the members voted to remain within the Consistorio, its end was foretold (eighteen votes in favor of continuance, nine against, two blank).[47] The fragmented evidence that survives points to financial problems and important differences between the rabbi and members of the Sephardi congregations.

On December 29, 1929, only a few days after the vote at the Congregación Israelita Latina de Buenos Aires on the future of its connection with the Consistorio, the steering committee received a letter from Rabbi Djaen in which he complained about a pamphlet authored and published by Benjamín Benzaquén that had not been condemned publicly by the institution's leaders.[48] There is another reference to the circulation of the pamphlet in the minute books of Kahal Kadosh, the Ottoman community, although it is not clear what the steering committee decided to do about it.[49] As the pamphlet has not survived, it is unclear what Djaen was being accused of; uncorroborated stories assert that he had complained about stores open on Shabbat, provoking the anger of (Moroccan) Sephardim, who were somewhat distant from strict religious observance.[50] We can be certain that the differences highlighted in the pamphlet were significant; it is after its publication that the Consistorio disappeared from newspaper coverage. It is safe to suggest that these conflicts led to the withdrawal of financial support on the part of some participating Sephardi communities, at a time when the economic reality was very trying indeed. In the end, Etz HaḤaim and the Círculo Social Israelita (both of Ottoman origin), decided not to continue supporting the Consistorio.[51]

The history of the consistory's demise is as invisible as the conflicts that precipitated it. In August 1930, the CILBA divorced itself from the Consistorio, and it was stated in the November 9 meeting minutes that the rabbinical council was dissolved. The rabbi (not grand rabbi anymore) continued his relationship with the Ottoman community of Camargo (Kal Kadosh), although it is clear from the evidence that they could not afford his salary much longer. They attempted fundraising among members, but the amount raised was not enough.[52] Relations between the rabbi and the communities who had supported the Consistorio until then were tense but cordial. On December 18, 1930, Moroccan, Jerusalemite, Aleppine, and Ottoman individuals "came to say they were ready to take on the support of Your Excellency Grand Rabbi Djaen," and although he was preparing to leave for Europe, he asked the Ottoman community to keep his position open until his return.[53]

The amicable state came to an end, however, with the publication of an article in *Mundo Israelita*, an Ashkenazi newspaper that was highly critical of Sephardim who had not, in the end, supported Djaen. (Most readers believed that Djaen had written the article, although it later became known that he did not.) In the piece, the Sephardim who criticized Djaen were accused of "wandering around the world, not displaying love for learning, for spiritual matters, or even love for the sages. . . . They have exchanged these Spanish virtues for Ottoman indifference, for Berber ignorance, for the materialism of oriental merchants." The author asked, "Is it surprising, then, that they would not appreciate those who wish to end their laziness and push them along the wide road of progress?" In closing, the reason for the failure of the Consistorio was attributed to the "manifested inferiority of the Sephardim, [and their] evident apathy for any type of intellectual activity."[54]

The piece angered Sephardim and they came together on February 22, 1931, to discuss the "insults suffered by the *colectividad Sefaradí* [Sephardim]." They debated whether to blame the newspaper or Djaen himself.[55] Although Djaen apologized for the article (not for writing it—since he had not—but for having aired his opinion with the journalist who penned the piece), Sephardim were deeply hurt by the assertion that they were inferior. "Perhaps some more than others, our people came here already educated," claimed a meeting participant during discussion of the article's claim that Djaen had been brought in to "enlighten" the Sephardi masses.[56] Djaen, although Sephardi himself, came to be seen as an other, both by Ashkenazim and Sephardim. And it was in connection to this discussion that the communities that had originally joined in the Consistorio, plus others who had not been part of it, raised the idea of creating an organization to defend their honor—what would eventually become the Confederación Israelita Sefaradí.[57] Thus while the Consistorio was dead, this meeting shows that the idea of a single Sephardi institution was not. Djaen may have failed at becoming the cultural and religious leader for Sephardim, but anger against him brought them, for a time, together again.

This question begs repeating: Why would an organization created to solve religious and cultural issues collapse if the same issues continued to exist? An analysis of the Consistorio's models, and especially how those did not apply, shows us distinctive features of Sephardi identity in Argentina at this time. The Consistorio Rabínico Sefaradí and its religious authority, in its short life, were largely an amalgam of the French consistories created in post-emancipation France and the position held by the chief rabbi (*ḥakham bashi*) after the nineteenth-century Ottoman reforms. These "institutions" were aimed at efficiently linking the Jewish community with the state. Napoleon created a hierarchical system with the central consistory located in Paris, and local consistories, representing Jewish communities in one or more *départements*. The consistories were made up of rabbis and lay members: the central consistory had three rabbis and two laymen, while local consistories had three lay members and one or two rabbis, depending on the size of the population.[58] The consistories, then, besides being in charge of practical aspects of the community's well-being, functioned as the Jewish representative body to the government. In the Ottoman context, the decree of 1865 that modified the relationship between Jews and the Ottoman state turned the ḥakham bashi into the highest government official in Jewish society.[59]

It is clear that Rabbi Djaen felt very comfortable in the role of chief rabbi, not just in Argentina during the years of the Consistorio, but even before. When he became the chief rabbi of Bitola, he received the blessing—in person—of Dr. Isaac Alkalay, chief rabbi of the Yugoslav communities. Djaen took the oath in front of Alkalay as well as the archbishop of Provo, the district governor, the regional military commander, the High Court justice, and other notable religious authorities and representatives of the state. Djaen walked the streets of Bitola preceded by a guard, who cleared the way for him by holding and waving a symbolic staff.[60] For the official event that marked the inauguration of the Consistorio, Djaen was "invited to sit [after an introduction by the Consistorio president] in a chair-throne of exquisite taste, made by request."[61] While touring South America on behalf of the World Confederation of Sephardi Jews, Djaen met the Spanish ambassador and foreign presidents.[62]

Even while the Consistorio did not become the representative of all Sephardim in Argentina (since the Syrian communities of Buenos Aires did not participate, given the weight of their own religious leaders), the public prominence it achieved did give it a certain authority with government officials. Unlike the early French consistories, however, the most visible member of the institution was Rabbi Djaen (and not the lay nobility). It is clear that Djaen wished to mold the figure of the Grand Rabbi of the Argentine Republic on the attributes of the Grand Rabbi of the Ottoman Empire (after the mid-nineteenth-century changes).[63] The new position in the empire allowed the government to deal with only one representative of the Jewish community, and although this was viewed by the Jewish community as an outside imposition on their internal affairs, and an affront to the power held by the lay leadership (who until then had represented the Jewish communities to Ottoman authorities), the position slowly came to be accepted toward the early twentieth century. The personality of the rabbi elected to the position usually defined how successful and influential his tenure would be, and for many years chief rabbis held no more power than local rabbis even when the Ottoman (and later Turkish) authorities considered them official representatives of the Jewish community.

Rabbi Djaen, notwithstanding the actual limited role exercised by chief rabbis, seemed to hope to turn the position into a relevant one. Djaen attempted to transform himself into the representative of Sephardim in Argentina. The official pictures of Grand Rabbi Djaen in ritual function show an impressive man, dressed in the traditional white robe and headgear (see figure 3.2). While on tour to the interior of the country, he met provincial governors, city mayors, police chiefs, and local political leaders.[64] In 1929, after news of the disturbances in Palestine reached Argentina, the rabbi published a "religious decree" (Becoaḥ HaTorah) declaring a day of mourning—which meant shops would close—and urging Sephardim to attend a public meeting that would end with the presentation, by a small committee, of a memorandum to the British ambassador in Argentina.[65] It was clear Rabbi Djaen saw himself as an intermediary between Sephardim—or perhaps Jews in general?—and secular authorities.[66]

It is likely that his wish to play this visible role (and what it ultimately represented) explains the short life of the consistory. It is clear that, from the start, Sephardim wanted to set up an organization led and controlled by lay people, with a rabbi who would guide but not decide. Instead the grand rabbi sought a central role. The Ottoman chief rabbinate was Djaen's model, but the early French consistory was the model the leaders of these communities wanted to follow, and the models were not compatible. Nor did the "savior" discourse around Djaen help him create a good relationship with the lay leadership. The consistory failed not for lack of agreement regarding ritual practices but a lack of agreement over the very idea of community the Sephardim wished to present to the Argentines. They were not simply a "religious" group that therefore required "religious" representation; they fought for an ideal of community stressing multiple aspects of its definition: philanthropy, culture,

Figure 3.2. Rabbi Djaen in Romania, 1937.

and social space. In fact, these Sephardim were already imbued with the Enlightenment notion that religion did not define status and belonging to the nation.

This does not mean that Sephardim became openly secular; nothing could be further from the truth. In fact, during the 1950s, many Sephardi congregations in Buenos Aires attracted important religious leaders to their communities. As a consequence of the disruption of the Sephardi world caused first by World War II and by the later Arab-Israeli conflict, famous rabbis, born and trained in the Old World, settled in Argentina. Saadiá Benzaquén from Morocco led the Moroccan community until his death in 1986. Aron Angel was born in Bulgaria, trained in Rhodes, and was Grand Rabbi of Egypt before his coming to Buenos Aires to serve the Ottoman community of Villa Crespo. Itzhak Chehebar, as noted above, came originally from Aleppo. Michael Molho, from Salonika, served for several years in the Ottoman community of Colegiales.[67]

In the end, the failure of the Consistorio suggests that as a single collective, Sephardim increasingly saw themselves as a "political" group making a statement about their singularity and wishing to act "as one" in matters that related to others. Religion and ritual, they realized, could continue to be addressed by each community individually and would remain an "internal" affair. But Sephardim did not wish to represent themselves as a single "religious" entity to others. In that sense, this attempt at creating a single Sephardi collectivity should be understood as one of many that existed within the Argentine Jewish community. The Federación Argentina Israelita, the Comité Central de Ayuda a las Víctimas de la Guerra (Central Committee to Aid Victims of War), and the Alianza, for example, set up a single voice in order to interact (among themselves and) with the state. Also by the 1930s, Ashkenazim had started to turn an existing organization (Ḥevra Kedusha) into a single society that served "internal" needs, a process that culminated with the creation of the AMIA.[68] Perhaps Sephardim wished to imitate Ashkenazim and create an organization to serve a similar purpose. It became clear, however, that the single voice would not be a "religious" voice, as it had been in the Old World.

CONFEDERACIÓN ISRAELITA SEFARADÍ AND THE FEDERACIÓN ARGENTINA DE SOCIEDADES ISRAELITAS

As mention of the Consistorio faded from newspapers and magazines, and the conflict with Rabbi Djaen took a more antagonistic turn after the appearance of the *Mundo Israelita* article, Sephardim, as noted above, began discussing the creation of another single institution. The reasons for its necessity were different, of course, from the reasons prompting the formation of the consistory. Religious and/or educational leadership were no longer primary concerns, at least as reasons for creating a unified Sephardi voice.

Sephardim worried both about the inability to defend their reputation as a collective (since there was no organization that could do so) and about the independence of individual communities if such a "collective" organization came into existence. The *Mundo Israelita* article was seen as an affront to all Sephardim, and they called on "a sovereign organization that could, when necessary, speak on behalf of all, and take a position," especially when the collective had been attacked.[69] But in the same breath with which they discussed the need for such organization, they clearly stated that "the important role to be played by the Confederación Israelita Sefaradí would not interfere in any way with the internal affairs of affiliated communities, who will remain autonomous."[70] The same language was repeatedly invoked in the many newspaper articles that chronicled the organizational meetings. The idea of a single collective was attractive, but not if the price was the "erasure" of particularities.

A significant majority of Sephardim supported the creation of such collective. Thirteen organizations—including burial, philanthropic, and social/recreational societies, as well as congregations—participated in the meeting held on June 14, 1931, and others continued to join after this event. The organizations came from all the main Sephardi groups—those from Morocco, Aleppo, Jerusalem, Damascus, and the Balkans—and from the various neighborhoods these groups had settled in, but representation was not based on place of origin. There were, for example, Jews from Damascus representing their burial society, their congregation in the Boca/Barracas neighborhood, and their congregation in Flores. The variety of organizations that wished to participate in the Confederación speaks about the appeal of a nonreligious entity. Whereas the Consistorio had focused its work on ritual and education—even when Rabbi Djaen visited recreational or social institutions—the Confederación had no such focus and thus had the potential to gather all Sephardi societies. Yet there is no evidence that suggests Sephardi organizations from the rest of the country joined in. In fact, an *Israel* reader complained about the creation of any such "singular" organization in Buenos Aires and suggested it be created in the center of the country (province of Córdoba, for example). He rhetorically asked, "When Rabbi Sabetay Djaen was called, the Consistorio said it represented Sephardi

The Limits of Community

Jews from all Argentina. Who did they consult and when?"[71] The conflict between Buenos Aires and the rest of the country did not begin with the Confederación project, nor did it end with it; this urban-provincial conflict was also not exclusive to the Jewish community. But it seems that Sephardi institutions in the provinces did not participate in the makeup of the new Confederación, a fact that perhaps constituted failure to achieve one of its aims: representativeness.

The initial negotiations to set up the Conferederación created a provisional steering committee with a president, secretary, treasurer, and five consultants. The initial commission was significantly enlarged a few months later, to six members plus thirty-five board members at large. This increase reflected the number of organizations that decided to join. The provisional presidency of the organization was granted to Ezra Teubal, an Aleppine Jew, accomplished industrialist and well-known philanthropist, and the vice presidency was given to Jacobo Bendahán, who was of Moroccan origin. This organization failed, but the reasons for its failure had little to do with personality conflicts or with questions regarding the kind of connection Sephardim wished to establish with government authorities, whether religious or not.

The intent to form a confederation among Sephardim came at the same time that other Jewish institutions in Argentina were attempting to do the same, for instance, B'nai B'rith Argentina, which proposed the creation of the Federación Argentina de Sociedades Israelitas. This local chapter of the international philanthropic Jewish organization had been created only a few months earlier, and, precisely around the time Sephardim began working on the creation of *their* confederation, the B'nai Brith began to push their new federation. Echoing language used by the Sephardim, the convener of the B'nai Brith meeting in July 1931 stated that "what we want is to help create an entity that can act on behalf of Jewish Argentines whenever necessary, in case of defamation, acts against the community, anti-Semitic events or similar problems."[72] The B'nai B'rith also wished to clarify, as Sephardim were doing with their own federation, that this new entity would "not intervene in the communities that belong to it, leaving each to their own."[73] Noting that this federation would be different from the Kehila, an organization that worked within the community, the Federación would be the link "between Jews and the government, between the Jews and the Argentine Press, to deal with 'foreign relations' issues, as it were."[74]

Sephardim decided to support the B'nai Brith's larger proposed project. Sixteen Sephardi institutions were present at the Federación's initial meeting, which was hosted by a Sephardi institution, and the Sephardi press followed developments closely.[75] Once the idea of the Federación was turning into reality, the project for a Sephardi-only confederation dropped out of sight. Although the need for an umbrella Sephardi institution had been born as a consequence of the perceived "insults" against them leveled by another Jewish institution (*Mundo Israelita*), and the perceived need for a unified Sephardi voice—even as the Federación Argentina de Sociedades Israelitas was being imagined as a spokesperson for the whole Jewish community against perceived acts of anti-Semitism and discrimination—Sephardim seem to have accepted the federation as able to perform some, if not all, of the roles they had planned for their own confederation. In particular, Sephardim cited an added benefit: that such an institution would "ensure a real connection between Sephardim and Ashkenazim, [and represent] a joint intelligent action on behalf of the rights of all [Jews]."[76]

The Federación Argentina de Sociedades Israelitas, however, failed to group all Jewish societies in 1932. Although meetings took place, and a committee was selected to draft bylaws, there was not a strong enough consensus as to what the organization's role would be. Newspaper accounts reference "campaña de calumnias" (defamation campaigns) on the part of some, and it is also important to note that it was the B'nai B'rith (and not the Ashkenazi Hevra Kedusha, for example) calling for the creation of such organization. At a time when the Hevra Kedusha was fighting to become the de facto Jewish Kehila—albeit mostly Ashkenazi—B'nai B'rith's efforts were perhaps viewed as a challenge to that centralizing vision, especially since the local chapter had been formed only a few months before. As an "American" organization, B'nai B'rith (founded in New York City in 1843) was ideologically suspect in some (Zionist) Argentine quarters, a subject I return to in chapter 4.

Despite the failure to create the Federación, it can still be argued that the organization that was formed in 1935, and that would become the umbrella Jewish association in Argentina until today, was linked to this initial effort. The pressing political reality of the early 1930s added a renewed sense of urgency, however. DAIA, as it came to be known, was formed in 1935, and it grew out of one organization founded in the early 1930s. This previous organization was called the Comité contra las Persecuciones de Judíos en Alemania (Committee against Persecutions of Jews in Germany), a name clearly showing that its origin was linked to the rise of Nazism, but it changed its name in 1934 to Comité contra el Antisemitismo (Committee against Antisemitism), which suggests more attention paid to the local climate.[77] Thus, international and Argentine political realities defined DAIA's objectives, which included, among others, "the struggle against the antisemitism 'imported' from abroad, and against the local 'exotic antisemitism' which was disturbing the harmony of the 'Argentine family.'"[78]

DAIA did attract a variety of Jewish institutions, from political Zionist organizations to philanthropic institutions to economic and cultural societies.[79] It indeed became the official voice of the community and the interlocutor with the state in cases in which the rights of Jews (to self-expression, for example) were threatened. Within the first few years, DAIA dealt with the state-mandated introduction of Catholic education in public schools, the creation of special registration for those not of the Catholic faith, and the prohibition of foreign languages in public meetings. It also denounced the appearance of anti-Semitic newspaper articles and attempted to influence state policy on international issues.[80]

UNIÓN DE ASOCIACIONES ISRAELITAS SEFARADÍES DE LA REPÚBLICA ARGENTINA

DAIA's 1935 achievement—the creation of a society to speak out in the defense of *all* Jews in Argentina—did not seem enough to Sephardim in 1942, when they faced a situation for which they wanted, yet again, an organization that would speak on behalf of Sephardim alone. With a war-ravaged Europe, and the need to aid surviving members of Jewish communities in the old countries, the Jewish Agency sought to reorganize itself to better deal with the situation at hand. Reorganization meant paying increased attention to Jewish communities not in Europe in order to augment fundraising efforts.

In April 1942, the CSS organized the Primera Convención Sefaradí de la República Argentina (First Argentine Sephardi Convention).[81] The meeting was attended by representatives of the main Argentine Sephardi organizations and delegates from Sephardi communities in Chile and Uruguay. In keeping with the Jewish Agency's intent to better organize fundraising efforts, Adolfo Arditti, a Sephardi representative of Keren Hayesod, attended, as did Dr. Mibashan, a Jewish Agency delegate from Jerusalem. Much of the discussion centered on the need to urge Sephardim to participate actively in that year's collections for the JNF, and on how to better connect Sephardi Zionist (fundraising) structures to other local and international groups. The plight of Sephardi communities in Europe was stressed in an attempt to create a sense of responsibility among Sephardim to help Sephardim.

The convention passed a number of resolutions; perhaps the most important was the creation of a committee that would eventually make it possible to have a Sephardi branch of the JNF.[82] A letter sent to a Sephardi community in the province of Chaco suggests that another resolution was the creation of a new Sephardi umbrella organization with the intention of helping Sephardim affected by the war in Europe. Stressing the plight of these Sephardim and their communities in Nazi-ravaged Europe, the newly created Unión de Asociaciones Israelitas Sefaradíes de la República Argentina made the case, not so subtly, that Sephardim were the responsibility of Sephardim. The objective of the organization, as explained in the letter, went further: "The Unión de las [sic] Asociaciones Sefaradíes de la Argentina was born from this urgent need [to support our brethren, and it aims] to create a well-organized center that could take on the common tasks of representing our colectividad [community] during these historic moments."[83]

But the organizers had in mind more than mere coordination to help those back in Europe. The Unión, they hoped, would also work on "all aspects of communal life [in Argentina]: ritual, philanthropy, education, youth and Sephardi culture," and pay special attention to supporting Sephardim in the interior, communities that were "small and isolated."[84] It seems that emphasizing responsibility toward brethren worldwide underscored their commonalities, and thus they seized the opportunity to take the next logical step—taking on common problems and issues in

Argentina—and broadened the organization's mission. Besides ensuring the spread of Zionist ideas among Sephardi communities in Argentina, the Unión adopted the representation of its Sephardim (representación del Judaísmo Argentino Sefaradí), as well, and sought to create a chief rabbinate and cultural center for Sephardi youth, coordinate the philanthropic work of all Sephardi institutions, and protect Sephardi immigrants.[85]

Sephardim did continue to work as one, but they threw their energy into the fundraising required by all Jews in the years prior to the creation of the state of Israel. This meant that the objectives set by the Unión to address common challenges they faced in Argentina were not achieved. The activity organized by the CSS (the focus of chapter 4) monopolized the time and energy of Sephardim; moreover, this organization (which had existed for a long time) became the de facto representative of Sephardim to other Sephardim, both in Argentina and abroad. The objectives of the creation of the Jewish state became paramount. The educational and religious objectives that the Unión had wished to address eventually were met by the arrival of new religious leaders, starting in the early 1950s, which invigorated Sephardi communities in Buenos Aires. Yet this was achieved by the efforts of individual communities and their leaders; Sephardi communities in the interior, for example, would not be as lucky. It would not be until 1972 that Sephardim would reconsider creating an umbrella organization. At the Convención de Comunidades e Instituciones Sefaradíes de la Argentina (Convention of Argentine Sephardi Congregations and Institutions) in the province of Córdoba, the Ente Coordinador Sefaradí Argentino (Sephardi Coordinating Body) was organized, with objectives similar to those stated by the Unión in 1942.[86] Yet again, the efficacy of such an institution remained doubtful.

CONCLUSION

Through these attempts at creating single institutions, Sephardim tested the limits of community. The organizations, and the goals they hoped to accomplish, show the objectives Sephardim believed they had in common and wished to pursue together; the failure of these institutions suggests that the strength they wished to gain by acting together was deemed, in many cases, not worth the cost. Above all, these stories confirm that Sephardi identity was never a given, but always in the process of being defined and acted on. Sephardim found issues that united them, just as we will see in chapter 4, and the institutions they created to pursue them were successful precisely because they appealed to a sense of responsibility. The Consistorio Rabínico, for a while, attempted to appeal to a shared religious identity that—Sephardim soon realized—no longer fit the way that Sephardim in Argentina wished to be identified. The Confederación Sefaradí and the Unión de Asociaciones Sefaradíes imagined common problems that were later addressed and fulfilled by other (sometimes not Sephardi, but Jewish) institutions. Sephardim tested the fine line that divided them from *and* united them with other Sephardim, other Jews in Argentina, and Jews in the diaspora, drawing and redrawing boundaries depending on the objectives and realities at hand.

FOUR

WORKING FOR THE HOMELAND

Zionism and the Creation of an "Argentine" Sephardi Community after 1920

> There are many Sephardi communities [in Argentina], but only one Sephardi Zionist Center.
>
> Baile de la Colectividad, 1945

> We must leave it to the historian and sociologists to explain the puzzling combination of all this national Jewish awareness and the desire to strike roots in Argentine agriculture or the ambition—in the urban centers—to become genuine Latin Americans.
>
> Moshe Kitrón, *Latin American Jewry in our Time*, 1964–1965

AN ARTICLE IN THE 1945 PROGRAM OF THE GRAN BAILE DE LA Colectividad (Grand Community Ball) read: "For most of the Ashkenazim, the Sephardi community [Colectividad Sefaradí] is an abstract nation with no content." The anonymous piece continued:

> For Sephardim, it [the community] is an assortment of people from various different origins with nothing in common. In fact, when a Sephardi Jew speaks of the community [*colectividad*], he thinks about the community he is from, and forgets that in this city there are many Sephardi sectors and many community organizations. There are more than twenty Sephardi temples.... some ten schools, a relatively important number of philanthropic organizations, and more than ten social and sports clubs.... [Yet despite the differences that exist today] there once was *one* "Sephardi world." This world was, in a sense, a reality, and it had a capital: the holy city of Jerusalem.... And it is the ideal Jerusalem, Zionism, which today serves as a link among the different Sephardi sectors. There are many [Sephardi] communities, but only one Centro Sionista Sefaradí, only one Keren Kayemet Department, and only one Youth Department.... In

> this country, differences in language and culture [will] disappear.... If Zionism does not take its place as the educator, the new mentality required for a new Jewish life will not be born. Sephardism [*Sefardismo*] would risk the danger of disappearing, with the erasure of the differences among the various sectors."[1]

This Sephardi Zionist writer went on, reflecting on the role he hoped Zionism would play among Sephardim in Argentina. Immersed in the post–World War II "euphoria" that characterized Zionist activity in those years, he reasoned that Zionism would help Sephardim in two ways: first, it would unite all different Sephardi groups under one banner—the "redemption of the land of Israel"—and, second, it would eventually save them from complete erasure as a cultural minority. Because Zionism could (and to a certain degree did) help unite Sephardim in a single Zionist organization, the writer believed that once all Jews in Argentina joined together—assuming that Sephardim and Ashkenazim would eventually become indistinguishable from one another, as he predicted—then this single Sephardi Zionist organization, and the identity it advocated, would preserve the minority group's cultural barriers. He ultimately called for a reconfiguration of Sephardi identity by creating new ideological boundaries to replace the geographical borders that were doomed, he claimed, to disappear.

In a sense, the writer was correct in his assumptions. Zionism did provide Sephardim with a space in common to create a new identity. For few projects did Sephardim come together as one group; for even fewer projects did they consider acting as a single entity.[2] On the one hand, there were practical reasons for joint activity. Cultural barriers made it hard for Sephardim to organize and work alongside the Ashkenazi Zionists in Argentina. Not only did these "other" Jews insist on speaking a language—Yiddish—that was not understood by Sephardim but Zionism had been experienced differently in Ashkenazi countries of origin.[3] On the other hand, Zionism allowed Sephardim the possibility of constructing a new identity, if only temporarily, by stressing their shared (though long gone, and not by all) past in Spain, when all Sephardim were together. The appeal to past origins was not a nostalgic journey through Sephardi history, however, but was used to highlight their present, shared responsibility in helping all Sephardim in Palestine and later Israel. This new role was necessary, Sephardim claimed, because the international leadership of the Zionist project was purposely discriminating against this minority. Because Ashkenazi leaders were not protecting the rights of Sephardim, Sephardim around the world had to step up to fulfill their duty to "brothers and sisters" who were settling in Palestine.

The appeal to an all-encompassing, even universal, "Sephardi" identity also provided the space for, and indeed required, the elaboration and configuration of the "Argentine" (*lo Argentino*). On the Zionist Jewish map, the Moroccan, Arab, and Ottoman Sephardim came to be identified (and to identify themselves) as "Argentine" Sephardim. As such, they financially supported the founding of colonies in Palestine for newly arrived Sephardim, and ensured that money collected in Argentina from Sephardim would be acknowledged as coming from the "Argentine Sephardi" community and used for projects they considered appropriate. These newly inclusive (Argentine) boundaries were predicated on both difference (from Ashkenazim) and similarity (the appeal to the Spanish past and Argentine present), and were created in conversation with local and international contexts.

This chapter examines Zionism in Argentina, paying special attention to how Sephardim responded to the nationalist project and how they navigated politically charged contexts, both at home and abroad. In particular, I stress how Zionism provided Sephardim with a legitimate platform to celebrate and defend their minority status, by fighting to retain control over donations, over investment of those donations, and over their communities. These actions created new borders around Sephardim living in Argentina. Rather than explore how Sephardim individually understood Zionism—the sources give far too little information to attempt that—I focus on the uses it was put to by Zionist Sephardi organizations.[4]

This story is a narrative that delineates how Zionism became an ideological glue that served an important purpose: to defend Sephardi visibility and the right to maintain their subethnic identities. But once the Zionist leadership had acknowledged that Sephardim wished to remain a distinct minority within the project, Zionist Sephardi organizations were consumed again by internal differences about whether to see themselves first as Sephardim or as Jews fighting for the state of

Israel. When their identity as Argentine Sephardim—distinct and separate from Ashkenazim—was legitimated, it was not as threatening to stress their own internal differences. By becoming "Argentine Sephardim," Moroccan, Ottoman, and Syrian Sephardim could continue to be subethnic groups and follow their own specific traditions.[5]

I begin with brief discussion of the development of Zionist organizations (mostly Ashkenazi) in Argentina to understand the context in which Sephardim developed their own groups and centers. Sephardi Zionist organizing can be divided into three stages:

1. From 1904, and the First Argentine Zionist Congress through the 1920s. This initial period was marked by conflict between the JNF and the World Union of Sephardi Jews (WUSJ) and witnessed the creation of the first Centro Sionista Sefaradí.
2. From the 1930s to the mid-1940s, a period that included the creation of Sephardi departments and branches of the JNF to the founding of a second Centro Sionista Sefaradí.
3. The post-1948 period, characterized by the increasing presence of the State of Israel in local affairs and by debate about the very meaning of Sephardi identity in the context of the new state.

In these moments, Sephardim interacted with and responded to their fellow Argentine Ashkenazim, fellow Sephardim in Palestine (later, Israel), and representatives of the Israeli state. These conversations informed and shaped their own understandings of the similarities and differences among the various Sephardi groups, among Argentine Jews, and among Jews of the Diaspora and those of Israel. I conclude with a description of Zionist activity among Sephardim in the interior of the country, highlighting how Zionism—considered a means to solidify ideas about a Jewish nation—contributed to cementing a new identity around the loyalty to the Argentine nation. By the 1960s, then, it is not surprising that Moshe Kitrón, whose words open this chapter, wondered about the close connection between Zionism (the longing to return to Zion) and the desire to remain Argentine.

ZIONISM IN ARGENTINA

Organized Zionist activity in Argentina (mostly among Ashkenazi Jews, given their earlier arrival) began at nearly the same time the First Zionist Congress took place in Basel, Switzerland, but the first decades were marred by internal conflict and a lack of centralized institutions. In August 1897 a handful of Buenos Aires Jews founded a Hovevei Zion society (organizations that came into existence in Eastern Europe in the 1880s, said to be the precursors of the Zionist movement), and soon after others created the "Dr. Hertzl League."[6] More organizations were set up in Buenos Aires, in several interior towns, and in JCA colonies. In 1898, at the Second Zionist Congress in Europe, there was even a delegate claiming to represent Argentine Jews.[7] All these new organizations, which included the "Spanish Congregation," (CILBA), sent delegates to the First Argentine Zionist Congress in 1904.[8]

One reason for the almost constant conflict between these organizations in this early period was that the leadership of the WZO wanted to name an official representative for Argentine Zionists. Eventually, and for that purpose, Argentine Jews founded a Federación Sionista Argentina (FSA) (Federation of Argentine Zionists) that shared recognition with the Dr. Hertzl League until 1908, when the WZO shifted support to Tiferet Tzion, a new Zionist organization.[9] Although these organizations spent much of their energy in internal battles for control of the community in order to secure recognition from the WZO, Argentine Zionists nonetheless found the time to organize schools (their main tool for disseminating Zionist ideals to the younger generation) and publish several periodicals (mostly in Yiddish), including *El Sionista* (The Zionist), in Spanish. This publication suggests that the readership included Spanish-speaking Jews (Sephardim) and perhaps Argentine society at large.

A new FSA, created in 1913, secured recognition from Zionist headquarters in Europe and a share of their collections, but increasingly came to represent the ideas of the General Zionists (HaTzionim HaKlaliym), only one ideological position of many on the wide spectrum of Jewish national movement ideologies. By then, Argentine Zionists belonged to Revisionist Zionism and the Orthodox-Zionist Mizrahi Party on the far right, the General Zionists in the center, and on the left, to Poalei Zion (socialist-Zionist labor party) and Hashomer Hatzair, the socialist-Zionist youth movement. There were also "apolitical" Zionist groups with large memberships such as WIZO and the Confederación Juvenil Sionista Argentina (Confederation of Argentine Zionist Youth). In 1943 the Consejo Central Sionista (Zionist Central Council), a new umbrella organization, replaced the FSA, which became the General Zionist Party in Argentina. In 1956, the Organización Sionista Argentina (OSA) (Zionist Organization of Argentina) came into existence, replacing the Consejo Central Sionista.[10]

Zionist parties participated actively in Argentine Jewish institutions, namely, in the Ashkenazi Kehila, later to become the AMIA. After the creation of the state of Israel, Zionist parties came to dominate the AMIA and the DAIA, dictating policies that ensured support for the new state, its culture, and Zionist ideology.[11] In that context of Zionist political hegemony in communal institutions, especially after 1949, non-Zionist groups (antinationalist Communist Jews and the Jewish Workers Bund) lost representation in the AMIA, and Communist Jewish institutions were expelled from the DAIA in 1952.[12]

SEPHARDIM, ERETZ ISRAEL, AND ZIONISM

First Period: Until the Early 1930s

Within a local Zionist context that was highly politicized—as it was elsewhere—Sephardim in Argentina had no space to act as a group. The structure of the Zionist movement developed along lines of political ideology, and as Sephardim were not a political party, they found it increasingly difficult to fit into that structure as a single unit.[13] The problem posed by Sephardi representation and participation would only be addressed by the WZO in the late 1940s, and it would not be fully resolved until the early 1950s. Until then, Sephardim fought very hard for their right to participate as their own group.[14] Of course individuals could join Zionist parties and participate as members of those parties but Sephardim chose, importantly, to work as *Sefaradíes*. This translated into the creation of Sephardi Zionist institutions and organizations that worked in parallel to Ashkenazi Zionist organizations. This policy was often interpreted by larger Zionist organizations as a lack of desire to participate in the Zionist movement; thus Sephardim spent a considerable amount of time and energy attempting to dispel that mischaracterization.

Among Sephardim, connections with Palestine and with the Jews living there did not occur only through Zionist institutions. In their countries of origin, many societies raised money for and offered help to those still living there, and that tradition crossed the Atlantic with them. In Buenos Aires, the congregation Or Torah, for example, helped support an old people's home in Jerusalem and wired money to rabbis there who lived in poverty.[15] The Aleppine Jews' organization Ahavat Shalom raised money for those living in Syria and Eretz Israel. Through financial support, these institutions participated in a larger exchange of help—part of a system of philanthropy that connected members of the diaspora—and were not necessarily taking a position on organized political Zionism.

But it would be wrong to assume that Sephardim connected to Palestine only through philanthropy. From early on, organized Zionist activity in Argentina included Sephardim, in particular Moroccan Jews, which confirms their support for the political project of creating a Jewish state. The Congregación Israelita Latina de Buenos Aires and its burial society were among the organizations that sponsored the First Argentine Zionist Congress; both the vice president and a member of this Congress were Moroccan Jews. CILBA also participated in the celebrations organized by the second FSA for the first anniversary of the Balfour Declaration by buying a theater box and by asking its members to close their stores to commemorate the anniversary.[16] The vice president and secretary of the first FSA were also Moroccan Jews, as was an editor of *El Sionista*.[17] Moroccans did not create specific "Zionist" organizations, but their community organizations (such as the burial society and the religious congregation listed above) participated in the activities of the FSA.

Other Sephardim created their own Zionist societies as soon as they arrived.[18] In 1914, Jews from Turkey and Rhodes founded Bene Sion, and in 1916 a group of men from Syria and Palestine created Geulat Sion.[19] The latter, for example, sent three delegates to the Fifth Conference of Argentine Zionists in 1919. Also, *El Sionista* reported the enthusiastic participation of individual Sephardim in Keren Kayemet (JNF) activities.[20]

In Buenos Aires, the CSS was established in early 1925. In August of the previous year, the FSA had published a letter in a Jewish newspaper (in Spanish) specifically requesting Argentine Sephardim to participate in Keren Hayesod's fundraising campaign.[21] It is difficult to gauge whether this public "shaming" of Sephardim—the FSA claimed there was no response after the letter—prompted the organization of the CSS, but its creation is the first documented attempt to centralize Sephardi participation in the movement. Rather than allow each Sephardi congregation or institution to send their collections independently to the FSA, the CSS wanted to act as a central body not only in raising money for the Zionist cause but also in spreading the Zionist ideal among the various Sephardi groups. The CSS organized subcommissions in Sephardi neighborhoods and enclaves,[22] and representatives of the center led conferences and walked the neighborhoods, collecting subscriptions.[23] CSS printed and distributed a variety of informational fliers, set up kiosks in the Moroccan congregation and in the temple on Camargo Street (where they sold roasted almonds to raise money), and organized a festival in the Etoile cinema, where they showed a "Palestinian film."[24]

Language was a practical reason prompting the creation of a separate Sephardi center. Shaul Seton Dabbah, rabbi of the Aleppine community, and one of the three members of Geulat Sion who attended the Conference of Argentine Zionists in 1919, walked out of it because "the majority of the speakers insisted on expressing their views in Yiddish."[25] Unaware (or purposefully dismissive) of this rightful complaint, Ashkenazim interpreted Sephardi reluctance to participate in a language they did not understand as unwillingness to participate in the movement itself. While language was identified as the main reason for the division between Ashkenazim and Sephardim, subtler cultural and historical contexts, as well as transnational events, lay underneath this "language" fight. The FSA claimed that Sephardim (when it was mostly Moroccan Jews) did not participate in Zionist activities on the grounds that "[as] some are religious fanatics, [they see] in Zionism a blasphemy of the Messianic idea."[26] For the FSA, religious adherence was considered incompatible with the secular political project of Jewish nationalism.[27] Yet their understanding of the contradictions between religious observance and political Zionism was the result of the ideologically charged Eastern European context from which they emerged, rather than from Sephardi reality. In the first meeting of the CSS, Mauricio Alacid, a founder, argued that Zionism was conceived of as a viable path to keep the "youth healthy and loyal to Judaism," in "liberal countries, where [it] slowly forgets its [Jewish] traditions."[28] Sephardim had found a way for Zionism—a movement imagined to be the result of modernity—and traditional conceptions of Judaism to coexist. Zionism, according to Alacid, provided Jews no longer living in traditional worlds with the means to remain in the folds of traditional Judaism.[29]

The idea that Zionism could keep traditional Judaism alive did not originate with Argentine Sephardim, of course. Zvi Zohar, in another context, forcefully argues that Sephardi rabbis were able to accept challenges to the law (halakha) because they were not immersed in the ideological European Jewish climate. This climate had forced rabbis in those lands to reject any challenge to the law on the grounds that it was an attempt to destroy it. The Haskalah, or Jewish Enlightenment, had moved Jews away from the Torah as the exclusive center of Jewish learning and life, and advocated the teaching of modern languages, science, and training in practical occupations. Perceiving this as a threat to the essence of Judaism, Orthodoxy in Eastern Europe had embarked on a campaign to fight against it.[30] But, as Zohar shows, the stories of Haskalah and Zionism (itself the result of the Jewish Enlightenment) in the Sephardi world were of a different kind. The Haskalah in Sephardi communities did not come, as it had in Eastern Europe, from within, but through European powers establishing colonial and economic presence in the Sephardi world. Therefore, modern Zionism (as opposed to traditional messianic Zionism) did not clash in the Sephardi world, with a traditional camp battling for survival against (local) forces of modernity. In his study of Haskalah's arrival in Mahdia, Tunisia, Yaron Tsur claims that given the nature of society there, "Zionism was perceived as a modern bridge for the purpose of restoring a former unity," that was broken by the arrival of modernity.[31] For Sephardim, the coming of modernity (thanks to the increasing presence of European-based organizations and ideas) had brought social disruptions that could be remedied by bringing all Sephardim within the folds of Zionism. In the Eastern European religious context, the idea that the ills of modernity could be neutralized with Zionism could not have been more far-fetched.[32] For Eastern European Jews, Zionism was ridden with conflict and myriad political positions; in contrast, Sephardim for the most part found a way to come together around it.[33]

Signs of visible opposition to Zionist plans within the Sephardim came from the leaders of the more religious Syrian communities, though the lines were not clearly drawn. For example, Ḥakham Setton Dabbah, rabbi of the Aleppine community, was opposed to teaching modern Hebrew in Jewish schools on the grounds that it was the sacred language of the Torah and could not be used for mundane tasks.[34] He also urged members of his congregation not to contribute to the JNF,[35] yet he was one of the three members of Geulat Sion who attended the 1919 Conference of Argentine Zionists. In another example, we find the reverse. Ḥakham Iaacov Mizrahi, a leader of the Damascene community in La Boca, clashed with the lay leadership and other members of the congregation over his vocal support for Zionism, leading to his resignation.[36] Yet his son was sent to study in Israel to become a rabbi by the same community leaders who had opposed his father.[37]

The effect of the language barrier was to highlight, perhaps too clearly, Sephardi minority status. The fact that most Jews present at meetings understood Yiddish and could participate in it left Sephardim outside decision-making positions, which they feared would leave them outside the Zionist project altogether.[38] As a response, Sephardi leaders in the Middle East and Europe founded the WUSJ (also known as the World Confederation of Sephardi Jews), and met in 1925 "under the auspices of many Zionist leaders" to ensure their minority position did not translate into concrete measures against Sephardim.[39] Although they claimed that nearly one-third of the Jews living in Palestine were Sephardim, these Jews were not receiving sufficient attention upon their arrival or adequate preparation prior to leaving their countries of origin. They therefore began a boycott of Keren Hayesod and sent representatives to countries with large Sephardi communities to raise money *among* Sephardim *for* Sephardim.[40]

The reservations Sephardim had about the leadership of the Zionist movement, and their role in it, and that Ḥakham Dabbah voiced by refusing to contribute to the JNF, provoked responses locally (in Argentina) and internationally. The FSA had requested as early as 1924 that the WZO help set up a campaign among Sephardim and send a delegate of Sephardi origin to work among them,[41] as it was believed a Sephardi would be able to convince other Sephardim that Zionism would benefit them and their communities in Palestine. Ariel Bensión, the delegate sent by the WZO in 1926,[42] arrived in the midst of the controversy that began when the WUSJ[43] asked Sephardim to send their contributions to them.[44] Although the existing literature claims that the CSS president told Bensión that they would not recognize his delegation unless all the money raised during his visit was sent to the WUSJ, there is no evidence to suggest a deep rift.[45] The CSS, the press announced, "is getting ready for the visit, and its role will bring about profitable results for Sephardi Zionism."[46] In this vein, the CSS president was named president of the campaign on behalf of Keren Hayesod in 1926.[47]

In any case, Bensión took this opportunity to assure Sephardim that the Zionist leadership was not discriminating against them. In a pamphlet compiled and published (in Spanish) during his stay among Argentine Sephardim, the WZO representative attempted to dispel some of the "misconceptions" held by local Sephardi communities by including a description of Keren Hayesod's work on behalf of Sephardim in Palestine. "In 1923, 2,104 Sephardim arrived in Jerusalem, as against 600 Ashkenazim. Keren Hayesod invested 2,969 Egyptian pounds on these immigrants, assigning 2,548 to the Sephardim."[48] The section concluded by assuring Sephardim that "no benefit and no responsibility is denied the Sephardim, who in ideal harmony, under the two-triangle symbol, and to the same labor tune, build the walls of the great edifice of our nation."[49]

In an effort to ensure that Sephardim sent donations to the WZO, Bensión founded three Bene Kedem groups during his visit: in Buenos Aires, Rosario, and Mendoza. They were the WZO's attempt to keep Sephardim within the fold, as against the threat posed by the WUSJ, which would have channeled money away from their coffers.[50] In the final report on his trip, Bensión requested that clear instructions be sent to Sephardim in Buenos Aires: "written in French," regarding where to send money. "[Use] very explicit instructions," he urged, "as if they were children, which indeed they are as far as our movement is concerned."[51]

In response to the WZO campaign among Argentine (and South American) Sephardim, in 1927 the WUSJ sent Rabbi Djaen to South and North America, to exactly the same countries and cities where Bensión had traveled before. Djaen toured several provinces in Argentina (Santa Fé, Mendoza, Córdoba), Uruguay, Brazil, Chile, Peru, Panama, Cuba, and New York.[52] In all these places, he created WUSJ branches and collected money for the work done for Sephardim by the Sephardi Confederation. His presence in Argentina created conflict, of course. The president of Bene Kedem in Argentina complained to the WZO that Djaen "made our Zionist work much more difficult.... trying to convince us to change our allegiance."[53] On the one hand, Bene Kedem explained, Djaen was in favor of Zionism as an ideal, but, on the other hand, he wanted the funds raised by local Sephardim to be sent to the WUSJ.[54] The Sephardim were indeed caught between two forces. If they did not contribute to the WZO and did to the WUSJ, they were accused of not being "true" Zionists; if they did not give money to the WUSJ, they were seen as disloyal Sephardim. In an interview with Rabbi Djaen, a journalist inquired if the creation of the WUSJ was not, in fact, a separatist move that highlighted difference rather than union.[55] Djaen replied that he believed that "in order to be a good Zionist, a Sephardi Jew had to be a good *Sefaradí* first."[56] In other words, helping Sephardim who needed aid must be a priority for Sephardim. In fact, Sephardim would continue to be caught between their sense of responsibility toward other Sephardim and their considering themselves Jews, part of a nationalist project that presumed the primacy of Jewish identity over all other ascriptions.

In 1928 Djaen returned to South America on another WUSJ mission. During this trip, he collected money for Keren Hayesod and Keren Kayemet Leisrael (KKL) but part of what he raised was sent to Palestine for the work organized and carried out by the Sephardi Confederation.[57] Indeed, in 1928, Argentine Sephardim could read in *Israel* magazine that the conflict dividing the WZO (together with the JNF and the KKL) and the WUSJ was resolved. "The WZO," an article read, "has understood the concerns expressed by Sephardi leaders and will try to fix the mistakes of the past."[58]

Although participation in Zionist activities by Sephardim in Argentina was always criticized as not enough, the Emergency Campaign of 1929 showed that the organizations (both within the WZO structure and outside it) among these Jews had succeeded in creating networks and in mobilizing various Sephardi communities.[59] After what came to be called the "Palestine riots" that year, Argentine Jews managed to contribute m$n 313,000 to the Emergency Fund. Of this amount, more than m$n 50,000 was raised by Sephardim among themselves. In Buenos Aires, where m$n 194,399.69 had been collected, m$n 35,661 had been contributed by Sephardim alone, a figure that amounted to almost 20 percent of the contributions among a population that accounted for less than 10 percent of the total Jewish community.[60]

Both Ashkenazim and Sephardim at home and abroad understood the practicalities of separate institutions. Language differences made it hard for Sephardim to participate in local meetings and events, while Ashkenazim considered that fundraising among Sephardim, through a single Sephardi organization, was a much more productive path than attempting to work with them in multiple small organizations. Sephardi groups around the world sought to highlight the responsibility of Sephardim to help Sephardim settling in Palestine. Separatism, then, was sought and maintained by all parties involved in this process.

Second Period: 1930s to 1948

The second Centro Sionista Sefaradí (referred to hereafter as Centro Sionista) was founded in 1932 by members of the defunct first CSS.[61] By then, the Bene Kedem organizations had disappeared as well, and it is likely their former members joined the newly created Centro Sionista.

Problems between Centro Sionista and the FSA did not abate, however. The use of Yiddish continued to be an issue, as a short exchange between the two Zionist groups illustrates. On March 21, 1936, Centro Sionista received a letter from the FSA requesting that Sephardim send representatives to a regional meeting of Argentine Zionist organizations.

Centro Sionista members protested that they could not understand the procedural requirements "because they are written in Yiddish" and requested a Spanish translation.[62] The FSA sent another letter, insisting Centro Sionista name representatives to the regional meeting, and Centro Sionista replied again that it would take no action until the bylaws were translated.[63] The following week, Centro Sionista received another letter from the FSA, "in Yiddish,"[64] announcing the agenda of the "upcoming Argentine Zionist Congress," and requesting the list of Sephardim representatives. Centro Sionista decided to demand a translation, yet again, but confirmed the names of two "permanent delegates" and four "substitute members." It added in its meeting minutes, however, that the designation of the delegates brought about "an interesting debate caused by the opposition of various members to the presence of our delegates to a Zionist Congress whose official language is Yiddish, a completely foreign language to the Sephardi community and the main source of apathy of our youth to the Zionist cause."[65] The following week, the FSA finally sent a letter with the "essential parts of the letter-invitation to the Congress translated into Spanish."[66]

A second conflict arose over the use of funds raised by Sephardim. Although the WUSJ-WZO rivalry had quieted by this time, and money was now sent to the WZO, it was clear that local Sephardim struggled to keep control over their collections. When Keren Kayemet requested donations in 1934, Centro Sionista responded that it would send one hundred pounds sterling through the FSA.[67] After further discussion, Centro Sionista decided to inform the FSA that:

1) We will always wire the money to both Keren Kayemet and Keren Hayesod through the FSA, *on the condition that there remains some evidence of our contribution* [my emphasis].
2) The FSA should not deduct any sum from the amount we give them to transfer to the central offices for the costs of propaganda or administration, etc., because the Centro Sionista pays for its own [such costs] out of its own budget.
3) The sums we transfer are dedicated to a special objective, in order to encourage our donors. This might be a piece of land under the name of local Sephardi Jews or something similar.

If the money sent by us is not enough to cover such a project [in full], we suggest opening an account [to save] for that aim.⁶⁸

The first resolution stressed the desire to ensure that Sephardim were recognized for the work done by them. If their contributions were simply added to those made by Zionist Ashkenazim, Sephardi efforts would indeed be lost to history. Their "invisibility" was not the result of nonparticipation but rather of minority status and they resolved to ensure that their donations and efforts would not be forgotten. Echoing this desire, in 1932 Bacri Halac (a Sephardi Jew living in Córdoba) declared that "it is high time that we take the place we deserve in the Zionist movement and not wait until the Ashkenazim request our contribution for KH [Keren Hayesod] or Keren Kayemet; this must be directed and organized by the Sephardim."⁶⁹ This position would eventually translate into the creation of Sephardi branches of Keren Kayemet and Keren Hayesod.

The second resolution made by Centro Sionista highlighted again the problems posed by the almost exclusive use of Yiddish by Ashkenazim. Because FSA material was mostly published in that language, Sephardim had set up their own administrative and propaganda machine to meet the needs of their work. This expense was financed by the monthly fee that all Centro Sionista members paid in dues, and therefore Centro members resented when a percentage was deducted from their donations on the grounds that the FSA needed that money to operate.

The third resolution, their wish to buy a piece of land and name it after themselves, had two interrelated objectives. First, it would serve as propaganda. In 1935, guided by Ezra Teubal (one of the wealthiest leaders of the Syrian Jewish community), Centro Sionista founded the Comité Intercomunal Sefaradí Pro-Gueulath Haaretz (Sephardi Inter-Communal Council in support of the Redemption of the Land), with the aim to fund a colony in Palestine that would bear the name República Argentina "as a testimony to the efforts made by Sephardim living there."⁷⁰ This committee was created, according to some of its participants, "to increase the number of contributions."⁷¹ The strategy used by the Comité was the same Centro Sionista employed. If Sephardim who were not members of Centro Sionista, but who made regular donations, knew how their money was being allocated, Centro Sionista might be able to raise more funds. Thus Zionism would become a "concrete" project rather than an abstract ideological position (which Sephardim were not very comfortable with).

The second reason for their third resolution was that by "naming" a project sponsored and funded by Sephardim, they would become visible within a nationalist project that placed them, both at home and abroad, at a disadvantage. They were participating in a transnational Jewish project that concerned them as Jews, but they were contributing to it as Argentine Sephardim, and, as such, they wanted to be noticed. In this last claim we can see that by participating in the construction of the Jewish nation, Sephardim came to recognize themselves as both members of the diasporic group (Jews) and their nation (Argentina).

At three conventions in the following years, Sephardim pursued solutions to these problems, taking decisions that institutionalized separate organizations. Representatives from provincial communities and from organizations in the city of Buenos Aires, Chile, and Uruguay met in 1942 for the Primera Convención Regional Sefaradí (First Argentine Sephardi Convention), in 1945 for the Primera Convención Regional Sefaradí del Keren Kayemeth Leisrael (First Argentine Sephardi Convention of Keren Kayemeth in Israel), and in 1948 for the Segunda Convención Regional Sefaradí (Second Argentine Sephardi Convention). The first and second conventions were organized by Centro Sionista, and three delegates from Palestine joined: Adolfo Arditti, Eliahu (or Eli) Eliashar (both representatives of Keren Hayesod), and Elias Castel (from the World Federation of Sephardi Communities, as was Eliahu Eliashar, too). These delegates suggested increasing the involvement of outside institutions in the construction of the Argentine Sephardi Zionist camp.

The Comité Sefaradí Argentino pro Keren Hayesod, KKL y Refugiados (Sephardi Committee of Argentina in support of Keren Hayesod, Keren Kayemet Leisrael, and Refugees) was created as a result of the first congress.[72] This was a first step to ensure that control over resources of the Sephardi communities was exclusively—and visibly—in the hands of a Sephardi organization. But the creation of this committee was confirmation, locally and transnationally, that Sephardim deserved to control the activities, propaganda, and means for meeting their financial obligations to the JNF. Independent from Centro Sionista, but led by many of the same men, the new organization used its resources exclusively for fundraising, freeing Centro Sionista from that task. This organization was not (yet) a branch of the JNF itself; it was a committee organized by Sephardim to more efficiently raise funds—in Sephardi communities—that would be sent to Palestine.

The committee was asked, in 1947, to "establish immediate and permanent contact with the Central Sephardi Community of Jerusalem," to better assess the needs of Sephardim in Palestine.[73] This link across national boundaries not only tightened the bond between Sephardim in Eretz Israel and Sephardim in Argentina (who shared a common past and future) but it strengthened ties between the various Sephardim *in Argentina,* as well. In a speech at the first convention, Nissim Teubal, a prominent Argentine Aleppine, proclaimed that "we, Sephardim, should demonstrate that we are able to rebuild the homes of thousands of Sephardim who have come to Jerusalem, and others who are about to arrive."[74] Jews from various origins thus became Argentine Sephardim, and, as such, they helped those Sephardim, themselves from a variety of origins, in Palestine.

Another purpose of this committee was to alleviate the plight of Holocaust victims. Although there were organizations with this exclusive objective, and Sephardim undoubtedly donated money as individuals, this Sephardi committee was an attempt to channel Sephardi help into a Sephardi organization, to help Sephardi survivors and communities.[75] A Sephardi desire to remain visible in the context of the Holocaust was evident in this institution and in other Sephardi decisions. For example, Sephardim were asked by the American Joint Distribution committee to send collected money to them, as opposed to wiring it to the World Jewish Congress (WJC). The "Joint" (as it was commonly called) claimed that aiding brother and sister victims of the Holocaust was not to be construed as a "political" act, and since the WJC was the political arm of the (then stateless) Jewish people, the Joint should be in charge of material aid.[76] And, the Joint further argued, since they "had been helping the Sephardim in Morocco, Turkey, Bulgaria, Greece, Yugoslavia and in Italy for thirty years. . . . [the] Argentine Sephardi community had the moral obligation to cooperate with the Joint."[77] The Joint appealed to a sense of responsibility Sephardim in the diaspora had toward Sephardim elsewhere, stressing not only their diasporic identity but their national (Argentine) identification, as well. Nevertheless, the Joint did not succeed in its bid for contributions.[78]

Further evidence of the role Zionism played in the creation of a national identity as Argentine Sephardim came in November 1945. The Convención Regional Sefardi del Keren Kayemeth Leisrael—convened by a group of Sephardi Zionists and eighty-one delegates from various organizations (not all of them Zionist per se)—created a Sephardi Department of the KKL. Until then, work for this fund was done by commissions in various Sephardi communities and by the Comité Argentino mentioned above. When the KKL founded its directory for Argentina, Centro Sionista officially created its KKL department in June 1944.[79] The work carried out by this department was successful, as it had managed to raise more than m$n 70,000 in its first two years as an independent branch.[80] The money was raised through various campaigns: the KKL tin box, inscriptions in the "Book of Children" and "Book of Trees," and balls.[81] With the creation of the Sephardi branch of the KKL in 1945, all Sephardi institutions (exclusively Zionist, such as Centro Sionista, as well as religious congregations) would be represented in this umbrella organization under the sponsorship of the KKL Argentine Branch.

The 1948 Segunda Convención Regional Sefaradí, with the attendance of two important delegates from the soon-to-be-born state of Israel, gathered almost all the Sephardi institutions in Argentina and created a Consejo Central Sefaradí (Sephardi Central Council), an entity that would centralize all Zionist Sephardi activity in Argentina. The council had as one of its main objectives to "care for the interests and rights of the Sephardim in Eretz Israel and in the diaspora," and it would keep close contact with the Comité Sefaradí Argentino pro Keren Hayesod, KKL, and Refugiados.[82]

This move toward centralized Zionist organizations took place outside the Sephardi community, as well.[83] In the 1940s, and partly as a result of a war-ridden Europe, the WZO began to pay more attention to the American continent as a source of money and help for the movement. Although the United States had the largest Jewish community and therefore the main fundraising efforts centered on them, Argentina and its Jewish community became a center of attention. The JNF created its Latin American office in Buenos Aires in 1941, and the KKL did so in 1943. The Jewish Agency founded a Latin American Department in New York, and it discussed the possibility of creating a South American office at the 1945 Primer Congreso Sionista de América Latina (First Congress of Zionists in Latin America). This branch of the WZO was created in 1947 and placed emphasis on the need to instill Zionist ideals through education and the formation of youth committees.

By 1948, then, the WZO had created local offices in Argentina, and within these organizations, Sephardim had formed their own departments. The division that had started in 1925, with the creation of the CSS, was not only institutionalized by the creation of these separate departments but was largely accepted by the Argentine Zionist movement, as well. At the second convention, the director of the KKL branch in Argentina concluded that "after listening to all the speakers, I now understand that the union being sought by the Sephardim [among Sephardim] does, in no way, imply an attempt at separatism."[84] The argument articulated by Djaen in 1927 was finally understood in 1948, a few months before the creation of the state of Israel.

The role played by the Holocaust in the consolidation of Zionism as the only solution to the "Jewish question" was undoubtedly important among the Sephardim. Although the success of the CSS/Centro Sionista in creating Sephardi branches of the main Zionist bodies, and in gaining international and local recognition, was the result of many factors, the war in Europe, and the horrors suffered by a Jewish population unable to escape, raised an awareness that translated into participation. The existing sources make it almost impossible to compare donations raised by Sephardim prior to the creation of the Sephardi branch of the KKL and after (pre– and post–World War II), but we see a significant increase in contributions that resulted from more participation by Sephardim. In 1946, for example, the Directorio Sefaradí del Keren Kayemeth Leisrael (Sephardi Directory of KKL) raised significantly less than in 1947, in all recorded items (festivals, donations, tin boxes), and the 1948 data show higher sums than those raised in the previous year.[85] More active participation by Sephardim was the result of not only the reorganization of the WZO (and the subsequent creation of the Sephardi branches) but of the painful reality of World War II and the realization that the state of Israel must be created.

During this period, Sephardim legitimized separate institutions—stressing Sephardi identity among an Ashkenazi majority—while developing a strong self-identification as Argentine Sephardim. As such, they integrated themselves into the transnational Zionist structure, adding another layer to their clearly Jewish and Sephardi identities.

AFTER THE CREATION OF THE STATE OF ISRAEL

The creation of the state of Israel began an important debate in Sephardi Zionist organizations in Argentina over the need to keep "separate" Sephardi organizations, and support for specific Sephardi populations and issues. Although the practical benefits of Sephardim working among Sephardim were not questioned, the existence of transnational Sephardi organizations raising money for Sephardim in Israel came under fire. For many Argentine Sephardim, the problems of those Sephardim should rightfully be addressed by the newly created state, not by "separatist" institutions; therefore their proceeds should be submitted to the FSA to be sent to Israel (after being duly noted as raised by Sephardim). Others, however, believed that the responsibility for Sephardim in Israel (and elsewhere in the diaspora, where there was danger or need) did not end with the creation of the Israeli state, and a share of collections should be wired to Sephardi organizations in Israel. Were Sephardim only the responsibility of other Sephardim? Or were Sephardim now seen as citizens of a state that would take care of them and not discriminate against them?

In this period, Zionist activity in the diaspora was increasingly organized along party lines, with each party putting up representatives and working to support their victory in local Jewish community elections.[86] In this highly politicized context, Sephardim had no place as their own "group"; possibilities for participating in local and transnational structures depended on a willingness to forgo "singleness" and to belong to political parties alongside Ashkenazim.[87] Yet this was hard to do—not only because of the language difference but because Sephardim had created useful and (to a degree) efficient structures that could be tapped.[88] They continued to see themselves as a singular group that went beyond political ascriptions. After much discontent, Sephardim would succeed in having their voices heard: the Jewish Agency would eventually create a department to deal with "communities," devising spaces in the bureaucratic structure to work with those not organized along party lines.

The strength of Sephardi unity and the issues surrounding its representation were brought to the fore when Eli Eliashar, leader of the Sephardi community in Jerusalem, traveled to Argentina on behalf of Keren Hayesod in 1948. Although Sephardim in Argentina were discouraged from organizing as a political group, and were asked to continue working independently (from Ashkenazim) for fundraising purposes, Eliashar managed to convince Argentine Sephardim of the need to raise money for Sephardi causes in Israel.[89] This was despite the fact that he was not very well received by some Argentine Sephardim, who wondered why "a Palestine emissary wants to convince us of the need to organize Sephardim in a world organization separate from the WZO especially now, when we are at war?"[90] Given the urgent situation, they chastised him for focusing on issues that would resolve once the state was created; they believed he was diverting attention from the armed struggle to defend the state before it had a chance to exist. "The Sephardi problem is the same as the Jewish people's problems: the consolidation of a Jewish nation that is now in danger," they claimed.[91]

Eliashar was also criticized for acting as if "he had become the only representative of Sephardim around the world, their tutor and *goel* [redeemer]," when many actors were vying to represent them.[92] Eliashar, who was involved in local Israeli politics and created a Sephardi political party there, wanted to revive the WUSJ and called to that end for a World Sephardi Congress in 1951.[93] In 1944, during the World Zionist Congress held in Atlantic City, a group of Sephardi delegates "without the right to be representing their communities" had revamped the World Federation of Sephardi Communities (WFSC), with their center in New York.[94] Although the WFSC's existence would be confirmed by elected delegates at a 1951 meeting in Paris (and not in Jerusalem as Eliashar proposed), Argentine Sephardim resented his desire to act as the spokesperson for all Sephardim.[95] In fact, Argentine Sephardim were deeply disappointed that Argentina's Sephardi community was not rightfully recognized, especially as they considered themselves the best organized in the Americas.[96] Their position in a country far from the accepted centers of Jewish and Sephardi life, they believed, impeded their chance to play a more important role in the recently reenergized Confederation.

The conflict provoked by the presence of Eliashar in Argentina in 1948 and his insistence on diverting contributions to Sephardim in Jerusalem resulted in a split among Argentine Sephardim. For the 1949 United Appeal, Sephardim divided into two groups: the Spanish-speaking Comité Argentino Sefaradí pro Campaña Unida (Argentine Sephardi Committee for the United Appeal) and the Arabic-speaking Consejo Central Sefaradí Argentino (Central Sephardi Council of Argentina).[97] The former group—which later formed the Delegación de Entidades Sefaradíes (DESA) (Delegation of Argentine Sephardic Entities)—said, "Only the State of Israel is capable of saving Sephardim in Turkey, the Balkans, Morocco, and the East in general," and therefore Argentine campaign proceeds should be sent to the Israeli state, and not to Sephardim in Jerusalem (who claimed to be speaking and acting on behalf of all Sephardim).[98] The Consejo Central Sefaradí Argentino was, according to the Spanish-speaking Comité Argentino, "free to act as they pleased."[99] Ezra Teubal, an important leader of the Arabic-speaking faction, countered that "just like it is our absolute obligation to make every effort to give the State of Israel our complete support and help, it is also absolutely necessary to help our brothers who are desperately crying in their captivity."[100] With the consolidation of the new WFSC, which agreed to work within the Zionist structure, Sephardim agreed to contact their local Jewish Agency leaders to negotiate sending a percentage of their collections to them.[101]

DESA, founded by the Spanish-speaking group, carried out an important "educational" campaign along with their work for United Appeal. They organized lectures, films, and social and "artistic" events on Jewish holidays, and their magazine carried a variety of articles on the development of the state of Israel.[102] They organized its youth groups in 1951 and its Women's Commissions in 1952, both of which became very active.[103] DESA's publications attempted to reconcile their ideological stand on Sephardi participation in the Zionist movement with the concrete reality Sephardim faced in Argentina.[104] "We do not believe in the need of a policy to defend *Sephardi* rights," they claimed, but only to defend "Jewish interests, and [to work] on behalf of Jewish national solidarity."[105] But they understood that Sephardim were left out of education and publication channels (Ashkenazim printed in Yiddish), and in that context, separate Sephardi institutions were essential for spreading the Zionist ideal.[106]

DESA was not the only Zionist Sephardi organization that flourished after the creation of the State of Israel. The Organización Sionista Sefaradí Argentina (Sephardi Zionist Organization of Argentina), for example, spent a lot of energy on both organizing lectures and educational events, and on "practical Zionism," supporting young men and women in their desire to make aliyah.[107] In particular, they supported Hejalutz-Tejezakna, a youth group created in 1951 by Sephardim from Argentina and Uruguay. The group prepared its members for aliyah, with young men and women "physically" trained in the province of Buenos Aires to prepare for settlement on Israeli kibbutzim.[108] Although the group organized as an "independent" Sephardi entity, "older" Zionist Sephardim founded a group to support their endeavors, and Hejalutz-Tejezakna sent an initial cohort of twenty to twenty-five Sephardi immigrants to Israel at the end of 1952.[109] The larger Dror movement (an existing Zionist youth group in Argentina, led by Ashkenazim) absorbed this Sephardic branch, diluting its Sephardi singularity and visibility.[110]

Sephardi Zionist groups, mostly of young people, developed in Buenos Aires neighborhoods, too. Acción Sionista (Zionist Action), for example, originally started in Flores, later organizing a Villa Crespo "branch." Its leaders (that later included not only Sephardim) actively participated in the Confederation of Argentine Zionist Youth, and one of its most prominent leaders became the central committee president.[111] The Centro Israelita Juvenil (Jewish Youth Center) was organized in La Boca/Barracas, and although it was not solely a Zionist organization, many of its activities were geared toward instilling Zionist ideals in youth.[112] In many other social Sephardi institutions, such as in Club Alianza and Chalom, Zionism became central to youth group activities.

It was in the 1950s that the Jewish Agency sent the first of three emissaries to Argentina to work among Sephardim. Josef Meiujas, the first of these *shliḥim*, arrived in 1958, and immediately set out to establish contact with youth groups who were active in Sephardi communities—both in Buenos Aires and the provinces—to incorporate them under the umbrella of the World Sephardi Federation.[113] One of his best remembered and praised projects was organizing the first of three three-month-long leadership seminars in Israel.[114] Eighteen Argentine Sephardim were sent in 1960, and a total of one hundred were trained at the three seminars combined. This leadership project did, in fact, create a new generation of Sephardi leaders who, upon return to Argentina, supported youth aliyah. Meiujas left Argentina in 1960, on the same boat as the first eighteen youth delegates, and the Jewish Agency did not orphan this newly initiated project, but sent a second *sheliaḥ* in 1962 and a third in 1966.[115]

The creation of the state of Israel made Argentine Sephardim question the need for transnational Sephardi institutions, especially any that helped only Sephardim. For many Argentine Sephardim, Israel meant the end of distinctions between Ashkenazim and Sephardim. Yet this did not mean that institutions that had been created specifically for fundraising and Zionist educational purposes among Sephardim were closed; in fact, they continued with their work, sending their duly recorded collections to the FSA and supporting youth pioneer groups. Argentine Sephardim defended their right to act as a group within the Zionist political structure but without developing a political party. Several Argentine Sephardim participated in Jewish communal politics by becoming Labor Party candidates, wishing to have Sephardi voices as representatives within the party structure.

SEPHARDI ZIONIST ACTIVITY IN THE INTERIOR

In the interior provinces, Sephardi Zionist centers were founded quite early on. By 1907, Moroccans had organized two small societies in the towns of Villa Mercedes (San Luis province) and Margarita and Rosario (both Santa Fé province).[116] In 1919 Sephardim from Morocco, Turkey, and Syria founded Geulat Aam.[117] Salta also boasted a Sephardi Zionist center that later joined the local Ashkenazi Zionist youth group.[118] In some provincial towns, support for the nationalist project did not necessarily translate into the creation of Zionist organizations. It was usually religious congregations or social clubs that—sometimes at the insistence of the CSS, the KKL (both the Sephardi Directory and the general KKL), or the FSA—organized collections, raised money for the JNF, or hosted speakers who traveled and spread Zionist ideas.[119] In 1929, for example, after hearing about the "need to help the victims of the conflict in Palestine," the Sociedad Israelita Latina Ḥesed VeEmet in Resistencia organized a collection among members, contributing one hundred pesos to the fund.[120] In Rosario, the Sociedad Etz HaḤaim contributed enough money to be entered in the "Golden Book" of the KKL and was awarded the corresponding diploma; they were the "first Sephardi group in Argentina, and the only Jewish organization in Rosario" to do so.[121]

The CSS tried to maintain close relations with Sephardi institutions in the provinces. In 1926, members of the Corrientes congregation visited the CSS in Buenos Aires and named the CSS president an honorary president of their society.[122] Also that year CSS delegates traveled to Rosario, an important interior city with a significant Sephardi population, to carry out a propaganda campaign.[123] There is also evidence that, after the creation of the Comité Sefaradí Argentino pro KK, KH, y Refugiados in 1942, its members toured interior cities.[124] Noting the interior had been unfortunately neglected, J. Adatto, who traveled to Rosario and Córdoba as a representative of the Centro Sionista and the Sephardi KKL, recommended that "sending speakers to the interior would have moral and material success for our cause."[125]

Rabbi Shabetay Djaen, emissary of the WUSJ and later of the Keren Hayesod, as well, visited interior towns on a mission to awake Zionist ideals and founded Sephardi centers affiliated with the Confederation of Sephardi Jews. He traveled to Córdoba, Rosario, Corrientes, and Mendoza, leading conferences and participating in Zionist events, sometimes with members of Ashkenazi organizations.[126] Death surprised him in 1947, during a visit to the city of Tucumán, hours after he gave several talks on Zionism to the local Jewish community.[127]

Contributions from interior cities were duly recorded by the CSS and the KKL. In 1938, for example, Centro entered in its minute books that it received a "donation from Santa Fé of m$n 1,500, from Corrientes m$n 2,500, and a large amount from Córdoba."[128] In 1941, Córdoba and Catamarca both wired money to aid World War II victims.[129] In 1946, the Sephardi branch of the KKL reported that m$n 1,582 was donated by Sephardi congregations in Villa Mercedes (San Luis), Concordia (Entre Ríos), Posadas (Misiones), Resistencia (Chaco), Tucumán, and Gualeguaychú (Entre Ríos).[130] These groups participated in other ways, too. Several organizations in the interior were listed as participants in the 1942 and 1948 Sephardi conferences. The list of participating organizations for the 1948 convention is more exhaustive, and it includes thirteen organizations from the interior that sent representatives.[131] The presence of Israeli emissaries contributed to closer connections between Buenos Aires and the provinces. In fact, several of the Sephardi young men and women who traveled to Israel in 1960, on the seminar organized by Meiujas, came from the interior provinces, in particular Córdoba.[132] This tendency to involve the Sephardim from the provinces continued into the 1960s and early 1970s.

The evidence of Sephardi participation in the Zionist movement in the interior provinces is, unfortunately, scanty. The material that has survived, however, presents a picture of involvement in Sephardi organizations in the Zionist camp. Both congregations in the interior and the Zionist centers in Buenos Aires tried to maintain ties, in furthering the effort to make Sephardi contributions visible and to spread the Zionist ideal outside Buenos Aires. This participation by provincial congregations and societies in the national Sephardi meetings further highlights the fact that a new identity emerged from involvement in the Zionist ideal and included all Sephardim in Argentina.

CONCLUSION

The complicated story of Sephardi Zionist organizations and their relationships with Argentine and international Zionist organizations signals how important it was for Sephardim to defend their minority status. They had found, in Zionism, a "legitimate" space from which to fight a battle for their identity as a distinct group. By "institutionalizing" difference, group identity became clear. The appeal to a common past became the foundation on which Sephardi communities gathered, now as Argentines, and from which they moved across the ocean to help Sephardim in Palestine. The institutionalization of difference was a slow process, reaching its zenith in the couple of years prior to the foundation of the state of Israel in 1948. Although the creation of these institutions happened only then, Sephardim had fought the battle from early on.

FIVE

BECOMING ARGENTINE, BECOMING JEWISH, BECOMING AND REMAINING SEPHARDI

Jewish Women and Identity in Twentieth-Century Argentina

> Having in mind the need to give a greater impulse to philanthropy, and considering that *el elemento femenino* is the most suited to perform it, we hereby resolve to get the help of the wives of our members.
>
> Congregación Israelita Latina de Buenos Aires, 1927

ON SEPTEMBER 26, 1937, A *TÉ DANZANTE* WAS HELD AT THE Alvear Palace Hotel. It was organized by the Sociedad de Damas de Beneficencia–La Unión (Women's Beneficence Society, La Unión), created in 1922 by a group of Sephardi women from the Ottoman community. *La Luz* noted:

> One of the most luxurious salons of the house [was] lit *"a giorno,"* [floodlit] [and] was prepared with exquisite taste ... [and] the efficient attention paid to all the guests by the untiring ladies of the group's organizing committee merits mentioning. With exquisite delicacy, the impressive turnout was served at small separate tables, giving way to cordiality and friendship. The famous orchestra of René Cospito with its singer Fernando Torres was in charge of the music.

"The success of the party," the story concluded, "was in every sense the worthy outcome of the unceasing activity of the organizers."[1]

Events such as this—organized by women's auxiliaries and groups, with social and philanthropic objectives in mind—were very common in the Jewish community. This chapter uses these parties to explore the role of women and the organizations they created in the construction of Jewish Argentine and Sephardi identities. The dances, social gatherings, fairs, theater productions, and cinema screenings arranged by these groups created Jewish spaces for the young to get together (and hopefully later marry), and for the community to strengthen its ties. But these events did more than that. First, they raised significant funds to keep community institutions and organizations going. Women's fundraising efforts translated into concrete benefits for the causes they chose to support and/or for the causes they were asked to contribute to. Second, these social occasions allowed the expression of a female Jewish identity in communities that reserved leadership positions for males. Women's work in these auxiliaries or women's societies turned them into visible communal actors, and although in many cases they could not control the funds they raised, their events and the publicity generated placed the women at the center of community continuity.[2]

The success of the events, however, rested on the incorporation of Argentine women's philanthropic methods and practices. The dance described above, for example, was held at the famous Alvear Palace Hotel, which was patronized by the most select of Argentine women's charitable organizations, including from other immigrant communities, and the elite of Buenos Aires.[3] It can be argued that these functions, aimed at preserving Jewish identity in the new land, allowed for the re-creation of, and fusion of, Argentine, Jewish, and Sephardi identities.

Philanthropic activity was a public means through which Sephardi women exerted control in articulating iterations of Argentine Sephardi Jewish identity, but it was not the only means. Cooking was a more private, personal way of doing the same. The foods women chose to serve their families and the foods they served for special occasions—and how these preferences changed over time—are more intimate acts of ethnic definition that contributed to continuity of the community and changed, in the process, the meaning of community itself.

This chapter, then, suggests that Jewish (including Sephardi) women also articulated precisely what it meant to be Jewish, Sephardi, and/or Argentine in ways that were modeled after upwardly mobile, elite Argentines. We examine how these layers of affiliation overlapped, at times conflicted, and changed over time. Sephardi women indeed transformed the Sephardi and broader Jewish community, both in the public sphere through philanthropic events, such as the dances that were prominent in the Sephardi/Jewish social world; through diaspora dynamics they cultivated in Zionist philanthropy; and, in the private sphere, through the transmission of food traditions, or lack thereof, to later generations.

JEWISH PARTIES, JEWISH PHILANTHROPY, JEWISH IDENTITY

The Jewish community, the evidence tells us, organized so many social events that Jews could count on having at least one party a weekend and, very often, several to choose from. *Mundo Israelita*, the Jewish weekly, had a section entitled "Parties You Should Attend" that listed the most important social events scheduled for the week(s) ahead. In March 1933, for example, this section listed: "[a] great fair at the Children's Orphanage," "a family gathering at the Zionist Cultural Youth Center," "two events organized by WIZO," "a children's party followed by an evening ball, both to be held at the Lasalle Hall," "a *té danzante* to benefit the Jewish hospital to take place at the Plaza Hotel," "a cocktail party at the Alvear Palace sponsored by the women's committee of the Society for the Protection of Jewish Immigrants," another "*té danzante* at the Alvear Palace," this time to raise money for the Young Girls Orphanage, and, finally, "the annual fair of the Argentine-Jewish Anti-Tuberculosis League which was to take place over a period of five Saturdays at the Les Ambassadeurs Dance Hall."[4]

Although such social occasions aimed to provide entertainment, these events were clearly primarily fundraising efforts. Advertising in newspapers and magazines was a tactic employed to promote audience participation. The Sociedad de Damas Israelitas de Beneficencia, in charge of the Asilo de Huérfanas (Young Girls' Orphanage) that was discussed briefly in chapter 2, for example, went so far as to publish the complete list of all events planned for a year.[5] Smaller groups, even without such funds and renown, chose to advertise in Jewish magazines. As this small sample shows, in the city of Buenos Aires, in 1918, and between 1931 and 1940, the Sephardi magazines *Israel* and *La Luz* published invitations to sixty-eight evenings, dances, and fairs (not related to religious festivities), and not always exclusively Sephardi. In Rosario, from 1918 to

1919, and from 1931 to 1940, there was reference to thirty-nine social events. In Córdoba city, of the twenty-four pieces related to activities of the Sephardi community, five short articles described social evenings and dances. Although these numbers seem small, they become significant when considered in proportion to the total number of news stories. In Buenos Aires, dances and parties represented 32 percent of all advertised news, whereas in Rosario, they amounted to 25 percent, and in Córdoba City, 20 percent. A look at the minute books of different communities shows that not all social events were advertised in these (national or local) magazines; the numbers above, then, should be read as low estimates. As an example, during the years 1950 to 1951 alone, Club Alianza (a Moroccan-Jewish social club) and its party subcommittee (staffed only by young women) organized twenty-four meetings, picnics, cultural evenings, and *tés danzantes*, none of which were published in any of the above-mentioned magazines.

While it is true that some of these events were organized only for members of these individual communities and others hoped to attract larger audiences—hence the investment in advertising—it is clear Jewish social life and philanthropy were inseparable. Social evenings were planned with the intent to raise money for various organizations that relied on public support for their work. Private social affairs like weddings, engagement parties, birthday parties, and even just social meetings yielded donations from guests. As one example, in 1926, the Jewish Hospital acknowledged a donation received at a wedding in Río Cuarto, in the province of Córdoba.[6]

Within these philanthropic societies, the role of (elite) women was central; even in Jewish organizations led by men, there was always a women's auxiliary whose focus was fundraising. The famous Hospital Israelita (Jewish Hospital), Comedores Israelitas (Jewish Soup Kitchen), Liga Israelita Argentina contra la Tuberculosis (Argentine-Jewish Anti-Tuberculosis League), Fondo Nacional Judío (Jewish National Fund), and the Bikur Jolim (association to aid the sick), to name but a few, all placed women in charge of organizing the functions, raffles, and other social events that raised money for their coffers.[7]

The financial survival of these organizations relied to a large extent on the work of these women, even if their participation was not always acknowledged as central. In her analysis of Jewish philanthropy in the nineteenth-century United States, historian Idana Goldberg argues that "Jewish men founded and formed the governing boards of almost all of the important institutions, leaving to Jewish women what they deemed auxiliary responsibilities, rather than the decision-making roles that would have allowed them to partner in planning for the future of these organizations."[8] It was only much later that women were able to sit in on the boards of important Jewish community organizations.[9]

ARGENTINE PHILANTHROPY

Ethnic groups in Argentina, as mentioned in chapter 2, developed their own networks of welfare organizations, which tended to the medical, financial, and social needs of their members. Argentine upper-class women were involved in philanthropy, as well, this arena being one of the few in which women could openly participate.[10] One of the most famous of these Argentine philanthropic organizations was the state-funded Sociedad de Beneficencia. As early as 1823, the society founded by Bernardino Rivadavia was put in charge of dispensing help to the poor. In the early decades of the twentieth century, with a perceived attack on the social health of the nation by the massive arrival of immigrants, Argentine women's charitable organizations took on a crucial role. The logic behind their work was that if the poor were helped, and their ill health treated, then their condition improved and they were able to procure better jobs. Then wives of poor families could return to the home, children would be supervised and educated, workers would not be attracted to extremist doctrines, and therefore the existing social structure would prevail.[11] The church and the state, both important defenders of the status quo, provided elite women a space from which to help the country retain its social and economic structures. As the anchors of family life, upper-class women were asked to play this decisive role.[12]

These Argentine charitable groups widely publicized their events. Under the heading *El Día Social* (Social Section), the local daily *La Prensa*, for example, announced some events, such as:

> Details are being finalized for an extraordinary show to be held tonight in the Cervantes Theater... to raise money for the St. Therese Clothes Fund....
> *The Refuge* will be performed tonight to benefit the philanthropic work supported by the Charity Workshops of Santa Rita.
> Next Thursday, and with the help of the children of our society, a children's party has been organized to benefit the Clothes Fund of the Poor....
> On the twenty-second of this month, a *té bridge* [tea party and bridge match] and rummy tournament has been organized by the *Obra Pro Asistencia Social* (Social Assistance Fund) to be held at the Alvear Palace Hotel.[13]

Some of these groups were local (from a particular church or parochial group), and some, like the Liga de Mujeres Católicas (League of Catholic Women) or the Confederación de Beneficencia (Confederation of Beneficence) worked on a national level.[14] The functions held by these groups raised money for clothes, workshops (*talleres*), various church-related funds, charity groups in other provinces, and help for orphans, babies, and even for bedridden patients. The organization that received the largest subsidy from the government, and in fact acted as a government agency from 1880 to 1943, was the Sociedad de Beneficencia.[15]

The types of events organized by the Argentine philanthropic groups, as well as the venues where these activities took place, were somewhat standard. Fundraising took the shape of theater productions, *té bridges*, dances, and fashion shows. Most of the philanthropic or fundraising events sponsored by Argentine women's organizations were held in the same few theaters, hotels, or dance halls. The Ateneo, Smart, San Martín, and Petit Splendid were the theaters and movie houses of choice, all of which were on famous avenues of downtown Buenos Aires. The most popular dance hall was the Salón Príncipe Jorge (Prince George Hall). Les Ambassadeurs was likewise a famous hall, with a spacious area for live bands.

Alvear Palace and the Plaza Hotel attracted the Argentine upper-class philanthropic groups for *té bridges* and *té danzantes*. Founded in the early 1930s, these hotels quickly became symbols in a city and country that wished to emulate the architecture and culture of Paris. They were chosen for fundraising activities, but charity was not the only thing drawing Argentines to their salons. The Alvear Palace and the Plaza Hotel were also where the Argentine upper class celebrated weddings, anniversaries, and "intimate gatherings," and the hotels were used by ambassadors to host official events. In the same section listing activities by charity organizations, *La Prensa* printed, for example, the following events:

> To bid farewell to Ricardo Miguel Quirno, who will soon travel to Europe, the following people gathered last night at the Alvear Palace....
> The day after tomorrow, at the Plaza Hotel, Alejandro Shaw will offer a dinner for a select group of his friends....
> The Minister of Venezuela, Dr. Pedro César Dominici will offer a lunch next Monday at the Alvear Palace in honor of Dr. José Santiago Rodriguez, official [Venezuelan] delegate to the Congress of American History. Many members of the congress and other gentlemen have already been invited to the event.
> A bachelor party for Anibal Noguera will take place at the Alvear Palace tomorrow.[16]

Thus the Alvear Palace and the Plaza Hotel were, in the imaginary of the day, places of glamour, spaces where the upper crust of Argentine society displayed its status and riches, venues that conjured up the right class connotations for any event organized within its walls.

USING ARGENTINE CULTURE TO DEFEND JEWISH IDENTITY

The parties, fairs, and dances organized by the Jewish community, including Sephardi groups, availed themselves of a vast industry of services. Jewish societies held their events in hotels, dance halls, parks (*residencias*) outside the city limits, and even on boats. This service industry was not necessarily provided *by* the Jewish community *for* the Jewish community.[17] Dance halls, boats, and sites outside the city for picnics and other summer events, together with caterers, orchestras, and singers, served not only the most famous Argentine philanthropic institutions but also other groups. Non-Jewish companies chose to advertise in Jewish magazines to market their facilities and services. In June 1933, for example, Salones Sarmiento (a banquet hall) bought an entire page in *Mundo Israelita* (see figure 5.1). Along with several pictures that showed the hall and a Jewish wedding reception, they announced:

> It is no longer a problem to find a reception hall where you can invite your family and friends to a respectable (*digno*) party, where you can provide them with the comfort necessary to create long-lasting memories. I now offer Salones

Figure 5.1. Advertisement for the Jewish Community *Mundo Israelita*, June 17, 1933, 3.

Sarmiento for the exclusive use of the Comunidad Israelita [Jewish community]. [The facilities] are ample and have all the elements necessary for a very memorable event.... I cordially invite all the Comunidad Israelita to visit it.[18]

The descriptions of parties organized by Argentine philanthropic groups show that Jewish women's organizations chose to hold most of their fundraising events in the same theaters or dance halls in which elite

Argentine women held theirs. The venues selected for parties, the language used to advertise and later describe the events in newspapers and magazines, the types of events selected, the orchestras hired to play,[19] and even the singers performing all suggest a culture of upper-class Argentine philanthropy that had, after years of existence, become so pervasive that other groups wished to imitate it.[20] Jewish women's organizations certainly did. The desire to consume "Argentine" venues and products was, as well, the result of concrete overtures made by the service companies that wanted to offer services to all possible groups.

This imitation, I believe, was not because Jewish women lacked imagination, but was the result of conscious decisions by organizing committees. More important, the decision to mimic upper-class Argentine culture was not, as one might imagine, solely driven by a desire to fit in, nor did it mean a loss of ethnic identity by adopting these practices. The consumption and use of the proper Argentine upper-class style, in fact, ensured the continuity of the Jewish community in the new land. Choosing the places where respected Argentine philanthropic organizations held their events was, in a sense, appropriating space that had become synonymous with philanthropy, refinement, and upper-class ambitions and culture. In his recent book on the Argentine middle class, Ezequiel Adamovsky suggests that prior to its formation, Argentines wished to consume that which had become synonymous with the upper class: "The services and goods offered became symbols of social status."[21] He continues, "Thus the market, through the supply of products and advertising, contributed to 'classify' the population according to their ability to recognize and acquire the necessary accoutrements of those with 'distinction' and 'good taste.'"[22] Thus the Jewish organizers of events, with no intention of being diverted from their fundraising endeavors, became jealous guardians of these Argentine class ideals. These women's groups capitalized on customs of Argentine philanthropic organizations and on the spaces in which the upper crust of Buenos Aires paraded their social position. Jewish organizers legitimized their events by consuming that which the hegemonic culture decreed symbols of distinction. By signaling their role as members of a class, and as respected philanthropic organizations for both Jews and Argentines alike, these groups practically guaranteed the success of the events they organized.

"Becoming Argentine," however, did not result in complete assimilation, nor was that the goal. It was by adopting *Argentine* norms and customs—that is, clearly selecting certain options over others available—that these organizers preserved their own identity as Jews in the new nation. After all, the events organized by these groups were aimed at supporting Jewish institutions in the new land. In the parties described above, we see that money was being raised to help Jewish orphans (both boys and girls) and old people, to care for Jewish tuberculosis patients, to keep a Jewish hospital running, to protect Jewish immigrants, and to raise money for Eretz Israel. In a context in which most of the help for those in need in Argentina took place in Catholic organizations headed by pious Catholic women, Jewish institutions provided a safe environment in which Jews who needed help could in fact remain inside Jewish networks.[23] Even after the arrival of Peronism, when the Catholic "threat" was somewhat diluted (as the state began to relieve the church from some of its traditional welfare activities), Jewish philanthropic organizations continued their work, unlike some Argentine women's groups.[24] By "utilizing" Argentine spaces, norms, and services, these Jewish philanthropic organizations raised sufficient money to enable Jews to continue being Jewish.

REMAINING SEPHARDI

If this chapter ended here, it would be titled "Becoming Argentine, Remaining Jewish." Yet there is another wrinkle to the story of Argentine philanthropic culture and Jewish identity, and it involves a struggle for identity and recognition by Sephardi Jews, the minority, in Argentina. Focusing on the participation of Sephardi women in the Zionist movement, I highlight the ways that seemingly similar organizations, events, and festivals acquired different meanings when placed in the context of Jewish identity in Argentina. While Sephardi women clearly organized to support the creation (and later sustenance) of the state of Israel, they stressed their own identity as Argentine Sephardim. They feared, as did Sephardi male-dominated Zionist organizations, that remaining within larger organizations risked Sephardim becoming invisible as a group.

There were three main independent women's Zionist organizations in Argentina: WIZO, the Organización Sionista de Pioneras, and the Orthodox women's Mizrahi.[25] WIZO, founded in 1920,[26] was the oldest and by far the most important organization, as it was the first international Zionist organization that brought women together to help women and children in Eretz Israel (see table 5.1). Until then, other female Zionist organizations existed—mainly Hadassah (The Women's Zionist Organization of America),[27] founded in 1912 by Henrietta Szold; the Federation of Zionist Women in Great Britain and Ireland, created in 1919; and the Verband Juedischer Frauen fuer Kulturarbeit in Palestine (Jewish Women's Group for Cultural Work in Palestine), created in 1907 in Germany—but none were international in scope.[28] WIZO's objectives were to help women and children in both Eretz Israel and the diaspora. It wanted to bring together "committed Zionist women" from around the world, spread Zionist ideals among women not yet committed to them, and raise funds to support colonization efforts under way in Palestine.[29] To affect these goals, WIZO federations were set up in "all the countries where there was a Jewish community."[30]

Argentina was one of the first countries to form its federation.[31] At a meeting held on August 30, 1926, "the assembly of women gathered in the offices of the Unión Sionista de la Capital [Zionist Union of the city of Buenos Aires], declared the creation of the Organización Femenina Sionista [Women's Zionist Organization] ... affiliated with WIZO."[32] Yet, "one should not think that the Argentine Jewish woman had remained indifferent to the national movement in the previous years."[33] In the first years of the twentieth century, the Liga Dr. Herzl (Dr. Herzl League) had a women's committee called "Deborah" that "organized dances and various social activities."[34] In 1921, the "Zirungs Fond" committee was created, "and ... was very successful."[35] In 1925, the women's committee of the Jewish National Fund (the seed from which the Argentine WIZO would grow) was founded in Buenos Aires under the auspices of a delegate of the World Zionist Organization. This committee, in its short one-year life, organized a festival and dance and raised funds for the purchase of land in Palestine.[36] It also participated in the meetings of the JNF committee in Capital Federal, as it recorded in minute books that it sent two members to its meetings.

Becoming Argentine, Jewish, and Sephardi

Table 5.1. Women's Zionist Organizations

Name of Organization	Year Founded (if available)
Comité de Damas del Fondo Nacional Israelita	1925–1926
Argentine WIZO (or OSFA: Organización Sionista Femenina Argentina)	1926
Organización Sionista de Pioneras	
Mizraḥi Orthodox Women	
Deborah (Dr. Herzl's League, women's committee)	1905, approximately
Zirungs Fond [sic]	1921
Comisión de Damas del Centro Sionista Sefaradí (became WIZO Sephardi section in 1946)	1945
Consejo Central de Damas Sefaradíes (another name for WIZO Sephardi section)	1949
Comité Femenino Sefaradí-Amigas de la Histadrut (later Amigas Sefaradíes de Na'amat)	1940s
Asociación Benot Yerushalaim (Comisión de Damas del Centro Sionista Sefaradí)	1947

In the women's committee's last session before it became independent from the JNF and affiliated with WIZO, Mrs. Gruman spoke about her recent visit to Palestine and described work done at a "women's farm" close to Rishon LeTsion (city in Israel, site of the first modern Jewish colony). She claimed that although the group of "pioneers" had received the land from the JNF, and the Keren Hayesod had financed the building of the facility, that help was not enough to support the project, especially because of the large number of girls waiting to join the farm. It was necessary, Mrs. Gruman said, to build "a house . . . [acquire] more land to extend their work . . . [and install an] irrigation system."[37] During her visit, she had promised the female leaders of the farm that the women's committee of the JNF "on behalf of the Jewish women of Argentina, would finance the work."[38] The committee upheld Gruman's promise and decided that they would "proclaim the beginning of the campaign in favor of the farm in an upcoming meeting . . . [and] would form an honorary committee of Argentine ladies presently residing in Palestine to participate in this work . . . and would get in touch with the farm in order to get material for propaganda."[39] In the next meeting, the Comité de

Damas del Fondo Nacional Israelita (Women's Committee of the National Jewish Fund) became the Organización Sionista Femenina Argentina (OSFA) (Organization of Argentine Zionist Women), affiliated with WIZO; what it had decided to do before it became part of WIZO would guide its activities in Palestine in the future. These women ceased to be a mere fundraising committee of a male-dominated organization and instead took it upon themselves to support a project of their liking.

Argentine WIZO and Sephardi Zionist activity became closely connected as Dr. Ariel Bensión and Ida, his wife, arrived in Argentina and sought to organize groups. Ida was instrumental in the creation of WIZO centers in the interior of Argentina;[40] just as Dr. Bensión had attempted to bring Sephardim under the control of WZO, she sought to bring these nascent independent women's Zionist organizations under the auspices (and control) of WIZO. In Rosario, the Círculo de Damas Sionistas (Zionist Women's Circle) was founded on November 2, 1926, during the couple's visit to the city, and in Mendoza, although the evidence is less clear, the creation of the women's center also seems to have taken place during their stay.[41]

As Argentine WIZO grew, centers were created in almost all cities with a Jewish population.[42] By 1948, there were 220 centers with a total of 22,000 members, by far the largest single Zionist organization of any kind in Argentina.[43] In 1961, the number of centers had risen to 338, and there were a total of 38,014 members.[44] The organization had an executive committee that acted as the central body for Argentina; the state was divided into several geographical regions, each of which had a regional center, which encompassed the smaller local centers. All centers belonged to their *regional* [regional office], with the exception of a few independent centers under the direct control of the central executive.

The activities of OSFA were varied. Locally the organization focused on spreading the Zionist ideal to women. The executive published a monthly magazine that included not only news about the homeland but also general information about Jewish festivities, Jewish history, and Zionist personalities. The executive's Department of Culture sponsored cultural seminars and Hebrew, Bible, and oratory courses. Fundraising events were usually organized around cultural activities like lectures, roundtables, and debates.

Funds to support this work were obtained through various campaigns and methods. An annual campaign set the tone for the work of the whole year, and it was usually proclaimed under "a slogan concerning the most urgent necessity in Israel."[45] Each *regional*, then, was responsible for raising a share for the campaign. This amount was collected through individual centers, each of which sponsored its own activities. Each member paid a monthly minimum membership fee, and those who wished to receive the magazine were charged a subscription fee. There were other traditional contributions, such as the *shekel* WIZO (a "tax" paid annually),[46] the WIZO flower, which each member (ḥaverah) received on her birthday, and for which she gave a contribution in turn,[47] and the Vacation Day contribution, given when a member went on holiday and donated the amount that she had spent on two days of vacation.[48]

Concrete work in Palestine and later Israel focused on supporting a farm and on sending educational supplies for schools and kindergartens. Sewing workshops were created in 1938, and each center sewed clothes and sent them to Palestine.[49] In a meeting prior to OSFA's birth as an independent organization, they discussed helping the Naylat Yehuda Colony directly, but Ida Bensión, present at their second meeting, said it was necessary to send money to London, to be added to WIZO's general budget. In OSFA's first Memoria y Balance (Annual Report and Balance Sheet), which described the work accomplished during the first year, they announced that "in order to take part in the work done in Palestine by WIZO, [we] decided to be in charge of the construction of a house in Afula [sic] in the name of the Organización Sionista Femenina Argentina."[50] Thus the original commitment to help the farm in Naylat Yehuda had been replaced with the farm at Afula, which became the practical work that connected the Argentine Zionist women to Palestine.[51] Subsequently, WIZO focused on the "Building" campaign, taking place in the last three months of the year, for the purpose of raising funds to continue building the farm (see figure 5.2). Later they took on the responsibility of raising a fixed amount of money for its upkeep and usually responded to urgent calls for specific projects, too.[52]

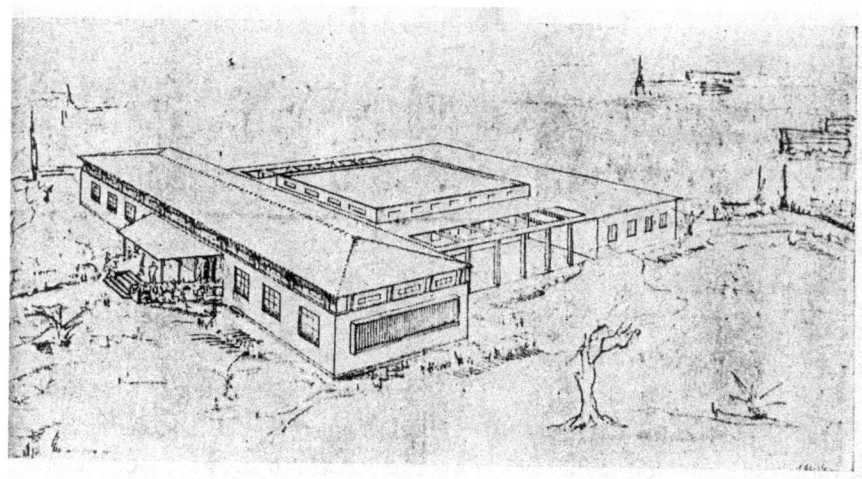

NUEVO COMEDOR DE AFULA

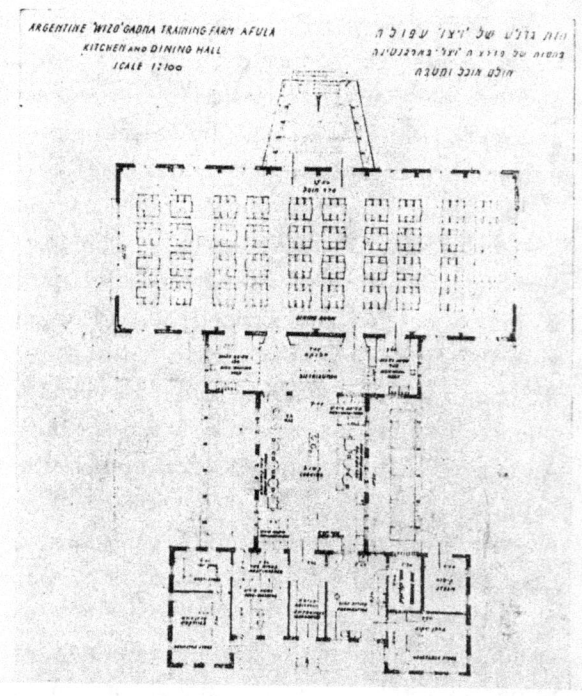

Figure 5.2. Organización Sionista Femenina Argentina: Announcement of the construction of a new cafeteria on Afula Revista OSFA, September 1954, 5.

The work of Zionist Argentine women and the work of Sephardi (male) Zionists resembled each other in the desire to leave evidence of it. Zionist women took it upon themselves to help a farm that would give refuge and education to female immigrants. The Sephardi Zionists wished to fund a specifically "Sephardi" colony in Palestine. Both found in these concrete projects a way to avoid their contributions being subsumed in the funds of the larger organizations in which they could not have an active voice.

Just as the issue of language had plagued the relationship between the Zionist organization and the Sephardi (male-dominated) groups, so it did among Jewish women. Although in 1935 OSFA requested the visit of a (female) "Yiddish" speaker, they realized the potential problem and solved it quickly.[53] The OSFA executive committee decided that "in order to solve the language difficulties posed by the German and Sephardi element, two [language] sections have been established."[54] By allowing these two "language" sections autonomy—more below—they remained within it. By 1948, the German section had founded eight centers and mobilized six hundred members.[55]

SEPHARDI WOMEN AND ZIONISM

The idea of bringing Sephardi Zionist women into the Argentine WIZO existed from early on, but it was not until 1946 that an "official" Sephardi section was created.[56] In a 1926 letter written to the WIZO representative in Rosario, Ida Bensión explained that "Mde. Yivoff is the Directora de la Sección Sefaradí' [in Buenos Aires] ... she is interested and I believe ... she will work and use all her influence on our behalf."[57] Also, in 1938, Dr. Mibashan, the delegate of the Keren Hayesod in Argentina, claimed that he had founded WIZO groups "of Sephardi, German-speaking and other ladies who already belong to the better class of local Jewry."[58] But in 1946, Sephardi Alegre Bonomo "visited the WIZO headquarters and [was] embarrassed to learn that out of the 74,000 members, only 80 were Sephardim."[59] The newly created Sephardi section had gathered five hundred members in its first eighteen months of work and had created four centers: Buenos Aires, Córdoba, Tucumán, and Paraná. Other centers were created later.

Just as Jewish women's participation in the Zionist movement did not start with the founding of WIZO, Sephardi women's participation in the Zionist project did not start with the creation of WIZO either. The Sephardi Zionist movement had also used "the female element" for fundraising activities for some time. In 1925, the first Centro Sionista Sefaradí, for example, selected a group of women to sell tickets for a festival they organized.[60] The second Centro Sionista Sefaradí asked a group of women to be in charge of the collection boxes (*alcancías*), because "given previous experiences, [we know] it will be successful."[61] These women, however, never created their own separate committee, and although as early as 1925 the idea of forming a Comisión de Damas was frequently discussed during meetings, it was not until 1945 that it actually happened.[62]

The climate created by Sephardi Zionist organizations and the drive toward celebrating and defending their minority status within Zionist organizations undoubtedly contributed to the creation of a Sephardi section of WIZO. As Sephardim had managed to consolidate their presence vis-à-vis the main male-dominated Zionist organizations, it seemed natural that they wished to extend their visibility in women's groups.

The relationship between OSFA and the Sephardi section went well at first, with activities mirroring those organized by other OSFA centers. They raised money for the KKL and for trees in Israel, collected donations during Brit Milah, Bnei Mitzvah, festivals, *té-bridges*, and other events. In the provincial towns where Sephardi OSFA opened their own chapters, Sephardi women's participation appears to have begun only with the creation of the center. The Ashkenazi centers were much older and had not been able to attract Sephardim, with a few exceptions.[63] In even smaller towns, however, single OSFA chapters were successful. Two examples are Presidente Roque Saenz Peña (Chaco province) and Gualeguay (Entre Ríos province), where Sephardim and Ashkenazim worked together raising money and organizing cultural meetings.[64] It was only in these small towns, coincidentally, where OSFA managed to attract "100 percent of the Jewish [female] population."[65]

The conflicts in the male Zionist Sephardi camp brought about with the creation of the state of Israel, and the fate of Sephardim living there (discussed in chapter 4), also threatened to split Sephardi women. In the

1946–1948 Executive Committee Report sent to the WIZO, the Argentine leadership reported:

> The Sephardi community, responding to directives from Jerusalem brought over by Mr. Eliaschar, organized a Consejo Central Sefaradí to tend to the needs of the Sephardi group both in and outside Argentina. This council covers all activities and includes everything related to Zionism, so that Sephardi participation in Jewish national life is now done through the council. They created a female council with the same goal, and asked the Sephardi WIZO to join the council, breaking away from the OSFA.[66]

Sephardi women who were already members in Sephardi WIZO centers were asked to join the newly formed council, but the evidence is ambiguous as to the effectiveness of the request. Disregarding the instruction to disband, Sephardi WIZO continued its work within OSFA until the 1980s, when it was wholly integrated into the organization.[67]

In fact, the Central Council of Sephardi Women worked *alongside* WIZO.[68] In 1951, OSFA-WIZO wrote to Tel Aviv in response to an inquiry regarding the existence of other women's Zionist organizations in Argentina. OSFA listed the "Women's Sephardi Council," the Orthodox Women's Mizraḥi Organization, and the Women's Pioneer Organization as existing organizations and further explained that "they send representatives to each of our big meetings and respond to the requests we make during our fund drives." The council decided to contribute to a campaign that raised money to build pavilions for infants in Israel, and the pavilion constructed with funds from this council on the Afula communal farm bore the name "Consejo Central de Damas Sefaradíes."[69] For its construction, the council donated "not only the amount asked of them, but twice as much. . . . and they are also prepared to give more, if it should be required."[70]

In order to keep Sephardi women involved in the project, the president of Argentine WIZO met with council leaders and showed them pictures of the building constructed with their donation. During this meeting, upon learning that the children of the kindergarten were only able to attend half a day for lack of funds, "[they] resolved to send a donation of m$n 6,000 for 6 months, which represents around US$300 for possible improvements."[71] Although the money pledged would not in the end be used for that particular purpose ("because it is important that mothers spend time with their children and learn how to take care of them"), WIZO hoped that the council "would feel happy and proud to see a sign [hung outside the entrance to the daycare center] that read: Consejo Central de Damas Sefaradíes—República Argentina."⁷²

Just as Afula had become an important symbol for OSFA, the children's pavilion on it became a source of pride for the Central Council of Sephardi Women. When the building was finished, the council requested that "more pictures were sent to them, [in which you could see] the whole building and the interiors of some halls."⁷³ When the pro-secretary of the council, Mrs. Mallah, traveled to Israel, she asked "to see up close the children's pavilion donated by this council."⁷⁴ When new contributions for further construction in Afula were wired to WIZO in Tel Aviv, the Argentine WIZO branch indicated that some of the donors belonged to the Consejo Central de Damas Sefaradíes, and further stipulated that the "donation was destined to the pavilion this institution supports in Afula."⁷⁵

The Central Council of Sephardi Women also engaged in other activities. In 1948, one magazine reported, this group "successfully" staged a play by Ben Hecht called *Nace una Bandera* (A Flag Is Born).⁷⁶ This women's group also had a youth subcommittee, Juventud Oriente Israel (Mizraḥi Israel Youth), that began in 1948 with "a series of cultural gatherings."⁷⁷ In November of the same year, the Department of Culture of the Consejo Central organized an evening in which "Rabbi Blum gave a speech . . . the soprano Simjá Kaplan sang some Hebrew songs, and, as a final treat, the Boca and Barracas youth choir sang various Israeli songs, finishing this wonderful evening with the words of the Hatikvá."⁷⁸ The play and the cultural evenings suggest that the council was, in fact, not only a fundraising organization but participated in the campaign to spread Zionist ideals to youth, with whom it worked in close contact.

In October 1945 there was another group of Sephardi women called Comité Femenino Sefaradí—Amigas de la Histadrut.⁷⁹ The Histadrut was founded in 1920 in Palestine as a Jewish workers' trade union, and it had always claimed that women held a prominent place in its ranks. In an article entitled "Women Hold an Important Space in the Histadrut," which appeared in the magazine of the Histadrut Sephardi Youth, they claimed that "the aims of the working woman's movement since its creation at the beginning of the century" were to "stimulate and develop the active forces of the working-class woman, reinforcing her position and placing her in decisive and important roles, with the same rights and obligations in the establishment of the Jewish working community in [her] national home."[80]

In Argentina, Judith Isajaroff, a Sephardi from Samarkand, Uzbekistan, who participated in Argentine Jewish politics as a member of the Mifleget Poalei Eretz Yisrael (Mapai) (Workers' Party of the Land of Israel), which controlled both the Histadrut in Israel and local Argentine Jewish politics, founded the Comité Femenino Sefaradí (Sephardi Women's Committee), later called Amigas Sefaradíes de Na'amat (Women Friends of Na'amat). In 1950, Isajaroff was one of four female candidates in the election of delegates to the twenty-third World Zionist Congress, a fact that was used by Mapai to show their commitment to placing women in the vanguard of the creation of the new state.[81] Surviving records reveal, however, that the activities of this Sephardi women's group centered on raising money for various causes: from helping defray the costs of buying a boat that would be used to "link Tel Aviv and Buenos Aires"[82] to supporting kindergartens and various vocational schools.[83] They also sponsored theater productions, art classes, Hebrew classes, Bible courses, and dances.[84] In 1947, they had five hundred members, all of whom were "conscious bearers of the Zionist ideal," who had created a sewing workshop, youth groups, and done much work in support of the JNF, as well.[85]

Sephardi women also created the Asociación Benot Yerushalaim (also known as Comisión de Damas del Centro Sionista Sefaradí), which sent money to Israel to carry "out a philanthropic and social work of wide-ranging proportions among the needy Sephardi community."[86] The Comisión de Damas del Centro Sionista Sefaradí sent just over m$n 16,000 collected through tea parties and other fundraising activities.[87]

As was the case of the male-dominated Sephardi Zionist organizations, Sephardi female participation in the Zionist movement managed to override distinctions of origin. Sephardi women participated in the Argentine women's organizations as Sephardim, regardless of where their families (or they themselves) had come from. And as *Argentine Sephardim*, they positioned themselves within a women's global project that responded to their women's concerns. Sephardi women's participation in the Zionist movement was extensive and served two purposes: to evidence Sephardi participation within general women's Zionist organizations and to create a space for women within specifically Sephardi Zionist organizations. They brought diversity to the women's organizations and women's concerns to the Sephardi movement. Within the general women's Zionist societies they made sure that Sephardi participation was evident and distinct. This was the case of Sephardi WIZO, the Amigas Sefaradíes de Na'amat, and the Central Council of Sephardi Women in their participation in WIZO work in Israel. They had fashioned these spaces in the hope that *all* Jewish Argentine women (not just Ashkenazi Argentines) were visible in the new state. Within the general "Sephardi" Zionist groups, women's organizations raised money for "women's" issues, as was the case of the CSS Women's Commission Benot Yerushalaim. But Sephardi women's groups did not focus solely on Zionist activities, ensuring the visibility of Sephardim within Ashkenazi institutions, or helping Argentine Sephardim in Palestine/Israel. As discussed in chapter 2, each Sephardi group was located in different parts of the city, and each founded its own philanthropic and social networks to help newcomers and, along with women's auxiliaries in Sephardi Buenos Aires congregations, supported the existence of these communities (see table 5.2). Their appearance dates from very early on. The Sociedad de Damas de Sión (Women's Society of Zion) organized raffles in 1899.[88] In 1908, Jewish women arrived from the Ottoman Empire founded El Socorro,[89] and in 1918, there were references to a philanthropic organization called Damas Israelitas Sefaradim de Buenos Aires (Sephardi Women of Buenos Aires), later called Asociación Argentina Israel de Damas Hebreas de Beneficencia de Buenos Aires (Association of Argentine Sephardi Women for Charity).[90] The community originally from Rhodes founded, in 1922, the Sociedad de Damas de Beneficencia–La Unión,[91] and the women's society from Damascus was founded in 1927.[92] In Flores, there were two women's groups: the Sociedad de Damas Israelitas de Flores (Jewish Women's Society of Flores) and the commission of the Club Juventud Israelita (Jewish Youth Club).[93] In the rest of the country, Sephardi women had also organized for charity (see table 5.3). In the city of Córdoba, for example, the Comisión de Damas

Becoming Argentine, Jewish, and Sephardi

Table 5.2. Sephardi Women's Philanthropic Groups in Buenos Aires

Name of Organization (Buenos Aires)	Year Founded (if available)	Origin (if available)
Sociedad de Damas Israelitas de Beneficencia		(Ashkenazi)
Sociedad de Damas de Sión	1899	Moroccan
El Socorro	1908	Ottoman
Damas Israelitas Sefaradim de Buenos Aires (later Asociación Argentina Israel de Damas Hebreas de Beneficencia de Buenos Aires)	1918	Moroccan (mostly)
Sociedad de Damas de Beneficencia–La Unión	1922	Ottoman (Rhodes)
Sociedad de Damas	1927	Damascus
Sociedad de Damas Israelitas de Flores		
Comisión de Damas del Club Juventud Israelita (Flores)		

de la Sociedad Israelita Sefaradí de Socorros Mutuos (Women's Commission of the Argentine Jewish Mutual Aid Society) was formed in October 1929, and reorganized in 1947.[94] In Santa Fé city, the Sociedad Israelita de Damas Sefaradí de Socorros Mutuos (The Sephardi Women's Mutual Aid Society) was founded in 1944.[95] The communities in Rosario, Mendoza, and Corrientes also had women's commissions in charge of philanthropy.[96]

Although women had organized early on, philanthropy was, in these early years, mostly in the hands of men; they distributed money to other men who could not support their families. Women were rarely the recipients of institutionalized help, only receiving support when their fathers or husbands died and no immediate male family member could provide needed assistance.[97] Such (male-led) societies carried out a job other men could not perform.

Women's auxiliaries acted in the shadow of these philanthropic organizations, and very little information on their activities has survived. The available evidence suggests that their work was confined to fundraising (the proceeds of which were later handed over to the male-dominated organizations) and/or distributing materials that were sewn, cooked, or made by the women themselves. But the fundraising led by

Table 5.3. Sephardi Women's Philanthropic Groups in Provincial Cities

Name of Organization	Year Founded (if available)	City
Comisión de Damas de la Sociedad Israelita Sefaradí de Socorros Mutuos	1929	Córdoba
Sociedad Israelita de Damas Sefaradí de Socorros Mutuos	1944	Santa Fé
Sociedad de Damas de Ḥesed VeEmet		Resistencia
Comisiones de Damas		Rosario, Mendoza, Corrientes

these auxiliaries was instrumental in helping their communities build synagogues and social halls, and thus for shaping the social structure of the Jewish community. In Resistencia, for example, the Sociedad de Damas of the Ḥesed VeEmet contributed m$n 45 for the construction of their social hall. In some cases, women's groups were formed for a specific fundraising objective. Ottoman Sephardim, who settled in Villa Crespo, for example, created an informal women's committee to raise funds to buy the parcel on which the community later built its synagogue. A community member, Marcos Emanuel, recalls that "women were sent by their husbands to the tenement homes, [and they would] say: 'We'll buy our own temple!' And people would donate, one, two, five pesos."[98] Ozer Dalim, the Moroccan philanthropic organization, created a "young ladies' commission to sell movie tickets that had been returned unsold [by our male members]."[99] It seems both groups disbanded after their objectives were met.

This reliance on women for fundraising became clear in 1925. The magazine *Israel* gladly announced that the president of the Congregación Israelita Latina de Buenos Aires had said that "philanthropy [*beneficencia*] should be carried out by women, since they are better prepared and have more free time at their disposal."[100] In 1927, the women's auxiliary was convened, although it "would totally depend on the steering committee of this congregation, a committee that would give it its constant support for the best management of their mission."[101]

It was in the late 1930s and early 1940s that most Sephardi women's philanthropic activities became more noticeable and more "elaborate," as well. Whereas soliciting donations door-to-door was sufficient for their purposes in the past, it now became important to hold fundraising events at the right places, with the right publicity, and with the right food and orchestra. It was about this time they began to follow the example of the Ashkenazi Jewish women's organizations that already enjoyed visibility in the community as a whole. In a context in which Sephardim were sometimes not viewed—by either Argentines or Ashkenazim—as "modern" Jews, imitating the Argentine upper-class culture of philanthropy (as employed by the Ashkenazi female groups) enabled them to claim a legitimate role as philanthropic organizations. They also came to defend what was Argentine and Jewish, as the Ashkenazi women's organizations had come to accept and defend existing unspoken rules about the proper way of doing philanthropy. For Sephardi women, philanthropy was thus an avenue to "becoming Jewish and Argentine."

The value of their work was not only economic contribution to their communities. Women's presence within community religious organizations was, as it had been in the old countries, rare. Even as late as 1945, women could not be members (*socios activos*) of the Congregación Israelita Latina.[102] Blanca Nahon de Essaya, for example, requested to be admitted after the death of her husband. The steering committee rejected her application and suggested, instead, that "she reserve her late husband's pew until her son became of age" not by paying a monthly *fee* (since she could not be a fee-paying member) but by making a monthly *donation* of the same amount.[103] While husbands and sons were able to express their "Jewishness" by following religious precepts and going to temple, women's Jewish identity, and their membership in the community, could be affirmed through the philanthropic and social events they organized.

THE STORY OF ETHNIC FOOD

Club Alianza's Youth Department (Moroccan community) minute books are replete with evidence of a busy social life. The group never advertised its events in national Jewish magazines or newspapers, yet it organized several formal activities a month in addition to regular weekly informal gatherings to play cards, dominos, or board games. Most of the "formal" activities (dance balls, cultural evenings, tournaments) involved, among other things, food. For example, we read that for the "ball" scheduled for September 28, they served a *copetín con 14 platitos* (vermouth with fourteen side dishes, tapas-style) with *pan negro* (dark rye bread). The drinks offered were "*sidra* [apple cider], vermouth, and gin," and the side dishes were "black olives, green olives, potato chips, pickles, peanuts, cheese, potato salad, sausage, *chizitos* [cheese sticks], beets, hard-boiled eggs, celery sticks, anchovies, and lima beans."[104]

For another social event, organized to celebrate "national flag day" on June 22, the committee decided to prepare an *asado criollo* (creole barbecue), with *chinchulines y chorizos* (intestines and sausage).[105] And for the celebration of the May Revolution, they settled on *chocolate con buñuelos* (chocolate with donutlike pastries), the typical food used to celebrate the national Argentine holiday.[106]

In 1996, many years after this group recorded their culinary choices for their social events, I asked Lida Azulay to teach me how to make couscous (*cuscus*).[107] I pleaded, to no avail. "Why?" she would ask me. "It is hard work." She would try to convince me that in this age of quick couscous in a box, easily bought in a supermarket, there was no need to learn to do it "by hand." I eventually won the battle, and one day I sat down in her kitchen to watch her work. I dutifully took down notes as she prepared the Bain Marie (double boiler), which I knew was a creative adaptation because she lacked the proper tool, a *cuscusiera* (couscous maker). After cooking the grain, I learned how to prepare the vegetables to go with it: sweet butternut squash, caramelized baby onions, walnuts, and raisins. The dish, once finished and served, is often sprinkled with a mixture of sugar and cinnamon.

What, if any, is the connection between these events—my wish to learn how to make couscous, and the group of young men and women descendants of Moroccan Jews who chose to celebrate national holidays and other social occasions eating "Argentine" traditional food? Is there a culinary trail that might suggest the workings of identity, both ethnic and national? If anything, the two events narrate, I believe, the changing meaning of food as it was (or was not) prepared by different generations of immigrants. Azulay remembered learning to make couscous from her mother, but she did not pass the skill on to her own daughter, Luna. And Luna enjoyed eating it but did not make it. I, on the other hand, wished to learn how to do it. Lida, by learning from her mother how to prepare couscous and many other dishes, in Sauce, Corrientes province, Argentina, learned how to be a Moroccan Jew. Luna, a member of the youth group of the Club Alianza, was an *Argentine* Jew; as such, she had no "need" to make couscous herself. In fact, she celebrated with her friends (also descendants of Moroccan Jews) by serving *chinchulines, chorizos,* and *chocolate con buñuelos*. Last, I am learning to be a (half) Sephardi Argentine Jew by asking Lida to pass on knowledge of couscous and other foods, and including in my culinary repertoire dishes such as *sharope* (white jam), *boios* (knishes), *trabaditos* (stews), baklava, gefilte fish, and even matzo balls.[108]

In this last section, I wish to discuss private food over food as a public expression.[109] It is to the home that I now turn, away from the richly decorated grand halls of the Alvear Palace Hotel, guided by the belief that it was also in the home where families and women came to experience and enact their ethnic identities. It was in the home that mothers taught and passed on recipes to their daughters.[110] It was also there that Argentine ways became part of an "ethnic" family food repertoire. It was there where the "meaning" of food was reconfigured, readapted, and reinterpreted by different generations.[111]

Preparing food was what women of Lida's generation did. Most of the participants of the oral history workshop I held in a Sephardi Jewish social club recalled their mothers spending most of their day thinking about and cooking food.[112] Family activities were clearly divided along gender lines, with women in charge of domestic tasks and men working outside the home to support the household. Even when women did work outside the home (often by helping their husband run a store, or working as a seamstress in a small textile workshop), they also were responsible for the housework; they either did the work themselves after their paid work ended or they paid another woman to do it.[113] Food was central in women's daily lives, an important component of their identity as women.[114]

Food was (and still is) central in family and religious celebrations. The Jewish sacred calendar revolves around food: the preparation, cooking, and eating of specific delicacies.[115] Fasting, or the absence of food, is also central in the Jewish calendar. Friday night dinners, Pesach Seders, Rosh

Hashanah gatherings, the breaking of Yom Kippur fasts, Purim carnivals, and Mimona (post-Passover) celebrations are all observed with dishes selected from a standard (but limited) traditional menu. The religious memory of Jews is grounded in sensations of the palate. Life cycle events, associated with religious traditions, were also marked by a selected repertoire of foods and delicacies. As Mesody, a woman born in Tangier, recalls, when her brother Elías was circumcised:

> Each person who arrived [at the party] was offered a big glass of *horchata* [a refreshing drink], and then a piece of *pasta real*... *Azahar* [orange blossom] sweets, eggplant sweets, and bitter orange sweets were offered too. There were no tables set; instead, each guest would get, upon leaving, a big paper cone tied with a ribbon, full of *marronchinos* [cookies], sweets, almonds, and chocolates.[116]

Beatriz, a Sephardi woman who came to Argentina after World War II, recalled that for Tu B'shvat (New Year of the Trees), "our mothers made little bags which were filled with seven fruits: walnuts, almonds, chestnuts, raisins, prunes, figs, carob, and chocolate-filled candy."[117] For Purim, she continued, "we would eat ḥalvah [sesame-based sweet hard paste], *rosquitas de aljashuv* [ring-shaped sweets filled with nuts], Haman's hair [or beard] [thin pasta]."[118] The pervasive presence of religious practices in all aspects of community life was not a given once migration had taken place; more often than not, it was absent. As mentioned in chapter 2, some communities in the interior did not have enough men to form the necessary minyan to perform religious services, and buying kosher food was not an option in most provincial towns. Some important provincial centers made it a priority to obtain matzah for Passover but were not able to hire a rabbi for celebration of the High Holidays.[119] It is in this context that family and community actions acquired more religiously symbolic meanings. In the past, and across the ocean, cooking Shabbat dinner took place alongside community, family, and religious activities. Stores closed before sundown; all houses were cleaned and readied for the arrival of Shabbat; the shammas (sextons) walked the streets calling on families to attend services; children came together from religious/Jewish school, anticipating the holy day. Now, in the new country, the cooking and eating of special foods together was probably the only reminder of that past, and the only symbolic marker of a religious occasion. As Lucha Funes said, "The most vivid memories I have of being Jewish in Paso de los Libres, Corrientes, was sitting at my grandmother's table, eating homemade sweets for Rosh Hashanah."[120]

In her study of Jewish women and English households, Ricki Burman similarly noted that in a "context [of increasing secularization] women's traditional domestic practices acquired a new significance." She continued, "What had previously been merely an accepted part of daily life, the observance of Jewish dietary laws and the preparation for Sabbaths and Festivals, now assumed a greater prominence as religious acts which served to define the Jewish identity of the household, and to distinguish the homes of Jewish families from those of their gentile neighbors."[121] Argentine Sephardi families did not necessarily live in a context of deliberate secularization—as in most cases Sephardi groups attempted, as much as possible, to maintain their religious life—thus less attention to ritual was, more often than not, a result of lacking the means to keep those rituals alive.[122] Also, there were significant differences between "Jewish life" in Paso de los Libres, province of Corrientes, and Villa Crespo, a Jewish neighborhood in Buenos Aires, where large numbers of Jews lived in close proximity to one another. The consumption of kosher food, which Burman cites as an important element kept by "secular" Jews in Great Britain, was in Argentina followed more strictly by some communities than by others. In particular, Arabic-speaking groups made it a priority to create and then financially support kosher butchers.[123] Or Torah, the religious congregation of the Damascene Jews in La Boca, for example, gently reminded members of another Jewish Damascene society to patronize the butchers Or Torah sponsored.[124] In the oral history workshops, participants recalled kosher butchers in the neighborhood of Villa Crespo, but no sources show official community financial support.[125] Yet I believe that Burman's argument can be applied to Argentina, which had a very different Jewish environment from Great Britain. The preparation and eating of Jewish food acquired, in Argentina, a new meaning that, by the very absence of other elements, took on religious and ethnic overtones.

Yet the food itself, together with its eating and preparation, was not only a marker of "Jewish" identity. It became associated with a strong "intra-ethnic" component. *Borrekas* (phyllo pastries), couscous, and kibbe signaled to Ottoman, Moroccan, and Arabic-speaking Jewry more clearly than last names did. A workshop participant, speaking to a mostly Ottoman Jewish group of women, said "My food has nothing to do with yours."[126] When Lida learned how to make couscous, she was learning the ways and traditions of *Morocco*, even though she was born in Sauce, a dusty small town in Corrientes province.

A story told by Bulisa, a woman whose parents had been born in Istanbul, also shows the close connections between food (and its rituals) and community tradition and identification. She described the Turkish Jewish tradition of the "serving set for sweetmeats" (*tavlá de dúlse*), a community ritual that clearly signaled who belonged and who did not. By custom, a host passed around this silver serving set—consisting of a tray, a silver cup filled with water, with a silver spoon and fork hanging from the rim, and matching small plates where jam was placed—to guests while all were sitting down, enjoying a cup of coffee (itself an important culinary tradition among all Sephardi groups). Each guest took a spoon or fork (depending on the jam's consistency), took a small amount of it, and placed it in her mouth. After tasting the jam, the spoon or fork was rinsed in the cup of water and rehung on the rim of the water cup. Sharope was the most famous jam, because of both its special taste and because the complicated procedure involved in making it certified a woman's excellence as a cook. It was notoriously sweet, and a small amount went "a long way." Bulisa, laughing, recounted a story involving her mother, Jewish friends, and a non-Jewish neighbor who were all invited to her mother's house for coffee one afternoon in Concordia, province of Entre Ríos. The neighbor, unfamiliar with the overwhelming sweetness of sharope, took a rather big portion when the serving set reached her. No one remarked on it, but it was clear by looking at the non-Jewish guest's face that she did not at all enjoy it.[127]

Yet food as a clear ethnic marker was not static. Generational differences and varying cultural contexts rewrote the very meanings of culinary symbols. When the first generation of Argentine Sephardi women were learning how to make Ottoman, Moroccan, or Syrian Jewish food, there were no cookbooks to learn from.[128] This was, as confirmed by the women I interviewed, a tradition that was passed orally to the next generation. The way this generation lived and experienced food was wrapped up in the preparation itself. Whenever I asked a woman of this generation to describe a specific dish for me, the language used was that of experiential knowledge: "mix it until the spoon can move around only so slowly.... add a pinch of salt."[129] Lida could not have *told* me how to make couscous; she had to sit down and *show* me how to do it, the same way she had learned it from her mother. Even when cookbooks with Sephardi recipes were eventually published, the fact that they had been collected from informants who had learned how to make the dishes by watching was reflected in the language: "Add salt, but not so much."[130]

The next generation of Sephardi (Moroccan, Ottoman, or Syrian) Jewish-Argentine women lived in a different environment. Most of the immigrant (or first-generation, Argentine-born) informants I interviewed recalled that notions regarding "health" affected the types of food their daughters prepared. Luna explained that "our food was too greasy and oily.... we can't eat those foods now."[131] This new focus on health pushed traditional dishes off the daily table, reserving them for special occasions. Another reason, mentioned by women in the workshop, for the abandonment of "traditional" food as everyday nourishment was that some ingredients were hard to come by. Bulisa recalled that her mother had gone to the extreme of planting her own okra garden. I asked Bulisa if she too kept a garden after she was married, and she replied in the negative, as she "moved to Buenos Aires and lived in an apartment building," but more important, "it was too much work."[132] What was probably left unsaid was that cooking *bamias* (okra) had been more important to her mother than to her. Her mother, born and raised in Izmir (and who had prepared *boios* for sale in Turkey), thought of okra as an integral part of what she cooked; changing her ways was, if possible, not contemplated. Bulisa added that her husband suffered from a heart condition, and thus cooking the "old way" was medically proscribed.

Joelle Bahloul argues that the types of food cooked and served by the French Jews she studied depended on whether the recipient of food was family (that is, community) or other Frenchmen and women (that is, outsiders).[133] I found that this was not necessarily the case in Argentina. Even in the private space of the home dinner table, Sephardi (and I suspect Ashkenazi) women began to cook things they thought were more healthful (less greasy), easier to make, and more readily available. They also came into contact with a much wider repertoire of cooking traditions as they interacted with local communities. Esther A., a woman whose parents were born in Morocco and arrived in Argentina as youngsters, recalled that "my mother rarely made Moroccan food." She had adopted *criollo* (creole) recipes and made "pasta, stews, [and] roasted meat" for the family.[134]

The only documents I located that revealed culinary choices made by Sephardi Jews stressed that dishes that came to be known as "Argentine" tradition (itself a complex mingling of Spanish, Italian, and creole traditions) became the food around which Jewish functions were planned. Only one side dish, of the fourteen chosen to be served at the Alianza Social Club ball, had a "real" Sephardi flavor: lima beans. The reasons for other choices made by these youths, in the list of fourteen dishes, are ambiguous. The celery stick and the egg, for example, suggest dishes served on the traditional Passover Seder plate. Some side dishes are clearly "Argentine": salami, *palitos* (cheese sticks), and *papas fritas* (potato chips); some seem to be "Ashkenazi" choices, such as the dark rye bread served with the side dishes. But rather than focusing on the origin of the foods chosen, or considering whether they were chosen because of those origins, the important point here is that the culinary repertoire from which this generation chose had been, not surprisingly, broadened by contact with other groups. Dishes that were not previously included in social celebrations appeared, and some that were ubiquitously present were left out. For the May 25 celebration, the group served *chocolate con buñuelos*, after rejecting the suggestion to prepare *fiyuelas* (thin strips of fried dough), a typical (delicious) Moroccan fried dish that required painstaking attention and time-consuming preparation.

For this generation of Argentine-born Jews, preparing only Moroccan, Ottoman, or Syrian food was neither a necessity nor a requisite. They were "Argentine Jews," with traditions that combined the ethnic culture their parents brought with them, the culture of other Jewish groups they encountered in various Jewish contexts, and Argentine culture, transmitted through mass media outlets like television, radio, newspapers, and magazines, which even their parents were slowly incorporating into their everyday lives.[135]

In *Memoria e Sociedade* (Memory and Society), Eclea Bosi claims that old people become the repositories of family and community memory when their more active roles in society come to an end on account of their age.[136] In the case of immigrant communities, the role of memory becomes more central and essential, as what is at stake is an ethnic identity that time will eventually reshape.[137] Thus Sephardi grandmothers were defending not just "Jewishness" but Moroccan, Ottoman, or Syrian traditions and rituals. Jewishness continued being an element in the identity of newer generations (in some more clearly than in others), but "ethnic" ways of being Jewish ran the risk of being forgotten as "hegemonic" ways of being Jewish took over. Lucha F., the woman born in Paso de los Libres, province of Corrientes, prepared traditional sweets at her home in Argentina (the same ones she enjoyed for Rosh Hashanah as a child with her grandmother) and "smuggled" them into the United States for the bar mitzvah of her grandson. Asked why she did this, she responded with a matter-of-fact shrug: "There was only going to be 'Russian' [Ashkenazi] food there [at the party]; that is not right."[138]

Ashkenazi culture became hegemonic in Argentina not merely because there were more Ashkenazi Jews but because restaurants and caterers who provided Jewish food for celebrations until recently prepared mostly "Ashkenazi" dishes.[139] Even supermarkets boasting a "Jewish" section sold only Ashkenazi items, thus "teaching" Argentines that Jewish food was Ashkenazi. Sephardi culinary traditions did not move from the private kitchens of grandmothers into mainstream locations, and if they did, they became associated with Middle Eastern food, not necessarily Jewish. Thus Lucha felt that it was up to her to provide "Sephardi" food at her grandson's celebration.

Because the defense of ethnic food identity was and is done in the face of Ashkenazi cultural dominance, Sephardi groups took it upon themselves to make sure that this important distinction was maintained and celebrated. The Sephardi WIZO in Argentina and Brazil and the Argentine Comité Femenino Sefaradí Amigos de la Histadrut have all published "Sephardi" cookbooks in the last twenty years.[140] This new development—the cultural transmission of culinary Sephardi traditions through the written word—confirms the perceived need to teach Sephardi culture to two Sephardi (or half-Sephardi) generations: one that purposefully decided not to learn it and a younger generation with the desire to learn. And although these books were intended primarily for a domestic Sephardi audience (which is a telling fact in itself), they seem to have opened up this culture to non-Sephardim who might never have been exposed to borrekas, couscous, or trabaditos. The fact that a major Argentine newspaper, in October 2003, published only Sephardi recipes in a section reserved for "Jewish food for the New Year" might very well mean that Sephardi culinary traditions have managed to survive, despite their grease, hard-to-find ingredients, and the legacy of an Ashkenazi majority.

CONCLUSION

Parties, social gatherings, dances, cinema and theater productions, and food were more than simple entertaining events, as the survival of the community was at stake. These boundaries were specific, for they did not encircle only "Jews" but the identities of these smaller communities, as the majority threatened to engulf all. Yet within these boundaries, everything was not "Jewish." Rather, the meaning of "Jewish" was being reconfigured by succeeding generations. Argentine food, Argentine fashion, Argentine hotels, and Argentine national holidays were integral mechanisms by which Sephardi communities defended their own identity in the face of Ashkenazi majority. What better way was there to raise money for a Sephardi philanthropic group than in the Alvear Palace Hotel, dancing to the music of René Cospito and his orchestra and eating *chocolate* and *masas finas* (fancy finger pastries)!

SIX

MARRIAGES AND SCHOOLS
Living within Multiple Borders

Pero es un ruso!!

Lida G. De Azulay, 1960

We do not exaggerate when we affirm that the Jewish community in Argentina celebrates national holidays as well as its [own] holidays. And that is only natural.

La Luz, May 29, 1931

THE PLAY *UN ROMANCE TURCO* (A TURKISH ROMANCE) WAS written in 1920 by Pedro Pico, a journalist, dramaturge, and screenplay writer, and Samuel Eichelbaum, a leading Jewish-Argentine playwright, and performed in the same year by the famous Muiño-Alippi theater troupe.[1] The play narrates the developing romance between Judi, a young Sephardi Jewish woman, and Maraj, a Muslim young man. Set in the Buenos Aires fabric store of Judi's father, Abujar, Maraj is presented to the audience as a trustworthy person who has garnered the affection of all Judi's family. He is a successful traveling salesman who is missed even by Abujar when he is away. It is only through Sochin, an employee in Abujar's store who is also in love with Judi, that the audience learns that Maraj failed to tell Judi that he is not Jewish. Although the central plot is centered on Maraj and Judi's ill-starred romance, the audience also meets Arim, Judi's younger brother, who is falling in love with Felicia, a classmate who is not Jewish.

In the last scene of *Un romance turco*, which takes place on Friday evening, Sochin confronts Maraj and forces him to tell his secret to his loved one. Judi is at first shocked and feels deceived, insisting that she cannot marry Maraj against the wishes of her father and grandmother. As she is walking away with her family, Maraj pleads, "Aren't I the same as when you believed me Jewish? We can still be happy, Judi," to no avail. In a last attempt to convince her, Maraj points to the young couple—Arim and Felicia—who are also witnessing the scene, and exclaims: "Look at them, Judi. They love each other; for them, there are no obstacles, neither in heaven nor on earth. That is why they love each other so much. Here Judi: we represent the old; with us is the God that divides men; *they* [Arim and Felicia] represent youth, this new land in which one can love without impediment."[2] The play concludes as Judi frees herself from her grandmother and runs toward Maraj, exclaiming: "Don't go Maraj.... *you* are my God ... Wait for me!"

This chapter focuses on the identity issues raised by the play. Argentina represented, in the liberal imaginary so prevalent in the last decades of the nineteenth century and early twentieth century, a land in which religious atavism had no place, a country where modernity—always secular—was bound to replace traditions brought from the Old World.[3] For the immigrant generation themselves, as exemplified by Abujar and the grandmother, marrying out of the faith was a sure sign of dangers lurking ahead, a sure indication that assimilation—the loss of culture—was around the corner. To avoid assimilation, marriage within the group was encouraged, and Judi initially suggests she understands what is at stake. Besides presenting the dangers (and the lure) of intermarriage, the play introduces another "threat" to the immigrants' cultures: the school. Arim, Judi's younger brother, attends the local state school, where he learns about "modern" topics and reads novels; it is there he meets his girlfriend, Felicia, a fellow classmate who is presented as less concerned about parental authority than Judi is, as Judi at first attempts to do what she believes her father wants. The generation being schooled in Argentine institutions, like Arim and Felicia, has learned, the authors of the play suggest, to be less attached to their own communities and to see themselves as sharing something in common, even as they come from different backgrounds: they are Argentines. Judi, on the other hand, has a harder time seeing Maraj as an equal after his religious beliefs are revealed to her, and appears, for a moment, to be like the old generation of her grandmother and father.

The play did not focus on how this new country threatened the existence of immigrant cultures that should be saved; on the contrary, it suggested that Argentina was able to successfully modernize newcomers, turning them into Argentine men and women who found in each other fellow citizens who willingly shed their previous traditional traits. The spirit of the play is, therefore, unequivocally triumphant, welcoming both the erasure of immigrant culture and the birth of a modern national identity without ethnic particularities. But I would suggest that the authors of *Un romance turco* were perhaps too optimistic in their desire that immigrants leave their pasts behind and become Argentines. The fictional treatment of this topic, like the liberal ideal that inspired the play, is simplistic; real life was significantly more complicated than that. This chapter, which focuses on Jewish marriages and community schools, reminds us, first, that adopting Argentine norms and learning the country's history and geography in its public schools did not necessarily entail the end of an immigrant's communal and religious affiliations; second, marrying within your own subethnic group, or otherwise maintaining communal and/or religious loyalties, did not mean that immigrants did not see themselves as Argentines. In fact, if we look at marriages between Sephardim and Ashkenazim, which become more common toward the mid-twentieth century, it can be argued that "being" Argentine is what brought them together and allowed them to continue to express their Jewish identity. And, likewise, attending community schools did not create isolated pockets of Jewish life but spaces in which the nation, the present, and the past merged.

TRUE MARRIAGE STORIES

While *Un romance turco* staged the desires of an immigrant generation regarding the power of Argentina to create new men and women, real marriage stories of two Sephardi women reveal some concrete issues they faced in their marriage choices. Lida, the daughter of Moroccan parents, who lived with them and her twelve brothers and sisters in a small dusty town in the province of Corrientes, was never secretive about the fact that her husband, Jacobo, another Moroccan Jew, was not the first man she loved in her life. Her first (and truest?) love, as my grandmother told me many times, was the town's *maestro* (teacher), a Catholic man who sent furtive letters to her through her sister, and who arranged secret rendezvous at the house of two spinsters who helped the young couple. The end to this platonic relationship came not because the *maestro* decided to run off with the young woman, or because they were discovered and forbidden to see each other again, but because the town sheriff (*comisario*) asked Lida's father for her hand in marriage. Her father was polite in response, stressing that the request was an honor, and he finished by saying that, if not for the fact that Lida was affianced to a man in Buenos Aires, they would be happy to accept the proposal. This was, of course, a ploy.

Lida was not engaged, but the sheriff, a gentile, could never have been accepted as her husband, though nor could it be stated plainly because of fear of a possible retaliation. That evening, at the dinner table, Lida's father informed his wife that the young lady was leaving for Buenos Aires on the next morning's train. And indeed Lida left, leaving behind what seemed the problem, the sheriff, but also the love of Lida's life—the *maestro*—as well. In Buenos Aires, she stayed with friends of the family who found Jacobo, a "nice young man" from the same Moroccan town as Lida's parents. They were married shortly after meeting for the first time. It was the early 1930s.

The second story took place about thirty years later, when in the late 1950s Luna, the daughter of Lida and Jacobo, met and fell in love with Sergio, an Ashkenazi university student like she was. Both families expressed concerns about the match, though the reservations clearly focused on "imagined" differences and failed to consider similarities they shared. As Luna recalls, "But he is a ruso!" was her parents' response when she told them about the relationship. Unlike her mother, however, Luna was not shipped away to a distant city. She indeed married Sergio, her own choice for a husband.

Both stories speak about perceived threats. Lida's father perceived the danger of marriage outside the Jewish community, and he sent her away to find a husband among those he knew and trusted: a man from the same town he had come from. Luna's parents' reaction to her choosing a (Jewish) ruso as a husband also highlights the threat of crossing boundaries. Who was an acceptable partner, even if Jewish, and who was not, was informed by what each generation considered to be a member of the group. Focusing on marriage records in Buenos Aires among Sephardi Jews, this section argues that Jewish identity was bound by changing notions of what constituted community and that these notions were closely related to and influenced by the experiences of this immigrant community (like many others) in Argentina. The constitution of Argentine identity was *also* in the process of being constructed by those old and new to the country. Thus "lo Argentino," was not static either. But this chapter, unlike previous scholarship on immigrant marriage patterns, is not necessarily interested in discovering either a melting pot or assimilation behind Lida's and Luna's decisions; that is to say, I am interested in marriages between Jews not because they constitute a sign that they were avoiding "assimilation." In fact, these marriages, and the decisions that made them happen, were deeply embedded in Argentina's realities.

A short note on methodology and sources is pertinent here. This chapter is based on the records of five different synagogues. Three are Sephardi: the Moroccan community, with marriage records spanning 1920 to 1960; the Ottoman (Rhodes) community of Chalom, with records from 1937 to 1960; and the Ottoman community on Camargo Street, with marriage records from 1930 to 1960 (with very few records for 1950s, as the synagogue was then being renovated). The other two synagogues are Ashkenazi: CIRA-Templo Libertad, with marriage records from 1920 to 1950, and Templo Paso, in the Once neighborhood, with records from 1928 to 1933. The materials placed obvious limitations on this study. Only religious Jewish marriages are examined, no Arabic-speaking congregations are represented, and only institutions in Buenos Aires were studied. An analysis of marriages in the communities from Aleppo and Damascus might have helped prove (or challenged) the perception that Arab Jews had a higher incidence of intracommunity marriages. Records of Jewish synagogues in the provinces, on the other hand, might have allowed an in-depth analysis of intracommunity relations in these centers and provided stronger evidence to support the thesis that provinces witnessed the growth of a more inclusive Jewish identity earlier than in Buenos Aires. As this study centers on configurations of ethnic and subethnic identity within community boundaries, there was no need to work with state records of marriages between Jews and non-Jews.[4] I have used more than eighteen thousand burial records from all the Buenos Aires Sephardi cemeteries to ascertain the origins of the Sephardim whose marriage licenses I analyzed, as the particular cemeteries Sephardim chose to be buried in provided strong clues to their community of origin. Besides marriage records, I also used various Sephardi magazines and interviews with Sephardi women, which have added an attitudinal dimension to the study.

ETHNIC MARRIAGES

Of course, this is not the first study that pays attention to marriage choice as a window into ethnic and national identities. Gino Germani used marriage records to make his now famous claim that immigrants to Argentina had, by 1930, successfully assimilated to their new society. Assimilation was evident, Germani noted, in that marriages with Argentines had come to "almost" replace marriages among co-nationals (Italians with Italians, Spaniards with Spaniards, and so on). Samuel Baily and Mark Schuzman, U.S. historians of immigration to Argentina, realized Germani had overlooked a significant detail.[5] When paying special attention to the nationality of the *parents* of the bride and groom, a different story emerged. Argentine-born children of immigrant parents and newly arrived immigrants, they showed, continued to marry within their familial ethnic groups, therefore creating a pluralistic society that celebrated and maintained difference. Germani's theory, the victory of the "melting pot," was, thus, proven wrong.

After that initial attack on Germani's positions, a second generation of historians continued to study his assertion and the corrections of Baily and Schuzman. They focused on big cities, small towns, Italian and Spanish immigrants, and smaller immigrant groups, and tested the theory in urban and rural settings. Without rejecting the notion that marriage choice was greatly influenced by the ethnic origin of the families, these scholars eventually concluded that brides and grooms had paid attention to more than just "nationality" when making their marriage choices.[6] Sex ratios, economics, and other variables, like educational and "spatial" considerations, had played a role, as well. Without necessarily arguing for abandoning marriage licenses as evidence that provided answers to questions about how nationalism and ethnic identity worked, these historians called for attention to other indicators.

Marriage patterns have also been the focus of historians who work on the Jewish community of Argentina in particular.[7] Steeped in the historiographical debate over whether Jews assimilated rapidly into the host society or not, these historians also addressed questions raised by the Jewish case, in particular. Diana Epstein, who wished to test the oft-cited argument that Moroccan Jews had assimilated much more easily than other Jewish groups to Argentine society, worked in state archives, looking for marriages to non-Jews. Rosa Geldstein and Fabiana Tolcachier, working with smaller Jewish groups (the former concentrating on the area around a Jewish agricultural colony, the latter on an interior capital), also tested Germani's assertion. Geldstein concluded that in Salta, intermarriage was influenced not just by a declining number of Jews in the region but by the slow but constant secularization of the community; in the case of the province of Buenos Aires, Tolcachier showed the strong loyalty exhibited by immigrants from the same town/city of origin was evolved to incorporate Jews from other points of origin and nearby colonies.

Whether they focused on the Jewish community in particular or the immigrant community in general all these historians shared the assumption that marriage choice revealed degrees of assimilation. In this framework, by marrying "others," Jews stopped being Jews to become Argentines. This notion was not only scholarly; recall how Judi's father and grandmother reacted to her possible attachment to Maraj in *Un romance turco*. The Sephardi Jewish press in Argentina indeed echoed these assumptions when it published articles concerned about the fate of those Jews (usually women) who decided to marry outside the faith. For example, on July 3, 1931, *La Luz* published an article about a Jewish woman living in Rosario. Never identified by name, the woman told the journalist: "It has been five years since I married a goy, and to be frank, I feel quite miserable."[8] The reason for so much unhappiness resided, she said, in three possible culprits:

1. Herself, her immaturity, and her "weakness." She noted, "I was perhaps blinded by love and fell hard for my beau's sweet words."
2. Her father was also guilty in her opinion, since he was "only nominally Jewish." A more religious household would perhaps have taken her down a different path.
3. The anonymous woman attacked her mother at greatest length. "Where was she," she asked, "when she failed to explain things to me, and neglected to bring me to the dances and other social gatherings where I could have met a nice Jewish young man?"[9]

Although it is clear that the mother was imagined as central to the preservation of ethnic identity, the article suggests that the whole family had a role to play in preventing young women from forming families outside communal boundaries. The magazine wished to alert Jewish families to the dangers posed by Argentina and by young women who were not properly supervised and maintained within the boundaries of the community.

Jewish *men* marrying outside the faith was a reality addressed by religious sanction, but Jewish magazines did not discuss the issue, nor did they cite it as a serious concern. As mentioned in chapter 3, Aleppine Rabbi Shaul Setton Dabbah (residing in Buenos Aires), together with Rabbi Aharon Goldman (Ashkenazi rabbi of the JCA colony of Moisesville) and Yosef Yedid (rabbi of the Aleppo community in Jerusalem), passed a ban on conversion in Argentina. Appalled at the lack of religious observation, especially because Jewish men married gentile women who had converted without following the proper rules, Setton announced in 1927 that no more conversions would take place in Argentina "until the end of time."[10] Many immigrants recall that, in order to avoid marrying outside the faith, men would write to their families back in the old country to request the "sending" of young women whom they would marry as soon as they disembarked.[11]

The stories, together with the reaction from the rabbis, suggest that (many) Jews agreed that marriage to non-Jews posed dangers for ethnic survival, and that the desire to remain within community boundaries was indeed strong. But an analysis of Sephardi marriage records in

Table 6.1. Moroccan Congregation Marriage Records (1920–1960)

Weddings	1920–1930	1931–1960
Among Sephardim	32 (29 couples of same origin)	88 (66 couples of same origin)
Between Sephardim and Ashkenazim	1 (1920s)	23 (3 in 1930s, 3 in 1940s, 16 in 1950s, 1 in 1960)
Total	33	113*

*It is impossible to ascertain geographical origins in three records. One groom came from a "mixed" (Ashkenazi-Sephardi) family, so the record was included in the Ashkenazim-Sephardim total.

Buenos Aires strongly indicates that the community boundaries they were preserving were those of their communities or origins, not exclusively those of "Jewishness." While there were few marriages between Sephardim and Ashkenazim (see tables 6.1, 6.2, and 6.3), which increased as the century went on, Sephardim married almost exclusively other Sephardim from their same towns/countries. "Ethnic" identity, for Sephardim, did not merely mean *Jewish*, but *Sephardi* from the same subethnic group.

The high incidence of marriage among Sephardim of the same origin, higher in the earlier decades of the twentieth century (1920–1940) than in the latter (1940–1960), is not a surprise. In fact, the previous chapters argued that in Buenos Aires, Sephardim tended to live their lives in neighborhoods that gathered people of the same origin, at least in the early years of these communities. This meant that social, cultural, and religious activities that brought together young men and women mostly occurred within these imaginary (neighborhood) walls.

Many of these marriages (twenty-five in the Moroccan congregation, three in the Camargo Temple, and twenty-one in the Chalom Temple) were among Sephardim of the same origin but in the synagogue of another Sephardi community (see tables 6.1, 6.2, and 6.3). The choice of a different synagogue (located in neighborhoods that were intimately linked to other communities) might be explained by the dates of construction of these temples. The Moroccan temple was the first Sephardi synagogue to be built in the city, followed by Camargo and later by

Table 6.2. Ottoman Congregation Marriage Records (Camargo Temple) (1930–1960)

Weddings	1930–1960
Among Sephardim	295
	(261 couples of same origin)*
Between Sephardim and Ashkenazim	53
	(8 in 1930s, 36 in 1940s, 5 in 1950s, 4 in 1960)
Total	381**

*In sixty-six records, the specific Sephardi origin was not clear.

**In thirty-nine records, it could not be determined whether the bride and/or groom were Sephardi or Ashkenazi.

Table 6.3. Ottoman Congregation Marriage Records (Chalom Temple) (1937–1960)

Weddings	1937–1960
Among Sephardim	415
	(332 couples of same origin)*
Between Sephardim and Ashkenazim	127
	(1 in 1930s, 40 in 1940s, 77 in 1950s, and 9 in 1960)
Total	592**

*Eighty-six records were not calculated in this number, as there was no obvious information about Sephardi origin, or the bride and groom came from a mixed (Ashenazi-Sephardi) marriage.

**In some records, it was not possible to evaluate origin

Chalom. For about ten years then—from 1920 to 1930—Sephardim who wanted a religious ceremony in a synagogue had only one option. Camargo was under renovation for most of the 1950s, so it is not surprising that many Ottoman Jews married in Chalom, the temple of another Ottoman community (mostly from Rhodes), located in a different neighborhood. Sephardim also, as the century progressed, moved out of neighborhoods where they had first settled. Chalom, for example, was located in a neighborhood where there were few other Jewish institutions. Choosing the temple that was closest to where Sephardim resided also explains why a particular wedding venue was chosen.[12] Although these synagogues were similarly constructed, including decoration and

Marriages and Schools

Table 6.4. Number of Marriages between Sephardim of Different Origins

	Number of Marriages among Sephardim of Different Origins
Moroccan Congregation (1920–1960)	22 (18.3% of total Sephardi marriages) (2 in 1920s, 1 in 1930s, 6 in 1940s, 12 in 1950s, 1 in 1960)
Ottoman Congregation (Camargo Temple) (1930–1960)	15 (5% of total Sephardi marriages) (5 in 1930s, 5 in 1940s, 4 in 1950s, 1 in 1960)
Ottoman Congregation (Chalom Temple) (1937–1960)	47 (11% of total Sephardi marriages) (10 in 1940s, 35 in 1950s, 2 in 1960)

architecture, aesthetic preferences surely played a role, too. All this suggests that even when Sephardim were strengthening the identities of their communities, Argentina, through its geography, its cities and neighborhoods, its aesthetics and architecture, played an important role in providing new alternatives and new ways of defining boundaries.

Although few in number, marriages among Sephardim of different origins did occur (see table 6.4). Let us recall the story of Estela Levy, who found her husband among Sephardim from Damascus, in the neighborhood her family had moved into. It is clear that, overall, those marriages steadily increased as the century moved on. (Camargo is the exception; very few marriages were performed in the 1950s.) That Sephardim of different origins were choosing each other as partners suggests, again, that new spaces came into existence that allowed for them to meet, whether in neighborhoods, more inclusive institutions, or even in non-Jewish venues (such as state schools). Yet it should be stressed that marriages among Sephardim of different origins were less common than marriages between Sephardim and Ashkenazim.

The story that emerges from the documents of the Ashkenazi congregations is somewhat different (see table 6.5). While there are few marriages between Ashkenazim and Sephardim until the late 1950s, we do find a number of marriages among Sephardim. That Sephardi couples would choose to hold their weddings at Ashkenazi congregations clearly illustrates how the meaning and boundaries of Jewish identity were complex and in flux. Ashkenazim, to Sephardi parents, were sometimes not good enough as marriage partners (as Lida's reaction to her daughter's

Table 6.5. Number of Sephardi Marriages in Ashkenazi Synagogues and Ashkenazi Marriages in Chalom Congregation

	Number of Marriages out of Total Marriages (by decade)
Paso Synagogue (Sephardi)	24 out of 189 (2 in 1920s, 22 in 1930s)
Libertad Synagogue (Sephardi)	350 out of 1,101 (13 in 1920s, 52 in 1930s, 284 in 1940s, 1 in 1950)
Chalom Synagogue (Ashkenazi)	11 out of 592 (1 in 1930s, 5 in 1940s, 5 in 1950s)

engagement reminds us), but their synagogues seemed to be Jewish enough for religious events. The same reasons given above, regarding Sephardi couples marrying in Sephardi synagogues other than their own, apply here. New settlement patterns, new more inclusive institutions, and aesthetic differences mattered. Both Ashkenazi synagogues (the Sephardi ones, too) were grand constructions that imitated the style of the Reform synagogues in Germany, with the bimah located at the end of a central aisle and with the seated congregation facing it (rather than a bimah in the center, with the congregation seated around it). This special configuration was reminiscent of Catholic churches, as well.

The strongest commonality between Luna and Sergio—what united them, before their wedding—was their being Argentine. They were children of endogamous marriages, but they were raised in an Argentine city, educated in Argentine schools and universities, participated in Argentine political parties, drank mate (a yerba mate drink), and ate Argentine food. Even Lida, who had reacted with "Pero es un ruso" to the news of her daughter's engagement, was extremely happy when the wedding was celebrated in CIRA's Templo Libertad, which had acquired, by the mid-twentieth century, a clear class status, as the elite of Jewish Buenos Aires (even Sephardim) chose to marry within its walls. The boundaries of Jewish identity were indeed multiple and flexible, even when they elicited initial opposition.

But Argentina was present even before the native-born children selected marriage partners "across the aisle" (Ashkenazi-Sephardi unions) or chose to marry in synagogues belonging to other communities. For many Sephardi immigrant men and women, Argentina was the place where the transition from "tradition" to "modernity" took place, and it is not surprising to see that this "modernity" adopted an Argentine style. This style, as noted before, was itself in flux, attempting to replicate European and French dictates in particular. Children of immigrants grew up learning about these modern ideals.

As Ezequiel Adamovsky demonstrated in his study of the Argentine middle class, the Argentine "ideal" assigned women a "secondary but nonetheless important role as the guardian of morality and of the home."[13] Marriage was seen as the ideal state for women, as it granted decency and honor, and (ideally) kept women within the walls of the home. This elite ideal coincided, as well, with a "Jewish" ideal for women and marriage, but the ways that ideal was celebrated and publicized were in dialogue with existing images, prescriptions, and proscriptions of Argentine middle-class respectability. *Israel* magazine, for example, ran a section (1931–1935) entitled "Nuestras Novias" (Our Brides), showcasing young women who were engaged to be married or had recently married. They usually appeared alone, and their maiden names (and the names of their husbands) were duly noted (see figure 6.1). The photographs highlighted the role these women would play as guardians of their Sephardi homes, and they stressed the dignity and respectability of them and their families.

Jewish marriage "á la Argentina" was always present in the pages of the Sephardi magazine *Israel*. In addition to "Our Brides," *Israel* published marriage announcements in the "Vida Social" (Social Life) section of the magazine, which listed births, trips to Europe, and other indicators of social mobility and prestige, such as finishing university or new jobs. In many issues, a wedding announcement was accompanied by photographs of the wedding itself, and it sometimes included a list of attendees (see figure 6.2). These were opportunities for the Sephardi elite to show off their daughters and sons, and the advantageous marriages that joined elite Sephardi families. These newspaper sections and announcements allowed Sephardi elite to broadcast their commitment to and acceptance of the Argentine ideals that Sephardim complied with and utilized, even as they stressed their loyalty to their own immigrant communities.

Figure 6.1. *Israel,* "Our Brides," August 12, 1932.

Marriages and Schools

Figure 6.2. *Israel,* Vida Social section, April 7–14, 1933, 26–27.

The wedding attire seen in the photos published in *Israel* was not the traditional type usually worn in the old country. Although "modern" wedding clothes were introduced in Jewish communities from the Ottoman Empire and northern Africa by the Alliance Israelite School (provoking strong reaction from those weary of change), most of the pictures showed women wearing local Argentine fashion styles.[14] *Israel* published two pictures of women (who lived in interior towns) dressed in the traditional Moroccan wedding dress. This dress—elaborate, with intricate gold designs sewn on expensive velvet—was usually worn by the married woman on important occasions even years after her wedding.[15] Thus, this dress in particular signaled not only marital status but class status, as well. These two photographs, unlike those in the sections showcasing weddings, are ambiguous as to the occasion being celebrated. It does not appear that the photos announce the weddings of the women pictured, as there are no grooms present alongside them, one of them is clearly already married, given the magazine uses "señora" (Mrs.) with her name. What is clear, though, is that these women (and their families) are being presented as members of the elite. "The distinguished lady, Mrs. Clara S. de Benmarqui," reads the caption of the photo, is wearing "the lavish traditional Moroccan dress."[16] The other photo shows "the señorita [Miss] Esther Abecasis, with the classic and expensive Moroccan dress."[17] Thus rather than treating traditional clothes as backward, both the women and *Israel* used the dresses to highlight class and marital status in "modern" Argentina.

Another important change in Jewish marriage, as suggested by the stories that opened this chapter, was the appearance of love (or, at least, personal choice) as the basis for marital unions. While Lida accepted Jacobo, a decision made for her by her family, and many others of her generation entered marriage without even knowing their future spouses, personal choice based on love, as in Luna's case, became more prevalent as the century went on. This was not, evidently, an exclusively Argentine phenomenon, but an ideal that came to be learned and consumed through "Argentine" stories available in cinema, serial publications, and on the radio. In his study of Argentine radio and cinema from 1920 to 1946, for example, Matthew Karush noted that while tango lyrics described "love affairs [that] were invariably illegitimate and fleeting, [the love stories presented in] weekly novels endorsed the bourgeois ideal of marriage and the constitution of the family as the route to happiness." Marriage was thus increasingly predicated on personal choice and love.[18] However, Beatriz Sarlo reminds us that "love is *not* stronger than social barriers," so challenging class distinctions was not done. *Israel*, then, through the photos it published on its pages, also reminded its (young) readership that the marriages worthy of space in the magazine (and therefore worthy of showing) were those between social equals.

Two examples from *Israel* demonstrate these ideals of personal choice and love. In a section called "Readers' Pages," to which the public contributed, we find two short paragraphs, one signed by "Palomita" (little dove), and one by "R. Valentino Riocuartense" (R. Valentino, from the town of Rio Cuarto). "Palomita" wrote that she was twenty years old and had a strong desire to marry. She was in love with Alberto, "his last name starts with LOP," and hoped that this short piece would reach his eyes so he would learn of her feelings. R. Valentino hoped that a "dark-haired woman, who enjoys the warmth of home, dances well. . . . and belonged to a distinguished family" would contact him to initiate a relationship.[19] Also, in 1933, the magazine published "The Tug of Love," a short story by Israel Zangwill that tells the story of Elias and Fanny, whose love triumphs over the dictates of traditional marriage. Interestingly, the version published by *Israel* included an extra ten lines at the end that explicitly spelled out the defeat of a marriage broker, and had Fanny returning affections, which were, in the original, expressed only by Elias.[20] It was through such pieces that *Israel* made clear to its readers that it supported the move away from traditional marriage arrangements and welcomed young people's involvement in determining their future lives. But *Israel* also made sure these young readers understood that class and social standings should not be challenged. While R. Valentino advertised his desire for a woman who liked to dance, he reminded possible mates that they had to "belong to a distinguished family." Modern marriage was to be encouraged, as it brought order and honor—if social-class distinctions were preserved—and was a good fit for a country that was striving to find its modernity, as well.[21]

Sephardim, like other immigrants and their descendants, adopted these changing norms that were embedded in the local context and transmitted through a variety of cultural products (Jewish and non-Jewish). Young Sephardim mostly found marriage partners (increasingly without familial input as the century moved on) among those who belonged to institutions of their communities of origin. As they moved to new neighborhoods, or frequented organizations that gathered Jews from a variety of origins, or even in non-Jewish spaces where they met other Jews, marriages between Sephardim and Ashkenazim, and among Sephardim of different origins, became more common. Who was acceptable as a marriage partner changed over time, but even when Sephardim from the same origin chose each other, their marriage was profoundly influenced by local circumstances.

EDUCATING ARGENTINES IN JEWISH COMMUNITY SCHOOLS

Most Sephardi groups in Buenos Aires founded Talmud Torahs (elementary schools) almost as soon as they created their main community organizations (see table 6.6). Some communities included educational objectives in the bylaws of their societies,[22] and the names of communal organizations evidenced their intention to focus on schools: for example, Sociedad Kahal Kadosh y Talmud Tora La Hermandad Sefaradí (Villa Crespo Ottoman Jews) and the Asociación Israelita Talmud Tora Sefaradim Yesod Hadat (Aleppine Jews in Once). Sephardim also founded schools in provincial capitals. The Sociedad Israelita Sefaradí Talmud Torah, for example, formed in 1921, gathering both Aleppine and Damascene Jews in the city of Córdoba,[23] and in Santa Fé, the Sociedad Israelita–Shalom VeReut, created in 1931 by Ottoman Jews, organized a Talmud Torah in 1933.[24] Schools also opened in the cities of Salta, Rosario (Etz HaḤaim), Catamarca, Corrientes, and Posadas (Misiones).

In a comprehensive study of Jewish education in Argentina, Efraim Zadoff defined these Talmud Torahs as attempts by Jews to retain their cultural specificities.[25] In the face of an appealing (and free) universal educational system set up by the Argentine government, Zadoff reasoned, Jewish communities used these schools to avoid the loss of identity that might result from close contact with Roman Catholicism, a fundamental of Argentine culture ingrained in its educational project.[26] Unlike other types of Jewish schools founded by other Argentine Jewish groups, Sephardim mostly focused their attention on Talmud Torahs, which almost exclusively, Zadoff argues, taught boys to read Hebrew and therefore to be fluent in saying prayers.[27] Susana Bianchi, in *Historia de las religiones en la Argentina: Las minorías religiosas* (The History of Religion in Argentina: Minority Religions), agrees with Zadoff's characterization of Sephardi educational institutions, defining them as "very close-knit" projects that allowed for "very little connection among the various Sephardi groups and no contact at all with Ashkenazim."[28] M. Fernanda Astiz, in a recent article on Jewish acculturation and education, likewise suggests that "Sephardim were largely apolitical. . . . [and

Marriages and Schools

Table 6.6. Sephardi Schools

Province/City	Name	Origin*	Neighborhood
Buenos Aires	Chalom	Ottoman	Colegiales
	Yesod Hadat	Aleppo	Once
	Or Torah	Damascus	Boca
	Agudat Dodim	Damascus	Flores
	Talmud Torah	Aleppo	Flores
	Hatikvah	Jerusalem	Once
	Talmud Torah	Morocco	Sud
	Talmud Torah	Ottoman	Villa Crespo
	Talmud Torah	Aleppo	Ciudadela
Misiones	Hijos de Sión	Ottoman	
Córdoba	Sociedad Israelita Siria de Córdoba	Syria	
Corrientes	Talmud Torah	Ottoman and Moroccan	
Salta	"La Unión"	(unknown)	
Santa Fé	Shalom VeReut (later Sociedad Hebrea Sefaradí)	Ottoman (later Moroccan)	
Rosario	Etz HaḤaim	Morocco	

(Mentioned in this chapter.)

*For provincial cities, I have listed the origin of the members of the organization that first founded the schools. Almost all provincial institutions merged Sephardi groups from different origins soon after their creation.

therefore it was] easier for them to remain faithful to their communal traditions."[29]

It is easy to see why these Sephardi educational institutions came to be characterized as isolated community bulwarks against assimilation. The Talmud Torahs that Sephardim founded were indeed part of the organizational structures of their groups and, as such, were supported by members and the leadership.[30] Teachers themselves were usually drawn from the community of origin to which the schools belonged, and at a time when settlement choices reflected subethnic belonging, the pupils came from the same communities of origin, as well. Schools were supervised by subcommittees of the main community institutions or by steering committees that had some (small) degree of independence, even when their members were sometimes also community leaders. The rituals taught in these schools, and the practices adopted, replicated the traditions followed in their places of origin.[31]

Nevertheless, I believe that the prevailing interpretation of these schools—as sites exclusively focused on preserving immigrant identity—is perhaps too simplistic. The problem is both conceptual and methodological. On the one hand, scholars have stressed the apolitical nature of Sephardim (always compared with the highly politicized environment of Eastern Europe that Ashkenazim experienced in their countries of origin and brought with them to Argentina) and therefore the centrality of geography (not ideology) as the source of community organization. As noted earlier, it has been assumed that these organizational strategies were based on a Sephardi essence; the assumption of the existence of that essence permeates most interpretations of Argentine Sephardi institutions and community activities. Because Sephardim remained on the periphery of the Jewish political discussions of the day and gathered around their own, the tacit argument goes, their actions were never imagined as being affected by the larger community, or as having had any impact outside communal spaces (always defined very narrowly), or as having changed through time. These conceptual assumptions lead to faulty methodological approaches. While it is true that few documents have survived that can chart the history of these educational projects, and that most of the surviving documents are organized community records and magazines, the potential of this existing material has been overlooked. Nonetheless, it is precisely in anecdotal references found in community records, narratives, descriptions, and magazine and newspaper articles that we can clearly see the much more nuanced role that Sephardi schools played among Sephardim, within the Jewish community at large, and as Sephardim became part of Argentine society.

I would like to propose, then, that even when mostly religious in orientation and objectives, these Sephardi schools nevertheless participated in discussions that connected Sephardi organizations with Argentines, Ashkenazi Jews, and other Sephardi communities in multivocal conversations over financial support, national (Argentine and Jewish) loyalty, neighborhood participation, and ethnic singularity. In attending these schools, Sephardi children not only learned their prayers but also became part of their communities, their multiethnic neighborhoods, and their nation. Close evaluation shows that Sephardi schools were an integral part of a discursive and "performative" field that allowed for many forms of identification, none necessarily contradictory and all valid.

The various Sephardi groups that settled in Buenos Aires founded schools in the neighborhoods where they settled. It was clear from the start that, although these institutions were educational in nature, control was in the hands of the community, not the teachers. The schools represented the community, and, as such, their leaders constantly chastised teachers for their behavior if it was thought to be detrimental to the public image of the organization. The steering committee of Agudat Dodim in Flores, for example, drafted a Reglamento (set of regulations) in an effort to avoid conflict between students, parents, and the association that would represent the community in a bad light to the rest of the neighborhood.[32] Complaining that disorderly children stained the honor of the whole community, they insisted that teachers exercise more authority. But the call to employ more authority did not mean permission to use physical punishment: community leaders made it clear that if children behaved badly, they would ultimately decide whether and how to reprimand the students and their families.[33] These were imagined as "modern" schools in which physical punishment had no place.

Sephardi schools also opened in most provincial capitals, although educational projects in the country's interior appear to have held lower priority, especially during the early years of a community's founding, when the needs for a social hall, synagogue, and cemetery occupied the members' minds and informed their budgetary decisions. Hijos de Sión, the Sephardi community in Posadas, for example, struggled constantly to keep its school open; appropriate classroom space could not be found, so sessions were first held in a member's home, and when the school was finally moved to its own quarters in 1948, it proved difficult to staff it with qualified teachers.[34]

Without a central organization to unify these Sephardi educational projects, or standardize teacher qualification requirements, or provide or vet religious and other curricula,[35] these Sephardi schools followed directives stipulated by each community. Two attempts to create a central organization were unsuccessful. The first was the Consistorio Rabínico Sefaradí, discussed in chapter 3, and the second was a proposal, supported by *Israel*, the Sephardi magazine, that a "Conference of Hebrew Teachers in Argentina" should be convened.[36] This call was prompted by the threatened closure of schools in Jewish Colonization Association areas (where most of the teachers were Sephardim), not by a specific desire to centralize Sephardi educational policy.[37] There is, however, no evidence that this conference ever took place.

The lack of a central body meant the absence of common educational objectives, but it was ultimately differences among Sephardim (in terms of economic positions and ideologies, and institutional objectives, such as building a temple or purchasing a cemetery) that resulted in the existence of such diverse schools. Sephardi Talmud Torahs varied in many respects: the sex and number of students, the language of instruction, the type and condition of facilities, and the life span of the schools. Yesod Hadat had 200 students in 1921, and the number grew to 450 in 1931; the school in Villa Crespo ranged from 20 to 70 students for the same years.[38] The Agudat Dodim congregation in Flores, claiming to have about 200 students, was "building a new section for girls in their new building," and the Moroccan Jewish community was already teaching girls.[39] Or Torah, the Aleppine Talmud Torah in Ciudadela, and the Sephardi congregation in Villa Crespo, on the other hand, taught only boys.[40] While Yesod Hadat's rabbi did not allow Hebrew to be used as a modern language in the 1920s, the Hatikvah school taught it.[41]

While the physical space of some schools was severely limited, others managed to fund a purpose-built school or rented decent rooms.[42] The Talmud Torah of the Sephardi community in Villa Crespo, for example, raised m$n 20,000 from its members to build a school.[43] Damascene Jews in La Boca used profits derived from the sale of kosher meat to subsidize their Talmud Torah, and parents who did not frequent kosher butchers were asked to pay monthly fees for their children's education.[44] The schools of these various institutions came into their own at different times: although some became visible in the early 1930s (the Moroccan Talmud Torah and Hatikvah, which disappeared from the public eye in the next decade), others reached their peak in the late 1940s and 1950s (Yesod Hadat, Agudat Dodim, Chalom). Some institutions were able to keep their teachers for longer periods of time (Agudat Dodim), while others had trouble retaining them (Or Torah). Most communities taught children of elementary school age, but some attempted to reach young children and create kindergartens.[45] Some schools held classes daily, while others did so only a few days per week.[46]

Diversity also existed in the curricula. Although the surviving material does not allow for a clear picture of what was taught in these schools, they obviously differed in what children were exposed to. Hatikvah, for example, taught Hebrew as well as "our origins and our history, the lives of our heroes and the biographies of those men who have fought for the rebirth of our nation in our holy land."[47] Children attending the Etz HaḤaim school in Rosario learned *canto, lectura, escritura, lenguaje, historia, geografía y Religión* (singing, reading, writing, language, history, geography, and religion),[48] while Agudat Dodim hired a *maestro de temas patrios* (teacher of national [Argentine] topics).[49] Clearly boys (and sometimes girls) attended these schools to learn how to pray and read the scriptures, and in many cases, religion was their main focus, but there is also evidence of students reciting poetry (in Hebrew, Spanish, and French), dancing "classic Hebrew dances,"[50] putting on plays,[51] and learning about Palestinian geography.[52] Communities were able to decide, on their own, what constituted Jewish education and how to best achieve their objectives.

Given the fact that Sephardi institutions in general were very diverse in terms of ideology, economic power, membership, and geographic location, among other issues, this educational diversity should not be surprising. Yet while the existing literature on Sephardim in Argentine has always highlighted the diversity and isolation of these groups, it has nonetheless long assumed that their educational institutions were similar.[53] The related assumption of an unchanged commonality among Sephardim of the same origin and within the same communities over time is also incorrect. While Damascene Jews in La Boca did not accept girls as students, for example, Damascene Jews in Flores did. While Aleppine Jews in Once at first resisted educating girls and using Hebrew (instead using Arabic translations),[54] these policies were reversed in the 1930s, when modern methods for teaching Hebrew were introduced and girls were accepted alongside boys.[55]

While it is important to stress that Sephardi educational institutions were diverse, to counteract the literature's tendency to portray all Sephardim and their institutions as "the same," it is perhaps equally important to put an end to the idea that the centrality of the community of origin meant that these Jews were not in contact with other Sephardim. Sephardi schools created networks of help, support, and advice among all Sephardim, even when their educational projects belonged to groups from diverse origins. In 1931 the Hatikvah school responded to a call from the Sephardi community in the province of Salta, sending it "syllabi, books, charts, the list of books used in classes and important reports on the teaching of Hebrew."[56] The Hatikvah school received periodic visits from members of other communities who had started their own educational projects and wished to learn about the methods and materials used there, as did, for example, José Halac, president of the Talmud Torah of the Sociedad Israelita Siria de Córdoba in August 1929.[57] Etz HaḤaim, a society of Ottoman Jews in Buenos Aires, lent the Talmud Torah Hatikvah "benches for the schoolchildren."[58] And in 1933, Chalom, the Sephardi community in Colegiales (Jews from the Balkans, Rhodes, and Salonika), loaned Hatikvah some benches.[59] These examples suggest that Sephardim, while interested in preserving traditions from their countries of origin, fostered a Sephardi identity and saw themselves as a larger group whose members supported and learned from one another.

Sephardi communities expressed pride at the performance of their schoolchildren, and almost all public community events involved the participation of the "young ones." The end of the academic year would usually be celebrated with a "show," to which everyone in the community would be invited. The best students were recognized, and prizes were handed out.[60] Children recited poems, read prayers, sang, and danced, even when the events being celebrated were not related to the school. During a social gathering organized by the Sociedad Israelita Sefaradí de Villa Crespo pro-Medicamentos, an event aimed at raising funds for purchasing medicine, the children of the community Talmud Torah recited monologues and prayers and put on an allegorical play entitled *Helping the Destitute*.[61] They also played the violin and "a piano version of the Hatikvah."[62]

These performances provided institutions with an occasion to demonstrate the success of their educational projects, and not just to themselves but also to others. Members of other Sephardi communities were invited to participate by handing out prizes, for example, or by acting as jurors and testing the young children's knowledge. In 1931, members of the Hatikvah school board attended the public exam given to Yesod Hadat students.[63] In the same year, during an *acto infantil* (children's public performance) organized by the Congregación Israelita Latina de Buenos Aires, members of the Hatikvah school (teachers and members of the steering committee) and the Agudat Dodim school in Flores handed out prizes to advanced students of the Moroccan congregation Talmud Torah.[64] Also present at this event was a representative of the Comunidad Israelita Sefaradí de Buenos Aires. Education had become an important measure of success, and these communities took every chance to demonstrate to others the degree of their achievements.

Besides the sharing of resources among Sephardi schools in Argentina, there is evidence that financial support for education crossed the Atlantic. Although it was clear that the Sephardi communities in Argentina were not conceived of as transitory, links with their communities of origin remained strong. On December 26, 1935, for example, members of the Sephardi community in Colegiales (Chalom) sent a money order to the Escuelas Israelitas in Rhodes.[65] A letter to the community in Rhodes announced the soon-to-arrive check and the names of those who had contributed. Likewise, Jews from Aleppo settled in Once collected money to support religious schools in Jerusalem.[66] Pride in education, then, was not focused on schools in just Argentina; it reached into the countries of origin and Palestine/Israel, as well.

These Sephardi schools and their leaders, far from remaining apart from the broader Jewish community, strengthened ties with Ashkenazim and their institutions. Some teachers in the Sephardi schools were, in fact, Ashkenazim. Moisés Klein, for example, was the director of the school of the Chalom congregation,[67] and Matilde Hertszcovich taught in the Agudat Dodim Talmud Torah. At Yedida Efrón's suggestion, the school in Posadas, Misiones, employed Batia Goldrig in 1948 to teach Hebrew. Also at his suggestion, Or Torah school in La Boca hired Mrs. Rabinovich, the director of Cursos Religiosos (Religious Courses).[68]

An organization originally set up in connection with the JCA and the CIRA, Cursos Religiosos supervised schools in JCA agricultural colonies and financially supported Jewish schools in Buenos Aires. Or Torah probably would not have been able to survive without its support.[69] And while Cursos Religiosos did not necessarily determine the curriculum of the Or Torah school, it was able to negotiate changes that were incorporated into the school's functioning. Or Torah was thus the first Arabic-speaking community that changed its language of instruction from Arabic to Spanish.[70] The opposite could also be true: some Sephardi institutions supported Ashkenazi schools. Chalom's Talmud Torah, for instance, bought tickets in 1935 for an event organized by the Wolfsohn School (a renowned Ashkenazi institution), which was located in the same neighborhood.[71]

Connections with Ashkenazim were established not only between institutions but between individuals, as well. Given that communities used celebrations, festivals, and other social events to showcase their educational projects, it is not surprising that Sephardi congregations invited famous Ashkenazi men to such events. Max Gluksman, the president of the Ashkenazi CIRA and a well-known entrepreneur, was invited to an event the Moroccan Talmud Torah organized in 1931. Leopoldo Hirsch, president of B'nai B'rith, was invited to the same celebration. Educational events clearly became opportunities for the leaders of these Sephardi institutions to socialize with their Ashkenazi peers.

Ashkenazi and Sephardi children also found a space to share in schools. Although such intracommunity development would become more visible from the 1950s onward, we find that as early as the 1930s, Hatikvah school had several Ashkenazi students.[72] With the creation of *escuelas integrales* (integrated schools), Jewish schools that taught the Argentine curriculum, as well as Hebrew and religious topics, some Sephardi schools attracted large numbers of Ashkenazim. In 1972, for example, Chalom opened its Escuela Hebrea Integral (Integrated Hebrew School), with many Ashkenazim in attendance.[73] Parents now made Jewish educational choices with multiple considerations in mind: geography, convenience, and price.

But while conversations over schools among Sephardim and between Sephardim and Ashkenazim existed, available stories remind us that the schools, although clearly Jewish and Sephardi, were part of multiethnic neighborhoods. Picture La Boca neighborhood on June 26, 1927, at 12:45 p.m.: a procession has started in Hernandarias 831; leading it are the Argentine and "Hebrew" flags,[74] which are followed by the Jewish Orphanage Music Band, the students of the Damascene Talmud Torah, members of Unión Israelita Sefaradit Or Torah's *comisión directiva* (steering committee), and guests. The schoolchildren are "dressed in white *guardapolvos* [uniforms worn by all Argentine schoolchildren] and carrying *escarapelas* [flag buttons] and Argentine flags," and they march to the beat of the songs (*marchas*) being played by the band; all proudly walk along the streets Hernandarias, Pinzón, Patricios, and Brandsen. After five blocks, and "cheered on by the public parked on the streets," the group stops at Brandsen 1444, site of the future temple and Talmud Torah of this neighborhood's Syrian Jews. On a "well-lit and conveniently adorned" stage are the *comisario* (local chief of police) of the neighborhood, señor Atilio Palacio, on behalf of the *jefe de la policía de la capital* (chief of police of the city of Buenos Aires); the *sub-comisario* (deputy chief of police); the justice of the peace señor Garibaldi; the *oficial de justicia* (judge) señor Calabrini; and "close to 2,000 people [who] stood around the makeshift *palco* [box]." At 1:30 p.m. sharp, Rabbi Shabetay D'Jaen makes his entrance, and the event starts. The band plays both the Argentine and the Hebrew anthems, with students leading the singing. Letters from the Argentine president, the *intendente municipal* (mayor), and the Consejo Nacional de Educación (National Education Council) president are read in order, and the founding stone for the new building is finally laid in place.[75] As the president of Or Torah later put it, *"Aquello [fue] realmente imponente"* ("That was really impressive").[76]

The official opening of the synagogue of Brandsen Street two years later, in 1929, was even more impressive, according to the organization's minute books. Students of the Talmud Torah marched on April 14, 1929, again wearing white *guardapolvos* and waving Argentine flags. They were again accompanied by members of the *comisión directiva*, the Music Band of the Jewish Orphanage, and two "silk" flags: Argentine and Hebrew. The route the procession followed was the same, and the audience in Brandsen 1444 was as prestigious: *el intendente municipal* Dr. José Luis Cantilo and Comisario Días, along with delegates from various Jewish and Argentine institutions. Students intoned the lyrics of the Argentine national anthem and the Hatikvah and sang Hebrew chants in front of a Sefer Torah. Two students "correctly pronounced" Hebrew prayers, which were translated into Spanish by a member of the *comisión directiva*. The Club Boca Juniors, a neighboring organization, sent a letter congratulating them on such a joyous occasion.

Let us move to another Buenos Aires neighborhood and another Sephardi community. In 1931, the Ottoman Jews of Villa Crespo celebrated the anniversary of the May Revolution (May 25). *La Luz* reported that the event, held at the Comunidad Israelita Sefaradí de Buenos Aires on Camargo 870 on May 21, began with a welcome speech given by the organization's president, Don Aaron Levy. After the Argentine national anthem was sung by students and guests alike, Remigio Iriondo, one of the education councillors for the VII education district, gave a patriotic speech highlighting events leading up to the May Revolution and the accomplishments of the first Argentine Patriotic Government. After his talk, David Elnecavé (editor of *La Luz*) and Isaac Bensignor (secretary of the Talmud Torah) addressed the audience. Later, guests moved on to the classrooms, where they enjoyed champagne while the Unión de Damas Israelitas distributed clothes donated by Mois Chami & Alderoqui and Yohai & Acrech (two famous Jewish-owned clothing stores). Many important members of the community attended this event, as did Romulo Magnani, the *comisario* of the neighborhood; Mr. Flauquin, the chief of police's secretary; Carlos Ferrari, the former chief of police; and various delegations from Ahavat Aḥim (from Flores neighborhood), the Argentine League against Tuberculosis, the Social Jewish Club from Villa Crespo, the Chalom center, and others. David Boton was in charge of providing the music.[77]

The magazine descriptions of the opening of the temple/Talmud Torah in La Boca and the celebration of the anniversary of the May Revolution provide us with moving scenes. We see these Sephardi Jews marching in the streets, cheered on by passersby, making the neighborhood theirs, as it were, playing a visible role in their shared *barrio*. Representatives of other neighborhood societies joined them (such as the Club Atlético Boca Juniors), as did *intendentes* (mayors), *comisarios, subcomisarios,* and *jueces de paz* (justices of the peace). It is clear that Argentina ultimately played a central role in these stories and schools, although not only through the presence of Argentine "officers," such as the members of the Consejo Nacional de Educación and *jefes de policía*, who were invited to all special occasions. Argentina was present in the wearing of *guardapolvos blancos*, the waving of Argentine flags, the singing of the Argentine national anthem, the celebration of *fechas patrias* (national holidays), and the hiring of non-Jewish teachers for the instruction of *temas patrios* (patriotic themes).[78]

It is true that the government attempted to regulate these schools, as it did all immigrant schools. There was a fear that Argentina was becoming too "foreign" by allowing newcomers to instruct their children in their languages of origin, thus allowing for the immersion of educational institutions in "local" (meaning, of their countries of origin) political and educational contexts.[79] In 1938 and 1939, the Consejo Nacional de Educación passed resolutions forcing all "language and religious" schools to display Argentine national symbols, maps, and portraits of historical figures, and to teach Argentine topics. Students were also expected to learn about the meaning of the national anthem. Teachers were required to pass tests administered by government educational authorities in order to teach, and textbooks, even those in "foreign" languages, had to incorporate Argentine topics.[80]

But while it is true that in the late 1930s the government mandated that "foreign" institutions celebrate Argentine history, the above-described events in La Boca and Villa Crespo took place before the laws were passed. These schools, then, which provided religious instruction to Jewish boys and girls, became spaces in which the history of the nation was exalted and celebrated alongside a variety of neighborhood and official guests. These representatives of the state were not distant bureaucratic workers but members of the community, as well. They worked in the neighborhood where this Jewish community had settled and as such were not strangers to the members of these Jewish societies and their affairs.

The relationship between Argentine (educational) authorities and Sephardi institutions was cordial. Yesod Hadat's school, for example, celebrated the anniversaries of the May Revolution and Independence Day and received strong support from the *inspector de educación* (education inspector), the officer charged with ensuring schools followed the law.[81] The education inspector often participated in events organized by Sephardi communities, as we can see from the opening of the temple in La Boca, described above.

Many examples confirm that the celebration and exaltation of the nation was not performed only because the government legislated it.[82] In the 1930s, members of the Sephardi community in Colegiales (Chalom) raised funds to buy an Argentine flag to donate to the local state school, and they did so not as individuals but as representatives of the Sephardi congregation. The school then organized an *acto* (public ceremony) in their honor, and the congregation, in return, purchased drinks and food for the event.[83] In 1931, the recently founded Jewish magazine *La Luz* announced in an editorial that the "anniversary of the May Revolution has been enthusiastically celebrated by this glorious Argentine nation, jealous of its freedom and independence." The editor went on:

> Our coreligionists living in this blessed country, coming from all political persuasions and convictions, have also celebrated this holiday, and patriotic parties have been organized in all [Jewish] centers. We do not exaggerate when we affirm that the Jewish community in Argentina celebrates the national holidays as well as its [own national] holidays. And that is only natural. For Israel, free countries are like air to mankind. Jews, much like all other elements of the Argentine population, work toward the country's prosperity, for its progress and greatness. We [Jews] are happy living in this welcoming land. We only have one aspiration, a single wish, which is to see our new *patria* [homeland] ranked among the best nations of the Universe.[84]

This text, because of its thinly veiled Zionist rhetoric, presents the discursive possibility that the national and the ethnic were not conceived as separately compartmentalized identities. Had this text made reference to "Jews" as a religious group, the dichotomy between national and ethnic identities would have existed, but it would not have presented any contradiction; because Judaism was a religion, Jews could be citizens of any country with no question of their allegiance. The writer of this editorial, however, used language that, although vague and purposefully ambiguous (especially the reference to *patria* at the end), made no effort to explain any seeming incongruity between the organization accepting the national Argentine holidays as its own and keeping the Jewish holidays,

Marriages and Schools

as well. In fact, Jews—referred to as "Israelitas"—were made equal to all other immigrants working for the future greatness of the country where they lived.

The Argentine "patriotic past," usually celebrated by "performing" children, was also used as the foundation for "Jewish" nationalism in Argentina. In an editorial published in *La Luz* after the July celebration of Argentine Independence Day, the writer began by reminding readers of the "iron will and character of Belgrano and San Martín in their fight for [Argentine] Independence." He closed by noting, "At times when the Jewish people are making efforts to obtain their total freedom and independence, we are sure they will fight, like those men did in 1816, to achieve it."[85] For Sephardi intellectuals, like the editor of *La Luz*, General Don José de San Martín and Manuel Belgrano, great national heroes and "founders" of the nation, had become examples to follow in the fight for the Jewish state. The patriotic past, the weapon thought to instill nationalist (Argentine) beliefs, was here used to strengthen ethnic, in this case "Jewish" nationalist desires.[86]

Sephardi Talmud Torahs were not simply religious spaces used by Sephardi communities to avoid the "loss of ethnic particularity" in the face of Catholic education. They were also conceived as a way to "create" members of the new country, not members outside the rest of society. Sephardi schools were institutions that groups from various origins supported and helped, thereby strengthening a shared common "Sephardi" identity born in Argentina. Sephardi leaders from other communities and Ashkenazim participated in "educational" events, and the achievements of students were publicly celebrated, displaying a shared belief in the importance of education, itself an important tenet of Argentine liberalism. Staging events in which students wore white *guardapolvos* and sang the Argentine national anthem and the Hatikvah in front of the *intendente municipal* and the *inspector de educación* was not a contradictory choice. In fact, sharing Hebrew, Arabic, French, and Spanish, singing national anthems, and learning about Domingo Faustino Sarmiento and Theodor Herzl were ways these Sephardi immigrants constructed and acted out their Argentine and Jewish identities; Sephardi religious schools were thus instrumental in helping immigrants become Argentines.

CONCLUSION

At the beginning of *Un romance turco*, Judi and Maraj seemed doomed to remain apart, but the ambiguous ending leaves open the possibility they will choose to be together, despite Judi's initial hesitation and familial and religious differences. Judi's brother, Arim, immersed in the public education system, on the other hand, is presented as unequivocally moving toward a life of learning and an Argentine non-Jewish wife. For both Judi and Arim, Argentina, with its mixture of people and its liberal and modernizing project, represents drastic change and a dramatic rupture with the past. In contrast to that perceived unstoppable march toward a modern future that we see in the play, Sephardim warned and acted against these threats; they wrote about the consequences for marrying outside the faith, passed religious sanctions about improper conversions, shipped daughters off to other cities with more coreligionists, complained about their children's marriage choices, and sent their children to Jewish schools.

But reality was not as starkly divided along sharp black-or-white camps: an unwavering attachment to the traditional past or its complete erasure. The marriage records of Sephardi and Ashkenazi institutions suggest that Sephardim chose partners from their communities of origin but increasingly met and interacted with other Sephardim and Ashkenazim as the realities of Argentina, its neighborhoods, institutions, and practices changed. Jewish schools, although deeply committed to the maintenance of ethnic (and subethnic) identity, participated in discussions that provided for the construction of a new Jewish identity and that inculcated national (Argentine) feelings among their students. Sephardim may have married mostly their own and attended schools of their communities, but it is clear that those choices were colored, lived in, enacted, and embedded within Argentina.

POSTSCRIPT

ON JULY 18, 1994, A SUICIDE BOMBER DROVE A VAN PACKED with explosives into the AMIA building in Buenos Aires. The explosion destroyed the building, killed eighty-five people, and injured more than one hundred. It remains the deadliest terrorist attack in Argentina. More than twenty years later, with the ongoing investigations marked by incompetence and/or cover-ups, the masterminds have yet to be identified or punished. In the days immediately after the attack, most Argentines reacted to the horrific event by expressing solidarity and showing their anger, surprise, and pain.[1] Three days after the attack, in a silent march that brought together 150,000 people outside the Plaza de los dos Congresos, signs that read, "Todos somos judíos" (We Are All Jews) could be seen. The AMIA attack, however, despite its savagery, had not inspired the phrase. Rather, Mario Diament, an Argentine journalist, writer, and playwright, had used the phrase in an *El Cronista Comercial* article written the day after an attack on the Israeli Embassy in Buenos Aires more than two years earlier, on March 17, 1992. "Yesterday," he wrote, "not only the building of the Israeli Embassy was blown up. A piece of our city and our dignity blew up, too. Our people were hurt and killed. Yesterday, whether we like it or not, we were all Jews."[2]

The reemergence of the phrase after the AMIA bombing showed that these two events were seen as inextricably linked not only because of the similarity of the targets but, most important, because of the reaction to the attacks on them. If "a piece of our city and our dignity blew up" along with the embassy of a foreign country—and even when that foreign country was Israel—then the destruction of "our" Argentine Jewish community building "deserved" the phrase even more.

In the aftermath of the AMIA bombing, the need for justice, the finding and punishing of those responsible, and the fear of governmental cover-up and collaboration took the shape of meaningful performative acts, many repeated for decades to come, organized by the relatives of victims and their supporters. "Their activism," claim editors Natasha Zaretsky and Annette H. Levine in a recent book on the aftermath of the attack, "firmly places Jewish Argentines within the public register of citizenship and the struggle against impunity in a way some would argue is integral to the contemporary Argentine national imaginary."[3] While the bombings may be read as evidence of the precarious situation of Jews in Argentina, the responses to them generated discussions that made it clear that, by the mid-1990s, Argentines understood the indissoluble presence of Jews as part of Argentine society.

The "We Are All Jews" placards, so visible in the aftermath of the AMIA bombing, are not unlike those we see in marches or on social media in countries around the world when minorities (or otherwise defined civilians) are the target of violent attacks. The sentiment in all these instances is/was the same: minorities are part of the larger whole, and an assault on one is an affront to all. In the case of Argentina and its Jews, "We Are All Jews" evidenced, perhaps without awareness, another reality. Unlike what Estela Levy experienced in 1919, when she was spared by assailants because she and those around her were not seen as Jews, Sephardim in the 1990s were imagined (both by non-Jews and Ashkenazim) as being part of the Jewish community. The AMIA building housed not only the main Ashkenazi mutual aid organization but others, including the offices of the DAIA, the political body that represents Jewish institutions to the state. It was then headed by Rubén Beraja, a highly visible (Sephardi) community member recognized by all (Jews and non-Jews alike) as a Jewish leader. Thus by the 1990s Sephardim had become part of mainstream Jewish institutions, and, in Argentine society, they were no longer invisible as Jews. "We Are All Jews" signs also meant that both Ashkenazim and Sephardim were included in the word *Jews*.

This book has focused on the boundaries, always contingent and fluid, and therefore historical, that demarcated belonging. The book asked how Jews who were not seen as Jews by Argentines in 1919, and who were seen as "different Jews" by Ashkenazim, came to lead Jewish Argentine institutions that were imagined to be so "Argentine" that Argentines decried their destruction in 1994. The book charted the ways in which Sephardim lived in and maintained multiple diasporic identifications while at the same time creating new ties both to the land on which they had settled and to those living there, Jews and non-Jews alike. The focus of the book has been diasporic, yet it highlighted the existence of several overlapping diasporas that connected Argentine Sephardim to not only the promised land but to the lands of their long-gone and more immediate ancestors. But the book, while attentive to these ties, has also uncovered the ways in which *lo nacional* (the national) wove itself into this (multiple) diasporic story, creating new belongings and strengthening old ones. Sephardi (and Jewish) identity was never a given, an a priori essence; it was always in the making, in flux, a choice, and a strategy.

The boundaries that Sephardim chose to define themselves as members of multiple diasporas varied depending on the time, location, and issue at hand. For example, Argentine provincial settings (with fewer people and less resources) allowed Moroccan Jews and their descendants to contribute to both the building of the cemetery walls in Tétouan and the Moroccan synagogue in Buenos Aires. They buried their dead in cemeteries they shared with other Sephardi groups (in some smaller towns, they even shared a cemetery with Ashkenazim), worshiped among them, and financially supported the World Union of Sephardi Jews (founded in Vienna in 1925). Moroccan Jews in Buenos Aires, on the other hand, buried their dead in a cemetery exclusively reserved for Moroccan Jews, belonged to (almost) exclusively Moroccan social and religious organizations, and supported the Jewish Hospital (led by Ashkenazim), but were part of the Centro Sionista Sefaradí alongside other Sephardim.

Living in Argentina created new bonds that emphasized old diasporic identifications and formed new ones. All Sephardim attempted, at various points, to create "Argentine-wide" organizations that represented them vis-à-vis Ashkenazim as well as provided them with leadership. Some of those organizations did not last—especially those religious in nature, such as the Consistorio—but some did, such as the

Centro Sionista Sefaradí, therefore delimiting new boundaries around those who now lived in Argentina and understood their shared experience in that country as constituting a new group identity. Argentine culture also helped Sephardim defend their minority status among the Argentine Jewish community; philanthropic associations, for example, organized fundraising events in venues where Argentine organizations held theirs, and, adopting Argentine upper-middle-class ideals, they succeeded in financially supporting institutions that enabled them to assert their presence "as Sephardim" within a Jewish community that was largely Ashkenazi.

These historical processes, together with some not discussed given the temporal scope of the book (the impact of the military dictatorship and the neoliberal governments of the 1990s, for example) affected the reality of Jews in Argentina today. Many years ago, I attended the memorial service that usually takes place between Rosh Hashanah and Yom Kippur at the Sephardi cemetery in Resistencia, Chaco. The participants, however, were not only Sephardim; both Ashkenazim and Sephardim had organized this event together. The first stop was at the Sephardi burial ground, and after prayers, the group went on to repeat the ceremony in memory of the Ashkenazi dead, buried in their community space. Both services were led by members of the congregations as there was no rabbi in Resistencia to fulfill this role.

That memorial ceremony was not the only one that both groups of Jews in Resistencia shared. Friday night services were held alternatively in the Ashkenazi and Sephardi synagogues. In the absence of a permanent rabbi, each community was in charge of the service whenever it was performed in its communal center. But both Sephardim and Ashkenazim attended. In fact, most of the couples present at the Shabbat service I participated in when I visited the provincial capital were Ashkenazi-Sephardi pairs. This present reality was in stark contrast to the past that I had gleaned in their minute books, when these communities initially kept separate social centers, synagogues, and cemeteries. The picture of Jewish life now in the provinces of Argentina is similar to that in Resistencia. When I visited Tucumán and Corrientes, for example, the presidents of the Sephardi organizations underlined how much of the work was now being done *in conjunction* with Ashkenazim. Temporary hiring of rabbis for the High Holidays, support of the Jewish

Postscript

school, even municipal *actos*, now found both groups acting as a single entity, even when the existence of two synagogues, two social centers, and two cemeteries was a physical testament to the division that had once existed.

One of the reasons often cited for this "merging" of Sephardim and Ashkenazim in the interior is the shrinking number of total Jews living in these towns. By the year 2000, in the city of Corrientes, for example, there were about 150 families, of which 35 to 40 were Sephardim.[4] Although there are no exact records that would allow us to make an accurate comparison, I identified about eighty-one different Sephardi family names in the burial records of the Sephardi community for the early part of the twentieth century. Because a single family name could in fact represent two or three family units, at least, these numbers suggest a sharp decline in the existing population.[5] Migration away from interior towns to Buenos Aires, however, is by no means a Jewish phenomenon, but it becomes perhaps more evident because of the small numbers that made up these communities to start. These now even smaller communities have begun to pool the limited resources of those who remain, further reconfiguring Jewish identity.

Even in Buenos Aires, where Sephardi organizations have fared better with regard to numbers, marriages between Ashkenazim and Sephardim have altered the membership of these communities. In particular, Sephardi organizations, with fewer members than the much larger Ashkenazi organizations, suffered more clearly. "Mixed" families, in which both traditions are represented, made belonging to a Sephardi or an Ashkenazi organization no longer a given, no longer an easy choice. Whereas in the past marriage choice for the young usually involved a partner from the same geographical community, it is clear from the information presented in chapter 6 that newer marriages were not necessarily all endogamous. The percentage of intracommunity weddings continued to rise as these communities moved into the 1980s and 1990s.[6]

Another important development among Sephardi congregations in Argentina, and not discussed here, given the chronology, is the recent (for most) move toward stricter religious observance. Sephardi identity has been reshaped in conversation with religious beliefs and practice, but whereas these were not the only axes in the past, Sephardi identity today for members of these congregations is deeply embedded in stricter

Orthodox observance. Sephardi congregations in the past provided a space that was primarily religious but not exclusively so; now even that social aspect is wrapped up in religious practices and rituals.

These developments have undoubtedly reconfigured the present meaning of the term *Jewish community* in Argentina. Whereas insistence on endogamous marriages (especially by the members of Sephardi communities) once assured continuation of the identity of these communities, the now reconfigured boundaries have moved outside geographically specific groups to include Jews who in the past had clearly not belonged. Dwindling numbers, however, should not be assumed to be the only reason for this change. The growth and creation of Jewish institutions employing a discourse of belonging that stressed "Argentine" character undoubtedly contributed to the existence of other Jewish spaces for social interaction. Whereas Sephardi youth had once only attended dances or other social events organized by their own Sephardi organizations, the growing importance of places like Sociedad Hebraica Argentina (Argentine Jewish Society), Organización Hebrea Argentina Macabi (Jewish Argentine Organization–Maccabi), and Club Naútico Hacoaj, for example, undoubtedly allow for the social "mixing" of Jewish youth.[7] These new (Argentine) social spaces are also, in large part, responsible for the reconfiguration of existing boundaries.

It is true that these new institutions (or old ones, evolving) would not have been successful in bringing into their membership mixed Jewish groups if the potential members themselves did not find reference to their "Argentineness" true and meaningful. The generations that came after the 1960s, who were born and raised in Argentina, clearly understood their ethnicity in different terms than their parents did. Their connection to the new country presented commonalities no longer centered on their ethnic past, but on a present that allowed for the evaluation and re-creation of their understanding of ethnicity. While this book has not examined in detail how the understanding of ethnicity changed for this generation, its reconfiguration highlights, once more, the need to conceive *ethnicity* and *community* as terms that are historical in nature, and thus susceptible to, and the product of, change.

The story this book tells may sound like a negative progression toward the death of individual communities, as it contrasts the strong

Postscript

desire of groups in the past to keep firm boundaries around their co-nationals (or those from the same regions) to a present characterized by a much more inclusive understanding of the term *Jewish community*. Minorities, it can be argued, may attempt to defend their visibility but end up suffering the seemingly unstoppable advance of the hegemonic group's practices. Although there is a reference to the now "Argentine" character of the Jewish community—which would seem to indicate neither a fully Ashkenazi nor a fully Sephardi identity—the fact remains that Ashkenazi culture is still much more prevalent.

But these new configurations of Jewish Argentine identity do not mean now, as they did not mean in the past, the erasure of particular inherited memories and traditions. (Jewish) Argentines can now attend events coordinated and sponsored by two Sephardi educational organizations that continue to emphasize the experiences of past generations in specific locales; Jewish Argentines can learn about Moroccan brit milah practices, hear about Maimonides and mysticism, and about the emigration of Jews from the Arab world starting in the 1940s; they can take weekly Ladino lessons and attend Ladino concerts. There is a weekly radio program that discusses Sephardi issues and topics of interest, as well as an annual international research conference on Sephardi Studies.[8] A very diverse and exciting offer in terms of Ashkenazi culture is, of course, also available.

Ultimately, the study presented in this book, and the reality of Argentine Jewish life today reminds us that diaspora(s) can be multiple, and are made up of flexible, changing, and overlapping but nonetheless strong ties to real and imagined lands, people, and practices. That a Jewish Argentine (whose parents came from Morocco very early in the twentieth century), living in Buenos Aires, frequents a synagogue founded by Jews from Rhodes, sent her children to state schools, attended parties in Buenos Aires organized by the Moroccan Embassy to celebrate the birthdays of King Hassan II and King Mohammed VI, spends weekends in the Jewish Social Club Macabi, continues to serve Moroccan Jewish delicacies to her family (now made up of Ashkenazim, Sephardim originally from Rhodes, and non-Jews), and drinks *mate* every morning illustrates the complex but meaningful ways in which Jews relate and maintain connections to their multiple pasts and diverse presents.

NOTES

INTRODUCTION

1. "Ashkenazim" are those Jews whose culture developed in the Rhine River Valley and northern France, moving eastward from the eleventh through the thirteenth centuries, and back to Western Europe in the seventeenth and eighteen centuries. *Sephardim* is the term used to describe those Jews who lived on the Iberian Peninsula until their expulsion in 1492. See Zohar, "A Global Perspective on Sephardic and Mizrahi Jewry," 6–8.

2. Levy, *Crónica de una familia sefaradí*, 79. *Turcos* was an umbrella term used to describe immigrants from the Ottoman Empire, regardless of religion.

3. Feldman, "Buenos Aires, 1919."

4. Ibid., 35.

5. Levy, *Crónica de una familia sefaradí*, 11.

6. Moya remarks on this desire of immigrants to emphasize the "individual" character of their migratory experience, but confirms that "most emigrated as part of social networks rather than as isolated individuals." See *Cousins and Strangers*, 391.

7. Most scholarly material and memoirs by Sephardi immigrants were indeed published in the last decades of the twentieth century. See, for example, Arditti, *Izmir, París, Buenos Aires*; Levy and Reinoso, *La vida, según Marcos Levy*; Gutkowski, *Erase una vez ... Sefarad*; Centro Educativo Sefaradí (CES), *Presencia sefaradí*; Silberman de Cywiner, *Inmigrantes sefardíes, memoria y tradición*; Bejarano, "Los sefaradies de la Argentina." There are, of course, some exceptions; see, for example, Elnecave, "Los sefaradies en la Argentina."

8. Her memoirs, and Levy, *Cocina sefaradí*.

9. Levy, *Crónica de una familia sefaradí*, 12.

10. Moisés Camji, another Sephardi, was vice president in the 1980s. See CES, *Presencia sefaradí*, 130, 78.

11. All quotes in this paragraph are from Levy, *Crónica de una familia sefaradí*, 12.

12. For a description of how diasporas are constituted both negatively and positively, see Clifford, "Diasporas," 310–11.

13. Zenner, *A Global Community*, chap. 2.

14. Levy, *Crónica de una familia sefaradí*, 50–52.

15. Ibid., 92.

16. Ibid., 91.

17. Ibid., 73.

18. Ibid., 91.

19. Ibid., 92.

20. Ashkenazim had their own institutions (ibid., 91). Non-Jewish turcos and árabes also settled in different parts of the city. See Flores, *La integración social de los inmigrantes*, 47–51, 69–72.

21. Levy, *Crónica de una familia sefaradí*, 91.

22. Ray, "New Approaches to the Jewish Diaspora."

23. Some scholars even suggest that diaspora is indeed what has defined Jewish identity, and not a claim to a land; see Boyarin and Boyarin, "Diaspora," 723.

24. Kobrin, *Jewish Bialystok and Its Diaspora*, 18. Phillips Cohen also showed the process by which Sephardim became attached to, and expressed their loyalty to, the Ottoman Empire; see *Becoming Ottomans*.

25. Kobrin, *Jewish Bialystok and Its Diaspora*.

26. Bejarano and Aizenberg, *Contemporary Sephardic Identity in the Americas*, xv.

27. Horowitz discusses a similar process in Israel among Arab Jews: the construction of a pan-ethnic Mizrahi community alongside their strong connections to their "particular homes in specific Muslim countries"; see *Mediterranean Israeli Music*, 34.

28. These terms signal, according to their users, the centrality of the diasporic/transnational (Latin American Jews) or the ethno-national/regional (Jewish Latin Americans). See Lesser and Rein, "New Approaches to Ethnicity and Diaspora in Twentieth-Century Latin America," 24–25.

29. Ibid., 25.

30. See, for example, Avni et al., "Cuarenta años de cambios"; Liwerant and Senkman, "Diásporas y transnacionalismo."

31. For a few examples of the re-diasporization of Latin American Jews, see Roniger and Babis, "Latin American Israelis"; Brodsky, "Belonging to Many Homes."

32. Lesser and Rein, "Challenging Particularity."

33. Those Jews autochthonous to the Middle East who remained there after AD 70 are called Oriental or Mizrahi Jews. See Zohar, "A Global Perspective on Sephardic and Mizrahi Jewry"; Shohat, "The Invention of the Mizrahim."

34. Rodrigue, "The Sephardim in the Ottoman Empire," 177.

35. Levy, *Crónica de una familia sefaradí*, 18, 54.

36. See Gutkowski, *Erase una vez... Sefarad*, chap. 7.

37. Rodrigue, "Eastern Sephardi Jewry," 84.

38. Abitbol, "The Integration of North African Jews in France," 249.

39. Ben-Ur, *Sephardic Jews in America*.

40. Miller, "Kippur on the Amazon." Yet her focus remained on Morocco.

41. Bejarano and Aizenberg, *Contemporary Sephardic Identity in the Americas*.

42. Contreras, "Family and Patronage"; Hordes, "Inquisition and the Crypto-Jewish"; Lazar, "Scorched Parchments and Tortured Memories"; Silverblatt, "New Christians and New World Fears"; Kagan and Morgan, *Atlantic Diasporas*.

43. Aizenberg, "Nuevos mundos halló Colón," 31–32.

44. Ibid.

45. Germani, *Política y sociedad*, 198. The other countries are the United States, Canada, Brazil, Australia, and the British West Indies.

46. Ibid. Germani asserts that in the United States the proportion of immigrants per total population never exceeded 14.4 percent, a figure that represents the lowest percentage in the history of immigration to Argentina (in 1947).

47. Solberg, *Immigration and Nationalism*; Castro, *The Development and Politics of Argentine Immigration Policy*.

48. The reports issued by the Argentine immigration authorities focused on the nationality of the newcomers. The reports included numbers for "declared religion," but we can assume not all Jews reported this fact. The Jewish organizations in charge of immigration, on the other hand, only kept track of some Jews (those using the services of these organizations), and not of those coming from the Sephardi world or of those who came on their own. See, for example, Alsina, *Memoria de la Dirección de Inmigración Correspondiente al año 1909*.

49. Della Pergola, "Demographic Trends of Latin American Jewry," 92; Baily, *Immigrants in the Lands of Promise*, 59; Moya, *Cousins and Strangers*, 149.

50. Castro, *The Development and Politics of Argentine Immigration Policy*.

51. Huberman, *Gauchos and Foreigners*; Ludmer, *The Gaucho Genre*.

52. Horowitz, *Israeli Ecstasies/Jewish Agonies*, 138.

53. Gerchunoff, *The Jewish Gauchos of the Pampas*.

54. Much has been written about Gerchunoff and his idea of Jewish assimilation. For recent examples, see Aizenberg, *Books and Bombs in Buenos Aires*; Freidenberg, *The Invention of the Jewish Gaucho*.

55. JCA, *Jewish Colonization Association*, 93.

56. Avni and Seibert, "La agricultura judía en la Argentina," 537.

57. See Della Pergola, "Demographic Trends of Latin American Jewry," 113; Winsberg, "Jewish Agricultural Colonization in Entre Ríos, Argentina," 295.

58. *Sephardim* was not, of course, a term used in the census questionnaire. See Cohen, "Aspéctos sociodemográficos," 64.

59. Censo Nacional de Población, 1960.

60. Weill, *Población israelita en la República Argentina*, 11.

61. Elnecave, "Los sefaradíes en la Argentina," 57.

62. American Jewish Committee, *Estudio demográfico de la colectividad sefaradí*; Elnecave, "Los sefaradíes en la Argentina"; Mirelman, *Jewish Buenos Aires*; Avni, "Argentine Jewry"; Rodgers, *Los judíos de Alepo*.

63. See Vilar, *Tetuán en el resurgimiento judío contemporáneo*, chap. 3.

64. For Moroccan immigration to Brazil and Portugal, see Vilar, "La emigración judeo-marroquí a la América Latina"; Miller, "Kippur on the Amazon"; Dias, "The Jewish Community in the Azores."

65. Many Moroccan Jews who married in Buenos Aires were born in Brazil or Venezuela. Their dates of birth range from 1893 to 1929. See Congregación Israelita Latina, Actas de Matrimonio, No. 25, 41, 55, 59, 64, 70, 86, 91.

66. Bunis, "Modernization and the Language Question among Judezmo-Speaking Sephardim of the Ottoman Empire," 239.

67. CES, *Presencia sefaradí en la Argentina*, 78.

68. Klich, "Arabes, judíos y árabes judíos en la Argentina de la primera mitad del novecientos," 121–122.

69. Ibid., 113–114.

70. By 1960, 84 percent of the members of the organized Jewish community lived in this city and its suburbs. Sephardim seem to follow this trend, as sixty-four of the eighty-seven main Sephardi institutions are located in Buenos Aires. See information by Schmelz and Della Pergola cited in Cohen, "Aspéctos sociodemográficos de la comunidad sefaradita de la Argentina."

71. Avni, *Argentina and the Jews*.

72. Lvovich, *Nacionalismo y antisemitismo en la Argentina*, 158, 62; Deutsch, *Las Derechas*.

73. Rein, *Los muchachos peronistas judíos*.

74. Moya, *Cousins and Strangers*, chap. 4; Baily, "Patrones de residencia de los italianos en Buenos Aires y Nueva York, 1880–1914."

75. Levy, *Crónica de una familia sefaradí*, 50.

76. Horowitz, *Argentina's Radical Party*, 50.

77. Most of these leftist activists were Ashkenazim. For women's participation, see Deutsch, *Crossing Borders, Claiming a Nation*, chaps. 6 and 7.

78. Rein, *Los muchachos peronistas judíos*.

1. BURYING THE DEAD

1. Englander, *The Ministry of Special Cases*, 1; Yehuda Amichai, "Ha-'ananimhem ha-metim ha-rishonim," in *Shirim*, 128. I thank Adriana X. Jacobs for her input on the translation of Amichai's line.

2. This organization is best known as Zwi Migdal, a name taken in 1927, at the request of the Polish ambassador and the Esras Noschim society (local branch of the London-based Society for the Protection of Girls and Women). It was originally Sociedad Israelita de Socorros Mutuos Varsovia (Jewish Mutual Aid Society of Warsaw), and it jointly purchased land to enlarge the cemetery with the Sociedad Israelita de Socorros Mutuos Ashkenasum (Jewish Mutual Aid Society Ashkenazim). See Brá, *La organización negra*, 27; Alsogaray, *Trilogía de la trata de blancas*, 123–124; Levy, *La mancha de la Migdal*; Yarfitz, "Polacos, White Slaves, and Stille Chuppahs."

3. Liachovitzky, *Zamlbuch*, 89ff., cited in Mirelman, *Jewish Buenos Aires*, 208.

4. Barth, "Ethnic Groups and Boundaries," 301.

5. Ibid.

6. Hall, "Cultural Identity and Diaspora."

7. Boyarin and Boyarin, "Diaspora: Generation and the Ground of Jewish Identity," 721.

8. Voekel, *Alone before God*; Reis, *Death Is a Festival*.

9. Meyer, *Ethnicity and the American Cemetery*; Ferro, "El oficio de los muertos"; Mato and Vizzari, *Angeles de Buenos Aires*; Pereira, *À flor da terra*.

10. Ehl, Parik, and Fiedler, *Old Bohemian and Moravian Jewish Cemeteries*; Halporn, "American Jewish Cemeteries"; Ben-Ur and Frankel, *Remnant Stones*.

11. See Toker and Weinstein, *Sitios de la memoria*, 19.

12. See, for example, (Moisesville Archive) Escritura [land title] No. 43, August 31, 1940.

13. Gallo, *Farmers in Revolt*, 5.

14. Curzón, "Presencia judía en la ciudad de Santa Fé," 6.

15. According to Jewish law, the dead can be moved only from a non-Jewish cemetery to a Jewish cemetery, or from a Jewish cemetery in the diaspora to one in Israel.

16. It is difficult to calculate the exact number of Jews living in Santa Fé in the first decades of the twentieth century. Forty families founded the cemetery in 1895, and fifty-four founded the Ashkenazi cemetery in 1916. Not many more than one hundred families were likely settled in the city by then. See Curzón, "Presencia judía en la ciudad de Santa Fé."

17. Among the groups who settled in the province there were Swiss, German, Austrian, and British immigrants, many of whom were not Catholic. Because cemetery lands had been consecrated by the Catholic Church, city governments understood the desire of other religious denominations to bury their dead according to other rites (and *not* in consecrated land). It is interesting to see that the provision included Arabs. See ibid., 7; Gallo, *Farmers in Revolt*, 6.

18. The term *dissident* refers to Protestants. The first Dissidents' Cemetery was founded in 1821, located in Juncal, between Cerrito and Carlos Pellegrini. Although it was ordered to close in 1824, it was used until 1831, when the second cemetery was purchased. See Nuñez, *Almario de Buenos Aires*, 27–28, 46–47; Bianchi, *Historia de las religiones*, 27.

19. See Nuñez, *Almario de Buenos Aires*, 64.

20. Although it seems that the British and German communities told the Jewish community as early as 1897 that they could no longer use their land, Jewish burials still took place until 1900. See Mirelman, *Jewish Buenos Aires*, 80.

21. This is the official date of the constitution of this organization. In 1885, a commission from CIRA acted as a de facto Hevra Kedusha both in petitions to the government for permission to open a burial ground and in matters of ritual in burials in the Dissidents' Cemeteries. See Lewin, *La colectividad judía*, 45; Mirelman, *Jewish Buenos Aires*, 78–82.

22. Although the legal name was Congregación Israelita de la República Argentina, it sometimes was called Congregación Israelita de Buenos Aires; CIRA, Libros de Actas [Minute Books], from September 6, 1885, to October 20, 1894. The topic of the cemetery came up in the meetings of July 29, 1886; September 30, 1888; and September 4, 1890. They petition the city government for a property on November 14 and December 27, 1888.

23. I have identified two Moroccan last names from the minutes of the CIRA for the years 1885 and 1890: Benzaquén and Hassan.

24. This group created a Bikur Holim (organization to provide medical care), and later a school. See Wolff, Schalom, and Zago, *Judíos y argentinos*, 16.

25. For example, Buenos Aires Rabbi Joseph, married to a Protestant German woman (who later converted to Judaism), and whose daughter married out of the Jewish faith, in his will requested to be buried according to Jewish ritual.

26. Mirelman cites Moroccan Jews living in Rio Cuarto (Córdoba), and in Tucumán, who were members of the Ashkenazi Hevra Kedusha. See Mirelman, *Jewish Buenos Aires*, 79.

27. Ibid., 80–81.

28. For a description of the extent of the white slave trade, see Bristow, *Prostitution and Prejudice*; Guy, *Sex and Danger in Buenos Aires*. For an investigation of the "construction" of the very notion of the "white slave" trade, see Yarfitz, "Polacos, White Slaves, and Stille Chuppahs."

29. This was mostly an Ashkenazi phenomenon. For a thorough discussion

of numbers of Jewish prostitutes and prostitutes of other origins, see Yarfitz, "Polacos, White Slaves, and Stille Chuppahs," 92.

30. The fear of "infiltration" extended into later decades, as well. See "Por la salud moral de la colectividad," *Mundo Israelita*, June 18, 1927, cover: "It is the duty of the leaders of [Jewish] organizations to make sure, by any means, that our community [*organismo social*] remains uncontaminated." In the same newspaper, there was a report on the rejection of a donation made to the "Ḥevra Kedusha" "because of moral reasons, as the origin of such a donation could not be ascertained." See *Mundo Israelita*, March 15, 1924, 2. See also "Una elogiable iniciativa de la Chevrah Keduschah [*sic*]" in *Israel*, February 13, 1925, 1.

31. See Yarfitz, "Sociedad Varsovia as Voluntary Society; Mirelman, *Jewish Buenos Aires*, chap. 9. For a description of a similar organization in Brazil, see Brá, *La organización negra*; Kushnir, *Baile de mascaras*.

32. The Guemilut Ḥasadim records give 1898 as the date of death of the first burial. It is unclear, however, if the plot was used before the official paperwork was ready, or if this is another case of a body originally buried in a non-Jewish cemetery. The property was purchased in the names of José Roffé and Abraham Sefaty, who promised to register it in the name of Guemilut Ḥasadim once the organization was legally accepted by the state. See Guemilut Ḥasadim, Burial Record lists, and "Entusiasta demostración pública," *Israel*, May 27, 1927, 11.

33. There was another "impure" cemetery outside Rosario, province of Santa Fé, located inside the municipal cemetery grounds. See Levy, *La mancha de la Migdal*, 269; Resta and Borga, *Pichincha y después*, 61–85.

34. The source historians make reference to is Jacobo Liachovitzky, the founder of the first Zionist organization in Buenos Aires; see his *Zamlbuch*. This theory has been repeated by some historians of the Jewish community in Argentina; see Bejarano, "El cementerio y la unidad comunitaria," 14; Armony, "Los cementerios judios de Buenos Aires," 24.

35. "Although we had nothing to do . . . [with the Zwi Migdal], we still take care of it [their cemetery]; Guahnon, "Cuenta tu pueblo, y contarás el mundo," 6.

36. See Brá, *La organización negra*, especially chap. 3; "La mutual de los rufianes"; Levy, *La mancha de la Migdal*, 77–78. The dates for the purchase of the "impure" cemetery differ by five years in various accounts. The "impure" association seems to have purchased more land in 1926 to expand the cemetery. See Yarfitz, "Sociedad Varsovia as Voluntary Society."

37. Jews continued being buried in Flores until 1935, well after the opening of Liniers. Historian Boleslao Lewin claims that eight hundred Jews were buried there; see *Cómo fué la inmigración judía a la Argentina*, 61. The Argentine Jewish Genealogical Association (AGJA) has been able to identify 887 dead buried in this cemetery who were later transferred to the Jewish cemetery in Liniers. See Armony, "Cementerio de Flores," 26–27.

38. Municipal Council Resolution, December 30, 1921. Cited in Alfonsín, "La historia del cementerio israelita no habilitado de La Paternal," 24.

39. See the annual balance of the Executive Committee of the Ḥevra Kedusha in *Mundo Israelita*, January 23, 1927, 2.

40. According to oral legend, some burials had taken place even before it

officially opened; Alfonsín, "La historia del cementerio israelita no habilitado de la Paternal," 25.

41. After this resolution, no new cemetery has ever opened within Buenos Aires city limits. Cited in ibid., 24. Nuñez, *Almario de Buenos Aires*, 78–79.

42. "La cuestión del nuevo cementerio Judío," *Mundo Israelita*, January 9, 1926, 2.

43. See Mirelman, *Jewish Buenos Aires*, chap. 10.

44. See chapter 3 for more on these institutions.

45. See, for example, "Ḥevra Kedusha: Memoria y balance: Subsidios y ayuda a los menesterosos," *Mundo Israelita*, January 9, 1926, 2.

46. Ḥevra Kedusha Minute Book, November 11, 1931, cited in Mirelman, *Jewish Buenos Aires*, 230. Although the new constitution was presented in 1931, it took nearly two decades to actually transform the Ḥevra Kedusha into the Kehila.

47. "La Cuestión del Nuevo Cementerio Judío," 2.

48. Ibid.

49. This last purchase had been an Ashkenazi Orthodox cemetery created in 1952 by an independent Orthodox organization as a result of conflict over a subsidy for religious schools. When the AMIA refused to continue supporting the Orthodox schools, the parent organization left the AMIA and bought their own cemetery plot for their members. In 1957, the dispute was settled, with the subsidy reinstated, and the threat to AMIA's control over Ashkenazi death and burial dissipated; see Armony, "Historia de cementerios," 136. For the only Ashkenazi cemetery (besides the one owned by the "impure" Zwi Migdal) in the province of Buenos Aires that does not belong to the Ashkenazi Ḥevra Kedusha, see Rebrij, "Comunidad judía de Lomas de Zamora."

50. A similar argument is made by Gabriel Ferro in his analysis of Italian mutual aid societies in Santa Fé, Argentina; see "El oficio de los muertos."

51. Ḥesed VeEmet, Minute Book, May 21, 1905.

52. Ḥesed VeEmet was challenged by Kanfe Yona, founded at the end of the 1920s. See chapter 2 for more on this.

53. See Bene Emet, Minute Books, November 1913, December 30, 1913, January 19, 1914, and July 15, 1914.

54. Steps toward purchasing a cemetery seem to have started in 1921; see Rodgers, *Los judíos de Alepo*, 42.

55. They began discussions with the Ashkenazi Ḥevra Kedusha in 1928 and signed the agreement in 1929. See Ḥesed Shel Emet Sefaradit, Minute Books, November 12, 1928, and September 8, 1929.

56. Indeed the Ladino-speaking community participated in the purchase by advancing the money needed; Ḥesed Shel Emet, Minute Books, July 4, 1926, and July 18, 1926.

57. The 1930 coup d'état was the first in Argentina, removing democratically elected President Hipólito Yrigoyen from power. The suggestion that Lieutenant General José Félix Uriburu signed off such a big parcel to a (relatively small) Jewish community may corroborate the thesis proposed most recently by Daniel Lvovich regarding the existence of different positions on the "Jewish question" among nationalists during the early 1930s; see his *Nacionalismo y antisemitismo*, chap. 5.

58. Interview with former president of AHASM, Alberto Amiras, August 1998. The official story of the Ashkenazi Ḥevra Kedusha, however, says that they bought the parcel and gave parts of it to the AHASM. Amiras forcefully rejected this position, claiming the title was in the name of AHASM, which was the

organization that received the donation, and then the AHASM gave parts of the cemetery to the Ashkenazi group. For the official Hevra Kedusha version, see AMIA, *Comunidad judía de Buenos Aires 1894–1994*, 154. For the Sephardi version, see CES, *Presencia sefaradí*, 74.

59. Cited in Mirelman, *Jewish Buenos Aires*, 79–80.

60. Ibid., 79.

61. See Dobrinsky, *A Treasury of Sephardic Laws and Customs*, chap. 5. Cohen, *Becoming Ottomans*, 45–46.

62. See story regarding Ornstein in Armony, "Historia de cementerios," 149–150.

63. See, for example, Bene Emet, Libro de Cuentas [Account Book], 1914. Entries show Bene Emet paid the Ashkenazi Hevra Kedusha for the burial of three members.

64. Hesed Shel Emet Sefaradit, Minute Books, 1927. Jewish law requires that burials take place as soon as possible.

65. See, for example, Hesed Shel Emet, Minute Book, November 8, 1925.

66. The same complaint regarding the Ashkenazi burial society's imposing "lucrative requirements" was voiced by the Sephardim of San Juan province as justification for purchasing land for a "Sephardi" cemetery. See "La Sociedad Israelita Latina de Socorros Mutuos adquiere terreno y permiso para cementerio," *Israel*, August 14, 1925, 19.

67. See Hesed Shel Emet, Minute Book, April 25, 1926.

68. Guemilut Hasadim, Minute Book, February 20, 1930.

69. See Hesed VeEmet, Minute Book, July 31, 1909.

70. Ibid.

71. Jewish honor has been discussed in the literature on the Argentine Jewish community, in connection with the existence of prostitution rings and white slavery. "Honorable" Jews were those who did not participate in such activities, and those who did have been described as "outsiders." See, for example, Mirelman, "The Jewish Community versus Crime."

72. See, for example, the Estatutos (bylaws) of the Asociación Israelita Latina de Corrientes (Spanish Jewish Association of Corrientes), 1924: "All those wishing to become members, should fill out a form.... The request for admission will be made public and shown on the walls of our social club for fifteen days. Members who question the moral standing of the candidate should address the Steering Committee with a written statement." And the bylaws of Hesed VeEmet, 1928: "To become a member, the candidate should a) be an Argentine or foreign Jew (regardless of age and sex) and have a good reputation."

73. I have found evidence of various incidents in Resistencia in which the organization was asked to intervene in disputes between members who had "offended" each other's good name. See, for example, Hesed VeEmet (Resistencia), Minute Books, October 13, 1932, October 18, 1932, and November 5, 1933.

74. There is evidence of a personal card, belonging to a very influential member, being attached to another person's application for membership in a communal organization. I have found no evidence of this in connection with burial, though. See, for example, letter written by Aljadeff, Johai y Galante on behalf of Sr. Yeuscua Soriano [*sic*], July 24, 1934, to ACISBA.

75. CAHJP, Primer libro de entierros [First Book of Burials], Hesed VeEmet, Resistencia.

76. Registro de entierros [Register of Burials], Asociación Israelita Latina de Corrientes.

77. For Santa Fé, Resistencia and Córdoba immigration patterns, see Curzón, "Presencia judía"; Rubin, *Historia de la comunidad israelita sefaradí*; Mazo, *Historia de los ashkenazim de Resistencia*.

78. A comparison of the founding dates of Ashkenazi social or religious organizations to the dates of the opening of their cemeteries shows the latter opened much later.

79. AGJA, register of burials in Santa Fé Cemetery.

80. Register of burials in the Resistencia Sephardi cemetery. See also Mazo, *Historia de los ashkenazim de Resistencia*, 224.

81. Register of burials in the Corrientes Sephardi cemetery.

82. See Curzón, "Presencia Judía," 10.

83. The currency of Argentina from 1881 to 1970 was the peso *moneda nacional*, abbreviated here as m$n.

84. Ḥesed VeEmet, Resistencia, Minute Book, May 27, 1933.

85. Ibid., January 22, 1933.

86. Ibid., October 17, 1933.

87. CAHJP #7672/1, Letter to the President of Ḥesed VeEmet, October 2, 1935.

88. CAHJP #7672/2, Letter to the President of Ḥesed VeEmet, January 4, 1937.

89. Ḥesed VeEmet, Resistencia, Minute Books, October 1, 1928.

90. Ḥesed VeEmet, Resistencia, Minute Books, January 1, 1930.

91. Stillborn babies do not require burial, but babies born alive do.

92. Ḥesed VeEmet, Resistencia, Minute Book, May 19, 1933.

93. Ashkenazi Ḥevra Kedusha, Minute Books, cited in Curzón, "Presencia judía," 8.

94. The Sociedad Israelita Salteña "La Union" de Socorros Mutuos was founded in October 1917, only two months before the purchase of the land. See *Israel* A. 2 No. 18, 385.

95. See *Israel*, July 9, 1918, 425.

96. See Rubin, *Historia de la comunidad israelita sefaradí*, 5.

97. CES, *Presencia sefaradí*, 119.

98. See the bylaws of "Asociación Fraternal Israelita de Pcia. R. S. Peña, Chaco," founded in September 1923.

99. Silberman de Cywiner, *Asociación Israelita Sefaradí de Beneficencia de Tucumán*.

100. See "La chevrah Keduschhah [sic] de Paraná," *Israel*, November 6, 1927, 3.

101. See *Israel*, July 9, 1918. See map 2.3.

102. First book of burials, Ḥesed VeEmet.

103. The members living in Sáenz Peña stopped paying their dues to the Resistencia association in 1923, the year the local Jewish cemetery opened. See Book of Burials, Asociación Fraternal Israelita de Presidencia Roque Sáenz Peña.

104. The Jewish community in Tucumán was granted a section of the Cementerio del Norte and used it until 1926, when the Burial Society purchased land for the Jewish cemetery that is still in use today. See Blumenfeld, *Historia de la comunidad israelita de Tucumán*, 49; Cohen de Chervonagura, *La comunidad judía de Tucumán*; and *La Luz*, Año 1, no. 27, 524.

105. The persistence of the idea of "Sephardi superiority" also served as the basis for an "essential" identity among Sephardim; see Ben-Ur, *Sephardic Jews in America*, chap. 2.

106. For a recent journal issue that stresses the multiplicity of Sephardi identities, see Lehmann, "Introduction: Sephardi Identities."

107. See Bejarano, "El cementerio y la unidad comunitaria"; Mirelman, "Sephardic Immigration to Argentina"; and Cohen, "Aspéctos socio-demográficos."

108. *All* cemetery walls mark, first and foremost, the distinction between death and life.

2. HELPING THE LIVING

1. "Legión de Voluntarios Kanfe Yona (Sefaradí)," *Israel*, June 3, 1927, 8.

2. Ibid.

3. "La Labor Encomiable de la 'Legión de Voluntarios Kanfe Yona,'" *Israel*, September 23 and 30, 1927.

4. Club Alianza, Minute Book, December 23, 1952.

5. "La Labor Encomiable."

6. It is impossible to ascertain whether non-Moroccans ever became members or received aid from Kanfe Yona, since no books from the organization have survived, but I think this unlikely.

7. CAHJP #7672/1, letter written by Marcos Botbol, Kanfe Yona president, to the Jewish community Ḥesed VeEmet in Resistencia, on September 3, 1929.

8. See, for example, Penslar, *Shylock's Children*; Green, "To Give and to Receive."

9. The process of Ottoman modernization, especially in the second half of the nineteenth century, has been the focus of many studies. For the ways this relates to Jewish communities and philanthropy, see Rodrigue, "The Sephardim in the Ottoman Empire"; Daccarett, "Jewish Social Services in Late Ottoman Salonica"; and Harel, *Syrian Jewry in Transition*, 58–76.

10. Meir, "From Community Charity to National Welfare"; Green, "Sir Moses Montefiore and the Making of the 'Jewish International'"; Penslar, *Shylock's Children*, especially chap. 5.

11. Kobrin, "The Politics of Philanthropy."

12. Some oral histories were carried out by the author, while others were collected in a book and a chapter by Gutkowski. Gutkowski, *Erase una vez ... Sefarad* and "Estampas del mundo sefaradí,"

13. Gutkowski, "Estampas del mundo sefaradí," 36.

14. Ibid.

15. Gutkowski, *Erase una vez ... Sefarad*. Jaime Angel was the owner of the pharmacy that gave medicine to the poor, and was paid by Bikkur Ḥolim.

16. Ibid., 204. This organization fed around 850 children daily; Daccarett, "Jewish Social Services in Late Ottoman Salonica," 43.

17. Gutkowski, *Erase una vez ... Sefarad*, 396. M. Mitchell Serels cites the same practice in Morocco; see "Aspects of the Effects of Jewish Philanthropic Societies in Morocco."

18. Cited in Serels, "Aspects of the Effects of Jewish Philanthropic Societies in Morocco," 107.

19. In some very big cities, like Istanbul or Izmir, Jews lived in different sections. Most prominent members could afford homes outside the usually poorer Jewish quarter. Many events were designed to bring together those providing support and those receiving it. See, for example, the "Halbasha" Ceremony—also spelled "Albascha"—during which orphans received clothes and shoes; "Recordando la fiesta de la 'Albascha' en Monastir," *Israel*, July 1929, 13; and Daccarett, "Jewish

Social Services in Late Ottoman Salonica."

20. Gutkowski, *Erase una vez... Sefarad*, 366; Molho, *Usos y Costumbres*, 169.

21. Gutkowski, *Erase una vez... Sefarad*, 261.

22. Ibid., 278.

23. Ibid., 279.

24. Angel, *The Jews of Rhodes*, 123.

25. This process was not without violence and conflict, of course; see Bushnell and Macaulay, *The Emergence of Latin America*.

26. There were, of course, mutual aid organizations around specific trades that predated massive immigration to Argentina; see Munck, "Mutual Benefit Societies in Argentina," 577. Existing philanthropic organizations were, if not ethnic, most likely with close ties to the church.

27. See ibid.; Martinez, *Tercer censo nacional, levantado el 1° de junio de 1914*; and Comisión Interparlamentaria, "Censo de mutualidades."

28. The literature on these societies is vast. For some of the newer material, see Guy, *Women Build the Welfare State*; Baily, "Las sociedades de ayuda mutua"; Devoto, "Las Sociedades Italianas de Ayuda Mutua"; Devoto and Miguez, *Asociacionismo, trabajo e identidad étnica*; Devoto, "La experiencia mutualista italiana en la Argentina"; Fernandez, "El mutualismo español"; Moya, *Cousins and Strangers*, especially chap. 6; Bestene, "Formas de asociacionismo"; Boulgourdjian, "Inmigrantes armenios en Buenos Aires"; Munck, "Mutual Benefit Societies in Argentina"; Otero, "El asociacionismo francés en la Argentina."

29. Comisión Interparlamentaria, "Censo de mutualidades."

30. Ibid.

31. The breakdown is as follows: two in the city of Buenos Aires, seven in the province of Buenos Aires, one in San Juan province, and one in Salta province (ibid.). As far as I can ascertain, none of the institutions counted were Sephardi.

32. Guy, *Women Build the Welfare State*, 152.

33. Ibid.

34. "Legión de voluntarios Kanfe Yona: Manifesto al público," *Israel*, July 1929, 13.

35. For other immigrant groups' hospitals and orphanages, see Bryce, "Paternal Communities"; Loyudice, *Hospital Italiano*; Fraser, *The British Hospital of Buenos Aires*.

36. See, for example, Schroeter, *The Sultan's Jew*, 91–92.

37. The first Jewish organization was the CIRA. Although organized in 1891, the Congregación Israelita Latina only became a legal organization in 1915. Before they founded their own institutions, the few Moroccans who lived in Buenos Aires belonged to the main Ashkenazi organization. The Argentine census of 1895 shows there were 110 Moroccan Jews, and the census of 1914 shows 927. Cited in Vilar, "La emigración judeo-marroquí a la América Latina," 36.

38. CILBA, Minute Book, August 13, 1913.

39. Ḥesed VeEmet, Minute Book, May 13, 1905.

40. Jose Roffé's family lived in the temple for many years; interview, May 2001.

41. Quoted in CES, *Presencia sefaradí*, 47.

42. For the argument that the cemetery was the only organization that brought unity within the Sephardi communities, see Bejarano, "El cementerio y la unidad comunitaria."

43. Vilar, *Tetuán en el resurgimiento judío contemporáneo*, 112. He estimates that the number of Jews living in Tétouan from 1860 to 1866 was seven thousand.

44. Harel, *Syrian Jewry in Transition*, 74.

45. Interview with Raquel Mehaudy, November 1998.

46. Interview with José Roffé, May 2001.

47. "Templo Etz-Ajaim-Bet Raquel," *Israel*, June 24, 1933, 3.

48. CILBA, Minute Book, September 5, 1950.

49. Interestingly, Serels describes the same incident in Tangier in 1863: Hebrat Ḥesed Ve Emet challenged the existing Hebrat Geummelout Hasadim [sic]; see "Aspects of the Effects of Jewish Philanthropic Societies in Morocco," 109.

50. Ḥesed VeEmet, Minute Book, May 13, 1905. Ḥesed VeEmet incorporated also an existing organization called "Ḥesed Laalafim," which had no leaders at that time.

51. Ibid., May 21, 1905.

52. Estatutos de la Asociación de Beneficencia, "Merced y Verdad," October 26, 1947.

53. CILBA, Minute Book, April 23, 1934.

54. Ozer Dalim, Minute Book, September 1, 1916.

55. Other activities included guaranteeing rent, sending men to pray in the memory of a woman, and helping Jews who suffered during Tragic Week. See Ozer Dalim, Minute Books, May 5 and 20, 1917; February 20, March 26, November 11, 1918; and April 11, 1919.

56. Ozer Dalim, Minute Book, September 27, 1917.

57. "Legión de Voluntarios Kanfe Yona: Manifesto al Público," and "Legión de Voluntarios 'Kanfe Yona,'" *Israel*, October 10–17, 1935, 36.

58. "Legión de Voluntarios 'Kanfe Yona."

59. CES, *Presencia sefaradí*, 95.

60. For a much more detailed description of this community's institutions, see Azar and Duer, "Judíos de Damasco en Argentina."

61. Or Torah, Minute Books, December 19, 1921 and January 20, 1923; Asamblea general extraordinaria, March 19, 1924; and December 12, 1929.

62. Or Torah, Minute Book, September 4, 1920.

63. Ibid., November 2, 1931.

64. Bene Emet, Minute Book, May 21, 1941; CES, *Presencia sefaradí*, 95; and Azar and Duer, "Judíos de Damasco en Argentina," 129.

65. Agudat Dodim, Minute Books, June 22, 1936, September 14, 1936, and September 13, 1943.

66. Ibid., September 6, 1944. Only men were accepted as members, and they usually joined when they married. Thus my assumption is that each male member represented at least three people (including himself).

67. Agudat Dodim, Minute Book, September 23, 1937.

68. Rodgers, "La comunidad judía alepina en Buenos Aires."

69. Ḥesed Shel Emet gave money to "the poor in our community." Cited in Rodgers, *Los judíos de Alepo en Argentina*, 106.

70. There were, of course, other smaller *minyanim* in the area (ibid., 28).

71. Ibid., 103.

72. Teubal, *El inmigrante*, 177–78.

73. See Rodgers, *Los judíos de Alepo en Argentina*, 297–309; CES, *Presencia sefaradí*, 106–107.

74. See Bertoni, "De Turquía a Buenos Aires."

75. *Israel*, July 31, 1918, 450.

76. Kahal Kadosh, Memoria y Balance General, October 1–September 30, 1946.

77. CES, *Presencia sefaradí*, 62.

78. The organization spelled its name this way.

79. Chalom, Minute Book, September 11, 1926.

80. Solicitudes de Ingreso, Chalom, 1946–1955.

81. Asociación Hebraica Argentina de Socorros Mutuos, Minute Book, July 12, 1932.

82. For example, AHASM, July 27, 1932.

83. Bejarano, "Los sefaradíes de la Argentina," 40; and CES, *Presencia sefaradí*, 111–112.

84. CES, *Presencia sefaradí*, 114–115.

85. For some examples of support to other organizations within the Sephardi communities, see Agudat Dodim, Minute Books, September 23, 1937; Guemilut Hasadim (Moroccan Ḥevra Kedusha), Minute Books, June 18, 1929; Fiesta de la Colectividad, October 18, 1947.

86. Curzón, "Presencia Judía," 7–8.

87. Ibid., 9–10.

88. See *La Luz*, October 2, 1931; Curzón, "Presencia Judía," 13.

89. Etz HaḤaim, 1ra Asamblea Gral. Extraordinaria, December 14, 1919.

90. For Círculo Cultural, see *La Luz*, December 4, 1931, 649; January 8, 1932, 15; July 8, 1932, 410; September 11, 1931, 438; and February 5, 1932, 55. For the Círculo Juvenil, see *La Luz*, August 14, 1931, 356; and November 13, 1931, 595.

91. See *La Luz*, June 9, 1932, 362; May 5, 1932, 190; and July 28, 1933, 342.

92. Ibid., December 4, 1931, 649.

93. Ibid., April 20, 1932, 189.

94. Etz HaḤaim, Minute Book, September 6, 1920.

95. Ibid., March 2, 1930.

96. *Israel*, April 11, 1918, 620. The mutual aid society Débora published its financial status, which indicates fundraising activity not reserved solely for purchasing the cemetery.

97. Saidman, "Colectividad Judía de Posadas."

98. Estatutos de la Asociación Israelita de Socorros Mutuos Hijos de Sión, Posadas, Artículo 3. These bylaws were published in 1945, according to Decreto Ley No. 24.499/1945, which affected all mutual aid organizations.

99. *La Luz*, April 10, 1931, July 31, and December 4.

100. CES, *Presencia sefaradí*, 120; "La Asociación Israelita Latina de Corrientes ha celebrado el 55 aniversario de su creación," *El Litoral*, June 19, 1969, Corrientes.

101. The first Sephardim buried in the cemetery date from 1917.

102. *Israel*, A. 2 no. 16, and 23.

103. *La Luz*, December 4, 1931, 655. *Presencia sefaradí*, however, cites 1927 as the date of creation; CES, *Presencia sefaradí*, 121.

104. *La Luz*, March 4, 1932, 101; *Mundo Israelita*, April 17, 1926, 2, and June 12, 1926, 4.

105. Benasayag, in his study of La Sábana, claims that of a population of two thousand, two hundred were Sephardim, 95 percent of whom were from Tétouan, Morocco; see "Sefaradíes Tetuaníes en La Sabana del Chaco Austral—Argentina."

106. Interview with Meri Benasayag de Muscar by Angeles de Martina, 1999, unpublished.

107. "Territorio Nacional del Chaco," *Israel*, September 28–October 5, 1928, no page.

108. Sociedad Israelita Latina Ḥesed VeEmet, Minute Books, November 4, 1928; October 30, 1930; June 21, 1931.

109. As shown by the origin of those buried who were members of the organization, and by the names of the steering committees.

110. "Instituciones de Córdoba," *Israel*, July 9–16, 1926, 5–6.

111. *La Luz*, September 18, 1931, 456.

112. Rubin, *Historia de la comunidad israelita sefaradí de la Provincia de Córdoba*, 5; and "Instituciones de Córdoba," 4–5.

113. Interview with Esther Acrich, May 19, 1997.

114. Blumenfeld, *Historia de la comunidad israelita de Tucumán*, 92–93; and Silberman de Cywiner, "Los sefarditas en Tucumàn," 155–158; and *Asociación Israelita Sefaradí de Beneficencia de Tucumán*, 26.

115. See *La Luz*, A. 1 No. 4, 21, 25, 26, 29, 31, 32, 33, A. 2 No. 12, 15, 16, A. 3, No. 3; *Israel*, A. 2 No. 18, 20.

116. Grinblat, *Historia de la comunidad judía en la Provincia de Salta*, 22.

117. *La Luz*, August 26, 1932.

118. Asociación Israelita Sefaradim de Catamarca de Socorros Mutuos, Minute Book. Cited in Altabef and Barbieri de Guardia, "Itinerarios, experiencias y conflictos," 12.

119. The Sociedad Israelita de Socorros Mutuos in 1927 had "more than 100 members." See *Israel*, April 22–29, 1927, 37, and *La Luz*, A. 1, no. 4, 77; no. 27, 537; and no. 31, 656.

120. Benasayag's grandfather had come from Tétouan, but before he settled in La Sábana, he had tried his luck in Mendoza, San Juan, Santa Fé, and Calchaquí (province of Santa Fé). Also, members of the Sociedad Ḥesed VeEmet from Resistencia discussed the possibility of appointing representatives of their society to "similar societies," like the Sociedad de Socorros Mutuos de Mendoza and the Sociedad Israelita Latina de Socorros Mutuos de San Juan; Benasayag, personal conversation, February 15, 2002; Ḥesed VeEmet, Minute Book, September 20, 1929.

121. *La Luz*, October 10, 1931.

122. *Israel*, June 11, 1926, 18. Some members of this organization were not Moroccan, but Sephardim of other origins.

123. CILBA, Minute Book, April 5, 1932.

124. Or Torah, Minute Book, October 6, 1924.

125. Ḥesed Shel Emet, Minute Book, July 4, 1926.

126. Or Torah, Minute Book, January 20, 1923.

127. CILBA, Minute Book, January 9, 1929.

128. Ḥesed Shel Emet, Minute Book, May 25, 1919.

129. "Pro-cementerio israelita-sefaradí en San Juan," *Israel*, August 14, 1925, 19.

130. Or Torah, Minute Book, May 6, 1926.

131. Bene Emet, Minute Book, August 5, 1936.

132. See letter written by the secretary of Ḥesed VeEmet (Buenos Aires) to the president of the Jewish hospital in the same city, November 9, 1942.

133. CAHJP #7672/4, letter from the Sociedad Jóvenes Israelitas Sefaradim (Latinos) de Corrientes to the president of the Asociacion Israelita Latina de Resistencia, May 11, 1935.

134. "Nota rosa y beneficiencia," *Israel*, July 2, 1926, 22.

135. "Pro-cementerio israelita-sefaradí."

136. Libro de socios [Members' Registry], Sociedad Israelita Latina Ḥesed VeEmet de Resistencia.

137. The first book covers membership from 1922 to 1927; the second book covers 1927 to 1929. I have excluded fifty-eight members who appear in the first book but stopped paying dues sometime before 1929. In some cases they stopped early on, but in others they remained in the association until late in 1929. Some members died in this period.

138. There are towns with significant Sephardi populations that are not listed, such as Presidencia Roque Saenz Peña. The interesting fact is that there are new towns that had not appeared in previous records, like Corrientes. Some other towns evince a decline in the number of Sephardim living there, such as La Sabana, Quitilipi, and Machagai.

139. Sociedad Israelita Latina Ḥesed VeEmet del Chaco, Minute Book, May 31, 1931.

140. Ibid., November 30, 1930.

141. Ozer Dalim, Minute Book, September 15, 1916.

142. From the 268 members (not all Moroccan, but all Sephardim), 139 were listed as living in the provinces. Ozer Dalim, Minute Book, list of members, November 1, 1917.

143. CILBA, Minute Book, November 16, 1919.

144. CES, *Presencia sefaradí*, 57.

145. Or Torah, Minute Book, October 3, 1927.

146. CILBA, Minute Book, September 18, 1918.

147. Ibid., December 17, 1916.

148. Ibid., January 7, 1906.

149. Or Torah, Minute Book, September 9, 1922.

150. Ibid., January 20, 1923; and Asamblea General Extraordinaria, March 19, 1924. In the first case, they sent money to three rabbis from Damascus who "were living in indigence," and the second one was for the old's people's home.

151. CILBA, Minute Book, October 27, 1910. I believe this was in response to the 1907 riots in the city.

152. "Ecos de una iniciativa expuesta en Israel," *Israel*, June 11, 1926, 8; "Por el cementerio de Alcázarquivir," *Israel*, April 22 and 29, 1927, 43.

153. "Los muros del cementerio de Tetuán," *Israel*, April 24, 1931.

154. There were Jewish hospitals in Tangier, Salonika, Izmir, and Istanbul. See Serels, "Aspects of the Effects of Jewish Philanthropic Societies in Morocco," 111; Daccarett, "Jewish Social Services in Late Ottoman Salonica." Danon, "Por bien de la sivdad i por amor del puevlo"; Cohen, "Fashioning Imperial Citizens."

155. Chalom's objective as an institution was not philanthropy; they spent m$n 341 from 1929 to 1932 on J. F.'s medical care. Chalom also raised funds from its members to pay hospital bills; see Minute Book, October 16, 1932.

156. See Comisión de Recetas, AHASM, Minute Books, 1932. In October 3, 1945, AHASM thanked a "Dr. Levy who saw patients on behalf of the organization."

157. See Bene Emet, Minute Book, August 21, 1935; Teubal, *El inmigrante*, 177–78; Kahal Kadosh, Minute Books, Balance General al 30 de Septiembre, 1946; and "Gran solemnidad alcanzó el gran acto con motivo de la inauguración del dispensario y sede social de la Comunidad Israelita Sefaradí de Buenos Aires," *Israel*, December 1947, 11–13, and 19.

158. Kahal Kadosh, ibid.

159. Ḥesed VeEmet, Memoria Administrativa, April 1, 1941.

160. "Liga Antituberculosa Israelita Sefaradí," *Israel*, May 27, 1932.

161. The Liga Israelita Argentina contra la Tuberculosis was still active in the 1950s. See figures quoted in Mirelman, *Jewish Buenos Aires*, 190.

162. "La obra humanitaria de la Liga Antituberculosa Israelita Sefaradí," *Israel*, January 12, 1934.

163. Mirelman, *Jewish Buenos Aires*, 188–189.

164. "La cooperación de los Sefardim," *Mundo Israelita*, September 13, 1930, cover; "La amplia contribución de la colectividad sefaradi a las instituciones Ascheknazim [sic]," *Israel*, July 26, 1935, cover; letter sent by the president of Ḥesed VeEmet to the president of Ezrah, November 9, 1942; Ḥesed VeEmet, Memoria Administrativa, April 1, 1943; Agudat Dodim, Minute Book, September 23, 1937.

165. "Un pabellón sefaradí en el Hospital Israelita," *Israel*, April 19–26, 1929, 11–12.

166. "Asilo Argentino de Huérfanas Israelitas, Arévalo 2026," *Israel*, May 6, 1927.

167. For a history of the girls' orphanage, see Guy, "Women's Organizations and Jewish Orphanages in Buenos Aires"; Lerner, "La historia del Asilo Argentino de Huérfanas Israelitas." For support for the girls' orphanage by Sephardim, see, for example, Bene Emet, Minute Books, 1930s, and Memoria y Balance correspondiente al ejercicio 1943; Agudat Dodim, Minute Book, September 30, 1936. For "Semana de la Huérfana" events, see, for example, "La Semana de la Huérfana," *Israel*, May 13, 1926, 7.

168. "Síntesis Histórica de los Asilos," 1944, 13–24.

169. Kal Kadosh, Minute Book, August 23, 1931; and "El Asilo de Huérfanos Israelitas y los Sefaradim," *Israel*, November 13, 1931, 8.

170. Chalom, Minute Book, December 21, 1931.

171. Bene Emet, Minute Book, December 2, 1936, and Memoria y Balance correspondiente al ejercicio 1943. "Niños sefaradim en el Asilo Israelita Argentino de Huérfanos y Ancianos," *Israel*, November 18, 1927, 19.

172. See CES, *Presencia sefaradí*, 95.

173. Bene Emet, Minute Book, September 2, 1936; and Jorge O. Bestene, "La inmigración sirio–libanesa en la Argentina."

174. Bene Emet, Minute Book, February 15, 1939.

175. Cited in Rodgers, *Los judíos de Alepo en Argentina*, 109.

176. Mirelman, *Jewish Buenos Aires*, 184.

3. THE LIMITS OF COMMUNITY

1. Ḥesed VeEmet, Steering Committee, Minute Book, October 24, 1933.

2. CILBA, Minute Book, November 13, 1933. They decided to send a letter to Tetuán, Morocco, in order to get a "qualified" answer.

3. CAHJP #7672/4, Letter from Saul Sedero to Jaime Azulay, president of the Sociedad Ḥesed VeEmet, Resistencia, November 9, 1933. His was the only response found in the documents of the society.

4. Ḥesed VeEmet, Steering Committee, Minute Book, December 3, 1933. They decided to vote on the suggestions in the following ordinary session, but I did not find further discussion of the topic.

5. Saidman, "Colectividad judía de Posadas," 22.

6. Guemilut Ḥasadim, Minute Book, June 1, 1932. The minutes do not list the letter's questions. Guemilut Ḥasadim decided to write to Tétouan as "we do not feel capable to respond."

7. CILBA, Libro de Actas de Comisión Directiva, October 12, 1928.

8. Note my hesitation in choosing terms to describe these attempts: collective, umbrella organization, single organization.

9. See, for example, advertisements offering the services of mohel, *shoḥet*, and *ḥazan* (cantor) in *Israel*, April 22 and 29, 1927, 47; Mohel Yomtob Egozi offered services as mohel and "officiant" for marriages in *Israel*, April 24, 1931, 14; advertisements for Mohel David Freue, who performed circumcisions "following hygienic laws," and not charging the poor, in *Israel*, December 1947, 19.

10. This did not affect the JCA colonies, as they all had rabbis, shoḥets, and mohels.

11. Zemer, "The Rabbinic Ban on Conversion in Argentina," 85.

12. Quoted in ibid., 84.

13. Zemer claims that the ban most likely expressed Rabbi Goldman's positions (rather than Dabbah's), given a previous exchange of letters between them concerning conversion of an "uncircumcised one" in 1915 (ibid.).

14. Rodgers, *Los judíos de Alepo en Argentina*, 38.

15. Zemer, "The Rabbinic Ban on Conversion in Argentina," 93.

16. He was succeeded by David Sutton Dabbah.

17. Rodgers, *Los judíos de Alepo en Argentina*, 87–92.

18. Rodgers argues that between 1930 (Dabbah's death) and 1953 (Chehebar's arrival), the Aleppine community tried to walk the fine line between traditionalism and integration; ibid.

19. Duer, "El rol del *Jajam* en las primeras inmigraciones damascenas a la Argentina"; Azar and Duer, "Judíos de Damasco en Argentina."

20. CILBA, Minute Book, May 22, 1927.

21. CILBA, Libro de Actas de Comisión Directiva, May 22, 1927.

22. "Actividades del Gran Rabino D. Sabetay Djaen," *Israel*, May 20, 1927, 9–11.

23. Ibid.

24. "Estos son los países del porvenir," *La Voz del Interior*, June 3, 1927. There is evidence too that Djaen was named "Gran Rabino Sefaradí de la República Argentina" in May 1927. See "Actividades del Rabino Djaen," *Israel*, May 27, 1927, 13. See chapter 4 for more information on the World Confederation of Sephardi Jews and Djaen's mission on its behalf.

25. "Arribó a nuestro país el Gran Rabino de Rumania Dr. S. Djaen," *Mundo Israelita*, October 1945.

26. The biographical information was taken from Lebel, "Ivrit baḥotsut Monastir hanaḥrevat."

27. "La voz de un gran sefaradí," *Israel*, April 22–29, 1927, 13.

28. "Cursos de Hebreo," *Israel*.

29. "Esther," *Semanario Hebreo*, June 14, 1929.

30. "Actividades del Gran Rabinato Sefaradí de la R. Argentina," *Israel*, January 1, 1929.

31. "Mensajes de Pesah," *Israel*, and "Actividades del gran Rabinato Sefaradí de la R. Argentina," *Israel*, January 4, 1929.

32. "Gran Rabinato Sefaradi: Información oficial," *Israel*, February 1, 1929, 5.

33. CAHJP #7672/2, "Propósitos y Programa del Gran Rabinato."

34. "Ha vuelto el gran Rabino D. Sabetay Djaen," *Israel*, September 28–October 5, 1928.

35. "Gran Rabinato Sefaradí de la R. Argentina," *Israel*, January 25, 1929, 10.

36. Ibid.

37. "Gran Rabinato Sefaradí," *Israel*, January 18, 1929, 16.
38. "Gran Rabinato Sefaradí de la R. Argentina."
39. Kahal Kadosh, Minute Book, May 19, 1929.
40. CILBA, Minute Book, March 3, 1929.
41. Ibid., October 12, 1928.
42. "Actividades del gran Rabinato Sefaradí de la R. Argentina," *Israel*, January 4, 1929.
43. "Propósitos y programa del Gran Rabinato."
44. "Creación del Consistorio Rabínico Sefaradí," *Semanario Hebreo*, (n/a).
45. "El mensajero de Jerusalém," *Israel*, April 22–29, 1927, 9; "Un gran huésped Sefaradí," *Israel*, May 6, 1927, 10; "Siguen efectuándose los agasajos y las conferencias del eminente Rabino Sr. Djaen," *Israel*, May 13, 1927, 5.
46. CILBA, Minute Book, November 17, 1929.
47. Ibid., December 8, 1929.
48. Ibid., December 29, 1929.
49. Kahal Kadosh, Minute Book, August 11, 1929.
50. Personal communication with Rabbi Djaen's grandson, August 2011.
51. Kahal Kadosh, Minute Books, June 23, 1930, and August 24, 1930.
52. Ibid., August 24, 1930, November 9, 1930, and November 30, 1930.
53. Ibid., December 18, 1930.
54. "La actuación del gran Rabino D. Sabetay J. Djaen," *Mundo Israelita*, January 24, 1931.
55. Kahal Kadosh, Minute Book, February 22, 1931.
56. Ibid.
57. "Conferederación Israelita Sefaradí," *Israel*, June 19, 1931. More below.

58. See Albert, *The Modernization of French Jewry*, especially chap. 3.
59. See Weiker, *Ottomans, Turks and the Jewish Polity*, 152.
60. See Lebel, "Ivrit baḥotsut Monastir hanaḥrevat."
61. "Acontecimiento histórico: Solemne proclamación del Gran Rabino sefaradí de Buenos Aires y constitución del Consistorio Rabínico Central," *Renacimiento de Israel*, January 15, 1929, 7.
62. "Estada de S.E. Gran Rabino Sabetay Djaen—Visita a la Presidencia," *Israel*, February 1, 1929, 17.
63. See Levy, "Haham Başi (Chief Rabbi)"; and "*Millet* Politics."
64. "Gran Rabino Sabetay Djaen," *Semanario Hebreo*, March 8, 1929; "Llegó ayer el rabino de Monastir," *El País* (Córdoba) March 1, 1929; "Se encuentra en Córdoba el doctor Sabitaj J. Djaen," *La Voz del Interior* (Córdoba), March 1, 1929.
65. "Manifesto del Gran Rabinato Sefaradí," *Israel*, August 29, 1929, 14. The literal translation of *Becoah HaTorah* is "by the power of the Torah." I thank David Brodsky for his help with this translation.
66. There was no official Argentine grand rabbi. The position of "head" of the Ashkenazi Bet Din was established during Perón's years—and held by Amram Blum—only to disappear once Perón was out of power. See Rein, *Argentine Jews or Jewish Argentines?*, 139–141.
67. "Actividades del Rabino Michael Molho," in *La Luz*, April 28, 1950, 206.
68. See chapter 1 for more information on this process.
69. "Confederación Israelita Sefaradí," *Israel*, July 3–10, 1931, 7.
70. "Conferederación Israelita Sefaradí: Una sesión memorable," *Israel*, June 19, 1931.

71. "Las encuestas de Israel: Cuál debe ser la función de una federación argentina de sociedades israelitas?," *Israel*, October 30, 1931, 6.

72. "Federación arg. de sociedades israelitas," *Israel*, July 3–10, 1931, 32.

73. Ibid.

74. "Federación y comunidad," *Israel*, July 10–17, 1931, 7.

75. "Sera pronto una realidad la iniciativa de la Bene Brith," *Israel*, August 14, 1931, 7.

76. "La constitucion de la FASI es un hecho histórico en el judaismo argentino," *Israel*, April 1, 1932.

77. See Deutsch, *Las Derechas*, 225–232.

78. "Fines de la DAIA," October 5, 1935, quoted in Avni, "Argentine Jewry," 164.

79. Twenty-eight organizations (from Buenos Aires) joined at the beginning, and the DAIA opened offices in the rest of the country. Jewish communist organizations, however, were not part of the DAIA, and they created their own society to fight anti-Semitism.

80. For more details on DAIA accomplishments and challenges during the Perón years, see Avni, "Argentine Jewry."

81. See "Significativos contornos alcanzó la Primera Convención Regional Sefaradí," *La Luz*, April 17, 1942, 176–179. The Centro Sionista Sefaradí is the focus of chapter 4.

82. More on this in chapter 4.

83. CAHJP # 7672/3, Letter written by Unión de Asociaciones Israelitas Sefaradíes de la República Argentina, September 1942.

84. Ibid.

85. CAHJP # 7672/3, "Estatutos de la Unión de las Asociaciones Sefaradís de la Argentina," Buenos Aires, 1942.

86. "Convención de comunidades e instituciones sefaradíes de la Argentina," *Adama*, June 1972, 1, 4.

4. WORKING FOR THE HOMELAND

1. Gran Baile de la Colectividad, program "La Colectividad Sefaradí de Buenos Aires," Buenos Aires, 1945, 18.

2. See chapters 2 and 3 for examples.

3. More on these differences below.

4. For an analysis of the Zionist discourse of the magazine *Israel*, see Rein and Lewis, "Judíos, árabes, sefaradíes y argentinos."

5. Collections among Sephardim were later done by two "Sephardi" groups that "divided" their work among various communities. To participate in the 1949 United Campaign, Ladino-speaking Jews founded DESA and CSS worked among the rest.

6. Hovevei Zion societies appeared in Russia and Romania in the early 1880s. They were part of the Hibbat Zion Movement (pre-Zionist movement), with the aim was to raise money to create agricultural projects in Palestine to bring Jews back to their land. See Ettinger, "Part VI," 727–1096, 894–897.

7. My knowledge of early Zionist activity in Argentina is based on the work of Siskel, "Los comienzos de la actividad educativa sionista en Argentina," 7–23; Mirelman, "Early Zionist Activities among Sephardim in Argentina," 190–205; Schenkolewski-Kroll, "La conquista de las comunidades," 191–201; Schenkolewski-Kroll, "Cambios en la relación de la organización Sionista Mundial," 149–166; Avni, "Argentine Jewry," 192.

8. Fifteen hundred shekel-paying members attended. See "The First Argentine Zionist Congress," *Jewish Chronicle*, May 20, 1904, 15ab.

9. For more details on the shift in support, see Schenkolewski, "The Organization of Zionism in Argentina," 62–89, 63.

10. Schenkolewski-Kroll, "Los sionistas generales en Argentina, de federación a partido," 369–374.

11. See Schenkolewski-Kroll, "La conquista de las comunidades," "The Influence of the Zionist Movement," and "Zionist Political Parties in Argentina."

12. See Bell, "Bitter Conquest."

13. Their apolitical stance also stemmed from their experience encountering Zionism in the first place. More on this below.

14. The creation of the Shas party in Israel, however, changed the "apolitical" position of many Sephardim. See Rodgers, "Los judíos sirios en Buenos Aires frente al sionismo y al estado de Israel," 181.

15. See Or Torah, Minute Books, January 20, 1923; Asamblea General Extraordinaria, March 19, 1924. In the first case, they sent money to three rabbis from Damascus who "were living in indigence," and the second was for the senior citizens' home.

16. CILBA, Minute Book, October 30, 1918.

17. As Camji aptly put it, "it is important to remark that the newspaper was in Spanish, rather than in Yiddish, evidence that there was an interest in keeping non-Yiddish speakers involved in the movement" ("A 100 años de sionismo," 4). I would add that Yiddish speakers were not as numerous then as they would be later.

18. Sephardim were exposed to Zionist ideology prior to arrival in Argentina, of course. Laskier dates the arrival of Zionism in Morocco as 1897 to 1900; see *The Alliance Israélite Universelle*. Haskell claims that organized Zionist activity appeared in Bulgaria as early as 1864; see "The Sephardic Culture in Bulgaria." The rabbi of the community in Mahdia, Tunisia, requested money from Hovevei Sion to set up a Zionist journal in 1885; see Tsur, "Haskala in a Sectional Colonial Society," 156. Persian Jews became increasingly involved in Zionism after the Balfour Declaration; see Netzer, "Persian Jewry and Literature," 250.

19. Geulat Sion was formed in 1916, but it formally became a Zionist center in 1918. See *Israel*, September 21, 1918, 532; Mirelman, "Early Zionist Activities," 194; and Rodgers, "La comunidad judía alepina en Buenos Aires," footnote 23. The Arabic-speaking community published *Al Gala*, a Zionist newspaper in Arabic.

20. Siskel, "Los comienzos de la actividad educativa sionista," 12.

21. "El silencio de los sefaradim," *Semanario Hebreo*, August 23, 1924, cover; "Sobre una resolución del noveno Congreso Sionista Argentino," *Israel*, November 14, 1924, 13.

22. CSS, Minute Book, November 26, 1925.

23. "Sionismo sefaradí," *Israel*, September 23, 1925, 7.

24. "Centro Sionista Sefaradí," *Israel*, September 18, 1925; CSS, Minute Books, October 12, 1925, and November 26, 1925.

25. *Habima Haivrit*, 1 no. 6 (Elul-Tishre 1921): 11–12, cited in Mirelman, "Early Zionist Activities," 194.

26. "Report on the History of Zionism in Argentina," by J. L. Liachovitzky, A. Crenovich, G. Dabin, and G. Zeitlin, March 14, 1907, 22, cited in Mirelman, "Early Zionist Activities," 197. For Ashkenazi (mis)conceptions of Sephardi connections to the Zionist project, see "Atracción de los sefardíes al movimiento

nacional judío," *Mundo Israelita*, October 2, 1926.

27. There were several types of Zionism: general Zionism (advocated the primacy of Zionism over class, party, or personal interests); political Zionism (stressed the importance of political action in establishing the state of Israel); practical Zionism (emphasized concrete action in Palestine, such as the building of cities, settling of agricultural colonies, and immigration); religious Zionism (emphasized importance of establishing the rule of Jewish law in the new land); synthetic Zionism (the merging of political and practical Zionism, adopted after the Eighth Zionist Congress in 1907); and revisionist Zionism (called for change in the moderate position adopted by the WZO toward the British, began by Vladimir Jabotinsky in 1925, who "revisited" Hertzl's ideas). Zionists were for the most part secular Jews who no longer accepted rabbinical authority or Jewish law. Thus, Zionism was initially rejected by most of the Eastern European Orthodoxy, who viewed the struggle for the State of Israel as a secular and political project.

28. CSS, Acta de Fundación, April 25, 1925.

29. This was the argument that Zionists in Bulgaria used, as well. See Haskell, "The Sephardic Culture in Bulgaria."

30. See, among many others, Berkowitz, *Zionist Culture and West European Jewry before the First World War*, chap. 1.

31. Tsur, "Haskala in a Sectional Colonial Society," 157.

32. In the Sephardi world, Zionism was attacked by the Alliance Israelite Universelle, itself a product of the Enlightenment. Afraid of losing its influence in Sephardi communities, the Alliance sought to dissolve any Zionist cells created by local groups. "The AIU," writes Laskier, "aspired to transform and liberate the Jews in their respective countries and what it could do was to fight for legislative reforms, bringing the Jews closer to France. The Zionists, on the other hand, called for the solution to the 'Jewish problem' not through assimilation but rather by physically uprooting Jews in the diaspora and placing them in a homeland of their own. Such a solution was unacceptable to the AIU for quite some time." The AIU rejected numerous objectives espoused by Zionists; an important conflict was over the return to Palestine itself. The AIU believed that Palestine would not be able to absorb all diaspora Jews, and conflict with peoples already settled on the land would make it almost impossible to succeed. Additionally, French (and Spanish) authorities in Northern Africa (some of whose interests were defended by the Alliance) saw a threat to their colonial power in any nationalist aspirations. See Laskier, *The Alliance Israélite Universelle*, 195–202.

33. But it would be wrong to assume that all Sephardim then became Zionists.

34. Rodgers, "La comunidad judía alepina en Buenos Aires," 45–64.

35. Mirelman, "Early Zionist Activities," 199; Rodgers, "La comunidad judía alepina en Buenos Aires." For opposition (not to Zionism, but to the policies sought by Zionist organizations) in Morocco, see Serels, *A History of the Jews of Tangier*, 117–118.

36. "Homenaje en Memoria del Rabino Jacobo Mizrahi," *La Luz*, April 28, 1950, 206; interview with his son, Adolfo Mizrahi, February 1, 2012.

37. Rodgers argues that a certain weakening of the ties with Israel (and a strengthening of orthodoxy) took place

among Sephardim in the Aleppine community after the 1960s; see "Los judíos sirios en Buenos Aires," 171.

38. Of course Yiddish was not the language used by the leadership of the movement in Europe; they used primarily French and German. See also "Confederación Mundial de Judíos Sefaradim," *Israel*, June 1925, 7, where the editors state that during the upcoming World Zionist Congress, "Sephardim should attend not as mere listeners, like it has happened until now, but with the right to speak out."

39. "Con Sabetay J. Djaen, enviado de la Confederación Universal Sefaradí," *Semanario Hebreo*, Buenos Aires, April 30, 1927. The WUSJ was also called "Confederation of Sephardi Jews."

40. J.C.A., Box 14, File 129, "Confederation Universelle des Juifs Sepharadim, Propagande, 2ème Année No. 17. Comité Exécutif, Jerusalem," August 31, 1927.

41. "Sobre una resolución del noveno Congreso Sionista Argentino," *Israel*, November 14, 1924, 13; Mirelman, "Early Zionist Activities," 195. See also "Atracción de los sefardíes al movimiento nacional judío," *Mundo Israelita*, October 2, 1926.

42. In the "Message to the Sephardim by Doctor Chaim Weizmann, President of the World Zionist Organization" in the booklet published by the Bene Kedem, Weizman claimed that Bensión "had been very successful in the Sephardic communities of Spain, Portugal, Morocco, Tunis, Baghdad, as well as in the Asian continent." Laskier noted Bension's late 1920s arrival in Morocco, and his work in the Spanish zone and Tangier, as well as in French Morocco. Bension succeeded Nathan Halpern, an emissary of Keren Hayesod, who arrived in Morocco in the early 1920s. Bene Kedem, *Los Sefaradim*, 21;

Laskier, *The Alliance Israelite Universelle*, 203; "El famoso sefaradí que visitará a los sefaradim de la América del Sur," *Israel*, January 22, 1926, 9; *Mundo Israelita*, September 18, 1926.

43. The World Union of Sephardi Jews "has denounced the World Zionist Organization to the Council of the League of Nations Union as not doing anything for the Sephardim. Just like our enemies, the Arab agitators and the Agudath Israel. Now, something must be done to show the world what they are." WIZO archives, Letter written by Ida Bensión (Ariel Bensión's wife) to Fanny Wachs, November 4, 1927; Bensión wrote two more letters to Wachs regarding Djaen's work and his connection to the WUSJ.

44. This might have been why Shaul Setton Dabbah refused to contribute to this campaign. See note 35.

45. Mirelman, "Early Zionist Activities," 197–198.

46. "Centro Sionista Sefaradí," *Israel*, February 12, 1926, 22; "Sionismo sefaradí," *Israel*, June 11, 1926, 8.

47. "El Centro Sionista Sefaradí y la campaña del Keren Hayesod," *Israel*, May 13, 1926, 8.

48. This section was taken from the Boletín del Departamento de Trabajo de Jerusalem, but included in the pamphlet under the title: "What the Keren Hayesod does for the Sephardim living in Erez Israel"; Bene Kedem, *Los Sefaradim*, 66–71.

49. Ibid., 71.

50. "Estatutos provisorios de la Organización Sionista Sefaradí Argentina 'Bene Kedem,' " *Israel*, January 6, 1928, 17.

51. CZA, Ariel Bensión, "Final Report on Keren Hayesod work amongst the Sephardim in Argentina," November 26, 1926.

52. For his visit to Rosario, see WIZO archive, invitation to a meeting where the "distinguished poet and orator, Rabbi Sabetay Djaen" will give a talk on "the role of the Jewish woman in the Jewish rebirth," Rosario, May 1927. For his visit to Chile, see letter by Robert Levy to *Nosotros*, August 27, 1927. For his visit to New York, see the letter written by the Congregation of Peace & Brotherhood of Monastir, Inc., New York, on November 14, 1927, to John H. Levy, Esq., regarding the dinner to be offered in honor of "Reverend Sabetay J. Djaen."

53. Cited in Mirelman, "Early Zionist Activities," 200.

54. (OSFA) Letter written to Wachs by Ida Bensión, September 29, 1927. "We have heard from Graiver in another letter that he spoke with Dr. Cadoche, the Secretary of Bene Kedem in Buenos Aires who told him that Djaen told them privately not to support the Zionist Organization, but only the Confederation [WUSJ]."

55. Djaen was accused of not being a Zionist by Ida Bensión. See WIZO archive, letters written to her WIZO friend in Rosario, September 29, 1927, July 21, 1927, and November 4, 1927.

56. "Con Sabetay J. Djaen, enviado de la Confederación Universal Sefaradí."

57. J.C.A., Box 14, File 129, Boletín de la Confederación Universal de los Judios Sefaradim. Comité Ejecutivo, Año 3, No. 22, Agosto 28, 1928, Jerusalem, 1–2.

58. This does not mean that Sephardim dropped this concern all together. See "La inteligencia entre las instituciones nacionales y la Confederación Universal de los Judíos Sefaradim," *Israel*, September 28–October 5, 1928.

59. Sephardim in Resistencia donated money, as well, although it is not clear if it was at the CSS's insistence. See Sociedad Israelita Latina Hesed VeEmet, Resistencia, Chaco, Minute Book, September 3, 1929.

60. Cited in Mirelman, "Early Zionist Activities," 202.

61. The exact date Centro Sionista was founded is not clear. A short article appeared in *La Luz* in June 1933, describing it as being founded "some months ago." The first written evidence of a Centro Sionista meeting is December 4, 1932. Yet the first written minutes of the meeting claimed that "a letter had been written to the president of this Centro Sionista," which might indicate that it had been active earlier. *La Luz*, June 9, 1933, 271; CSS, Minute Book, December 4, 1932.

62. CSS, Minute Book, March 21, 1936.

63. Ibid., March 28, 1936.

64. Ibid., April 4, 1936.

65. Ibid.

66. Ibid., April 11, 1936.

67. Even in 1946, the CSS requested the creation of a separate account so money wired to the KKL in Palestine by the KKL in Argentina would duly note the amount contributed by Sephardim. CSS, Minute Book, September 8, 1946.

68. CSS, Minute Book, July 21, 1934.

69. *La Luz*, January 13, 1933, 10.

70. CSS, Minute Book, August 8, 1935; José Camji (CSS delegate), "El informe sobre la contribución de los sefaradim," [speech given at Primer Congreso Sudamericano Pro-Eretz Israel], *La Luz*, May 27, 1938, 243–245.

71. Camji, "El informe sobre la contribución de los sefaradim," 244.

72. *La Luz*, "Significativos contornos alcanzó la Primera Convención Regional Sefaradí," 179.

73. CZA F26/3, CSS, Minute Book, June 24, 1947.

74. "Discurso del Sr. Nissim Teubal," *La Luz* 12, No. 8, 180.

75. The Comité contra el Racismo y Antisemitismo, for example, requested donations from the CSS. Later, the Comité Central Pro Socorro a las Víctimas Israelitas de la Guerra y Refugiados was created. This committee, not exclusively Sephardi or Ashkenazi, was presided over by a Moroccan Jew: Moisés Cadoche. See CSS, Minute Book, June 3, 1939; CES, *Presencia sefaradí*, 124.

76. JDC Archives, AR 45/54, Folder # 891, Letter sent to Nissim, Elías, and Moisés Teubal by the Joint Distribution Committee, Buenos Aires, September 20, 1945.

77. Ibid.

78. The WJC spent considerable resources to keep Sephardi donations coming toward them. See AJA, Collection WJC, Box Number H233, Folder 5, "Grupos sefarditas en la Argentina," November 10, 1949.

79. "Primera Convención Regional Sefaradí del Keren Kayemeth Leisrael Realizada los días 24 y 25 del mes ppdo," *Israel*, November 1945, 13. See also Schenkolewski-Kroll, "Cambios en la relación," 158.

80. "Informe del Keren Kayemet Sefaradí por el Sr. Y. Shabtay," *Israel*, May 31, 1948, 20.

81. The KKL tin box, with a Jewish flag painted on it, was placed in private homes, where hosts encouraged guests and family to contribute coins. The boxes were placed and picked up by volunteers. The KKL instituted the practice of entering the name of newly born children into the "Book of Children" when collections were carried out by family and friends in honor of the birth; those people who donated money to buy a tree had their names entered in the "Book of Trees." For a discussion of these campaigns, see Berkowitz, *Zionist Culture*, chap. 7.

82. "Resoluciones aprobadas en la Segunda Convención Sefaradí Argentina, llevada a cabo los días 8, 9 y 10 de Mayo de 1948," *Israel*, May 31, 1948, 7.

83. See Schenkolewski-Kroll, "Cambios en la relación."

84. "Informe de la 2a. Convención Regional Sefaradi Argentina, celebrada durante los dias 8, 9 y 10 de Mayo de 1948," *Israel*, May 31, 1948, 14.

85. CZA F26/11, Directorio Sefaradí del Keren Kayemeth Leisrael, Entradas y Salidas Generales, 1946, 1947, and part of 1948. For example, the total wired to the KKL by this entity in 1946 was m$n 18,369.40, whereas for 1947 the sum was m$n 35,470.70. For 1948, we do not have final figures as the documentation only shows the revenue from January to May, and expenses incurred from January to March. The partial total recorded for January–March (total funds raised minus expenses) was m$n 13,934.10.

86. Bell, "Bitter Conquest."

87. It should be pointed out, however, that the Israeli Histadruth (Labor Federation) had a Sephardi branch in Argentina. But, of course, it did not run its own candidates list. See *Despertar*, the newspaper of its Sephardi Youth Group, which was published for a short time in Buenos Aires in the late 1940s.

88. See Ricardo Levy, "La juventud sefardí y los partidos políticos," *DESA*, May 3, 1956, 4.

89. IWO, Buenos Aires, Carpeta: Sefaradíes, Letter from Baruch Uziel (Tel Aviv) to the president of ACISBA, José Ventura, June 12 1949.

90. "Al márgen de la misión de un delegado sefaradí," *La Luz*, May 21, 1948, 205.

91. Ibid.

92. "Los sefaradím, simple instrumento," *La Luz*, January 26, 1951, 38.

93. Eliachar claimed he proposed this idea during his visit to Argentina. It would eventually take place in 1951 in Paris; see his *Living with Jews*, 134. "World Sephardic Congress Held, Paris, November 4–8, 1951," *The Sephardi*, December, 1951, 1–7.

94. "Acerca de la Federación Mundial de Comunidades Sefaradíes," *La Luz*, June 25, 1948, 258.

95. For a description of the 1951 Congress, see "World Sephardic Congress Held," *The Sephardi*.

96. "La comunidad sefaradí de Buenos Aires y el Congreso Sefaradí," *DESA*, 2.

97. The Campaña Unida (United Appeal) was a fundraising campaign that brought all Sephardi and Ashkenazi institutions together, aiming to avoid tiring donors with too many independent campaigns. The resulting funds raised would be divided according to predetermined percentages.

98. "Comité sefaradí pro-campaña unificada, 1949," *La Luz*, July 8, 1949.

99. Ibid.

100. "Discurso pronunciado por el Sr. Ezra Teubal durante el acto realizado en el Club Oriente," *La Luz*, April 13, 1949, 136.

101. "World Congress Opens Center in London," *The Sephardi*, September 1952, 1, 3; and "World Sephardi Conference in Paris," *The Sephardi*, January 1953, 2; Eliachar, *Living with Jews*, 150; and J.C.A., Box 38, File 420, Letter to Elías Teubal by the Fédération Mondiale des Communautés Sepharades, Jerusalem, August 27, 1954.

102. See, for example, "Conozcamos a Israel," *DESA*, May 3, 1956, 7.

103. "Juventud D.E.S.A." *DESA*, Nov. 17, 1951, 6; "Comité femenino de la D.E.S.A" *DESA*, November 27, 1952, 6.

104. Rein and Lewis, "Judíos, árabes, sefaradíes y argentinos."

105. Levy, "La juventud sefaradí y los partidos políticos," *DESA*, May 3, 1956.

106. Ibid.

107. "Dentro del cuadro general de las entidades," *La Luz*, July 8, 1949.

108. "Un movimiento jalutsiano sefaradí toma auge en nuestro medio," *DESA*, December 18, 1951, 7; "Jalutzim sefaradim," *DESA*, July 1952, 4.

109. "Jalutzim sefaradim."

110. Levy, "La juventud sefaradí y los partidos políticos." Interview with Judith Bartov, a participant who made aliyah in 1953 (July 2012). See also Bar-Gil, *Juventud*.

111. "Celebróse el VI Congreso Ordinario de la Confederación Juvenil Sionista Argentina," *La Luz*, October 22, 1948, 454–455.

112. Interview with Elena Masri, José Menasce, Ricardo Galante, Jose Alfie, Bs. As, May 18, 2010.

113. Ibid.

114. All expenses were paid for, but participants were asked to contribute a small amount. In the end, only one or two payments were collected by the agency, and the rest was pardoned (ibid.).

115. The history of Sephardi Zionist youth deserves its own study, and it remains to be told.

116. Mirelman, "Early Zionist Activities," 193.

117. *Israel*, January 1, 1919, 705.

118. *La Luz*, August 12, 1932.

119. See, for example, *Mundo Israelita*, February 4, 1933, 4. The article announced Jacobo Razili's visit (as emissary of the Histadrut) to Tucumán and Salta, where "Sephardim contributed greatly."

120. Sociedad Israelita Latina Hesed VeEmet, Resistencia, Chaco, Minute Book, September 3, 1929.

121. "En acto solemne hízose entrega a la Sociedad 'Etz HaḤaim' del Diploma de Honor," *Israel*, [1927?].
122. CSS, Minute Book, March 4, 1926.
123. Ibid.
124. "El Comité Sefaradí Argentino pro Keren Kayemeth, Keren Hayesod y Refugiados," Gran Baile de la Colectividad, Buenos Aires, 1948.
125. CSS, "Informa el compañero J. Adatto del viaje realizado conjuntamente con su Sra. Esposa," n.d.
126. See newspaper clippings of Djaen's visits. "Desde hoy es húesped de Córdoba, el Gran Rabino de Monastir Sabitaj José Djaen," *Córdoba*, June 1927; "el Gran Rabino Dr. Djaen organiza el sefaradismo en Sud América," June 1927 (in this article, written during his visit to Córdoba, there is mention of a newly created branch of the "Confederación Universal Sefaradí," with members from both the Syrian and the Ottoman communities, which until then had not participated together); "Rosario," *Israel*, July 1927, 10; "Confío en una renovación liberal," *La Palabra*, July 1927 (Mendoza?); "Rosario," *Semanario Israelita*, June 1927; photographs of his visit to Corrientes (December 1928).
127. "Arribó el Gran Rabino de la colectividad israelita," *Trópico*, Tucumán, November 6, 1947.
128. CSS, Minute Book, August 27, 1938.
129. Ibid., November 22, 1941.
130. Gran Baile de la Colectividad, March 30, 1946, Buenos Aires.
131. "Delegados de las sociedades, comunidades y centros que participaron en la Segunda Convención Regional Sefaradí Argentina," *Israel*, May 31, 1948, 21.
132. Interview with Elena Masri et al.

5. BECOMING ARGENTINE, BECOMING JEWISH, BECOMING AND REMAINING SEPHARDI

1. *La Luz*, October 8, 1937, 436–437.
2. See Deutsch, *Crossing Borders, Claiming a Nation*, chap. 8.
3. In a very interesting (but unrelated) turn of events, this hotel is now owned by an Argentine Sephardi family of Syrian origin. See Rodgers, "Identidad y prácticas económicas."
4. *Mundo Israelita*, March 18, 1933, 2.
5. See, for example, ibid., February 27, 1926, 2.
6. Ibid., January 30, 1926, 3.
7. For a description of the work of some of these organizations, see Mirelman, *Jewish Buenos Aires*, 187–196.
8. Goldberg, "Sacrifices upon the Altar of Charity," 44.
9. There were, of course, organizations exclusively led by women. See below.
10. Guy, *Women Build the Welfare State*, 58–59.
11. McGee, "Right-Wing Female Activists in Buenos Aires," 85–97; Deutsch, "The Catholic Church, Work, and Womanhood in Argentina"; Little, "The Society of Beneficence."
12. McGee, "Right-Wing Female Activists in Buenos Aires," 88–89; Little, "The Society of Beneficence," 1; Cianfardo, "La práctica benéfica y el control de los sectores populares de la ciudad de Buenos Aires." The existing literature on these groups (and on other organizations such as the Sociedad de Beneficiencia) has moved away from an interpretation that centered on the idea of social control to a more nuanced understanding of women's roles in solving concrete problems and in carving a new role for women in modern Argentina. For this interpretation, see, in particular, Mead, "Gender, Welfare and the Catholic Church in Argentina."

13. *La Prensa*, July 12, 16, 19, and September 3, 1937.

14. For a description of the work of the Catholic groups, see McGee, "Right-Wing Female Activists in Buenos Aires," 85–97, 90; Deutsch, "The Catholic Church, Work, and Womanhood in Argentina," 304–322. The Confederación de Beneficencia had several chapters in the provinces; I found references to groups (*círculos*) from Salta, San Luis, Entre Rios, and Córdoba, all organizing events in Buenos Aires.

15. Guy, *Women Build the Welfare State*, 45–48, 51–57.

16. *La Prensa*, July 1, 2, 12, 16, and 21, 1937.

17. There were, of course, kosher caterers. See *Israel*, November 9, 1934, 10.

18. *Mundo Israelita*, February 7, 1931, 2 and June 17, 1933, 3.

19. *La Prensa*, July 9, 1937.

20. Other ethnic philanthropic organizations used the same places and types of events. The Syro-Lebanese Patronage Circle, for example, "offered tea and dance at the Alvear Palace"; *La Prensa*, July 18, 1937.

21. Adamovsky, *Historia de la clase media Argentina*, 69.

22. Ibid., 72.

23. The Sociedad de Damas Israelitas expressed their fears about the presence of Jewish orphans in both Catholic and state institutions. See Guy, "Women's Organizations," 7–8.

24. Ibid., 12, 23.

25. There were, of course, many women's committees within the (male) Zionist organizations.

26. The organization was officially WIZO (Argentina branch), although most called it simply WIZO. In the late 1930s, the state began requiring all "foreign-named" institutions to go by a Spanish name; WIZO became OSFA (Organización Sionista Femenina Argentina), and thereafter used this term in official correspondence and publications, although the organization continued to be known colloquially as WIZO.

27. See Levin, *It Takes a Dream*, especially 41–42, chaps. 1 and 4.

28. See Shilo, "The Women's Farm at Kinneret, 1911–1917," 256.

29. Elnecavé, "Historia," 2.

30. Ibid.

31. In fact, only eight other countries had WIZO federations before Argentina joined. In 1926, three other countries besides Argentina joined; WIZO, "International Movement: WIZO."

32. *Mundo Israelita*, September 18, 1926, 2.

33. WIZO Archives, OSFA, "Memoria y balance, desde Agosto 1926 hasta Diciembre 1927," 1927, 1.

34. See Siskel, "Los comienzos de la actividad educativa sionista," 12.

35. OSFA, "Memoria y balance," 1. It is likely this name was misspelled in the publication. Perhaps the original name was Zidlung Fond (Yiddish for Settlement Fund). I thank Malena Chinski for her help with this translation.

36. Comité de Damas del Fondo Nacional Israelita, Minute Books, August 24, 1925, and November 1925.

37. Ibid., August 5, 1926.

38. Ibid.

39. Ibid.

40. *Israel*, November 1926.

41. See "Ecos de la visita de los ilustres propagandistas del Sionismo Dr. Ariel Bensión y Juana de Bensión," *Semanario Hebreo*, November 1926, 9; OSFA, "Memoria y balance," 6–7.

42. *La Luz*, A. 1 No.28, 556; A. 1 No. 30, 597; A. 2 No. 7, 147; and A. 4 No. 5, 118.

43. McCune makes the same point regarding Haddasah in the United States; "Social Workers in the Muskeljudentum," 162. OSFA, Informe del Ejecutivo de la Organización Sionista Femenina Argentina, 1946–1948, 1–2.

44. OSFA, Report on Activities, 1957–1961, 1–2.

45. Ibid., 4.

46. The payment of the "Zionist Shekel" was instituted by Theodor Herzl, as a way to fund Zionist activities. WIZO copied this practice, and members purchased their "shekel" every year.

47. Practice instituted in 1950; OSFA, *Vivencias*, 18.

48. Instituted in 1946 (ibid.).

49. The first shipment was sent in 1946 (ibid.).

50. OSFA, "Memoria y balance," 1926–1927, 2. Mrs. Bensión, in a letter written to her friend in Rosario, complained that "it is a pity that they are concentrating on Afuleh [sic]. They should help in all WIZO work and not only [for] one group." Apparently, Afula was at first exclusively a farm for women and children (which might have been the very reason OSFA chose to aid it). Mrs. Bensión explained that "groups of young women living alone and doing man's work is not normal, nor a natural life. Girls, I believe, should be trained to earn their own living, but in a normal way. They should be encouraged to marry and to have children, because we must increase the population by natural means." WIZO Archives, Letter written by Ida Bensión to Fanny Wachs, November 28, 1928.

51. It should be added, however, that the money raised for Afula was sent to WIZO central offices in London, and later Tel Aviv. Part of that money, it is safe to assume, was used to pay for the support of WIZO structure, as Mrs. Bensión explained to the Argentine women.

52. For the need to construct more dorm rooms, see OSFA, Informe de la Organización Sionista Femenina WIZO, Años 1936–1938, 6.

53. CZA F49/1, OFSA letter to WIZO president, September 18, 1935.

54. CZA F49/6, Informe del Ejecutivo de la Organización Sionista Femenina Argentina, 1946–1948.

55. OSFA, Informe del Ejecutivo, 1946–1948, 2. The number of members in the German section in 1961 is unclear, as the report claims there were 8 centers and 1,886 members in BOTH the Sephardi and German sections. OSFA, Report on Activities, 1957–1961, 2.

56. The Comisión de Damas, later to become WIZO had in fact been created in 1945, on the initiative of the Youth Department. See Programa de acción del departamento de juventud del Centro Sionista Sefaradí.

57. Letter from Ida Bensión to Fanny Wachs, November 24, 1926. Madame Yivoff was a member of the Comité de Damas del Fondo Nacional, and later of WIZO/OSFA. See Comité de Damas del Fondo Nacional, Minute Book, Actas no. 1, 2, 5, 6, 7, 8; and Memoria y balance, 1926–1927, Lista de Socias, Buenos Aires.

58. CZA F49/2, Letter by Dr. Mibashan, to Dr. Hantke, Buenos Aires, March 23, 1938.

59. "Informe de la Sra. Alegre de Bonomo," *Israel*, May 31, 1948, 8.

60. CSS, Minute Book, October 12, 1925. The names of the women suggest they were the wives and daughters of CSS members.

61. CSS, Minute Book, March 28, 1936. They again discussed the need to establish a permanent women's commission for the

purpose of placing and retrieving collection boxes, but decided to ask the Federación Sionista Argentina to do it, as they had the necessary manpower. See also CSS, Minute Books, October 17, 1936, December 5, 1936, February 5, 1937.

62. This is the group that later became WIZO Sefaradí. Programa de acción del Departamento de Juventud del Centro Sionista Sefaradí; and CSS, Minute Books, August 4, 1946, and May 29, 1947.

63. In Resistencia, for example, Mrs. Galimidi (related to a future president of the Sephardi congregation) was "a founder and one of the most effective members" of WIZO (non-Sephardi).

64. For Presidencia Roque Saenz Peña, see the 1938 list of its Executive Committee. For Gualeguay, see "Actividades de los Centros de Entre Ríos," Revista OSFA, October, 1948.

65. OSFA, Informe del Ejecutivo 1946–1948, 2.

66. Ibid.

67. The last evidence I found dates from April to September 1980. Revista OSFA, No. 321, 1980, 28.

68. Sometimes, the word *Central* was omitted from the full name, but it was the same organization.

69. CZA F49/10, Letter written to Fay Grove, Head of the OFSA Organization Department, Buenos Aires, April 16, 1951.

70. CZA F49/11, Letter written to Mrs. Hauser by OSFA, Buenos Aires, January 15, 1952.

71. CZA F49/12, ibid., September 24, 1952.

72. CZA F49/12, Letter sent to the Consejo Central de Damas Sefaradíes by Mrs. Hauser, December 31, 1952.

73. CZA F49/12, Letter sent to Mrs. Ginossar by OSFA, Buenos Aires, August 29, 1952.

74. CZA F49/13, ibid., February 5, 1953.

75. CZA F49/17, ibid., September 2, 1954.

76. *Hanoar Hasefaradí*, November 1948, 7.

77. Ibid., August 1948, 6.

78. Ibid., November 1948, 14.

79. The anonymous writer of "La Histadruth" in 1947 said that the group had been founded "two years ago." An "official" pamphlet gives October 31, 1945, as the founding date. Other (secondary) sources claim it was founded in 1948. Gran Baile de la Colectividad, March 29, 1947, "La Histadruth" and *Presencia sefaradí*, 129; Amigas Sefaradíes de Na'amat, n/a, 1.

80. CZA 1865, *Despertar*, Tribuna de la Juventud Sefaradí Histadrut, November–December 1947, 3.

81. Political campaign pamphlet of Mapai, November 1950. There were other three women on a list of twenty-six candidates.

82. CZA 1865, *Despertar*, Tribuna de la Juventud Sefaradí Histadrut, July 1947, 8.

83. CZA 1865, *Despertar*, 1947, 8; and pamphlet listing the activities of Naamat "Naamat-Pioneras, Tu Vínculo con el Pueblo de Israel," n/a.

84. CZA F26/3, CSS, Minute Book, May 29, 1947; pamphlet edited by the "Amigas Sefaradíes de Na'amat," n/a, 3–5.

85. Gran Baile de la Colectividad, "La Histadruth."

86. "Apoyemos la labor de la Asociación Benot Yerushalaim," in pamphlet "Gran Baile de la Colectividad," March 29, 1947.

87. "Adhesión de la Asociación de Damas Sefaradíes 'Benot Ierushalaim,'" *Hanoar Hasefaradí*, September 1949, 14; CZA F26/3, CSS, Minute Book, May 29, 1947.

88. CILBA, Minute Book, Buenos Aires, October 1, 1899.

89. *Presencia sefaradí*, 56.

90. *Israel*, August 23, 1918, 489.

91. *Presencia sefaradí*, 56; and *La Luz*, April 24, 1931, 77; Deutsch, *Crossing Borders, Claiming a Nation*, 214.

92. *Presencia sefaradí*, 97; Bene Emet, Minute Book, February 15, 1939.

93. *La Luz*, May 29, 1931, 151, and October 23, 1931.

94. Rubin, *Historia de la comunidad israelita*, 8, 13.

95. Curzón, "Presencia judía en la ciudad de Santa Fé."

96. *La Luz*, September 3, 1934, 118, and April 4, 1932, 189; Etz HaHaim, Minute Book, August 24, 1920. Photograph of the Sociedad de Damas Israelitas Sefardim de Corrientes, Corrientes, December 1928.

97. For examples of widows requesting aid (or wives whose husbands were unable to work because of illness), see Ozer Dalim, Minute Book, March 26, 1918; AHASM, Minute Book, July 12, 1932.

98. *Presencia sefaradí*, 57.

99. Ozer Dalim, Minute Book, June 17, 1917.

100. *Israel*, October 16, 1925, 14.

101. CILBA, Minute Book, June 7, 1927.

102. *Socios activos* participated in meetings and had a vote. Women were considered *socios pasivos*. They paid dues, but could not participate in decision making. In some Sephardi communities in the interior, Ashkenazim were accepted as *socios pasivos*.

103. CILBA, March 1, 1945, and April 18, 1945.

104. Club Social Alianza, Departamento de Juventud, August 24, 1958.

105. Ibid., June 1, 1958.

106. Ibid., May 12, 1958.

107. Couscous is a typical northern African dish made of semolina, and usually paired with stew.

108. I have respected the Argentine transliteration of these dishes. Lida Azulay and Luna Azulay also appear in chapter 6.

109. Joelle Bahloul has argued for a distinction between ritual time and ordinary time, the designation of which determined the food served; see "Food Practices among Sephardic Immigrants in Contemporary France," 485–496.

110. For the argument on the connection between women and food see Pilcher, "Recipes for Patria"; Shapiro, *Perfection Salad*.

111. This section is, by necessity, qualitative rather than quantitative. Several interviews with Sephardi Jewish women serve as the basis for most of the analysis.

112. The oral history workshops took place August to September, 1998, in Centro Israelita Sefaradí (CIS).

113. One of the participants in the oral history workshops told me that although she had to work outside the home, her mother, who lived with her, was in charge of cooking. "Until my mother died, I never cooked a single dish," she confessed.

114. There is an important, growing body of scholarly work on the ways that cooking became the battleground between immigrants and women's groups intent on "homogenizing" American culture. To my knowledge, there is not much work on this specific topic for Argentina. See Rose, "From Sponge Cake to *Hamentaschen*," 6; Joselit, *The Wonders of America*; Legath, "The Way to an Immigrant's Heart"; McClymer, "Gender and the 'American Way of Life,'" 8; and Shapiro, *Perfection Salad*.

115. Sephardi and Ashkenazi cookbooks are usually organized by main ingredients (meats, poultry) or courses (salads), but almost always include a section entitled "Holidays" that collects recipes associated with each religious festivity. The connection between religious festivity and food has been explored by Bahloul, "Food Practices among Sephardic Immigrants"; and Prosterman, "Food and Celebration."

116. Gutkowski, *Erase una vez... Sefarad*, 412.

117. Interview with Beatriz Rosanes de Samuilov, June 1997.

118. Ibid.

119. Ḥesed VeEmet, Minute Book, March 20, 1935.

120. Lucha Funes, in an interview conducted in June 1997. She lived in Paso de los Libres until 1940.

121. Burman, "She Looketh Well to the Ways of Her Household," 249.

122. "Restricted" means prioritizing expenditure. If a community decided to raise money for a ritual bath, it probably meant not using that money for something else.

123. Or Torah, Minute Book, January 30, 1922.

124. Ibid., August 4, 1930.

125. Because Villa Crespo was a neighborhood chosen by both Sephardim and Ashkenazim, the butcher shops might have been run and supervised by Ashkenazim.

126. Oral history workshop, August 27, 1998.

127. For a description of the many rituals associated with the *tavlá de dulses*, see Gutkowski, *Erase una vez... Sefarad*, 274.

128. Foods that came to be associated with particular "Jewish" Sephardi communities were also, needless to say, the result of many cultural borrowings in the countries of origin. Baklava, for example, came to be associated with Ottoman and Moroccan Jewry, but it was a typical Ottoman food, not just "Jewish."

129. Phrases gathered during the second CIS interview, August 20, 1998.

130. Levy, *Cocina sefaradí*, 34.

131. Oral history workshop, August 20, 1998.

132. Bulisa and I met three times to discuss her experiences in Concordia and later Buenos Aires. She was not part of the workshop, as she belonged to a different Jewish social club.

133. Bahloul, "Food Practices among Sephardic Immigrants."

134. Interview with Esther Acrich, May 19, 1997.

135. See Pite, "Entertaining Inequalities."

136. Bosi, *Memoria e sociedade*, 23.

137. The same argument is made by Hasia Diner: "The older immigrants served as repositories of Jewish knowledge, skills, and standards" (*Hungering for America*, 191).

138. By "Russian" she meant "Ashkenazi." Interview with Lucha Funes, June 1997.

139. There are exceptions, of course. *Borrekas* and phyllo dough finger foods (Sephardi traditional dishes) have become mainstream at Jewish celebrations. A major Argentine newspaper published Sephardi recipes for Rosh Hashanah celebrations in its culinary section; recipes and comments were provided by Miriam Kamenszein, one of the few caterers who prepares Sephardi food. See *Clarín*, Ollas y Sartenes, October 2, 2003.

140. Levy, *Cocina sefaradí*; Na'amat, *Cocinando al estilo sefaradí*; WIZO-Rio Grupo Aliyah, *Gostinho de saudade*.

6. MARRIAGES AND SCHOOLS

1. Pico and Eichelbaum, "Un romance turco," *Escena: Revista Teatral,* Suplemento No. 9, August 30, 1920.
2. Ibid., n.p.
3. Stein, *Making Jews Modern.*
4. For a contemporary study that focuses on "exogamous" marriages among Jews in Buenos Aires, see Erdei, *Choosing Each Other.*
5. See Baily, "Marriage Patterns and Immigrant Assimilation"; Szuchman, "The Limits of the Melting Pot."
6. Otero, "Una visión crítica de la endogamia"; Seefeld, "La integración social de extranjeros en Buenos Aires"; Maluendres, "Los migrantes y sus hijos ante el matrimonio"; Pagano and Oporto, "La conducta endogámica de los grupos migrantes"; Silberstein, "Inmigración y selección matrimonial." For a study of marriages among internal migrants, see Acha, *Crónica sentimental,* chap. 1.
7. Epstein, "Los judeo-marroquies"; Tolcachier, "Continuidad o ruptura de identidades étnicas"; Geldstein, "Matrimonios mixtos en la poblacion judía de Salta."
8. *La Luz,* July 3, 1931, 250.
9. Ibid.
10. See Zemer, "The Rabbinic Ban on Conversion," 84.
11. See Levy and Reinoso, *La vida, según Marcos Levy.*
12. This explains the number of Ashkenazi marriages in this synagogue, as shown below.
13. Adamovsky, *Historia de la clase media Argentina,* 86.
14. "The Marriage of Regina," in Rodrigue, *Jews and Muslims,* 91–93.
15. Simon, Laskier, and Reguer, *The Jews of the Middle East and North Africa in Modern Times,* 214.
16. *Israel,* April 22–29, 1927, 29.
17. "Sociales de Rosario," *Israel,* September 23–30, 1927, n.p.
18. Karush, *Culture of Class,* 105; Sarlo, *El imperio de los sentimientos,* 135.
19. *Israel,* April 22–29, 1927, 43.
20. *Israel,* July 7, 1933, 5–6.
21. The practice of using the mikvah before the wedding was described as a "backward" tradition, incompatible with "modern" norms of decorum and privacy. Discussion among participants in Oral History workshop, August–September 1998.
22. CILBA, Minute Book, August 13, 1913, and bylaws approved in 1915; Agudat Dodim, article 3 of bylaws, 1935.
23. *Israel,* July 9–16, 1926, 4–5; Rubin, *Historia de la comunidad israelita sefaradí de la provincia de Córdoba,* 5.
24. Curzón, "Presencia judía en la ciudad de Santa Fé," 13.
25. Zadoff, *Historia de la educación judía en Buenos Aires,* 54.
26. Ibid., 12.
27. Ibid., 54.
28. Bianchi, *Historia de las religiones en la Argentina,* 98.
29. Astiz, "Jewish Acculturation: Identity, Society and Schooling," 50.
30. Although some of the educational institutions founded by Sephardim were not mere Talmud Torahs, the literature tends to assume, to a large degree, that they were. See Mirelman, *Jewish Buenos Aires,* 153–155. Zadoff's work, however, is more attentive to these differences.
31. Zadoff, *Historia de la educación judía en Buenos Aires,* 54.
32. Agudat Dodim, Steering Committee, meeting minutes, January 20, 1936.
33. See Or Torah, Steering Committee, meeting minutes, December 12, 1927.
34. *Israel,* October 17, 1937; Saidman, *Colectividad judía de Posadas,* 22.

35. The Vaad Hajinuj (Central Organization for Jewish Education) was created in 1935 by three Ashkenazi organizations. Most Sephardi institutions did not join. See Zadoff, *Historia de la educación judía en Buenos Aires,* chap. 4.

36. *Israel,* January, 22, 1932, cover. The call for a congress seems to suggest the desire of the magazine's editors to organize teachers in an effort to defend their jobs. Ashkenazi teachers had created a "labor union" of sorts in the early 1930s. See Zadoff, *Historia de la educación judía en Buenos Aires,* 83–93.

37. For the role of Sephardi teachers in JCA areas, see Epstein, "Maestros marroquíes"; Zadoff, *Historia de la educación judía en Buenos Aires.*

38. Rodgers, *Los judíos de Alepo en Argentina;* "Registro Talmud Torah alumnos, turno de la manana y de la tarde," September 1929; Mirelman, *Jewish Buenos Aires,* 155.

39. *Israel,* January 8, 1932, 9.

40. "Entrevista con Ruben Beraja," in Archivo de la Palabra, Centro de Investigación Mark Turkow, interview no. 141; Talmud Torah of the Comunidad Israelita Sefaradí de Buenos Aires, "Registro Talmud Torah alumnos, turno de la mañana y de la tarde" (Register of students, morning and afternoon shifts), September 1929.

41. They "followed the Hebrew system of writing adopted in Palestine, the same used by the Ashkenazim" (*Israel,* June 5, 1931, 15; January 2, 1932).

42. The Talmud Torah Etz HaḤaim in Rosario complained bitterly about a defective ceiling that made it impossible to hold classes when it was raining.

43. *Israel,* August 9, 1929, 14.

44. Or Torah, Minute Book, February 8, 1932.

45. *Israel,* March 20, 1925, 7; School in Posadas, Minute Books, April 1949. For the kindergarten idea, see *Israel,* March 13, 1925, 9; March 20, 1925, 7; Or Torah, Minute Book, January 29, 1931.

46. See Rodgers, *Los judíos de Alepo en Argentina,* 37; printed material, *Chalom,* April 1955.

47. *Israel,* May 27, 1932.

48. Etz HaḤaim, Rosario, Subcomisión escuela, Minute Book, February 8, 1934.

49. Agudat Dodim, Minute Book, April 19, 1948. This inclusion of "Argentine topics" had to do with the Consejo Nacional de Educación resolutions of 1938 and 1939, which required that all "religious and language" schools teach Argentine history and geography.

50. *Israel,* January 8, 1932, 8; July 3–10, 1931, 13; January 8, 1932, 3.

51. *Israel,* May 27, 1932. Agudat Dodim students played a "biblical scene" during the celebration of the Hilula of Rebí Schimihon.

52. Etz HaḤaim, Rosario, Subcomisión escuela, Minute Book, February 4, 1934.

53. See Zadoff, *Historia de la educación judía en Buenos Aires;* Bianchi, *Historia de las religiones en la Argentina.*

54. The Damascene Jews of La Boca utilized this method of translation into Arabic, too, until they adopted Spanish (given the requirement of the Cursos Religiosos Israelitas). See Zadoff, *Historia de la educación judía en Buenos Aires,* 54; Mirelman, *Jewish Buenos Aires,* 154–155.

55. See Rodgers, *Los judíos de Alepo en Argentina,* 87.

56. *Israel,* June 5, 1931, 15.

57. Ibid., August 2–9, 1929.

58. Ibid., June 22–29, 1928, 7.

59. Letter written by Chalom to "Templo Jerusalem y Colegio Atikva [sic]," June 26, 1933.

60. *Israel*, January 8, 1932, 9; invitation to Chalom's "End of the Year Celebration," November 1954.

61. Ibid., May 27, 1932, 14.

62. Ibid.

63. Ibid., June 5, 1931, 15.

64. Ibid., January 8, 1932, 3.

65. Letter to the Rhodes community by Chalom, December 26, 1935.

66. Rodgers, *Los judíos de Alepo en Argentina*, 101.

67. *Israel*, July 21, 1933, 3.

68. Or Torah, Steering Committee, meeting minutes, May 17, 1934.

69. Ibid., June 22, 1936.

70. Mirelman, *Jewish Buenos Aires*, 154.

71. Chalom School to Wolfson School, letter dated July 28, 1935.

72. Zadoff, *Historia de la educación judía en Buenos Aires*, 71. This school was located in a neighborhood where both Ashkenazim and Sephardim lived.

73. Chalom Archives. See the 1972 invitation to the "bat mitzvah" of the female students of this school. Several of the girls had "Ashkenazi" last names.

74. Singing the Hatikvah and carrying the "Hebrew" flag in all official celebrations were requirements the Vaad Hajinuj established for its schools in the late 1930s; this school did not belong to the organization. See Zadoff, *Historia de la educación judía en Buenos Aires*, 285.

75. Or Torah, Minute Book, June 30, 1927.

76. Ibid.

77. *La Luz*, May 26, 1933, 244.

78. See Agudat Dodim, Minute Book, September 6, 1944. One of the teachers hired to teach *temas patrióticos* was Antonia Rossi de Luca; the other was Ashkenazi Matilde Hertszcovich.

79. See Zadoff, *Historia de la educación judía en Buenos Aires*, 191–192; Bertoni, *Patriotas, cosmopolitas y nacionalistas*; Bryce, "Between Community and Nation."

80. Zadoff, *Historia de la educación judía en Buenos Aires*, chap. 5.

81. Rodgers, *Los judíos de Alepo en Argentina*, 89.

82. *Israel*, May 29–June 5, 1925, 15.

83. Although the receipts are undated, it is clear that this event took place in the mid-1930s. See "Entrega y bendición de la bandera a la escuela no. 12, Consejo Escolar 10."

84. *La Luz*, May 29, 1931, 141. The original word used in text was *Israelitas* and not *Jews*.

85. Ibid., July 10, 1931, 262.

86. See Rein and Lewis, "Judíos, árabes, sefaradíes y argentinos."

POSTSCRIPT

1. See Zaretsky and Levine, *Landscapes of Memory and Impunity*.

2. Diament, "Todos somos judíos."

3. Zaretsky and Levine, *Landscapes of Memory and Impunity*, 2.

4. Figures given by Jaime Saúl Levy, the president of the Asociación Israelita Latina de Corrientes, September 2000. Other sources cite 120 Jews (both Ashkenazim and Sephardim). CES, *Presencia sefaradí*, 120.

5. I have counted each name only once. Given that families in the past tended to have more than one or two children, eighty-one family names does not necessarily imply eighty-one families but probably many more.

6. See Erdei, *Choosing Each Other*.

7. Sociedad Hebraica Argentina, Organización Hebrea Argentina Macabi,

and Club Naútico Hacoaj are Jewish sporting and social clubs. Although they were founded in the 1920s and late 1930s, they began to attract larger numbers in the 1960s.

8. Liliana and Marcelo Benveniste coordinate weekly cultural meetings (Raices de Sefarad) and maintain an online newsletter (eSefarad), as well as a weekly radio program (Magazín Sefaradí). The Centro de Investigación y Difusión de la Cultura Sefaradí (CIDiC-SeF) organizes the Ladino classes, a variety of cultural events, and the Annual International Conference for Sephardi Studies.

BIBLIOGRAPHY

ARCHIVES
American Jewish Archives (AJA), Cincinnati, Ohio, United States
Archivo de la Palabra, Centro de Investigación Mark Turkow, Buenos Aires, Argentina
Asociación de Genealogía Judía de la Argentina (AGJA), Buenos Aires, Argentina
Alliance Israélite Universelle, Paris, France
Center for Jewish History, New York, New York, United States
Central Archives for the History of the Jewish People (CAHJP), Jerusalem, Israel
Central Zionist Archives (CZA), Jerusalem, Israel
Chalom Archives, Buenos Aires, Argentina
IWO Archives, Buenos Aires, Argentina
Jerusalem City Archives (J.C.A), Jerusalem, Israel
Joint Distribution Committee (JDC), New York, New York, United States
Museo Histórico Comunal y de la Colonización Judía, "Rabino Aarón H. Goldman," Moisesville, Argentina
Organización Sionista Femenina Argentina (OSFA), Buenos Aires, Argentina
Sabetay Djaen papers, Buenos Aires, Argentina

MINUTE BOOKS, BURIAL RECORDS, AND MARRIAGE RECORDS
Agudat Dodim
Asociación Hebraica Argentina de Socorros Mutuos
Asociación Israelita Sefaradí Hijos de la Verdad–Bene Emet
Centro Sionista Sefaradí
Chalom
Club Alianza
Comunidad Israelita Sefaradí de Buenos Aires–Kahal Kadosh (ACISBA)
Congregación Israelita de Buenos Aires (CIRA)
Congregación Israelita Latina de Buenos Aires (CILBA)
Etz HaḤaim
Guemilut Ḥasadim
Ḥesed Shel Emet
Ḥesed Shel Emet Sefaradit
Ḥesed VeEmet (Buenos Aires)
Or Torah
Organización Sionista Femenina Argentina (OSFA), Buenos Aires
Ozer Dalim
Rachel Temple
Sociedad Israelita Latina Ḥesed VeEmet del Chaco

NEWSPAPERS AND MAGAZINES

Adama
DESA
Despertar
Hanoar Hasefaradí
Israel
La Luz
La Prensa
Mundo Israelita
Revista OSFA
The Sephardi

INTERVIEWS

Acrich, Esther. 1997. Interview by author. Buenos Aires, Argentina. May 18.

Amiras, Alberto. 1998. Interview by author. Buenos Aires, Argentina. August 13.

Bartov, Judith. 2012. Interview by author. Or Haner, Israel. July 26.

Benasayag de Muscar, Meri. 2001. Interview by author. Resistencia, Argentina. September 6.

Funes, Lucha. 1997. Interview by author. Buenos Aires, Argentina. June 25.

Masri, Elena; Menasce, José; Galante, Ricardo; Alfie, José. 2010. Interview by author. Buenos Aires, Argentina. May 18.

Mehaudy, Raquel. 1998. Interview by author. Buenos Aires, Argentina. November 8.

Mizrahi, Adolfo. 2012. Skype interview by author. Buenos Aires, Argentina–Madrid, Spain. February 4.

Oral History workshop at Circulo Israelita Sefaradí, August–September 1998.

Roffé, José. 2001. Interview by author. Buenos Aires, Argentina. May 18.

Rosanés de Samuidov, Betty. 1997. Interview by author. Buenos Aires, Argentina. June 29.

PRINTED PAMPHLETS/SHORT PUBLICATIONS

Alsina, Don Juan. *Memoria de la Dirección de Inmigración Correspondiente al año 1909*. Ministerio de Agricultura. Buenos Aires. 1910.

American Jewish Committee. *Estudio demográfico de la colectividad sefaradí de habla española de Buenos Aires*. Buenos Aires. 1969.

Asociación de Beneficencia "Merced y Verdad." *Estatutos*. Buenos Aires. 1947.

Asociación Fraternal Israelita de Presidencia Roque Sáenz Peña. *Estatutos*. Presidencia Roque Sáenz Peña. 1945.

Asociación Israelita de Socorros Mutuos Hijos de Sión. *Estatutos*. Posadas. 1945.

Asociación Israelita Latina de Corrientes. *Estatutos*. Corrientes. 1924.

Asociación Israelita Latina de Corrientes. *Estatutos*. Corrientes. 1939.

Bene Kedem. *Los sefaradim y el sionismo*. Buenos Aires. 1926.

Comisión Interparlamentaria del Seguro Nacional. *Censo de mutualidades correspondiente a su estado en el año 1926*. Buenos Aires. 1926.

Consistorio Rabínico. *Propósitos y Programa del Gran Rabinato*. Buenos Aires. 1928.

Gran Baile de la Colectividad. Programs. Buenos Aires. 1945–1950.

Jewish Colonization Association. *Jewish Colonization Association: Su obra en la República Argentina, 1891–1941*. Buenos Aires. 1942.

Martinez, Alberto B. *Tercer censo nacional, levantado el 1° de junio de 1914, ordenado por la Ley no. 9108 bajo la presidencia del Dr. Roque Sáenz Peña, ejecutado durante la presidencia del Dr. Victorino de la Plaza*. Buenos Aires: Talleres gráficos de L. J. Rosso, 1916.

"Síntesis Histórica de los Asilos." Buenos Aires, 1944.

Sociedad Cultural Israelita. *"Scholem Aleijem" en sus Bodas de Oro, 1917–1967*. Corrientes. 1967.

SECONDARY SOURCES

Abitbol, Michel. "The Integration of North African Jews in France." *Yale French Studies* 85 (1994): 248–261.

Acha, Omar. *Crónica sentimental de la Argentina peronista: Sexo, inconsciente e ideología, 1945–1955*. Buenos Aires: Prometeo, 2013.

Adamovsky, Ezequiel. *Historia de la clase media Argentina: Apogeo y decadencia de una ilusión, 1919–2003*. Buenos Aires: Planeta, 2009.

Aizenberg, Edna. *Books and Bombs in Buenos Aires: Borges, Gerchunoff, and Argentine-Jewish Writing*. Hanover: University Press of New England, 2002.

———. "'Nuevos mundos halló Colón,' or, What's Different about Sephardic Literature in the Americas?" In *Contemporary Sephardic Identity in the Americas: An Interdisciplinary Approach*, edited by Margalit Bejarano and Edna Aizenberg, 31–37. Syracuse: Syracuse University Press, 2012.

Albert, Phyllis Cohen. *The Modernization of French Jewry: Consistory and Community in the Nineteenth Century*. Hanover: University Press of New England, 1977.

Alfonsín, Jorge. "La historia del cementerio israelita no habilitado de La Paternal." *Toldot* 12 (2000): 24–25.

Alsogaray, Júlio. *Trilogía de la trata de blancas (rufianes, policía, municipalidad)*. Buenos Aires: Tor, 1933.

Altabef, Norma E. Ben, and Marta Isabel Barbieri de Guardia. "Itinerarios, experiencias y conflictos: Historias de vida de inmigrantes judíos en una provincia del NOA." Paper presented at the Crossroads of History: Experience, Memory, Orality. XI International Oral History Conference. Istanbul, 2000.

AMIA. *Comunidad Judía de Buenos Aires, 1894–1994*. Buenos Aires: Milá, 1994.

Amichai, Yehuda. *Shirim: 1948–1962*. Tel Aviv: Schocken, 2002.

Angel, Marc D. *The Jews of Rhodes: The History of a Sephardic Community*. New York: Sepher-Hermon Press, 1978.

Arditti, Elías. *Izmir, París, Buenos Aires: Odisea de un inmigrante*. Buenos Aires, 1993.

Armony, Paul. "Cementerio de Flores." *Toldot* 4, no. 14 (2001): 26–27.

———. "Historia de cementerios." In *Patrimonio cultural en cementerios y rituales de la muerte*, edited by Leticia Maronese, 123–162. Buenos Aires: Comisión para la preservación del patrimonio histórico cultural de la ciudad de Buenos Aires, 2005.

———. "Los cementerios judíos de Buenos Aires." *Toldot* 10 (1999): 24–26.

Astiz, M. Fernanda. "Jewish Acculturation: Identity Society and Schooling. Buenos Aires, Argentina (1890–1930)." *Journal of Jewish Identities* 3, no. 1 (2010): 41–66.

Avni, Haim. *Argentina and the Jews: A History of Jewish Immigration*. Tuscaloosa: University of Alabama Press, 1991.

———. "Argentine Jewry: Its Social Position and Organization. Part II: The Organized Jewish Community and Its Institutions." *Dispersion and Unity* 13–14 (1971): 161–208.

Avni, Haim, Judit Bokser Liwerant, Sergio Della Pergola, Margalit Bejarano, and Leonardo Senkman. "Cuarenta años de cambios: Transiciones y paradigmas." In *Pertenencia y alteridad: Judíos en/de América Latina: Cuarenta años de cambios*, edited by Judit Bokser Liwerant Haim Avni, Sergio Della Pergola, Margalit Bejarano, Leonardo Senkman, 13–83. Madrid: Iberoamericana, 2010.

Avni, Haim, and Sibila Seibert. "La agricultura judía en la Argentina ¿éxito o fracaso?" *Desarrollo Económico* 22, no. 88 (1983): 535–548.

Azar, María Cherro de, and Walter Duer. "Judíos de Damasco en Argentina: Una historia de más de 100 años." *Diversidad* 5, no. 8 (2014): 115–131.

Bahloul, Joëlle. "Food Practices among Sephardic Immigrants in Contemporary France: Dietary Laws in Urban Society." *Journal of the American Academy of Religion* 63, no. 3 (1995): 485–496.

Baily, Samuel. *Immigrants in the Lands of Promise: Italians in Buenos Aires and New York City, 1870–1914.* Ithaca, NY: Cornell University Press, 1999.

———. "Las sociedades de ayuda mutua y el desarrollo de una comunidad italiana en Buenos Aires, 1858–1918." *Desarrollo Económico* 21, no. 84 (1982): 485–514.

———. "Marriage Patterns and Immigrant Assimilation in Buenos Aires, 1882–1923." *Hispanic American Historical Review* 60, no. 1 (1980): 32–48.

———. "Patrones de residencia de los italianos en Buenos Aires y Nueva York, 1880–1914." *Estudios Migratorios Latinoamericanos* 1, no. 1 (1985): 8–47.

Bar-Gil, Shlomo. *Juventud, visión y realidad: Movimientos jalutzianos en Argentina, de Dror y Gordonia a Ijud Habonim, 1934–1973* [in translation of: Ne'urim, hazon u-metsiút]. Colección Testimonios. Buenos Aires: Editorial Milá, 2008.

Barth, Fredrik. "Ethnic Groups and Boundaries." In *Theories of Ethnicity: A Classical Reader*, edited by Werner Sollors, 294–324. New York: New York University Press, 1996.

Bejarano, Margalit Bacchi de. "El cementerio y la unidad comunitaria en la historia de los sefaradim de Buenos Aires." *Sefárdica* 1, no. 2 (1984): 13–30.

———. "Los sefaradíes de la Argentina." *Sefárdica* 1, no. 2 (1984): 37–43.

Bejarano, Margalit, and Edna Aizenberg, eds. *Contemporary Sephardic Identity in the Americas: An Interdisciplinary Approach.* Syracuse: Syracuse University Press, 2012.

Bell, Lawrence D. "Bitter Conquest: Zionists against Progressive Jews and the Making of Post-War Jewish Politics in Argentina." *Jewish History* 17, no. 3 (2003): 285–308.

Benasayag, Eduardo Muscar. "Sefaradíes tetuaníes en La Sabana del Chaco austral-Argentina." *Maguen*, 2008. https://revistamaguenescudo.wordpress.com/sefardies-tetuanies-en-la-sabana-del-chaco-austral-por-eduardo-fortunato-muscar-bensayag/.

Ben-Ur, Aviva. *Sephardic Jews in America: A Diasporic History.* New York: New York University Press, 2009.

Ben-Ur, Aviva, and Rachel Frankel. *Remnant Stones: The Jewish Cemeteries and Synagogues of Suriname. Essays.* Cincinnati, OH: Hebrew Union College Press, 2012.

Berkowitz, Michael. *Zionist Culture and West European Jewry before the First World War.* Cambridge: Cambridge University Press, 1993.

Bertoni, Liliana Ana. "De Turquía a Buenos Aires: Una colectividad nueva a fines del siglo XIX." *Estudios Migratorios Latinoamericanos* 9, no. 26 (1994): 67–93.

———. *Patriotas, cosmopolitas y nacionalistas: La construcción de la nacionalidad argentina a fines del siglo XIX.* Buenos Aires: Fondo de Cultural Económica de Argentina, 2001.

Bestene, Jorge O. "Formas de asociacionismo entre los sirios-libaneses en Buenos Aires (1900–1950)." In *Asociacionismo, trabajo e identidad*

étnica, edited by F. J. Devoto and
E. J. Miguez, 115–133. Buenos Aires:
CEMLA, CSER, IEHS, 1992.

———. "La inmigración sirio-libanesa en
la Argentina. Una aproximación."
Estudios Migratorios Latinoamericanos
9 (1988): 239–268.

Bianchi, Susana. *Historia de las religiones
en la Argentina: Las minorías religiosas*.
Buenos Aires: Sudamericana, 2004.

Blumenfeld, Israel. *Historia de la
comunidad israelita de Tucumán*.
Tucumán: Sociedad Union Israelita
Tucumana, 1971.

Bosi, Eclea. *Memoria e sociedade:
Lembrança de velhos*. São Paulo: Editora
da Universidade de São Paulo, 1973.

Boulgourdjian, Nélida. "Inmigrantes
armenios en Buenos Aires: Tensión
entre tradición e integración. Evolución
de su red asociativa (1900–1950)."
Estudios Migratorios Latinoamericanos
20, no. 59 (2006): 27–68.

Boyarin, Daniel, and Jonathan Boyarin.
"Diaspora: Generation and the Ground
of Jewish Identity." *Critical Inquiry* 19
(1993): 693–725.

Brá, Gerardo. "La mutual de los rufianes."
Todo es Historia 121 (1977): 74–92.

———. *La organización negra: La increíble
historia de la Zwi Migdal*. Buenos Aires:
Corregidor, 1982.

Bristow, Edward. *Prostitution and
Prejudice: The Jewish Fight against White
Slavery, 1870–1939*. New York: Schocken
Books, 1983.

Brodsky, Adriana. "Belonging to Many
Homes: Argentine Sephardi Youth in
Buenos Aires and in Israel, 1956–1976."
In *Transnational Histories of Youth in the
Twentieth Century*, edited by Richard
Jobs and David Pomfret, 213–235.
Basingstoke: Pallgrave, 2015.

Bryce, Benjamin. "Between Community
and Nation: British, French and
German Schools in Buenos Aires,
1880–1930." Paper presented at The
New Ethnic Studies: Issues and
Methods Conference. Tel Aviv
University, 2015.

———. "Paternal Communities: Social
Welfare and Immigration in Argentina,
1880–1930." *Journal of Social History* 49,
no. 1 (2015): 213–236.

Bunis, David M. "Modernization and the
Language Question among Judezmo-
Speaking Sephardim of the Ottoman
Empire." In *Sephardi and Middle
Eastern Jewries: History and Culture in
the Modern Era*, edited by Harvey
E. Goldberg, 226–239. Bloomington:
Indiana University Press, 1996.

Burman, Ricki. "'She Looketh Well to the
Ways of Her Household': The Changing Role of Jewish Women in Religious
Life, 1880–1930." In *Religion in the Lives
of English Women, 1760–1930*, edited by
Gail Malmgreen, 234–259. Bloomington: Indiana University Press, 1986.

Bushnell, David, and Neill Macaulay. *The
Emergence of Latin America in the
Nineteenth Century*. 2nd ed. New York:
Oxford University Press, 1994.

Camji, Moisés. "A 100 años de sionismo:
Importante activismo de la comunidad
sefaradí de la Argentina." Unpublished
manuscript.

Castro, Donald S. *The Development and
Politics of Argentine Immigration Policy,
1852–1914: To Govern Is to Populate*. San
Francisco: Mellen Research University
Press, 1991.

Centro Educativo Sefaradí, ed. *Presencia
sefaradí en la Argentina*. Buenos Aires:
Centro Educativo Sefaradí, 1992.

Cianfardo, Eduardo O. "La práctica
benéfica y el control de los sectores
populares de la ciudad de Buenos Aires,
1890–1910." *Revista de Indias* 54, no. 210
(1994): 383–403.

Clifford, James. "Diasporas." *Cultural Anthropology* 9, no. 3 (1994): 302–338.

Cohen, Julia Phillips. *Becoming Ottomans: Sephardi Jews and Imperial Citizenship in the Modern Era.* New York: Oxford University Press, 2014.

———. "Fashioning Imperial Citizens: Sephardi Jews and the Ottoman State, 1856–1912." PhD dissertation, Stanford University, 2008.

Cohen, Mario Eduardo. "Aspéctos socio-demográficos de la comunidad sefaradita de la Argentina." *Sefárdica* 3 (1985): 57–78.

Cohen de Chervonagura, Elisa B. *La comunidad judía de Tucumán: Hombres y mujeres, historias y discursos, 1910–2010.* Tucumán, 2010.

Contreras, Jaime. "Family and Patronage: The Judeo-Converso Minority in Spain." In *Cultural Encounters: The Impact of the Inquisition in Spain and the New World*, edited by Elizabeth Perry and Anne J. Cruz, 127–144. Berkeley: University of California Press, 1991.

Curzón, Marcos. "Presencia judía en la ciudad de Santa Fé." Paper presented at the III Encuentro de Historiadores "Dra. Hebe Livi." Junta Provincial de Estudios Históricos de Santa Fé, 1999.

Daccarett, Paula. "Jewish Social Services in Late Ottoman Salonica (1850–1912)." PhD dissertation, Brandeis University, 2008.

Danon, Dina. "Por bien de la sivdad i por amor del puevlo." Paper presented at the conference Crossing Boundaries: New Approaches to Modern Judeo-Spanish Cultures. Los Angeles, 2011.

Della Pergola, Sergio. "Demographic Trends of Latin American Jewry." In *The Jewish Presence in Latin America*, edited by Judith Laikin Elkin and Gilbert W. Merkx, 85–133. Boston: Allen and Unwin, 1987.

Deutsch, Sandra McGee. "The Catholic Church, Work, and Womanhood in Argentina, 1890–1930." *Gender and History* 3, no. 3 (1991): 304–322.

———. *Crossing Borders, Claiming a Nation: A History of Argentine Jewish Women, 1880–1955.* Durham, NC: Duke University Press, 2010.

———. *Las Derechas: The Extreme Right in Argentina, Brazil, and Chile, 1890–1939.* Stanford, CA: Stanford University Press, 1999.

Devoto, Fernando J. "La experiencia mutualista italiana en la Argentina: Un balance." In *Asociacionismo, trabajo e identidad étnica: Los italianos en América Latina en una perspectiva comparada*, edited by Fernando J. Devoto and E. J. Miguez, 169–185. Buenos Aires: CEMLA, CSER, IEHS, 1992.

———. "Las sociedades italianas de ayuda mutua en Buenos Aires y Santa Fé. Ideas y problemas." *Studi Emigrazione* 31, no. 75 (1984): 320–342.

Devoto, Fernando J., and E. J. Miguez, eds. *Asociacionismo, trabajo e identidad étnica: Los italianos en América Latina en una perspectiva comparada.* Buenos Aires: CEMLA-CSER-IEHS, 1992.

Diament, Mario. "Todos somos judíos." *El Cronista Comercial*, March 18, 1992.

Dias, Fátima S. "The Jewish Community in the Azores from 1820 to the Present." In *From Iberia to Diaspora. Studies in Sephardic History and Culture*, edited by Yedida K. Stillman and Norman A. Stillman, 19–34. Leiden: Brill, 1999.

Diner, Hasia R. *Hungering for America: Italian, Irish, and Jewish Foodways in the Age of Migration.* Cambridge, MA: Harvard University Press, 2001.

Dobrinsky, Rabbi Herbert C. *A Treasury of Sephardic Laws and Customs.* New York: Yeshiva University Press, 1988.

Duer, Walter. "El rol del *Jajam* en las primeras inmigraciones damascenas a la Argentina." Paper presented at the 4to Simposio Internacional de Estudios Sefaradíes. Buenos Aires, 2011.

Ehl, Petr, Arno Parik, and Jirí Fiedler. *Old Bohemian and Moravian Jewish Cemeteries*. Prague: Kynsperk nad Ohri, 1991.

Eliachar, Elie. *Living with Jews*. London: Weidenfeld and Nicolson, 1983.

Elnecavé, Bruria de. *Historia de la WIZO Mundial*. Buenos Aires: Depto. de Cultura de la Organización Sionista Femenina Argentina, 1950.

Elnecave, David. "Los Sefaradíes en la Argentina." In *50 años de vida judía en la Argentina: Homenaje a "El Diario Israelita" en su 25 aniversario*, edited by Hirsch Triwaks, 57–60. Buenos Aires, 1940.

Englander, Nathan. *The Ministry of Special Cases*. New York: Knopf, 2007.

Epstein, Diana. "Los judeo-marroquíes en Buenos Aires: Pautas matrimoniales 1875–1910." *Estudios Interdisciplinarios de América Latina y el Caribe* 6, no. 1 (1995): 113–133.

———. "Maestros marroquíes. Estrategia educativa e integración, 1890–1910." V Jornadas Interescuelas/Departamentos de Historia y I Jornadas Rioplatenses Universitarias de Historia: Montevideo, Uruguay, 1995.

Erdei, Ezequiel. *Choosing Each Other: Exogamy in the Jewish Community of Buenos Aires*. JDC International Centre for Community Development, 2014. http://www.bjpa.org/Publications/details.cfm?PublicationID=21933.

Ettinger, S. "Part VI: The Modern Period." In *A History of the Jewish People*, edited by H. H. Ben-Sasson, 727–1096. Cambridge, MA: Harvard University Press, 1976.

Feldman, Hernán. "Buenos Aires, 1919: Arbeit macht frei?" *Latin American Literary Review* 36, no. 71 (2008): 24–52.

Fernandez, Alejandro Enrique. "El mutualismo español en un barrio de Buenos Aires: San José de Flores (1890–1900)." In *Asociacionismo, trabajo e identidad étnica: Los italianos en América Latina en una perspectiva comparada*, edited by F. J. Devoto and E. J. Miguez, 135–168. Buenos Aires: CEMLA-CSER-IEHS, 1992.

Ferro, Gabriel. "El oficio de los muertos. Las sociedades italianas de socorros mutuos de la provincia de Santa Fé frente a la muerte." *Estudios Migratorios Latinoamericanos* 17, no. 51 (2003): 441–455.

Flores, María Alejandra. *La integración social de los inmigrantes. Los llamados turcos en la ciudad de Córdoba, 1890–1930*. Córdoba: Centro de Estudios Históricos, 1996.

Fraser, Hugh. *The British Hospital of Buenos Aires: A History 1844–2000*. Buenos Aires: n.p., 2001.

Freidenberg, Judith Noemí. *The Invention of the Jewish Gaucho: Villa Clara and the Construction of Argentine Identity*. Austin: University of Texas Press, 2009.

Gallo, Ezequiel. *Farmers in Revolt: The Revolutions of 1893 in the Province of Santa Fé, Argentina*. London: Athlone Press, 1976.

Geldstein, Rosa N. "Matrimonios mixtos en la población judía de Salta. Un análisis sociodemográfico." *Estudios Migratorios Latinoamericanos* 9 (1988): 217–235.

Gerchunoff, Alberto. *The Jewish Gauchos of the Pampas*. Translated by Prudencio de Pereda. Albuquerque: University of New Mexico Press, 1998.

Germani, Gino. *Política y sociedad en una época de transición*. Buenos Aires: Paidos, 1965.

Goldberg, Idana. "Sacrifices upon the Altar of Charity: The Masculinization of Jewish Philanthropy in Mid-Nineteenth Century America." *Nashim: A Journal of Jewish Women's Studies & Gender Issues* 20 (2010): 34–56.

Green, Abigail. "Sir Moses Montefiore and the Making of the Jewish International." *Journal of Modern Jewish Studies* 7, no. 3 (2008): 287–307.

Green, Nancy L. "To Give and to Receive: Philanthropy and Collective Responsibility among Jews in Paris, 1880–1914." In *The Uses of Charity: The Poor on Relief in the Ninenteenth-Century Metropolis*, edited by Peter Mandler, 197–226. Philadelphia: University of Pennsylvania Press, 1990.

Grinblat, Isaías. *Historia de la comunidad judía en la Provincia de Salta*. Salta: Asociación Alianza Israelita de SS. MM. y la Sociedad Israelita Salteña "La Unión," 1986.

Guahnon, José. "Cuenta tu pueblo, y contarás el mundo." *Un Orgullo de Cien Años*, October 1991, 5–7.

Gutkowski, Hélène. *Erase una vez ... Sefarad. Los sefaradíes del Mediterráneo; su historia; su cultura*. Buenos Aires: Editorial Lumen, 1999.

———. "Estampas del mundo sefaradí de ayer." In *Presencia sefaradí en la Argentina*, edited by CES, 25–39. Buenos Aires: Centro Educativo Sefaradí en Jerusalem, 1992.

Guy, Donna. *Sex and Danger in Buenos Aires: Prostitution, Family and Nation in Argentina*. Lincoln: University of Nebraska Press, 1990.

———. *Women Build the Welfare State: Performing Charity and Creating Rights in Argentina, 1880–1955*. Durham, NC: Duke University Press, 2009.

———. "Women's Organizations and Jewish Orphanages in Buenos Aires, 1918–1955." Paper presented at the Latin American Jewish Studies Association, Rio de Janeiro, 2002.

Hall, Stuart. "Cultural Identity and Diaspora." In *Diaspora and Visual Culture: Representing Africans and Jews*, edited by Nicholas Mirzoeff, 21–33. London: Routledge, 2000.

Halporn, Roberta. "American Jewish Cemeteries: A Mirror of History." In *Ethnicity and the American Cemetery*, edited by Richard E. Meyer, 131–155. Bowling Green, OH: Bowling Green University Popular Press, 1993.

Harel, Yaron. *Syrian Jewry in Transition: 1840–1880*. Oxford: Littman Library of Jewish Civilization, 2010.

Haskell, Guy H. "The Sephardic Culture in Bulgaria." In *From Iberia to Diaspora: Studies in Sephardic History and Culture*, edited by Yedida K. Stillman and Norman A. Stillman, 35–48. Leiden: Brill, 1999.

Hordes, Stanley M. "Inquisition and the Crypto-Jewish Community in Colonial New Spain and New Mexico." In *Cultural Encounters: The Impact of the Inquisition in Spain and the New World*, edited by Elizabeth Perry and Anne J. Cruz, 207–218. Berkeley: University of California Press, 1991.

Horowitz, Amy. *Mediterranean Israeli Music and the Politics of the Aesthetic*. Detroit: Wayne State University Press, 2010.

Horowitz, Joel. *Argentina's Radical Party and Popular Mobilization, 1916–1930*. University Park: Pennsylvania State University Press, 2008.

Horowitz, Louis. *Israeli Ecstasies/Jewish Agonies*. New York: Oxford University Press, 1974.

Huberman, Ariana. *Gauchos and Foreigners: Glossing Culture and Identity in the Argentine Countryside*. Lanham, MD: Lexington Books, 2011.

Joselit, Jenna Weissman. *The Wonders of America: Reinventing Jewish Culture: 1880–1950*. New York: Hill and Wang, 1994.

Kagan, Richard L., and Philip D. Morgan. *Atlantic Diasporas: Jews, Conversos, and Crypto-Jews in the Age of Mercantilism, 1500–1800*. Baltimore, MD: Johns Hopkins University Press, 2008.

Karush, Matthew B. *Culture of Class: Radio and Cinema in the Making of a Divided Argentina, 1920–1946*. Durham, NC: Duke University Press, 2012.

Klich, Ignacio. "Arabes, judíos y árabes judíos en la Argentina de la primera mitad del novecientos." *E.I.A.L* 6, no. 2 (1995): 109–42.

Kobrin, Rebecca. *Jewish Bialystok and Its Diaspora*. Bloomington: Indiana University Press, 2010.

———. "The Politics of Philanthropy: Migration, Emigration, and the Transformation of Jewish Communal Governance in Bialystok, 1885–1939." In *Studies in Jewish Civilization: The Jews of Eastern Europe*, edited by Leonard J. Greenspoon, Ronald A. Simkins, and Brian J. Horowitz, 233–254. Omaha, NE: Creighton University Press, 2005.

Kushnir, Beatriz. *Baile de mascaras: Mulheres judias e prostituçao. As "Polacas" e suas associaçoes de ajuda mutua*. Rio de Janeiro: Imago Editora, 1996.

Laskier, Michael M. *The Alliance Israélite Universelle and the Jewish Communities of Morocco, 1862–1962*. Albany: State University of New York Press, 1983.

Lazar, Moshe. "Scorched Parchments and Tortured Memories: the 'Jewishness' of the Anussin (Crypto-Jews)." In *Cultural Encounters: The Impact of the Inquisition in Spain and the New World*, edited by Elizabeth Perry and Anne J. Cruz, 176–205. Berkeley: University of California Press, 1991.

Lebel, Jennie. "Ivrit beḥotsut monastir haneḥrevat: Rabi Shabetay Djaen, toldotav shel rab, mahapkhan, vemaḥzaei tsitonei beLadino." *Dimui* 11 (1996): 22–30.

Legath, Jennifer Wiley. "The Way to an Immigrant's Heart." Unpublished paper, 2000.

Lehmann, Matthias B. "Introduction: Sephardi Identities." *Jewish Social Studies* 15, no. 1 (2008): 1–9.

Lerner, Gloria Rut. "La historia del Asilo Argentino de Huérfanas Israelitas." Unpublished manuscript.

Lesser, Jeffrey, and Raanan Rein. "Challenging Particularity: Jews as a Lens on Latin American Ethnicity." *Latin American and Caribbean Ethnic Studies* 1, no. 2 (2006): 249–263.

———. "New Approaches to Ethnicity and Diaspora in Twentieth-Century Latin America." In *Rethinking Jewish-Latin Americans*, edited by Jeffrey Lesser and Raanan Rein, 23–40. Albuquerque: University of New Mexico Press, 2008.

Levin, Marlin. *It Takes a Dream: The Story of Hadassah*. Jerusalem: Gefen Publishing House, 1997.

Levy, Avigdor. "Haham Başi (Chief Rabbi)." In *Encyclopedia of Jews in the Islamic World*, edited by Norman A. Stillman. Brill Online, 2016. <http://referenceworks.brillonline.com/entries/encyclopedia-of-jews-in-the-islamic-world/haham-bas-chief-rabbi-COM_0008940>

———. "*Millet* Politics: The Appointment of a Chief Rabbi in 1835." In *The Jews of the Ottoman Empire*, edited by Avigdor Levy, 425–438. Princeton, NJ: Darwin Press, 1994.

Levy, Estela. *Cocina sefaradí*. Buenos Aires: n.p., 1980.

———. *Crónica de una familia sefaradí*. Buenos Aires: Carcos, 1983.

Levy, Larry. *La mancha de la Migdal: Historia de la prostitución judía en la Argentina*. Buenos Aires: Grupo Editorial Norma, 2007.

Levy, Marcos, and Ricardo Reinoso. *La vida, según Marcos Levy: Biografía de un inmigrante de orígen sefardí*. Tucumán: n.p., 2002.

Lewin, Boleslao. *Cómo fue la inmigración judía a la Argentina*. Buenos Aires: Editorial Plus Ultra, 1971.

———. *La colectividad judía en la Argentina*. Buenos Aires: Alzamor Editories, 1974.

Liachovitzky, Jacobo Simon. *Zamlbuch*. Buenos Aires: n.p., 1938.

Little, Cynthia Jeffress. "The Society of Beneficence in Buenos Aires, 1823–1900." PhD dissertation, Temple University, 1980.

Liwerant, Judit Bokser, and Leonardo Senkman. "Diásporas y transnacionalismo. Nuevas indagaciones sobre los judíos latinoamericanos hoy." In *Judaica Latinoamericana. Estudios históricos, sociales y literarios*, edited by AMILAT, 11–71. Jerusalem: Magnes, the Hebrew University of Jerusalem, 2013.

Loyudice, Francisco. *Hospital Italiano: Testimonios y nostalgias*. Buenos Aires: Asociación Dante Alighieri, 1995.

Ludmer, Josefina. *The Gaucho Genre: A Treatise on the Motherland*. Durham, NC: Duke University Press, 2002.

Lvovich, Daniel. *Nacionalismo y antisemitismo en la Argentina*. Buenos Aires: Javier Vergara, 2003.

Maluendres, Sergio. "Los migrantes y sus hijos ante el matrimonio: Un estudio comparativo entre alemanes de Rusia, españoles e italianos en Guatraché (La Pampa, 1910–1939)." *Estudios Migratorios Latinoamericanos* 18 (1991): 191–221.

Martina, Angeles de. "Interview with Meri Benasayag de Muscar." Unpublished manuscript, 1999.

Mato, Omar López, and Hernán S. Vizzari. *Angeles de Buenos Aires. Historia de los cementerios de la Chacarita, Alemán y Británico*. Buenos Aires: Olmo Ediciones, 2011.

Mazo, Júlio. *Historia de los ashkenazim de Resistencia*. Resistencia, 1987.

McClymer, John F. "Gender and the 'American Way of Life': Women and the Americanization Movement." *Journal of American Ethnic History* 10, no. 3 (1991): 3–20.

McCune, Mary. "Social Workers in the Muskeljudentum: 'Hadassah Ladies,' 'Manly Men' and the Significance of Gender in the American Zionist Movement, 1912–1928." *American Jewish History* 86, no. 2 (1998): 135–165.

McGee, Sandra. "Right-Wing Female Activists in Buenos Aires, 1900–1932." In *Women and the Structure of Society*, edited by Barbara J. Harris and Jo Ann McNamara, 85–97. Durham, NC: Duke University Press, 1984.

Mead, Karen. "Gender, Welfare and the Catholic Church in Argentina: Conferencias de Señoras de San Vicente de Paul, 1890–1916." *The Americas* 58, no. 1 (2001): 91–119.

Meir, Natan M. "From Community Charity to National Welfare: Jewish Orphanages in Eastern Europe Before and After World War I." *East European Jewish Affairs* 39, no. 1 (2009): 19–34.

Meyer, Richard E., ed. *Ethnicity and the American Cemetery*. Bowling Green, OH: Bowling Green State University Popular Press, 1993.

Miller, Susan Gilson. "Kippur on the Amazon. Jewish Emigration from Northern Morocco in the Late Nineteenth Century." In *Sephardi and Middle Eastern Jewries: History and Culture in the Modern Era*, edited by Harvey E. Goldberg, 190–209. Bloomington: Indiana University Press, 1996.

Mirelman, Victor A. "Early Zionist Activities among Sephardim in Argentina." *American Jewish Archives* 34 (1982): 190–205.

———. *Jewish Buenos Aires, 1890–1930: In Search of an Identity*. Detroit, MI: Wayne State University Press, 1990.

———. "The Jewish Community versus Crime: The Case of White Slavery in Buenos Aires." *Jewish Social Studies* 46, no. 2 (1984): 145–168.

———. "Sephardic Immigration to Argentina Prior to the Nazi Period." In *The Jewish Presence in Latin America*, edited by Judith Laikin Elkin and Gilbert W. Merkx, 33–44. Boston: Allen and Unwin, 1987.

Molho, Michael. *Usos y costumbres de los sefaradíes de Salónica*. Madrid: Consejo Superior de Investigaciones Científicas Instituto Arias Montano, 1950.

Moya, José C. *Cousins and Strangers: Spanish Immigrants in Buenos Aires, 1850–1930*. Berkeley: University of California Press, 1998.

Munck, Ronaldo. "Mutual Benefit Societies in Argentina: Workers, Nationality, Social Security and Trade Unionism." *Journal of Latin American Studies* 30, no. 3 (1998): 573–590.

Na'amat, Amigas Sefaradíes de. *Cocinando al estilo sefaradí*. Buenos Aires, 1994.

Netzer, Amnon. "Persian Jewry and Literature: A Sociocultural View." In *Sephardi and Middle Eastern Jewries: History and Culture in the Modern Era*, edited by Harvey E. Goldberg, 240–255. Bloomington: Indiana University Press, 1996.

Nuñez, Luis F. *Almario de Buenos Aires: Los Cementerios*. Buenos Aires: Ministerio de Educación y Cultura, 1970.

Otero, Hernán. "El asociacionismo francés en la Argentina. Una perspectiva secular." *Estudios Interdisciplinarios de América Latina y el Caribe* 21, no. 2 (2010): 123–52.

———. "Una visión crítica de la endogamia: reflexiones a partir de una reconstrucción de familias francesas, Tandil 1850–1914." *Estudios Migratorios Latinoamericanos* 15–16 (1990): 343–378.

OSFA. *Vivencias: 70 Aniversario*. Buenos Aires: OSFA, 1996.

Pagano, Nora, and Mario Oporto. "La conducta endogámica de los grupos migrantes. Pautas matrimoniales de los italianos en el barrio de La Boca en 1895." *Estudios Migratorios Latinoamericanos* 4 (1986): 483–495.

Penslar, Derek J. *Shylock's Children*. Berkeley: University of California Press, 2001.

Pereira, Júlio César Medeiros da Silva. *À flor da terra: O cemitério dos pretos novos no Rio de Janeiro*. Rio de Janeiro: Editora Garamond, 2007.

Pico, Pedro E., and Samuel Eichelbaum. "Un romance turco." *La Escena: Revista Teatral* 3, no. 9 (1920).

Pilcher, Jeffrey M. "Recipes for Patria: Cuisine, Gender and Nation in Nineteenth-Century Mexico." In *Recipes for Reading: Community, Cookbooks, Stories, Histories*, edited by Anne L. Bower, 200–215. Amherst: University of Massachusetts Press, 1997.

Pite, Rebekah E. "Entertaining Inequalities: Doña Petrona, Juanita Bordoy, and Domestic Work in Mid-Twentieth-Century Argentina." *Hispanic American Historical Review* 91, no. 1 (2011): 96–128.

Prosterman, Leslie. "Food and Celebration: A Kosher Caterer as Mediator of Communal Traditions." In *Ethnic and Regional Foodways in the United States: The Performance of Group Identity*, edited by Linda Keller Brown and Kay Mussell, 127–144. Knoxville: University of Tennessee Press, 1984.

Ray, Jonathan. "New Approaches to the Jewish Diaspora: The Sephardim as a Sub-Ethnic Group." *Jewish Social Studies* 15, no. 1 (2009): 10–31.

Rebrij, Freida Geffner. "Comunidad judía de Lomas de Zamora." *Toldot* 5, no. 13 (2000): 14–15.

Rein, Raanan. *Argentine Jews or Jewish Argentines? Essays on Ethnicity, Identity, and Diaspora*. Boston: Brill, 2010.

———. *Los muchachos peronistas judíos*. Buenos Aires: Sudamericana, 2015.

Rein, Raanan, and Mollie Lewis. "Judíos, árabes, sefaradíes y argentinos: el caso del periódico *Israel*." In *Arabes y judíos en Iberoamérica: similitudes, diferencias y tensiones sobre el transfondo de las tres culturas*, edited by Raanan Rein, 83–115. Madrid: Fondo de las Tres culturas, 2008.

Reis, João José. *Death Is a Festival: Funeral Rites and Rebellion in Nineteenth-Century Brazil*. Chapel Hill: University of North Carolina Press 2003.

Resta, Laura, and Mabel Borga. *Pichincha y después... Ocaso del mundo prostibular, 1930*. Rosario: Editorial Ciudad Gótica, 2010.

Rodgers, Susana Brauner. "La comunidad judía alepina en Buenos Aires: de la ortodoxia religiosa a la apertura y de la apertura a la ortodoxia religiosa (1930–1953)." *Estudios Interdisciplinarios de America Latina y el Caribe* 11, no. 1 (2000): 45–64.

———. "Identidad y prácticas económicas: empresarios judíos y ortodoxos de orígen sirio en Argentina, desde el menemismo al kirchnerismo." Paper presented at LAJSA 16th International Research Conference. Austin, 2011.

———. *Los judíos de Alepo en Argentina*. Buenos Aires: Nuevos Tiempos, 2005.

———. "Los judíos sirios en Buenos Aires frente al sionismo y al estado de Israel, (1948–1990)." *AMILAT* 5 (2005): 169–184.

Rodrigue, Aron. *Jews and Muslims: Images of Sephardi and Eastern Jewries in Modern Times*. Seattle: University of Washington, 2003.

———. "The Sephardim in the Ottoman Empire." In *Spain and the Jews: The Sephardi Experience 1492 and After*, edited by Elie Kedourie, 162–168. London: Thames and Hudson, 1992.

Roniger, Luis, and Deby Babis. "Latin American Israelis: The Collective Identity of an Invisible Community." In *Identities in an Era of Globalization and Multiculturalism: Latin America in the Jewish World*, edited by Eliezer Ben-Rafael Judit Bokser Liwerant, Yossi Gorny, and Raanan Rein, 297–320. Leiden: Brill, 2008.

Rose, Elizabeth. "From Sponge Cake to *Hamentaschen*: Jewish Identity in a Jewish Settlement House, 1885–1952." *Journal of American Ethnic History* 13, no. 3 (1993–1994): 6.

Rubin, Jacobo. "Historia de la comunidad israelita sefaradí de la provincia de Córdoba R. A, 1904–1973." Unpublished manuscript, 1973.

Saidman, Sheila Nadia. "Colectividad judía de Posadas." Monografía de

Grado, Universidad Nacional de Misiones, 1999.

Sarlo, Beatriz. *El imperio de los sentimientos*. Buenos Aires: Norma, 2000.

Schenkolewski-Kroll, Silvia. "Cambios en la relación de la Organización Sionista Mundial hacia la comunidad judía y el movimiento sionista en la Argentina, hasta 1948." *Judaica Latinoamericana. Estudios Histórico-Sociales* 1 (1988): 149–166.

———. "The Influence of the Zionist Movement on the Organization of the Argentinian Jewish Community: The Case of the DAIA, 1933–1946." *Studies in Zionism* 12, no. 1 (1991): 17–28.

———. "La conquista de las comunidades: El movimiento sionista y la comunidad ashkenazi de Buenos Aires (1935–1949)." *Judaica Latinoamericana. Estudios Histórico-Sociales* 2 (1993): 191–201.

———. "Los sionistas generales en Argentina, de federación a partido." *World Congress of Jewish Studies* 11 (1994): 369–374.

———. "The Organization of Zionism in Argentina from Tifereth Sión to the Establishment of the Zionist Federation (1908–1913)." *Michael* 8 (1983): 62–89.

———. "Zionist Political Parties in Argentina from the Revolution of 1943 to the Establishment of the State of Israel." In *The Jewish Diaspora in Latin America. New Studies on History and Literature*, edited by David Sheinin and Lois Baer Barr, 239–249. New York: Garland Publishing, 1996.

Schroeter, Daniel. "Orientalism and the Jews of the Mediterranean." *Journal of Mediterranean Studies* 4 (1994): 183–196.

———. *The Sultan's Jew: Morocco and the Sephardi World*. Stanford, CA: Stanford University Press, 2002.

Seefeld, Ruth. "La integración social de extranjeros en Buenos Aires según sus pautas matrimoniales: pluralismo cultural o crisol de razas?" *Estudios Migratorios Latinoamericanos* 1, no. 2 (1986).

Serels, M. Mitchell. "Aspects of the Effects of Jewish Philanthropic Societies in Morocco." In *From Iberia to Diaspora. Studies in Sephardic History and Culture*, edited by Yedida K. Stillman and Norman A. Stillman, 102–112. Leiden: Brill, 1999.

———. *A History of the Jews of Tangier in the Nineteenth and Twentieth Centuries*. New York: Sepher-Hermon Press, 1991.

Shapiro, Laura. *Perfection Salad: Women and Cooking at the Turn of the Century*. Edited by Ruth Reichl. New York: Modern Library, 2001.

Shilo, Margalit. "The Women's Farm at Kinneret, 1911–1917: A Solution to the Problem of the Working Woman in the Second Aliya." In *The Jerusalem Cathedra: Studies in the History, Archaelogy, Geography and Ethnography of the Land of Israel*, edited by Lee I. Levine, 246–283. Detroit, MI: Wayne State University Press, 1981.

Shohat, Ella. "The Invention of the Mizrahim." *Journal of Palestine Studies* 29, no. 1 (1999): 5–20.

Silberman de Cywiner, María Esther. *Asociación Israelita Sefaradí de Beneficencia de Tucumán (1921–2006): Memoria y testimonios de su fundación y evolución*. Tucumán: Universidad Nacional de Tucumán, 2006.

———. *Inmigrantes sefardíes, memoria y tradición: Tucumán, pasado y presente. Documento de trabajo*. Tucumán: Universidad Nacional de Tucumán, 2001.

———. "Los sefarditas en Tucumán. Procedencia y asentamiento." Paper presented at the Primer Congreso Internacional sobre Patrimonio Histórico e Identidad Cultural. Tucumán, 1998.

Silberstein, Carina. "Inmigración y selección matrimonial: El caso de los italianos en Rosario, 1870–1910." *Estudios Migratorios Latinoamericanos* 18 (1991): 161–189.

Silverblatt, Irene. "New Christians and New World Fears in Seventeenth-Century Peru." *Comparative Studies in Society and History* 42, no. 3 (2000): 524–546.

Simon, Reeva Spector, Michael Menachem Laskier, and Sara Reguer, eds. *The Jews of the Middle East and North Africa in Modern Times*. New York: Columbia University Press, 2002.

Siskel, Dov. "Los comienzos de la actividad educativa sionista en Argentina a traves de la prensa judía local." In *El Keren Kayemet Leisrael y la educación judía en Eretz Israel y en Argentina*, edited by Instituto de Investigaciones Históricas del Keren Kayemet Leisrael, 7–23. Jerusalem: Keren Kayemet Leisrael, 1996.

Solberg, Carl. *Immigration and Nationalism. Argentina and Chile, 1890–1914*. Austin: University of Texas Press, 1970.

Stein, Sarah Abrevaya. *Making Jews Modern: The Yiddish and Ladino Press in the Russian and Ottoman Empires*. Bloomington: Indiana University Press, 2004.

Szuchman, Mark. "The Limits of the Melting Pot in Urban Argentina: Marriage and Integration in Cordoba, 1869–1909." *Hispanic American Historical Review* 57, no. 1 (1977): 24–50.

Teubal, Nissim. *El inmigrante: De Alepo a Buenos Aires*. Buenos Aires: Macagno, 1953.

Toker, Eliahu, and Ana E. Weinstein. *Sitios de la memoria: Protagonistas y forjadores de la comunidad judía argentina*. Buenos Aires: Milá, 2005.

Tolcachier, Fabiana S. "Continuidad o ruptura de identidades étnicas: el comportamiento matrimonial de los israelitas en el partido de Villarino, (1905–1934)." *Estudios Migratorios Latinoamericanos* 7, no. 20 (1992): 37–69.

Tsur, Yaron. "Haskala in a Sectional Colonial Society: Mahdia (Tunisia) 1884." In *Sephardi and Middle Eastern Jewries: History and Culture in the Modern Era*, edited by Harvey E. Goldberg, 146–167. Bloomington: Indiana University Press, 1996.

Vilar, Juan Vta. "La emigración judeo-marroquí a la América Latina en la fase preestadística (1850–1880)." *Sefárdica* 11 (1996): 11–54.

———. *Tetuán en el resurgimiento judío contemporáneo (1850–1870). Aproximación a la historia del judaísmo norteafricano*. Caracas: Centro de Estudios Sefaradíes de Caracas, 1985.

Voekel, Pamela. *Alone before God: The Religious Origins of Modernity in Mexico*. Durham, NC: Duke University Press 2002.

Weiker, Walter F. *Ottomans, Turks and the Jewish Polity: A History of the Jews of Turkey*. New York: University Press of America, 1992.

Weill, Simon. *Población israelita en la República Argentina*. Buenos Aires: Bene Brith, 1936.

Winsberg, Morton D. "Jewish Agricultural Colonization in Entre Rios, Argentina, I: Some Social and Economic Aspects of a Venture in Resettlement." *American Journal of*

Economics and Sociology 27, no. 3 (1968): 285–295.

WIZO. "International Movement: WIZO. Making It All Possible." Tel Aviv: WIZO, n.d.

WIZO-Rio Grupo Aliyah. *Gostinho de saudade: Al savor de muestras madres*. Rio de Janeiro: WIZO, 1995.

Wolff, Martha, Myrtha Schalom, and Manrique Zago. *Judíos y argentinos. Judíos argentinos*. Buenos Aires: M. Zago Ediciones, 1988.

Yarfitz, Mir. "Polacos, White Slaves, and Stille Chuppahs: Organized Prostitution and the Jews of Buenos Aires, 1890–1939." PhD dissertation, University of California, Los Angeles, 2012.

———. "Sociedad Varsovia as a Voluntary Society: Mutual Aid among Jewish Pimps in Buenos Aires, 1906–1930." *Journal of Latin American Studies*, forthcoming (2017).

Zadoff, Efraim. *Historia de la educación judía en Buenos Aires (1935–1957). Investigaciones*. Buenos Aires: Milá, 1994.

Zaretsky, Natasha, and Annette Levine, eds. *Landscapes of Memory and Impunity: The Aftermath of the AMIA Bombing in Jewish Argentina*. Leiden: Brill, 2015.

Zemer, Moshe. "The Rabbinic Ban on Conversion in Argentina." *Judaism* 37 (1988): 84–96.

Zenner, Walter P. *A Global Community: The Jews from Aleppo, Syria*. Detroit, MI: Wayne State University Press, 2000.

Zohar, Zion. "A Global Perspective on Sephardic and Mizrahi Jewry." In *Sephardic and Mizrahi Jewry: From the Golden Age of Spain to Modern Times*, edited by Zion Zohar, 3–22. New York: New York University Press, 2005.

INDEX

Note: Page references followed by an italicized f indicate information contained in a figure.

Acción Sionista, 135
ACILBA (Asociación Comunidad Israelita Latina de Buenos Aires), 60, 61, 65. *See also* CILBA (Congregación Israelita Latina de Buenos Aires)
ACISBA (Asociación Comunidad Sefaradí de Buenos Aires), 40, 60, 61, 70, 72
Acrich, Esther, 79–81
Adamovsky, Ezequiel, 148, 185
Adatto, J., 137
Afula, 158, 240nn50–51
AGJA (Argentine Jewish Genealogical Association), 218n37
Agudat Dodim (Flores), 61, 67, 69, 86, 94, 191, 193, 194, 195, 197, 224n66, 245n49
AHASM (Asociación Hebrea Argentina de Socorros Mutuos), 28, 41, 72, 86
Ahavat Aḥim (Flores), 200
Ahavat Aḥim (Lanús), 61, 67
Ahavat Shalom (Aleppine), 119
AISA (Asociación Israelita Sefaradí Argentina), 60, 62
Aizenberg, Edna, 11
Alacid, Mauricio, 121
Albascha Ceremony, 222n19
Alcázarquivir, Morocco, 85
Aleluya (congregation), 61, 62, 63, 64f
Aleppine Jewish community: Ahavat Shalom, 119; Asociación Israelita

Sefaradí Argentina (AISA), 60, 62; Asociación Israelita Sefaradí de Ciudadela, 62, 69; Asociación Israelita Sefaradí Shevet Aḥim (Rosario), 74, 75; Asociación Israelita Talmud Tora Sefaradim Yesod Hadat, 190; in Buenos Aires, 18, 67, 69; burial societies and cemeteries, 21, 28, 36, 40, 42, 43–44; in Ciudadela, 36; and Consistorio Rabínico Sefaradí, 92–96; dates of arrival, 16, 17; Habad Tsedek, 62, 69; Ḥesed Shel Emet Sefaradit, 28, 40, 219nn54–55; and Jerusalem Jewish community, 44, 72; marriage in, 177; religious orthodoxy of, 93–94, 229n18; schools, 191, 194, 195, 197; Shaarei Sion, 62, 69; Shevet Aḥim, 74, 79; Shuba Israel, 62, 69; Sociedad Israelita Sefaradí Talmud Torah, 74, 79, 190; Sociedad Jóvenes Israelitas Sefaradím (Latinos) de Corrientes, 74, 77; Yeshurun, 62, 69; Yesot Hadat, 62, 86, 92, 93, 191, 194, 201–202. *See also* Ciudadela (Buenos Aires); Dabbah, Shaul Seton; Flores (Buenos Aires); Once (Buenos Aires); Syrian Jewish community
Aleppo, 63, 92, 105
Alianza, 37, 105
aliyah, 135, 136
Alkalay, Isaac, 102

Alliance Israélite Universelle (AIU), 17, 187, 233n32
Alvear (Corrientes), 77
Alvear Palace Hotel, 140, 141, 145–146, 172
Amazon, 11, 17
American Joint Distribution committee, 129–130
AMIA Asociación Mutual Israelita Argentina (AMIA), 38, 105, 118, 205–206. *See also* Hevra Kedusha (Ashkenazi)
Amiras, Alberto, 219n58
Angel, Aron, 104–105
Angel, Jaime, 56
anti-Semitism, 20, 55
Arabic-speaking Jewish associations, 67–69, 68f
Arabic-speaking Jewish community, 4, 14, 16t, 17, 214n20, 214n27. *See also* Aleppine Jewish community; Damascene Jewish community; Syrian Jewish community
Arab nationalism, 10
Arditti, Adolfo, 110, 128
Argentina: census 1960, 16; immigration patterns and policies, 11–14, 19–20, 215n48; and Jewish education, 200–203; Jewish immigration to, 12–13, 215n48; liberality of, 57; marriage, 185–189; state and philanthropy, 144–146; welfare state condition, 57–59
Argentine Jewish Federation, 37
Argentine Jewish Genealogical Association (AGJA), 218n37
Argentine Jewish Organization (OIA), 21
Argentine WIZO. *See* WIZO (Argentina branch)
Ashkenazim: Argentinian, 213n1; cemeteries in interior Argentina, 47–49; education, 198–199, 244n35; food and hegemony, 171–172, 243n139; "head" of Bet Din, 230n66; hegemony of, 171–172, 210, 244n35; Hevra Kedusha of, 26, 29, 31, 32–39, 40, 43, 105, 118, 218n39, 219n46, 219n55, 219n58; as Jewish gauchos, 13, 14; Kehila, 36–39, 219n46; marriage, 183–185; in New York City, 11; and Sephardi cemeteries, 42–46, 47–49, 52

Asilo Argentino de Huérfanas Israelitas, 87, 142
Asociación Agudat Israelita Sefaradí de Concordia (Concordia), 74, 77–78
Asociación Argentina Israel de Damas Hebreas de Beneficencia de Buenos Aires, 160, 161
Asociación Argentina Sefaradí de Cultura y Beneficencia, 61, 68
Asociación Benot Yerushalaim, 151, 159, 160
Asociación Comunidad Israelita Latina de Buenos Aires (ACILBA), 60, 61, 65
Asociación Comunidad Israelita Sefaradí de Buenos Aires (ACISBA), 40, 60, 61, 70, 72
Asociación de Israelitas Oriundos de Yugoslavia en la Argentina, 62, 72
Asociación Hebrea Argentina de Socorros Mutuos (AHASM), 28, 41, 72, 86
Asociación Hebrea Argentina de Socorros Mutuos (Once), 61
Asociación Hebrea Argentina de Socorros Mutuos (Tablada), 28
Asociación Israelita Ahinu Atah (Rosario), 74, 75, 82
Asociación Israelita de Beneficencia (Tucumán), 74, 81
Asociación Israelita de Beneficencia Hijos de Sión (Posadas), 74, 82, 191, 193
Asociación Israelita Latina de Corrientes, 220n72
Asociación Israelita Sefaradí Argentina (AISA), 60, 62
Asociación Israelita Sefaradí de Ciudadela, 62, 69
Asociación Israelita Sefaradi Hijos de la Verdad (Bene Emet), 60, 61
Asociación Israelita Sefaradim de Socorros Mutuos (Catamarca), 75

Index

Asociación Israelita Sefaradí Pro-Medicamentos (V. Crespo), 61, 70, 71f, 86
Asociación Israelita Sefaradí Shevet Aḥim (Rosario), 74, 75
Asociación Israelita Talmud Tora Sefaradim Yesod Hadat (Once), 190
assimilation, 14, 58, 94, 149, 174–175, 177, 178–181, 187–188, 191, 215n54
Astiz, M. Fernanda, 190–191
Ateneo theater, 145
Avellaneda (Buenos Aires), 25, 35–36, 218n36
Aydin, 69, 70
Azulay, Lida, 164, 165, 175–177, 188, 242n108
Azulay, Luna, 164, 165, 176–177, 184, 188, 242n108

Bahia Blanca (Buenos Aires), 85
Bahloul, Joelle, 169, 242n109
Baily, Samuel, 178
baklava, 243n128
Balkans, 14, 16, 16t, 19, 69
Balkan Wars (1912–1913), 10
Bancalari (Buenos Aires), 40, 42, 44
Barracas al Sud (Buenos Aires), 35, 44–45
Barth, Fredrik, 26–27
Beirut Jewish community, 81
Bejarano, Margalit, 11
Belgrano, Manuel, 203
Benasayag, Meri, 78, 225n105, 226n120
Bendahán, Jacobo, 107
Bene Emet (Damascene), 28, 39–40, 43, 44–45, 67, 69, 83, 85, 86, 87–88
Bene Sion (Ladino-speaking), 61, 70, 119
Bensignor, Isaac, 200
Bensión, Ariel, 123–124, 152, 234n42
Bensión, Ida, 152, 153, 155, 240n50
Bentolila, Salomón, 78, 225n105
Ben-Ur, Aviva, 11
Benzaquén, Benjamin, 99, 104
Beraja, Rubén, 3
Berazategui (Buenos Aires) cemetery, 38, 219n49

Bet Rachel (congregation), 61
Bialystok (Poland), 6
Bianchi, Susana, 190
Bikur Ḥolim, 61, 67–68, 69
Bikur Jolim, 143
Blum, Abraham, 93, 230n66
B'nai B'rith Argentina, and Federación Argentina de Sociedades Israelitas, 107–109
Boca/Barracas (Buenos Aires), 18, 18f, 20, 40, 135, 158, 191, 194, 195, 197, 199–200, 245n54; Or Torah, 61, 67–68, 82, 83, 85, 94, 119, 195, 197, 198, 232n15
Bodrum, 69
Bolsheviks (Russian), 1
Bosi, Eclea, 171
Botbol, Marcos, 63
Boyarin, Daniel, 29
Boyarin, Jonathan, 29
Brazil, 17
Britain, 9
British community, 32, 217n20
Buenos Aires: Arabic-speaking Jewish associations, 67–69, 68f; foreign-born residents, 12; Jewish (Ashkenazi) burial societies and cemeteries, 26, 27f, 28t, 32–46, 33t; Ladino-speaking Jewish associations, 69–72, 71f; marriage among Sephardi in, 181–183; Moroccan Jewish associations, 62–67, 64f; neighborhoods of Sephardic settlement, 17, 18, 18f, 19, 20; philanthropic societies in, 60–72, 64f, 68f, 71f, 82–85; provincial migration to, 209; Sephardi cemeteries and burial societies, 39–42, 51; Sephardi instutions in, 216n70; Sephardi schools in, 191; Sephardi Zionist neighborhood groups, 135; theaters and hotels of, 145–146; Tragic Week riots, 1; women's events and groups, 142; women's philanthropic groups in, 159–163. *See also specific neighborhoods*
Bulgaria, 16, 19, 232n18, 233n27
Bulisa, 168, 169, 243n132

burial societies: Asociación Hebrea
  Argentina de Socorros Mutuos
  (AHASM), 28, 41, 72, 86; Bene Emet
  (Damescene), 28, 39–40, 43, 44–45,
  67, 69, 83, 85, 86, 87–88; Guemilut
  Hasadim (Buenos Aires) (Moroccan),
  28, 33–34, 35, 39, 44–45, 61, 66, 91,
  218n32, 228n6; Ḥesed Shel Emet
  Sefaradit (Aleppine), 28, 40, 219nn54–55;
  Hevra Kedusha (Ashkenazi), 28, 31,
  32–39, 40, 43, 49, 91, 105, 118, 218n39,
  219n46, 219n55, 219n58; Sociedad
  Israelita de Socorros Mutuos Varsovia
  (Zwi Migdal), 25–26, 28, 34–35, 216n2
Burman, Ricki, 167

Cadoche, Moisés, 3
Calchaquí, 50
Camargo (congregation), 181–183
Camargo (Kal Kadosh), 100
Campaña Unida, 134, 237n97
Cantilo, José Luis, 199
Casablanca, 85
Castel, Elias, 128
Catamarca, 50, 138; Asociación Israelita
  Sefaradim de Socorros Mutuos
  (Catamarca), 75
Catholic Church, 20, 190, 217n17
Catholic Workers' Circles, 58
Çeşme, Turkey, 57
Cementerio del Norte (Tucumán),
  221n104
Cementerio del Oeste, 32, 36
cemeteries, Jewish: Ashkenazi Hevra
  Kedusha, 26, 29, 31, 32–39, 40, 43,
  105, 118, 218n39, 219n46, 219n55,
  219n58; honor and membership, 45–46;
  inter-Sephardi conflict over, 42–46;
  list of, near Buenos Aires, 28; in Santa
  Fé, 30–32, 217nn16–17; scholarly
  study of, 29–30; Sephardi cemeteries in
  Buenos Aires, 39–42, 51–52; Sephardi
  cemeteries in the provinces, 46–49;
  walls and identity, 26–27, 29, 51–52,
  222n108; Zwi Migdal, 25–26, 216n2

Central Sephardi Community of
  Jerusalem, 129
Centro Argentino de Socorros Mutos
  (Salta), 75, 81
Centro Cultural y Recreativo Sefaradim
  (Concordia), 77–78
Centro Israelita Argentino (Rosario), 75
Centro Israelita Juvenil, 135
Çeşme, Turkey, 57, 69
Chacarita Cemetery, 32
Chaco, 17, 78, 79f, 83; Sociedad Israelita
  Latina Ḥesed VeEmet (Resistencia), 74,
  78, 137, 226n109
Chalom (congregation), 61, 70, 135,
  181–183, 191, 194, 197, 198, 202,
  227n155, 246n73, 246n83
Chehebar, Itzjak, 94, 105, 229n18
Chivilcoy (Buenos Aires), 82, 85
CILBA (Congregación Israelita Latina de
  Buenos Aires), 42–43, 61, 62, 64f, 65,
  82, 84–85, 94, 100, 117, 119, 140.
  See also ACILBA (Asociación Comunidad
  Israelita Latina de Buenos Aires)
CIRA (Congregación Israelita de la
  Repúblíca Argentina), 32, 38, 42–43,
  217nn21–22, 223n37
Círculo Cultural Israelita Sefaradí
  (Rosario), 75
Círculo de Damas Sionistas (Rosario), 152
Círculo Juvenil Israelita (Rosario), 75
Círculo Social Israelita, 100
Ciudadela (Buenos Aires), 18, 36, 40, 67,
  82, 191; Asociación Israelita Sefaradí de
  Ciudadela, 62, 69
Club Alianza, 64f, 95, 135, 143, 163–164, 165
Club Juventud Israelita, 160
Club Naútico Hacoaj, 210
Cohen Imach, Sión, 3
Colegiales (Buenos Aires), 19, 70, 105,
  191, 202
collective organizations, failed Sephardí:
  about, 90–92, 111–112; Confederación
  Israelita Sefaradí, 91, 105–109; Unión de
  Asociaciones Israelitas Sefaradíes de la
  República Argentina, 91, 109–111

Index

Colonia Romang, 50
Comedores Israelita, 143
Comisión de Damas de la Sociedad Israelita Sefaradí de Socorros Mutuos, 160–161, 162
Comisión de Damas del Centro Sionista Sefaradí, 151. *See also* WIZO (Sephardi section)
Comisión de Damas del Club Juventud Israelita (Flores), 161
Comisiones de Damas, 162
Comité Argentino Sefaradí pro Campaña Unida, 134
Comité Central de Ayuda a las Víctimas de la Guerra, 105
Comité Central Pro Socorro a las Víctimas Israelitas de la Guerra y Refugiados, 236n75
Comité contra el Antisemitismo, 109
Comité contra el Racismo y Antisemitismo, 236n75
Comité contra las Persecuciones de Judíos en Alemania, 109
Comité de Damas del Fondo Nacional Israelita, 151, 152
Comité Femenino Sefaradí—Amigas de la Histadrut, 151, 158–159, 160, 241n79
Comité Intercomunal Sefaradí Pro-Gueulath Haaretz, 127–128
Comité Sefaradí Argentino pro Keren Hayesod, KKL y Refugiados, 128, 130, 137
Communidad Israelita Sefaradí de Buenos Aires, 90
Communidad Israelita Sefaradí de Córdoba (Córdoba), 79
Comunidad Israelita Sefaradí de Buenos Aires, 200
Concordia (Entre Ríos), 77–78, 138, 243n132; Asociación Agudat Israelita Sefaradí de Concordia, 74, 77–78; Centro Cultural y Recreativo Sefaradim, 77–78
Confederación de Beneficencia, 145, 239n14
Confederación Israelita Sefaradí, 91, 105–108
Confederación Juvenil Sionista Argentina, 118
Confederation of Argentine Zionist Youth, 135
Congregación Israelita de la Repbulica Argentina (CIRA), 32, 38, 42–43, 217nn21–22, 223n37
Congregación Israelita Latina de Buenos Aires (CILBA), 42–43, 61, 62, 64f, 65, 82, 84–85, 94, 100, 117, 119, 140, 163
Congregación Israelita Latina Sefaradím de Santa Fé (Santa Fé), 73–75
Congregación Sefaradí de Enseñanza, Culto y Beneficencia Yesod Hadat, 69
Consejo Central de Damas Sefaradíes. *See* WIZO (Sephardi section)
Consejo Central Sefaradí Argentino, 130, 134
Consejo Central Sionista, 118
Consejo Nacional de Educación, 199, 201
Consistorio Rabínico Sefaradí, 91, 92–105, 194, 207
Constitución (Buenos Aires), 17, 18f
Convención Regional Sefardi del Keren Kayemeth Leisrael, 130
conversions ban, 93, 180, 229n13
cookbooks, 168, 169, 171–172, 243n115
cooking. *See* ethnic food preparation
Córdoba, 5, 18, 19, 49, 50, 78–81, 80f, 83, 85, 138, 143, 160–161, 190, 191, 214n20, 221n77; Comisión de Damas de la Sociedad Israelita Sefaradí de Socorros Mutuos, 160–161, 162; Communidad Israelita Sefaradí de Córdoba, 79; National Hospital Santa María, 86; Shevet Aḥim (Córdoba), 74, 79; Sociedad de Beneficencia Rofe Ḥolim (Córdoba), 74, 78; Sociedad Israelita de Beneficencia Sefaradí (Córdoba), 74, 78; Sociedad Israelita Sefaradí Talmud Torah (Córdoba), 74, 79, 190; Sociedad Israelita Siria de Córdoba, 191, 196

Corrientes, 17, 18, 47, 50, 52, 77, 83, 137, 138, 161, 190, 191, 209; Alvear, 77; Asociación Israelita Latina de Corrientes, 220n72; Comisiones de Damas, 162; Sociedad Jóvenes Israelitas Sefaradím (Latinos) de Corrientes, 74, 77
Cospito, René, 172
coup d'etat (1930), 219n57
couscous, 164, 242n107
Crypto-Jews, 11
CSS (Centro Sionista Sefaradí), 109, 111, 116, 120, 121, 123, 125–131, 137, 156, 207, 208, 231n5, 235n59, 235n61, 235n67
Curuzú Cuatiá (Corrientes), 77

Dabbah, Shaul Seton, 69, 92–93, 120, 122, 180, 229n13, 229n18
DAIA (Delegación de Asociaciones Israelitas Argentinas), 3, 109, 231nn79–80
Damascene Jewish community: Agudat Dodim, 61, 67, 69, 86, 94, 191, 193, 194, 195, 197, 224n66, 245n49; Ahavat Akhim, 61, 67, 82; Asociación Argentina Sefaradí de Cultura y Beneficencia, 61, 68; Asociación Israelita Sefaradi Hijos de la Verdad (Bene Emet), 60, 61; Asociación Israelita Sefaradí Shevet Aḥim (Rosario), 74, 75; Bene Emet, 28, 39–40, 43, 44–45, 67, 69, 83, 85, 86, 87–88; Bikur Ḥolim, 61, 67–68, 69; in Buenos Aires, 18, 67–69; Comisión de Damas del Club Juventud Israelita, 161; and Consistorio Rabínico Sefaradí, 92–96; dates of arrival, 4, 16, 17; Guemilut Ḥasadim, 61, 67, 69, 88; in La Boca, 194, 195, 245n54; Liga Antituberculosia Israelita Sefaradí, 86; marriage in, 177; Or Torah, 61, 67–68, 82, 83, 85, 94, 119, 191, 195, 197, 198, 232n15; philanthropic and religious organizations, 61; schools, 191; Shaare Tefilá, 61, 67; Sociedad de Damas, 160, 161; Sociedad de Damas Israelitas de Flores, 160, 161; Sociedad Israelita Sefaradí Talmud Torah, 74, 79, 190; and Zionism, 122. *See also* Boca/Barracas (Buenos Aires); Flores (Buenos Aires); Syrian Jewish community
Damascus, 10, 17, 18, 63
Damas Israelitas Sefaradim de Buenos Aires, 160, 161
Débora (Vera), 74, 77, 225n96
Deborah (Dr. Hertzl League), 150, 151
DESA - Delegación de Entidades Sefaradíes (DESA), 134–135, 231n5
Días, Comisario, 199
diasporas, 5–9, 19, 23, 24, 93, 112, 116, 119, 130, 132, 142, 150, 207, 211, 213n12
dietary laws, 167
Diner, Hasia, 243n137
Directorio Sefaradí del Keren Kayemeth Leisrael, 131
Dissidents' Cemetery (Second), 32, 34, 51, 217n18, 217n21
Djaen, Sabetay, 91, 94–103, 95*f*, 104*f*, 124–125, 137, 199, 229n24, 235n52, 235n54, 235n55, 238n126
domestic practices. *See* ethnic food preparation
Don Segundo Sombra (Güiraldes), 13
Dror movement, 135

Edirne, 69
education and schools, Sephardi, 97, 109; Ashkenazim connections, 198–199; in Buenos Aires neighborhoods, 193, 199–201; centralization of, 194, 244n35; and connections to community and nation, 192–193, 196, 197–198; control and management of, 193–194; curricula, 195; financial support, 197; government intervention and involvement, 200–203, 246n78; language of instruction, 198; list of Sephardi schools, 191; purpose of, 190–191; Talmud Torahs, 190–195, 244n30
Efrón, Yedida, 197
Egozi, Yomtob, 229n9
Eichelbaum, Samuel, 173

Index

Eliashar, Eli, 128, 133–134, 157, 237n93
Elnecavé, David, 90, 200
El Semanario Hebreo (Lutzky), 99
El Sionista (periodical), 117, 119, 120, 232n17
El Socorro, 40–41, 61, 72, 160, 161
Entre Ríos, 14, 18, 77–78; Asociación Agudat Israelita Sefaradí de Concordia (Concordia), 74, 77–78; Sociedad Israelita Sefaradí Shevet Aḥim (Paraná), 74
Epstein, Diana, 179
Escuela Hebrea Integral (Chalom), 198
Escuelas Israelitas (Rhodes), 197
Esquina (Corrientes), 77
Esther A., 170
ethnic food preparation, 163–172
ethno-national communities, 8
Etz HaḤaim (congregation), 40–41, 61, 70, 72, 100, 196
Etz HaḤaim (Rosario), 74, 75, 77, 191, 195, 245n42
Etz HaḤaim-Bet Raquel, 62

fascism, 20
fasting, 165–166
Favelukes, Jaime, 86
Federación Argentina de Sociedades Israelitas, 107–109
Federación Israelita, 37
Federación Israelita Argentina, 37
Federación Sionista Argentina (FSA), 117–118, 119, 120–121, 125–127, 241n61
Federation of Zionist Women in Great Britain and Ireland, 150
First Argentine Zionist Congress, 116, 117, 119, 231n8
Flores (Buenos Aires), 18, 18f, 19, 67, 69, 70, 160, 191, 193, 194, 195; Agudat Dodim, 61, 67, 69, 86, 94, 193, 194, 195, 197, 224n66, 245n49; Ahavat Ahim, 200; Comisión de Damas del Club Juventud Israelita, 161; Sociedad de Damas Israelitas de Flores, 160, 161
Flores cemetery, 36, 43, 218n37

Fondo Nacional Judío, 143. *See also* JNF (Jewish National Fund)
food preparation, ethnic, 163–172
Formosa, 50
France, 14, 16t
French Jewish communities, 16, 32
Freue, David, 229n9
Freue, Nissim, 94
FSA (Federación Sionista Argentina), 117–118, 119, 120–121, 125–127, 241n61
Funes, Lucha, 166–167, 171

Galimidi, Mrs., 241n63
García, Isaac, 94
gauchos, 13–14
Geldstein, Rosa, 179
General Levalle (Córdoba), 81
general Zionism, 233n27
General Zionists Party, 117, 118
Gerchunoff, Alberto, 14, 215n54
Germani, Gino, 178
German Jewish communities, 32, 217n20
Geulat Aam, 136
Geulat Sion, 119–120, 122, 232n19
Gluksman, Max, 198
Goldberg, Idana, 144
Goldman, Aharon, 92, 93, 180, 229n13
Goldrig, Batia, 197
Goya (Corrientes), 77
Gran Baile de la Colectividad, 113–114
Gruman, Mrs., 151
Gualeguaychú (Entre Ríos), 138, 156
Guemilut Ḥasadim (Buenos Aires) (Damascene), 61, 67, 69, 88
Guemilut Ḥasadim (Buenos Aires) (Moroccan), 28, 33–35, 39, 43, 44–45, 46, 61, 66, 91, 218n32, 228n6
Güiraldes, Ricardo, 13

Habad Tsedek, 62, 69
Hadassah, 150
Halac, Bacri, 127
Halac, José, 196
Hall, Stuart, 27

Halpern, Nathan, 234n42
Hara, Isaac Levy, 94
Hashomer Hatzair, 118
Haskalah, 121, 122, 233n32
Hatikvah Talmud Torah, 194, 196, 198, 246n72
Ḥaverim (congregation), 61, 65
Hebrew, 194, 195, 197, 245n41
Hejalutz-Tejezakna, 135
Hernández, José, 13
Hertszcovich, Matilde, 197, 246n78
Herzl, Theodore, 240n46
Ḥesed Shel Emet (Ladino-speaking community), 28, 40, 43, 44, 69, 70, 88
Ḥesed Shel Emet Sefaradit (Aleppine), 28, 40, 219nn54–55
Ḥesed VeEmet (Moroccan), 39, 44–45, 61, 66, 83, 86, 219n52, 220n72, 226n132
Ḥesed VeEmet de Socorros Mutuos (Santa Fé), 75
Ḥesed VeEmet of Resistencia, 47, 48–49, 50, 74, 78, 83–84, 90, 137, 226n109, 226n120, 227n137, 228n4
Hes Hayim, 61, 62, 64f
Ḥevra Kedusha (Ashkenazi), 28, 31, 32–39, 40, 43, 49, 91, 105, 118, 218n39, 219n58, 219n46, 219n55
Hibbat Zion Movement, 231n6
Hirsch, Baron Maurice de, 2, 13
Hirsch, Leopoldo, 198
Histadruth (Israeli Labor Federation), 236n87
Historia de las religiones en la Argentina (Bianchi), 190
holiday cooking, 165–167, 243n115
Holocaust, 10, 129, 131
Horischink, Leon, 37–38
Hospital Israelita Ezrah (Buenos Aires), 66, 83, 86–87, 143
hospitals, 86–87, 227n154
Hovevei Zion society, 117, 231n6, 232n18

immigration: groups organized around origin cities or regions, 6; individual character of, 2, 213n6; and Tragic Week riots, 1

Isajaroff, Judith, 159
Israel (magazine), 79, 90, 142, 185–189, 186f, 187f, 194, 229n9, 231n4, 245n36
Israeli embassy attack (1992), 205–206
Istanbul, 4, 10, 69, 70, 222n19
Istanbul Jewish community, 78
Italian Jewish communities, 16, 42, 72
Italian Peninsula, 9
Italy, 14, 16t, 19
Izmir, 69, 70, 222n19
Izmir Jewish community, 5, 10, 77, 78, 81

Jabotinksy, Vladimir, 233n27
JCA (Jewish Colonization Association), 13–14, 15f, 30, 194, 198
Jerusalem, 129
Jerusalem Jewish community, 42, 72, 81
Jewish Agency, 110, 136, 237n114
Jewish Colonization Association (JCA), 13–14, 15f, 30, 194, 198
Jewish Congregation of the Republic of Argentina, 32, 217nn21–22. *See also* Congregación Israelita de la Repbulica Argentina (CIRA)
Jewish Federation, 37
Jewish Hospital Ezrah, 66. *See also* Hospital Israelita Ezrah (Buenos Aires)
Jewish Latin Americans, 8, 214n28
Jewish Mutual Aid Society "Union" of Salta, 50, 191
Jewish National Fund (JNF), 96, 110, 120, 123, 129, 131, 143, 150
Jewish Orphanage (Buenos Aires), 8
Jewish World Congress, 8
Jews, Argentin, census, 16
Jews, diasporas as defining identity of, 6
Jews, immigration to Argentina: inexact data on, 215n48; rural colonies, 12–14; urban focus of, 14–16
JNF (Jewish National Fund), 96, 110, 120, 123, 129, 131, 143, 150
Jolita (congregation), 63
Joseph, Rabbi, 29, 42–43, 317n25
Juventud Oriente Israel, 158

Index

Kahal Kadosh, 40, 99
Kamenszein, Miriam, 243n139
Kanfé Yoná, 53–54, 59, 61, 64f, 66–67, 219n52, 222n6
Kaplan, Simjá, 158
Karush, Matthew, 188
Kavala, Greece, 56
Keren Hayesod, 110, 120, 123, 124, 126
Keren Kayemet (JNF), 120, 126, 131
Keren Kayemet Leisrael (KKL), 124, 128, 130–131, 235n67, 236n81, 236n81, 236n85
Kitrón, Moshe, 113, 116
Klein, Moisés, 197
Kobrin, Rebecca, 6
kosher food, 167

Labor Party, 136
Ladino-speaking community, 19, 40–41, 42, 43, 44, 69–72, 71f, 219n56, 231n5; Asociación Comunidad Israelita Sefaradí de Buenos Aires (ACISBA), 40, 60, 61, 70, 72; Asociación Hebrea Argentina de Socorros Mutuos (Once), 61; Asociación Israelita Sefaradí Pro- Medicamentos (V. Crespo), 61, 70, 71f, 86; Bene Sion (Once), 61, 70, 119; Chalom (congregation), 61, 70, 135, 181–183, 191, 194, 197, 198, 202, 227n155, 246n73, 246n83; El Socorro, 40–41, 61, 72, 160, 161; Etz HaHaim (congregation), 40–41, 61, 70, 72, 77, 100, 196; Sociedad Kahal Kadosh y Talmud Tora La Hermandad Sefaradí (Villa Crespo), 61, 70, 71f, 190. *See also* Colegiales (Buenos Aires); Flores (Buenos Aires); Hesed Shel Emet (Ladino-speaking community); Once (Buenos Aires); Ottoman Jewish community; Villa Crespo (Buenos Aires); Villa General Urquiza (Buenos Aires)
Ladino-speaking Jewish associations, 69–72, 71f
La Forestal, 78
La Luz (magazine), 90, 142, 179–180, 202

Lanús (Buenos Aires), 39–40, 67; Ahavat Akhim, 61, 67, 82
La Prensa (newspaper), 144–145, 146
Larache, Morocco, 17
La Rioja, 18, 49
La Sábana, 50, 78, 225n105
La Tablada (Buenos Aires) cemetery, 38, 41
Latin American Jews, 8, 214n28
Legion de Voluntarios Kanfe Yona, 53–54, 59, 61, 64f, 66–67, 219n52, 222n6
Les Ambassadeurs dance hall, 145
Levine, Annette H., 206
Levy, Don Aaron, 200
Levy, Estela, 1–5, 11, 13, 183
Levy, Samuel de A., 90
Lewin, Boleslao, 218n37
Liachovitzky, Jacabo, 218n34
Lida. *See* Azulay, Lida
Liga Antituberculosia Israelita Sefaradí, 86
Liga de Mujeres Católicas, 145, 239n14
Liga Dr. Hertzl, 117, 150
Liga Israelita Argentina contra la Tuberculosis, 86, 143, 200, 228n161
Liniers cemetery, 36, 40, 43, 52, 218n37
Lomas de Zamora (Buenos Aires), 39–40
Los Gauchos Judíos (Gerchunoff), 14
Luna. *See* Azulay, Luna
Lutzky, José, 99
Lvovich, Daniel, 219n57

Magnani, Romulo, 200
Manchester, England, 18
Margarita (Santa Fé), 50, 136
marriage, Sephardi: with Ashkenazim, 183–185, 209; assimilation and patterns of, 178–181; of Lida Azulay, 175–176; modernity of Argentinian norms, 185–189, 244n21; Moroccan Jews, 181–183; Ottoman Jews, 181–183; personal choice in, 188
"Martín Fierro" (Hernández), 13
"maximalists," 1
Mehaudy, David, 63
Meiujas, Josef, 136, 138

Memoria e Sociedade (Bosi), 171
memory and tradition, 171, 243n137
Mendoza, 9, 81, 83, 91, 152, 161;
  Comisiones de Damas, 162; Sociedad Israelita de Socorros Mutuos Rofe Ḥolim (Mendoza), 75, 81, 226n119
Mercedes (Corrientes), 77
Mesody, 56, 166
Mibashán, Dr., 110, 155
Mifleget Poalei Eretz Yisrael (Mapai), 159
Milas, 69
military, Argentine, 20
Miller, Susan, 11
Mirelman, Victor, 88
Misiones, 77, 191; Asociación Israelita de Beneficencia Hijos de Sión (Posadas), 74, 82, 191, 193
mitzvot, 55
Mizrahi, Iaacov, 94, 122
Mizraḥi community, 214n27, 214n33
Mizraḥi Orthodox Women, 151
modernity, 55, 120–122, 174–175, 185–189, 233n27, 244n21
mohels, 92, 229n9
Mois Chami & Alderoqui store, 200
Moisesville (Santa Fé), 30–32, 92
Molho, Michael, 105
Moroccan Jewish community, 217n23; Aleluya (congregation), 61, 62, 63, 64f; in the Amazon in 19th cent., 11; arrival of, 14–17, 16t, 215n65; Asociación Comunidad Israelita Latina de Buenos Aires (ACILBA), 60, 61, 65; Asociación Israelita Aḥinu Atah, 74, 75, 82; assimilation, 179; associations in Buenos Aires, 62–67, 64f; associations in provinces, 73–78; in Buenos Aires, 62–67, 64f, 207; burial practices and cemeteries, 25, 29, 33, 35–36, 42–46, 207, 217n26, 218n32; Club Alianza, 64f, 95, 135, 143, 163–164, 165; Congregación Israelita Latina de Buenos Aires, 42–43, 61, 62, 64f, 65, 84–85, 94, 100, 117, 119, 140, 163; Congregación Israelita Latina Sefaradím de Santa Fé, 73–75, 74; and Consistorio Rabínico Sefaradí, 98, 99–100; Damas Israelitas Sefaradim de Buenos Aires, 160, 161; Débora, 74, 77, 225n96; education and schools, 191, 194, 197, 198; ethnic food preparation, 164, 165, 167–168, 170; Etz HaḤaim (congregation), 40–41, 61, 70, 72, 77, 100, 196; Geulat Aam, 136; Guemilut Hasadim, 28, 33–35, 39, 43, 44–45, 46, 61, 66, 91, 218n32, 228n6; Haverim (congregation), 61, 65; Hes Hayim, 61, 62, 64f; Ḥesed VeEmet, 39, 44–45, 61, 66, 90, 219n52, 220n72; immigration to Brazil and Portugal, 215n64; Legion de Voluntarios Kanfe Yona, 53–54, 59, 61, 64f, 66–67, 219n52, 222n6; marriage, 175–176, 181–183, 187, 188; in Mendoza, 9; Ozer Dalim, 61, 66, 84–85, 86, 162, 224n55, 227n142; philanthropic organizations, 62–67, 64f, 73–78, 207; in provincial settings, 30, 77, 207; provincial settlement, 73–78; in Santa Fé, 30; settlements, 77; Sociedad de Damas de Sión, 160, 161; Sociedad Hebrea Sefaradí, 74; Sociedad Israelita Latina Ḥesed VeEmet (Resistencia), 74, 78, 137, 226n109; Zionism of, 115, 116, 119, 120, 136. *See also* Chaco; Corrientes; Santa Fé; Sud (Buenos Aries)
Morocco, 10, 17, 56, 57, 63, 77, 85, 224n49, 225n105, 226n120, 232n18
Mundo Isrelita (newspaper), 100–101, 105, 106, 142, 237n119
mutual aid societies, 58–59, 223n26. *See also* philanthropic societies, Sephardi

National Hospital Santa María (Córdoba), 86
nationalism, 1, 219n57
Netherlands, the, 9
New York City, 11
North Africa, 9, 10

Once (Buenos Aires), 18, 18f, 19, 20, 67, 69, 86, 190, 191, 197; Asociación Hebrea Argentina de Socorros Mutuos (Once), 61; Asociación Israelita Talmud Tora Sefaradim Yesod Hadat (Once), 190; Bene Sion, 61, 70, 119; Sociedad Israelita para Culto y Beneficencia Bene Mizrah, 61, 70; Sociedad Israelita para Culto y Beneficencia Bene Mizrah (Once), 61, 70
Organización Hebrea Argentina Macabi, 210
Organización Israelita Argentina (OIA), 21
Organización Sionista Argentina (OSA), 118
Organización Sionista de Pioneras, 150, 151
Organización Sionista Femenina Argentina (OSFA), 152. *See also* WIZO (Argentina branch)
Organización Sionista Sefaradí Argentina, 135
Oriental Jewish community, 4, 214n33
Ornstein, Rodolfo, 42
orphanages, 87
Orthodox-Zionist-Mizrahi Party, 117
Or Torah (La Boca), 61, 67–68, 82, 83, 85, 94, 119, 191, 195, 197, 198, 232n15
Ottoman Empire, 9, 10, 17, 55, 102–103, 214n24, 222n9
Ottoman Jewish community, 85, 98, 99–100, 102, 200, 243n128; arrival of, 19; Asociación Comunidad Israelita Sefaradí de Buenos Aires (ACISBA), 40, 60, 61, 70, 72; Asociación Hebrea Argentina de Socorros Mutuos (Tablada), 28; Asociación Israelita de Beneficencia Hijos de Sión (Posadas), 74, 82, 191, 193; Asociación Israelita Sefaradim de Socorros Mutuos (Catamarca), 75; burial societies and cemeteries, 21, 28; Chalom (congregation), 61, 70, 135, 181–183, 191, 194, 197, 198, 202, 227n155, 246n73, 246n83; and Consistorio Rabínico Sefaradí, 98–105; education and, 190, 191, 196; El Socorro, 40–41, 61, 72, 160, 161; Etz HaHaim (congregation), 40–41, 61, 70, 72, 77, 100, 196; marriage, 181–183; philanthropic and religious organizations, 70, 71, 74, 82, 85, 94; Sociedad de Damas de Beneficencia—La Unión, 140, 160, 161; Sociedad Hebrea Sefaradí (Santa Fé), 74; Sociedad Israelita de Beneficencia Sefaradí (Córdoba), 74, 78; Sociedad Israelita Shalom VeReut (Santa Fé), 74, 75, 190, 191; Sociedad Kahal Kadosh y Talmud Tora La Hermandad Sefaradí (Villa Crespo), 61, 70, 71f, 190; women, 140; Zionism and, 115–116. *See also* Colegiales (Buenos Aires); Flores (Buenos Aires); Hesed Shel Emet (Ladino-speaking community); Ladino-speaking community; Once (Buenos Aires); Villa Crespo (Buenos Aires); Villa General Urquiza (Buenos Aires)
Ozer Dalim, 61, 66, 84–85, 86, 162, 224n55, 227n142

Palestine, 9, 19
Palestinian Jewish community, 16, 77
Panigel, Dr., 93
Paraná (Entre Ríos), 50, 77
Paso de los Libres (Corrientes), 77, 167, 171
Passover matzah, 166
Perón, Juan Domingo, 20, 21, 59
Petit Splendid theater, 145
philanthropic societies, Sephardi: about, 88–89; and Argentine government, 57–58; in Buenos Aires, 60–72, 64f, 68f, 71f; hospitals built, 86–87, 227n154; interconnectedness of, 82–85; Matanot Laevionim, 56; in Old World, 55–57; orphanages, 87; in the provinces, 73–81, 76f, 79f, 80f; resources and industry services, 146–149; supporting "Jewish" institutions, 86–87; supporting non-Jewish institutions, 87–88; women's roles and groups, 140–144. *See also specific organizations*

Plaza Hotel, 145–146
Poalei Zion, 118
Poale Zedek, 33, 217n24
political Zionism, 233n27
Portugal, 9
Portuguese colonial period, 11
Posadas (Misiones), 19, 50, 90, 138, 190, 193
poverty and economic hardship, 10
practical Zionism, 135, 233n27
Presidencia Roque Saenz Peña (Chaco), 156, 227n138
Primera Convención Regional Sefaradí, 128
Primera Convención Sefaradí de la República Argentina, 110
prostitution, 25–26, 34, 217nn28–29, 220n71
Protestants, 217n18
Punta Alta cemetery, 36, 218n40

Rabinovich, Mrs., 197
Radical Party, 20
Raquel-Aleluya (congregation), 62, 63, 64f, 65
Razili, Jacobo, 237n119
Reconquista, 50
religious Zionism, 233n27
Resistencia (Chaco), 47, 48–49, 50, 52, 78, 83–84, 91, 137, 138, 162, 208, 220n73, 221n77, 221n103, 235n59, 241n63; Sociedad de Damas de Ḥesed VeEmet, 162; Sociedad Israelita Latina Ḥesed VeEmet, 47, 48–49, 50, 74, 78, 83–84, 90, 137, 226n109, 226n120, 227n137, 228n4
revisionist Zionism, 233n27
Revisionist Zionism Party, 117
Rhodes, 3, 19, 42, 56, 57, 69, 70, 105, 119, 160, 161, 177, 182, 197, 211. *See also* Chalom (congregation)
Rio Cuarto (Córdoba), 217n26
Río de Janeiro, 17
ritual matters, disputes and resolutions. *See* Consistorio Rabínico Sefaradí
Rivadavia, Bernardino, 144
Roffé, José, 65, 218n32
Roque Sáenz Peña, 50, 221n103

Rosario (Santa Fé), 18, 19, 50, 75–77, 82, 85, 136, 137, 142–143, 152, 161, 179–180, 191, 218n33, 235n52; Asociación Israelita Aḥinu Atah, 74, 75, 82; Asociación Israelita Sefaradí Shevet Aḥim, 74, 75; Centro Israelita Argentino, 75; Círculo Cultural Israelita Sefaradí, 75; Círculo de Damas Sionistas, 152; Círculo Juvenil Israelita, 75; Comisiones de Damas, 162; Etz HaḤaim, 74, 75, 191, 195, 245n42
Rossi de Luca, Antonia, 246n78
Rubin, Léon, 78
rusos, 1
Russian Jews, 33

Sáenz Peña Law (1912), 20
Saidman, Sheila, 90
Salama, Iaacov Cohen, 94
Salama, Isaac, 94
Salones Sarmiento banquet hall, 146–147
Salonika, 19, 42, 56, 57, 69, 105
Salón Príncipe Jorge dance hall, 145
Salta, 18, 49–50, 81, 136–137, 179, 190, 191; Centro Argentino de Socorros Mutuos, 75, 81; Jewish Mutual Aid Society "Union" of Salta, 50, 191; Sociedad Israelita Salteña La Unión, 74, 81
Samarkand, 19
San Juan, 49, 81, 83; Sociedad Israelita Latina de Socorros Mutuos de San Juan, 75, 81
San Luis, 50
San Martín, Don José de, 65–66, 203
San Martín theater, 145
Santa Fé, 14, 17, 19, 30, 47, 49, 52, 85, 161, 190, 191, 221n77; Asociación Israelita Aḥinu Atah (Rosario), 74, 75, 82; Asociación Israelita Sefaradí Shevet Aḥim (Rosario), 74, 75; Congregación Israelita Latina Sefaradím de Santa Fé city, 73–75; Débora (Vera), 74, 77, 225n96; Jewish cemeteries in, 30–32, 217nn16–17; philanthropical societies in, 73–75; Sociedad Hebrea Sefaradí, 74;

Sociedad Israelita de Damas Sefaradí de Socorros Mutuos, 161, 162; Sociedad Israelita Sefaradí Etz HaḤaim (Rosario), 74, 75; Sociedad Israelita Shalom VeReut, 74, 75, 190, 191; towns where Sephardim settled, 76f
Sauce (Corrientes), 77, 165, 175–177
schools. *See* education and schools
Schuzman, Mark, 178
secularization, 29, 55, 57, 120–122, 167, 179, 233n27
Sedero, Saúl, 90
Sefaty, Abraham, 218n32
Segunda Convención Regional Sefaradí, 128, 130
"Semana de la Huérfana," 87
Semana Trágica. *See* Tragic Week riots
Sephardi diaspora (from Spain), 9–10, 51, 55–57, 114–115
Sephardi immigration (to Argentina): dates of arrival and origins, 14–15, 16t; history of, 17–19, 18f; independent nature of, 2; from Old World, 10–11; political integration, 20–21; published memoirs of, 2, 213n7
Sephardim, Argentine: about, 213n1; apoliticality of, 118, 192, 232nn13–14; Argentineness of, 210; burial societies and cemeteries in Buenos Aires, 39–46, 51; burial societies and cemeteries in interior Argentina, 46–50; communal life in Buenos Aires, 19; and Consistorio Rabínico Sefaradí, 91, 101–105; contemporary merging with Ashkenazim, 208–209; defined in previous research, 7; diasporic identity of, 5–9; history, 9–11; identity defined by Levy, 3–4; invisible as Jews in Argentina, 1–2, 127, 149; marriage of, 178–183, 185–189; need for single organization for voice of, 105–106; population estimates, 16; Sephardi superiority, 221n105; stricter religious observance of, 209–210; unity and representation, 132–133; urban-provincial conflict, 106–107; visibility attestations of Levy, 2–3, 4. *See also* Zionism/Zionist organizations
Sephardim, in Americas, literature on, 11
Setton, Jacobo, 93
Shaarei Sion, 62, 69
Shaare Tefilá, 61, 67
Shabtai, Hizkiya, 93
Shas Party (Israel), 232n14
Shevet Aḥim (Córdoba), 74, 79
Shomke, Alfredo, 48
Shuba Israel, 62, 69
Six-Day War (1967), 10
Smart theater, 145
Sociedad de Beneficencia, 144, 145, 238n12
Sociedad de Beneficencia Pro-Hospital Sirio-Libanés, 87–88
Sociedad de Beneficencia Rofe Ḥolim (Córdoba), 74, 78
Sociedad de Damas, 160, 161
Sociedad de Damas de Beneficencia—La Unión, 140, 160, 161
Sociedad de Damas de Ḥesed VeEmet, 162
Sociedad de Damas de Sión, 160, 161
Sociedad de Damas Israelitas, 87
Sociedad de Damas Israelitas de Beneficencia (Ashkenazi), 161
Sociedad de Damas Israelitas de Beneficencia, 142
Sociedad de Damas Israelitas de Flores, 160, 161
Sociedad Etz HaḤaim, 137
Sociedad Hebraica Argentina, 210
Sociedad Hebrea Sefaradí (Santa Fé), 74
Sociedad Israelita de Beneficencia Sefaradí (Córdoba), 74, 78
Sociedad Israelita de Damas Sefaradí de Socorros Mutuos, 161, 162
Sociedad Israelita de Socorros Mutuos Dr. Theodore Hertzl, 28
Sociedad Israelita de Socorros Mutuos Rofe Ḥolim (Mendoza), 75, 81, 226n119
Sociedad Israelita de Socorros Mutuos Varsovia (Zwi Migdal), 25–26, 28, 34–35, 216n2

Sociedad Israelita Latina de Socorros Mutuos de San Juan (San Juan), 75, 81
Sociedad Israelita Latina Ḥesed VeEmet (Resistencia), 47, 48–49, 50, 74, 78, 83–84, 90, 137, 226n109, 226n120, 227n137, 228n4
Sociedad Israelita para Culto y Beneficencia Bene Mizrah (Once), 61, 70
Sociedad Israelita Salteña La Unión (Salta), 74, 81. *See also* Jewish Mutual Aid Society "Union" of Salta
Sociedad Israelita Salteña "La Union" de Socorros Mutuos, 50
Sociedad Israelita Sefaradí de Villa Crespo pro- Medicamentos, 196
Sociedad Israelita Sefaradí Etz HaḤaim (Rosario), 74, 75
Sociedad Israelita Sefaradí Shevet Aḥim (Paraná), 74
Sociedad Israelita Sefaradí Talmud Torah (Córdoba), 74, 79, 190
Sociedad Israelita Shalom VeReut (Santa Fé), 74, 75, 190, 191
Sociedad Israelita Siria. *See* Sociedad Israelita Sefaradí Talmud Torah (Córdoba)
Sociedad Israelita Siria de Córdoba, 74, 79, 81, 191, 196
Sociedad Jóvenes Israelitas Sefaradím (Latinos) de Corrientes (Corrientes), 74, 77
Sociedad Kahal Kadosh y Talmud Tora La Hermandad Sefaradí (Villa Crespo), 61, 70, 71*f*, 190
Sociedad Obrera Israelita, 33
Spain, 9, 10, 16, 16t, 114
Spanish colonial period, 11
Spanish Jewish Association of Corrientes, 220n72
Spanish Jewish Congregation of Buenos Aires, 42
Spanish-Moroccan War, 17
strikes, 1
Sud (Buenos Aries), 191
Suli, Elias, 94

Suli, Iaacov, 94
synagogues, 63
synthetic Zionism, 233n27
Syria, 10, 85, 119
Syrian Jewish community: Asociación Israelita Sefaradí Argentina (AISA), 60, 62; Asociación Israelita Sefaradi Shevet Aḥim, 75; as autochthonous, 4; in Buenos Aires, 102, 199; commerce, 17–18; in Córdoba, 5, 78, 83; dates of arrival, 16; Geulat Aam, 136; and Ḥesed VeEmet, 44–46; in Lanús, 82; in provinces, 18; in Rosario, 82; Sociedad Israelita Salteña La Unión (Salta), 74, 81; Sociedad Israelita Sefaradí Talmud Torah (Córdoba), 74, 79, 190; Sociedad Israelita Siria de Córdoba, 74, 79, 81, 191, 196; Zionism and, 122. *See also* Aleppine Jewish community; Córdoba; Corrientes; Damascene Jewish community; Entre Ríos; La Rioja; Salta
Szold, Henrietta, 150

Talmud Torahs. *See* education and schools
Tangier, Morocco, 17, 85, 224n49
Tétouan, Morocco, 17, 56, 57, 63, 77, 225n105, 226n120
Teubal, Ezra, 107, 127, 134
Teubal, Nissim, 69, 129
Tiferet Tzion, 117
t'meym (impure), 34–35, 218n30, 218n33
Tolcachier, Fabiana, 179
Tragic Week riots, 1, 20
Tsur, Yaron, 121
Tucumán, 19, 50, 81, 138, 221n104; Asociación Israelita de Beneficencia (Tucumán), 74, 81
"The Tug of Love" (Zangwill), 189
Tunisia, 232n18
turcos, 213n2, 214n20
Turkey, 14, 16t, 19, 69, 78
Turkish Jewish community, 16, 136, 168
tzedakah, 55–57

Index

Unión de Asociaciones Israelitas Sefaradíes de la República Argentina, 91, 109–111
Unión de Damas Israelitas, 200
Unión Sionista de la Capital, 150
United States, 215n46
Un Romance Turco (Pico), 173–175, 179, 204
Uriburu, José Félix, 219n57
Urla, 69

Vaad Hajinuj, 244n35, 246n74
Venezuela, 17
Ventura, Enrique, 3
Véra (Santa Fé), 29, 50, 63, 77
Verband Juedischer Frauen fuer Kulurarbeit in Palestina, 150
Vicente Lopez (Buenos Aires), 44
Villa Angela, 50
Villa Atuel (Mendoza), 88
Villa Crespo (Buenos Aires), 18f, 19, 70, 72, 105, 135, 167, 190, 191, 194, 200, 243n125; Asociación Comunidad Israelita Sefaradí de Buenos Aires (ACISBA), 40, 60, 61, 70, 72; Asociación Israelita Sefaradí Pro- Medicamentos, 61, 70, 71f, 86, 196; Sociedad Kahal Kadosh y Talmud Tora La Hermandad Sefaradí, 61, 70, 71f, 190
Villa General Urquiza (Buenos Aires), 18f, 19, 41, 72
Villa María (Córdoba), 82
Villa Mercedes (San Luis), 50, 136, 138

"We Are All Jews," 205–206
Weill, Simon, 16
Weizmann, Chaim, 234n42
Western Cemetery, 32
white slave trade, 25–26, 34–35, 217nn28–29, 220n71
WIZO (Argentina branch), 150–155, 154f, 156–158, 171–172, 239n26
WIZO (Sephardi section), 151, 155–158, 241n62
WIZO (Women's International Zionist Organization), 3, 118, 150, 239n31
Wolfsohn School (Ashkenazi), 198

women: as central protector of ethnic identity, 180; and ethnic food preparation, 163–172, 242n110; as guardians of morality and home, 185; marriage and, 179–180, 185; political activism of, 20–21; as reciepient of institutionalized help, 161, 242n97; and white slave trade, 25–26, 34–35, 217nn28–29, 220n71
women's philanthropic and social groups and events, Jewish: about, 140–142; adoption of Argentine society norms and customs, 144–149; fundraising focus of, 142–144, 162; Sephardi groups in Buenos Aires, 159–163; Sephardi groups in provinces, 162–163; Sephardi women's groups, 155–163
women's Zionist organizations, 150–163. *See also specific organizations*
World Federation of Sephardi Communities (WFSC), 128, 133, 134, 136
World Jewish Congress (WJC), 129, 236n78
World War I, 10
World War II, 20
World Zionist Organization, 8, 118, 123–125, 126, 130–131, 234n43
WUSJ World Union of Sephardi Jews (WUSJ), 122, 123–125, 126, 207, 234n43, 235n54

Yedid, Yosef, 92, 180
Yeshurun, 62, 69
Yesot Hadat (congregation), 62, 86, 91, 92, 93, 194, 201–202
Yiddish language, 114, 117, 120, 122, 125, 126, 127, 234n38
Yivoff, Mde., 155, 240n57
Yohai & Acrech store, 200
Young Turks, 10
Yrigoyen, Hipólito, 1, 219n57
Yugoslav Jewish community, 16, 42, 62, 72

Zadoff, Efraim, 190
Zangwill, Israel, 189
Zaretsky, Natasha, 206

Zionism/Zionist organizations: after creation of state of Israel, 132–136; R. Djaen and, 96–97, 124–125, 235nn52, 235n54, 235n55; early activity in Argentina, 118–125; national and ethnic identities, 202–203; in Old World, 232n18; overview of, 117–118; political parties, 117–118; and Primera Convención Sefaradí de la República Argentina, 110; in the provinces, 136–138; second period of activity, 125–132; secularity and modernity of, 120–122, 233n27; and Sephardi separatism, 113–116, 118–119, 125, 127; types of, 233n27; Unión de Asociaciones Israelitas Sefaradíes de la República Argentina, 91, 109–111; women and their activities, 150–163

Zirungs Fond, 150, 151, 239n35

Zohar, Zvi, 121

Zwi Migdal, 25–26, 34–35, 216n2

Born and raised in Buenos Aires, Argentina, Dr. Adriana M. Brodsky has focused her academic career on studying the Sephardi groups that settled in that country. She obtained her PhD at Duke University in 2004, and has lived in the United States for the last fourteen years. She is an associate professor at St. Mary's College of Maryland, where she has taught for eleven years. She resides in Alexandria, Virginia, and has two wonderful children.

www.ingramcontent.com/pod-product-compliance
Lightning Source LLC
Chambersburg PA
CBHW070754230426
43665CB00017B/2361